STERLING
Test Prep

SAT
PHYSICS REVIEW

Complete
Content Review

3rd edition

www.Sterling-Prep.com

3   2   1

ISBN-13: 978-0-9977782-6-7

Sterling Test Prep products are available at special quantity discounts for sales, promotions, academic counseling offices, and other educational purposes.

For more information, contact our Sales Department at:

Sterling Test Prep
6 Liberty Square #11
Boston, MA 02109

info@sterling-prep.com

© 2019 Sterling Test Prep

Published by Sterling Test Prep

Congratulations on choosing this book as part of your SAT Physics preparation!

Scoring high on SAT subject tests is important for admission to college. To achieve a high score on SAT Physics, you need to develop skills to properly apply the scientific knowledge you have to solve each question. Understanding key concepts, having the ability to extract information from the provided data and distinguishing between similar answer choices is more valuable than merely memorizing terms.

This book provides a detailed and thorough review of the topics tested on the SAT Physics Subject Test. The content covers foundational principles and theories necessary to answer related questions on the test. The information is presented clearly and organized systematically to provide students with targeted SAT Physics review tool. You can focus on one knowledge area at a time to learn and fully comprehend important concepts and theories or to refresh your memory. By reading these review chapters thoroughly, you will learn important physics concepts and the relationships between them so that you can answer related questions on the test. This will prepare you for the SAT Physics, and you will significantly increase your score.

All the material in this book is prepared by physics instructors with years of experience in applied physics, as well as in academic settings. This team of physics experts analyzed the content of the test, released by the College Board, and designed essential review that will help you build and solidify the knowledge necessary for your success on the test. The content was reviewed for quality and effectiveness by our science editors who possess extensive credentials, are educated in top colleges and universities and have years of teaching and editorial experience.

We wish you great success in your future academic achievements and look forward to being an important part of your successful preparation for the SAT Physics!

Sterling Test Prep Team
190117gdx

Our Commitment to the Environment

Sterling Test Prep is committed to protecting our planet's resources by supporting environmental organizations with proven track records of conservation, ecological research and education and preservation of vital natural resources. A portion of our profits is donated to help these organizations so they can continue their critical missions. These organizations include:

For over 40 years, Ocean Conservancy has been advocating for a healthy ocean by supporting sustainable solutions based on science and cleanup efforts. Among many environmental achievements, Ocean Conservancy laid the groundwork for an international moratorium on commercial whaling, played an instrumental role in protecting fur seals from overhunting and banning the international trade of sea turtles. The organization created national marine sanctuaries and served as the lead non-governmental organization in the designation of 10 of the 13 marine sanctuaries.

For 25 years, Rainforest Trust has been saving critical lands for conservation through land purchases and protected area designations. Rainforest Trust has played a central role in the creation of 73 new protected areas in 17 countries, including the Falkland Islands, Costa Rica and Peru. Nearly 8 million acres have been saved thanks to Rainforest Trust's support of in-country partners across Latin America, with over 500,000 acres of critical lands purchased outright for reserves.

Since 1980, Pacific Whale Foundation has been saving whales from extinction and protecting our oceans through science and advocacy. As an international organization, with ongoing research projects in Hawaii, Australia, and Ecuador, PWF is an active participant in global efforts to address threats to whales and other marine life. A pioneer in non-invasive whale research, PWF was an early leader in educating the public, from a scientific perspective, about whales and the need for ocean conservation.

With your purchase, you support environmental causes around the world.

Table of Contents

Table of Contents (*continued*)

Table of Contents (*continued*)

Table of Contents (*continued*)

Table of Contents (*continued*)

This book should be supplemented by

"SAT Physics Practice Questions" book

or online practice material

at www.Sterling-Prep.com

To access more SAT Physics questions online at a special pricing for book owners, see page 529

Please, leave your Customer Review on Amazon

About SAT Physics Subject Test

Recommended Preparation

- One-year introductory physics course on the college-preparatory level

- Laboratory experience: even though the test can measure lab skills only in a limited way (e.g., data analysis), lab skills are a significant factor in developing reasoning and problem-solving competencies.

Content

The College Board divided the test into six categories. Below is the breakdown of these topical categories with their respective percentages on the test. These percentages are estimations and can vary from test to test. This serves as a way to know where to focus your studies if you are particularly weak in a certain topic. Practice questions in this book cover all tested topics.

Content Category / Topic	% of the test

Mechanics:
    Kinematics
    Dynamics
    Energy and momentum
    Circular motion
    Simple harmonic motion
    Gravity
	36–42%

Electricity and magnetism:
    Electric fields, forces and potentials
    Capacitance
    Circuit elements and DC circuits
    Magnetism
	18–24%

Waves and optics:
    General wave properties
    Reflection and refraction
    Ray optics
    Physical optics
	15–19%

Heat and thermodynamics:
    Thermal properties
    Laws of thermodynamics
	6–11%

Modern physics:
    Quantum phenomena
    Atomic structure
    Nuclear and particle physics
    Relativity
	6–11%

Miscellaneous:
    General history of physics and questions that overlap several major topics
    Analytical skills (graphical analysis, measurement and math skills)
    Contemporary Physics
	4–9%

Questions on the SAT Physics test topics that are covered in any standard high school physics course. However, many differences depend on your school's curriculum, and many students will discover that there are topics that are not familiar to them. By using this book, you can fill in the gaps in your knowledge and maximize your score.

Format of the Test

There are 75 questions on the test that must be completed in 60 minutes. The test is divided into two parts. The first is Part A, which contains classification questions. The second is Part B, which contains five-choice completion questions. Part A is 12–13 questions and Part B is 62–63 questions.

Part A: Classification Questions

Classification questions are essentially multiple-choice questions. You are provided with five answer choices that pertain to a group of few questions. These types of questions require you to have a broader understanding of the topic because they present multiple questions on a single topic.

The difficulty level within each set of questions can vary. The beginning question won't always be easier than the last. However, with each set of classifications, the difficulty level increases as you go through the test. This means that questions 1–4 will normally be easier than questions 11–13.

Part B: Five-Choice Completion Questions

Part B consists of regular multiple-choice questions with five answer choices. This part of the test has no specific structure regarding the topic order. You might find questions that are similar or questions that test completely different topics near each other. Questions usually increase in difficulty as you progress through the test.

How Your Knowledge is Tested?

To better prepare yourself for the test, you should know that three different skills will be tested. Certain topics of physics will be tested in different ways. For example, kinematics questions often require the use of a formula, but questions on the atomic structure may ask to name a particular concept.

Skills covered in the context of physics:

1) Recalling and understanding the application of major physics concepts to solve specific problems.

   - *Fundamental knowledge*: remembering and understanding concepts or information (approximately 12%–20% of test). These questions test your understanding of basic knowledge. Either you know these questions, or you don't. There is no need for equations or calculations to solve these questions.

- *Single-concept problems*: applying a single physical formula or concept (about 48%–64% of test). These questions require you to recall physical relationships, formulas or equations to solve the problem. You might need to substitute numbers into an equation or recall the equation and solve for a variable. These questions focus on your knowledge of important functions and how to use them.

- *Multiple-concept problems*: integrating two or more physical formulas or concepts (about 20%–35% of test). These questions require you to combine two or more formulas or equations. These could be formulas from the same or different topics. These questions test your knowledge of relationships in physics and how to integrate more than one formula to solve a problem.

2) Understanding algebraic, trigonometric and graphical relationships, the concepts of ratio and proportion and the application of these to physics problems.

3) Application of laboratory skills in the context of the physics content

Fundamental knowledge questions are not always the easiest, and the multiple-concept questions are not always the most difficult. All three types of questions are found throughout the test with varying difficulty levels. Every question ultimately tests the same thing – whether you understand the basic principles of physics.

Scoring on SAT Physics

The scaled score on the SAT Physics test ranges from 200 to 800. These scaled scores are converted from raw scores, and ETS develops the formula at the time of the exam.

The raw score is comprised of 1 point for each correctly answered question (regardless of its difficulty) with 0.25 points subtracted for each question answered incorrectly. Questions without a response neither earn nor subtract any points.

On the next page is the approximate raw-to-scaled score conversion table for SAT Physics. This conversion formula is only an approximation and not an absolute measure.

Raw Score	Scaled Score	Raw Score	Scaled Score	Raw Score	Scaled Score
75	800	43	680	11	480
74	800	42	670	10	480
73	800	41	670	9	470
72	800	40	660	8	470
71	800	39	650	7	460
70	800	38	640	6	450
69	800	37	640	5	450
68	800	36	630	4	440
67	800	35	620	3	440
66	800	34	610	2	430
65	790	33	610	1	430
64	790	32	600	0	420
63	790	31	600	−1	410
62	780	30	590	−2	410
61	780	29	590	−3	400
60	780	28	580	−4	400
59	770	27	580	−5	390
58	770	26	570	−6	380
57	760	25	560	−7	380
56	760	24	560	−8	370
55	750	23	550	−9	360
54	740	22	540	−10	360
53	740	21	540	−11	360
52	730	20	530	−12	350
51	720	19	530	−13	350
50	720	18	520	−14	340
49	710	17	520	−15	340
48	700	16	510	−16	330
47	690	15	510	−17	320
46	690	14	500	−18	310
45	680	13	490	−19	310
44	680	12	490		

Test-Taking Strategies

The best way to do well on SAT Physics is to be good at physics. There is no way around that. Prepare for the test as much as you can, so you can answer with confidence as many questions as possible. With that being said, for multiple choice questions, the only thing that matters is how many questions were answered correctly, not how much work you did to come up with those answers. A lucky guess will get you the same points as an answer you knew with confidence.

Below are some test-taking strategies to help you maximize your score. Many of these strategies you already know and they may seem like common sense. However, when a student is feeling the pressure of a timed test, these common-sense strategies might be forgotten.

Mental Attitude

If you psych yourself out, chances are you will do poorly on the test. To do well on the test, particularly physics, which calls for cool, systemic thinking, you must remain calm. If you start to panic, your mind won't be able to find the correct solutions to the questions. Many steps can be taken before the test to increase your confidence level. Buying this book is a good start because you can begin to practice, learn the information you should know to master the topics and get used to answering physics questions. However, there are other things you should keep in mind:

Study in advance. The information will be more manageable, and you will feel more confident if you've studied at regular intervals during the weeks leading up to the test. Cramming the night before is not a successful tactic.

Be well rested. If you are up late the night before the test, chances are you will have a difficult time concentrating and focusing on the day of the test, as you will not feel fresh and alert.

Come up for air. The best way to take this hour-long test is not to keep your head down, concentrating the full sixty minutes. Even though you only have 48 seconds per question and there is no time to waste, it is recommended to take a few seconds between the questions to take a deep breath and relax your muscles.

Time Management

Aside from good preparation, time management is the most important strategy that you should know how to use on any test. You have an average time of 48 seconds for each question. You will breeze through some in fifteen seconds and others you may be stuck on for two minutes.

Don't dwell on any one question for too long. You should aim to look at every question on the test. It would be unfortunate to not earn the points for a question you could have answered just because you did not get a chance to look at it. If you are still in the first half of the test and find yourself spending more than a minute on one question and don't see yourself getting closer to solving it, it is better to move on. It will be more productive if you come back to this question with a fresh mind at the end of the test. You do not want to lose points because you were stuck on one or a few questions and did not get a chance to work with other questions that are easy for you.

Nail the easy questions quickly. On SAT subject tests, you get as many points for answering easy questions as you do for answering difficult questions. This means that you get a lot more points for five quickly answered questions than for one hard-earned victory. The questions do increase in difficulty as you progress throughout the test. However, each student has their strong and weak points, and you might be a master on certain questions that are normally considered difficult. Skip the questions you are struggling with and nail the easy ones.

Skip the unfamiliar. If you come across a question that is unfamiliar to you, skip it. Do not try to figure out what is going on or what they are trying to ask. At the end of the test, you can go back to these questions if you have time. If you are encountering a question that you have no clue about, most likely you won't be able to answer it through analysis. The better strategy is to leave such questions to the end and use the guessing strategy on them at the end of the test.

Set a Target Score

The task of pacing yourself will become easier if you are aware of the number of questions you need to answer to reach the score you want to get. Always strive for the highest score, but also be realistic about your level of preparation. It may be helpful if you research what counts as a good score for the colleges you are applying to.

You can talk to admissions offices at colleges, research college guidebooks or specific college websites, or talk to your guidance counselor. Find the average score received by students that were admitted to the colleges of your choice and set your target score higher than the average. Take a look at the chart provided earlier to see how many questions you need to answer correctly to reach this target score. You can score:

> 800 if you answered 68 right, 7 wrong, and left 0 blank
> 750 if you answered 58 right, 12 wrong, and left 5 blank
> 700 if you answered 51 right, 13 wrong, and left 11 blank
> 650 if you answered 43 right, 16 wrong, and left 16 blank
> 600 if you answered 36 right, 19 wrong, and left 20 blank

If the average score on SAT Physics for the school you're interested in is 700, set your target at about 750. To achieve that score, you need to get 58 questions right, which leaves you room to get 12 wrong and leave 5 blanks.

Therefore, you can leave some questions blank, get some wrong, and still achieve 750. If you have an idea of how many questions you need to answer correctly, you can pace yourself accordingly. Keep in mind that you'll likely get some answered questions wrong.

Understanding the Question

It is important that you know what the question is asking before you select your answer choice. This seems obvious, but it is surprising how many students don't read a question carefully because they rush through the test and select a wrong answer choice.

A successful student will not just read the question but will take a moment to understand the question before even looking at the answer choices. This student will be able to separate the important information from distracters and will not get confused by the questions that are asking to identify a false statement (which is the correct answer). Once you've identified what you're dealing with and what is being asked, you should be able to spend less time picking the right answer. If the question is asking for a general concept, try to answer the question before looking at the answer choices, then look at the choices. If you see a choice that matches the answer you thought of, most likely it is the correct choice.

Correct Way to Guess

Random guessing won't help you on the test, but educated guessing is the strategy you should use in certain situations if you can eliminate at least one (or even two) of the five possible choices.

On SAT subject tests, you lose ¼ of a point for each wrong answer. This is done to prevent blind guessing, but not to punish you for making an educated guess. For example, if you just randomly entered responses for the first 20 questions, there is a 20% chance of guessing correctly on any given question.

Therefore, the odds are you would guess right on 4 questions and wrong on 16 questions. Your raw score for those 20 questions would then be 0 because you get 4 points for 4 correct answers and lose 4 points for 16 wrong answers. This would be the same as leaving all 20 questions blank.

However, if for each of the 20 questions you can eliminate one answer choice because you know it to be wrong, you will have a 25% chance of being right. Therefore, your odds would move to 5 questions right and 15 questions wrong. This gives a raw score of 1.25 (gain 5 points and lose 3.75 points).

Guessing is not cheating and should not be viewed that way. Rather it is a form of "partial credit" because while you might not be sure of the correct answer, you do have relevant knowledge to identify one or two choices that are wrong.

SAT Physics Tips

Tip 1: Know the formulas

Since 70–80% of the test requires that you know how to use the formulas, it is imperative that you memorize and understand when to use each one. It is not permitted to bring any papers with notes to the test. Therefore, you must memorize all the formulas you will need to solve the questions on the test, and there is no way around it.

As you work with this book, you will learn the application of all the important physical formulas and will use them in many different question types. If you are feeling nervous about having many formulas in your head and worry that it will affect your problem-solving skills, look over the formulas right before you go into the testing space and write them down before you start the test. This way, you don't have to worry about remembering the formulas throughout the test. When you need to use them, you can refer back to where you wrote them down earlier.

Tip 2: Know how to manipulate the formulas

You must know how to apply the formulas in addition to just memorizing them. Questions will be worded in ways unfamiliar to you to test whether you can manipulate equations that you know to calculate the correct answer. Knowing that $F = ma$ is not helpful without understanding that $a = F/m$ because it is very unlikely that a question will ask to calculate the force acting on an object with a given mass and acceleration. Rather you will be asked to calculate the acceleration of an object of a given mass with force acting on it.

Tip 3: Estimating

This tip is only helpful for quantitative questions. For example, estimating can help you choose the correct answer if you have a general sense of the order of magnitude. This is especially applicable to questions where all answer choices have different orders of magnitude, and you can save time that you would have to spend on calculations.

Tip 4: Draw the question

Don't hesitate to write, draw or graph your thought process once you have read and understood the question. This can help you determine what kind of information you are dealing with. Draw the force and velocity vectors, ray/wave paths, or anything else that may be helpful. Even if a question does not require a graphic answer, drawing a graph (for example, a sketch of a particle's velocity) can allow a solution to become obvious.

Tip 5: Eliminating wrong answers

This tip utilizes the strategy of educated guessing. You can usually eliminate one or two answer choices right away in most questions. Also, there are certain types of questions for which you can use a particular elimination method.

By using logical estimations for quantitative questions, you can eliminate the answer choices that are unreasonably high or unreasonably low.

In classification questions (Part A), the same five answer choices apply to several questions. It is helpful to keep in mind that it is not often that one answer choice is correct for more than one question (though it does happen sometimes).

Some answer choices that you are confident to be correct for some questions are good elimination candidates for other questions where you're trying to use a guessing strategy. It is not a sure bet, but you should be aware of this option if you have to resort to guessing on some questions.

Roman numeral questions are the multiple-choice questions that list a few possible answers with five different combinations of these answers. Supposing that you know that one of the Roman numeral choices is wrong, you can eliminate all answer choices that include it. These questions are usually difficult for most test takers because they tend to present more than one potentially correct statement which is often included in more than one answer choice. However, they have a certain upside if you can eliminate at least one wrong statement.

Last helpful tip: fill in your answers carefully

This seems like a simple thing, but it is important. Many test takers make mistakes when filling in answers whether it is a paper test or computer-based test. Make sure you pay attention and check off the answer choice you chose as correct.

We want to hear from you

Your feedback is important to us because we strive to provide the highest quality prep materials. Email us if you have any questions, comments or suggestions, so we can incorporate your feedback into future editions.

Customer Satisfaction Guarantee

If you have any concerns about this book, including printing issues, contact us and we will resolve any issues to your satisfaction.

info@sterling-prep.com

We reply to all emails – please check your spam folder

Thank you for choosing our products to achieve your educational goals!

Chapter 1

Kinematics and Dynamics

- **Introduction: The Nature of Science**

- **Units and Dimensions**

- **Vectors, Components**

- **Vector Addition**

- **Speed, Velocity**

- **Acceleration**

- **Freely falling bodies**

Notes

Introduction: The Nature of Science

The first step toward scientific discovery is observation: recognizing patterns and anomalies in unexplained phenomena. Based on observations, theories are created to explain the phenomena and to predict what will happen under other conditions with different variables. Further observations determine whether the predictions were accurate, and the cycle continues as laws are established from these verified theories.

Models, Theories and Laws

Theories are detailed statements that provide testable predictions of the behavior of natural phenomena. They are established to explain observations, and then tested based on their predictions. If a theory accurately predicts the behavior of a certain phenomenon, a *model* is constructed to explain in detail the behavior of that phenomenon.

Theories are much vaguer and more encompassing than models; they provide the foundation upon which models are constructed. Models, however, are far more specific. They create mental pictures of physical phenomena following the predictions of scientific theories and can be very useful in the process of trying to understand these phenomena. Multiple models are often constructed to explain a portion or the entire scope of a theory.

Care must be taken to understand the limitations of a model and not to apply it dogmatically. A model is a basic representation of a part of a theory; it is not intended to provide a complete picture of every occurrence of a phenomenon under that theory, but rather to provide a familiar way of envisioning its fundamental aspects. When theories are proven accurate over a large scope of scenarios and environments, laws are developed based on these results. *Laws* are brief descriptions of how nature behaves in a broad set of circumstances. Laws are the products of multiple theories that have been tested and proven, culminating in a broad claim regarding those predictions.

Furthermore, laws are intended to be simple explanations that are widely applicable. Laws that make simple and broad claims are more robust than those who make claims on a narrower, more specific set of variables and parameters. Claims that are more specific and apply to a narrower range of phenomena are *principles*.

Units and Dimensions

Measurement and Uncertainty: Significant Figures

No measurement is exact; there will always be some uncertainty due to limited instrument accuracy and precision. The *accuracy* of an instrument depends on how well-calibrated that instrument is concerning the true quantitative value of a measurement. For example, an empty scale holding no objects that are initially calibrated to 0 grams of mass is more accurate than the same empty scale calibrated to 1 gram of mass. An instrument's *precision* is based upon the scale of the measurement, with measurements on a smaller scale being more precise than measurements on a larger scale. For example, a meter stick that includes millimeter markings (0.001 m) is more precise than a meter stick with only centimeter markings (0.01 m).

Estimated uncertainty of a measurement is written with a ± sign. For example, 8.8 ± 0.1 cm essentially reads as "8.8 centimeters, give or take 0.1 centimeters."

Percent uncertainty is the ratio of the uncertainty to the measured value, multiplied by 100. Taking the values from the previous example, the percent uncertainty in the measurement is:

$$\frac{0.1}{8.8} \times 100 \approx 1\%$$

The number of significant figures is the number of reliably known digits in a number. The way the number is written should indicate the number of significant figures:

- 22.41 cm has four significant figures.

- 0.058 cm has two significant figures (the initial zeroes before significant digits are ignored). If it has three significant figures, it is written as 0.0580 cm.

- 70 km has only one significant figure (zeroes that serve as placeholders without decimal points are not considered significant). If it has two significant figures, it is written as 70. km (notice that the decimal point changes the significance of the trailing zero). If it has three significant figures, it is written as 70.0 km.

When multiplying or dividing numbers, the result should have as many significant figures as the number with the fewest significant figures used in the calculation. For example:

12.5 cm × 5.5 cm = 68.75 cm, but because 5.5 cm has only two significant figures, the value 68.75 cm must be rounded to 69 cm.

When adding or subtracting numbers, the answer is no more precise than the least precise value used. In this case, it is best to round the quantity with higher precision to the same decimal place as the quantity with lower precision. For example:

68.75 cm - 32.1 cm = 36.65 cm, but 32.1 cm only has three significant figures. Therefore 36.65 cm must be rounded to 36.7 cm.

Calculators may not give the right number of significant figures; they either give too many or too few (i.e., if there are trailing zeroes after a decimal point).

Solving Problems

Here is a list of general guidelines for solving motion problems:

1. Read the whole problem and make sure to understand it.

2. Decide which objects are under study and what the time interval is.

3. Draw a diagram and choose coordinate axes.

4. Write all known (given) quantities, then the unknown ones that have to be found.

5. Determine which equations relate the known and unknown quantities. Are they valid in this situation?

   Solve algebraically and check that the result is sensible (correct dimensions).

6. Calculate the solution and round it to the appropriate number of significant figures.

7. Is the result reasonable? Does it agree with a rough estimate or guess (positive or negative, order of magnitude, etc.)?

8. Check the units. Do the units on one side of the equation match the units on the other?

Order of Magnitude: Rapid Estimating

A quick way to estimate a calculated quantity is to round off all numbers to one significant figure before calculating. The result should at least be the right order of magnitude. This can be expressed by rounding it off to the nearest power of 10. For example:

$$3{,}321 \times 401 = 1{,}331{,}721 \approx 13 \times 10^5$$

The result can be estimated by rounding 3,321 to 3×10^3 and 401 to 4×10^2 which gives:

$$(3 \times 10^3) \times (4 \times 10^2) = 12 \times 10^5$$

which is relatively close to the exact solution and is the same order of magnitude.

Dimensions and Dimensional Analysis

The dimensions of a quantity are the base units that make it up, and they are generally written using square brackets. For example:

Speed = distance / time, dimensions of speed: [L/t]

Quantities that are being added or subtracted must always have the same dimensions. Furthermore, a quantity calculated as the solution to a problem should have the correct dimensions, so dimensional analysis is useful for checking calculations:

- One dimension only contains the magnitude of quantities.

- Two dimensions contain quantities on a 2D plane (x and y coordinates).

- Three dimensions contain quantities in 3D space (x, y and z coordinates).

- Four dimensions contain quantities in 3D space at a given time (x, y, and z spatial coordinates plus a time coordinate t).

Units, Standards, and the SI System

Quantity	Unit	Standard
Length	Meter (m)	Length of the path traveled by light (in a vacuum) in 1/299,792,458 seconds
Time	Second (s)	Time required for 9,192,631,770 periods of radiation emitted by cesium atoms
Mass	Kilogram (kg)	Platinum cylinder in the International Bureau of Weights and Measures, Paris

Properties of Units in Different Dimensions

A unit is a label for a quantity. Thus, like the quantities they label, units also hold many similar properties:

- unit + unit = unit

- unit − unit = unit

- unit × unit = unit^2, unless multiplying quantities of different units (e.g., meter × second = m·s)

- unit / unit = no unit, unless dividing quantities of different units (e.g. meter / second = m/s)

- Dimensions are represented by powers of units:

  o unit = one dimension

  o unit^2 = two dimensions

  o unit^3 = three dimensions

- The product of operations involving all SI units is also in SI units.

In the SI system, the basic units are meters, kilograms and seconds.

More complex units such as units for velocity, force, and power can then be derived from these basic units.

Basic Translational Motion SI Units		
Quantity	SI Unit	Name
Length	m	Meter
Mass	kg	Kilogram
Time	s	Second

Complex Translational Motion SI Units		
Speed or Velocity	m/s	Meter per second
Acceleration	m/s^2	Meters per second squared
Area	m^2	Square meter
Volume	m^3	Cubic meter
Density	kg/m^3	Kilogram per cubic meter
Force	N (kg·m/s^2)	Newton
Energy	J (N·m)	Joule
Power	W (J/s)	Watt

$$Volume = \frac{kg}{1} \times \frac{m^3}{kg}$$

The kilogram terms cancel because they are on opposite sides of the division bar. Thus the units for volume are:

$$Volume = m^3$$

This is an example of a helpful method to keep track of units or solve for an unknown unit. As problems become more complex, always check the units to ensure that the solution represents the correct unit and that no errors have occurred.

These are the standard SI prefixes for indicating powers of 10. Many are familiar, while some are rarely used.

Metric (SI) Prefixes		
Prefix	**Abbreviation**	**Value**
peta	P	10^{15}
tera	T	10^{12}
giga	G	10^{9}
mega	M	10^{6}
kilo	k	10^{3}
deci	d	10^{-1}
centi	c	10^{-2}
milli	m	10^{-3}
micro	μ	10^{-6}
nano	n	10^{-9}
pico	p	10^{-12}

Converting Units

Converting between metric units involves powers of 10. For example:

$1 \text{ kg} = 10^3 \text{ g}$

$1 \text{ mm} = 10^{-6} \text{ km}$

$5 \text{ s} = 5 \times 10^3 \text{ ms}$

Converting to and from imperial units is considerably more work. For example:

$1 \text{ m} = 3.28084 \text{ ft}$

$1 \text{ kg} = 2.204 \text{ lbs}$

$1 \text{ km} = 0.621 \text{ miles}$

Vectors, Components

Kinematics in One Dimension: Reference Frames and Displacement

Any measurement of position, distance or speed must be made concerning a reference frame. For example, if a person walks down the aisle of a moving train, the person's speed concerning the train is a few miles per hour, at most. The person's speed with respect to the ground outside, however, is much greater; it is the combined speed of both the train and the person walking on the train. *Kinematics* is the description of how objects move with respect to a defined reference frame.

Within a reference frame, displacement is used to signify an object's change in position. There is a distinction between *displacement* and *distance*, as displacement (a solid line) is how far the object is from its starting point, regardless of how it got there, while distance traveled (a dashed line) is measured along the path of the object. In the image, the distance traveled is 100 meters, but the displacement is only 40 meters:

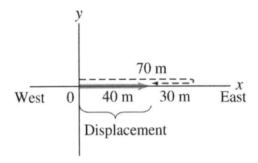

The displacement is written mathematically as $\Delta x = x_2 - x_1$. Since displacement involves direction, it can be positive or negative about the coordinate directions. Here is an example of positive displacement:

$\Delta x = x_2 - x_1$

$\Delta x = 30 \text{ m} - 10 \text{ m}$

$\Delta x = 20 \text{ m}$

Here is an example of negative displacement:

$$\Delta x = x_2 - x_1$$

$$\Delta x = 10 \text{ m} - 30 \text{ m}$$

$$\Delta x = -20 \text{ m}$$

It should be noted that an arbitrary choice of direction can be selected when setting up a coordinate system. The answer will be correct if all vector components are labeled and computed consistently concerning the chosen coordinate system direction.

Vectors and Vector Components

Quantities can be divided into two types: scalar and vector quantities. *Scalar* quantities represent a magnitude without a direction.

For example, length, time and mass are all quantities without an associated direction.

Vector quantities include both magnitude and direction. For example, displacement, acceleration, and force all contain a direction in which they are applied.

There are three trigonometric rules to follow when calculating vector components, which can be summed as SOH CAH TOA:

- **SOH**: $\sin \theta$ = **o**pposite / **h**ypotenuse

- **CAH**: $\cos \theta$ = **a**djacent / **h**ypotenuse

- **TOA**: $\tan \theta$ = **o**pposite / **a**djacent

"Opposite," "adjacent" and "hypotenuse" refer to the vectors about the angle θ.

For example, in the diagram below, the vector adjacent to θ_x is v_x, the vector opposite θ_x is the vertical dotted line (equivalent to v_y), and the hypotenuse is v.

Axis-vector components

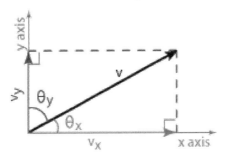

It may be helpful to create a mnemonic for "SOH CAH TOA" to memorize the different angle associations, such as "Some Old Hairy Camels Are Hairier Than Others Are."

Vector components are portions of the vector in a given direction. Typically, the components are calculated along the axis directions in a coordinate system.

For example, a vector can have a horizontal component and a vertical component in a 2D coordinate system (often represented as an x-component and y-component):

$$v_x = \vec{v} \cos \theta_x = \vec{v} \sin \theta_y$$
$$v_y = \vec{v} \cos \theta_y = \vec{v} \sin \theta_x$$

The magnitude of the resulting vector is calculated by the Pythagorean Theorem:

$$\vec{v}^2 = v_x^2 + v_y^2$$

Here are some examples of vectors and vector components in a 2D coordinate system:

Gravity components on slope

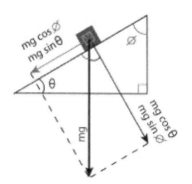

Vector-vector components

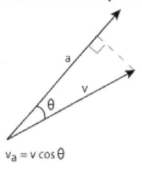

$v_a = v \cos \theta$

In a 3D coordinate system (as in, there exists a *z*-axis) a third *z*-component of the vector is included:

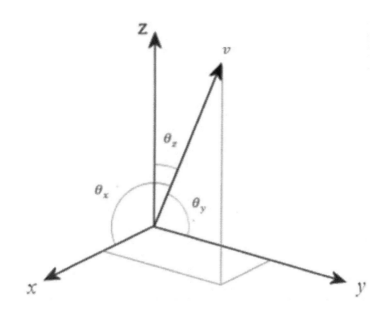

$$v_x = \vec{\mathbf{v}} \cos \theta_x$$

$$v_y = \vec{\mathbf{v}} \cos \theta_y$$

$$v_z = \vec{\mathbf{v}} \cos \theta_z$$

$$\vec{\mathbf{v}}^2 = v_x^2 + v_y^2 + v_z^2$$

Vector Addition

Vector addition can be done either graphically or by using components. Vectors can only be directly added if they are in the same dimension. Otherwise, the addition of each of the vectors' x-, y- and z-components must be performed. Since the sum of all components of a vector equals the vector itself, the resulting components make up the added vector, the resultant vector.

Operations involving two vectors may or may not result in a vector.

For example, kinetic energy derived from the square of two velocity vectors results in a scalar quantity. Operations involving a vector and a scalar always result in a vector, while operations involving a scalar and a scalar always result in a scalar.

For vectors in one dimension, addition and subtraction are all that is needed. Figure (a) demonstrates vector addition in one dimension:

(a)

$$8 \text{ km}_{East} + 6 \text{ km}_{East} = 14 \text{ km}_{East}$$

Figure (b) demonstrates vector subtraction in one dimension:

(b)

$$8 \text{ km}_{East} - 6 \text{ km}_{East} = 2 \text{ km}_{East}$$

Addition of Vectors — Graphical Methods

If there is motion in two dimensions, the situation is somewhat more complicated. Here, the travel paths are at right angles, so the displacement can be calculated by using the Pythagorean Theorem:

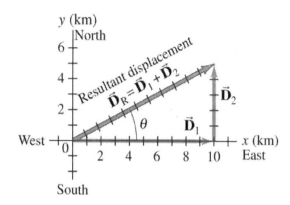

Adding the vectors in the opposite order gives the same result:

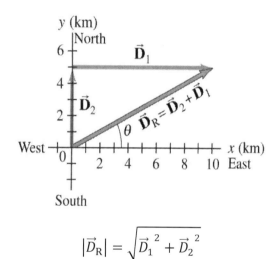

$$|\vec{D}_R| = \sqrt{\vec{D}_1^{\,2} + \vec{D}_2^{\,2}}$$

Even if the vectors are not at right angles, they can be added graphically using the "tail-to-tip" method. To use the "tail-to-tip" method, place the tail of each vector at the tip of the arrow of the vector before it. After all the vectors have been arranged tail-to-tip, draw the resultant vector from the tail of the original vector to the tip of the last vector added. Here is an example of using the "tail-to-tip" method with three vectors:

If there are two vectors, the "parallelogram" method may also be used. To perform the parallelogram method, arrange the two vectors such that their tails are connected. Starting from the tips of the two vectors, draw two dashed lines that complete the parallelogram. The resultant vector is drawn from the tails of the original vectors to the corner of the drawn parallelogram.

Here is an example of the "tail-to-tip" and parallelogram method with two vectors:

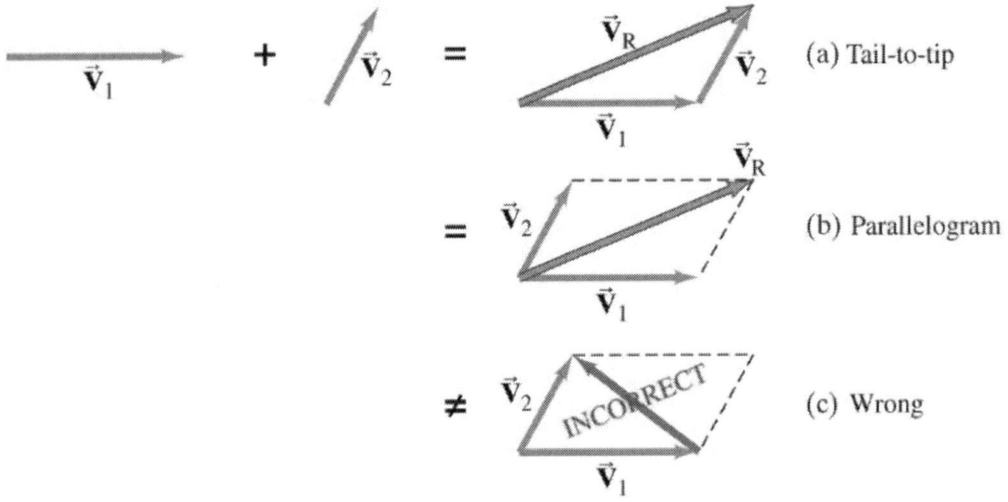

Subtraction of Vectors and Multiplication of a Vector by a Scalar

To subtract vectors, define the negative of a vector that has the same magnitude, but points in the opposite direction.

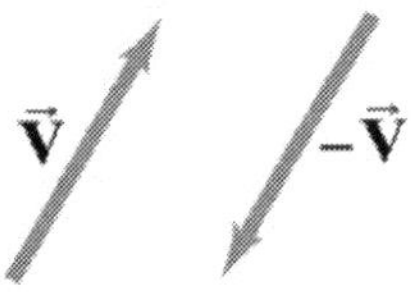

Then add the negative vector:

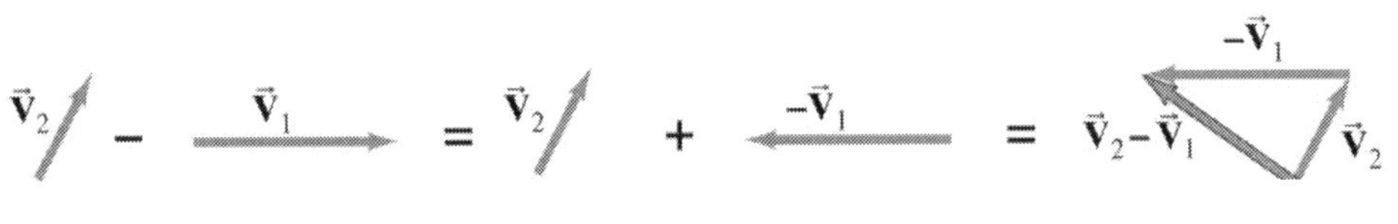

A vector $\vec{v}$ can be multiplied by a scalar c. The result is a vector that has the same direction, but a magnitude $c\vec{v}$. If c is negative, the resultant vector points in the opposite direction.

Here is an example of a vector $\vec{v}$ being multiplied by different scalars:

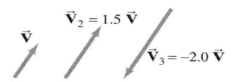

Adding Vectors by Components

Any vector can be expressed as the sum of its component vectors. The component vectors are usually chosen so that they are perpendicular:

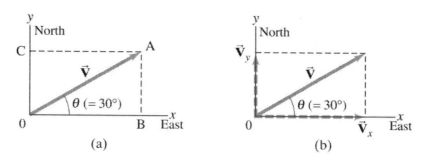

If the components are perpendicular, they can be found using trigonometric functions:

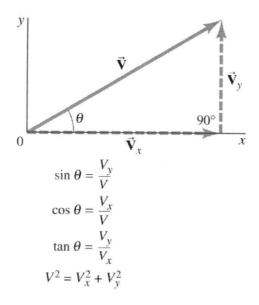

$$\sin \theta = \frac{V_y}{V}$$

$$\cos \theta = \frac{V_x}{V}$$

$$\tan \theta = \frac{V_y}{V_x}$$

$$V^2 = V_x^2 + V_y^2$$

The components are effectively one-dimensional, so they can be added arithmetically:

$$V_{Ry} = V_{1y} + V_{2y}$$

$$V_{Rx} = V_{1x} + V_{2x}$$

$$\left|\vec{V}_R\right| = \sqrt{\vec{V}_{Rx}^2 + \vec{V}_{Ry}^2}$$

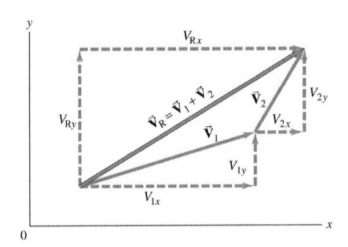

When adding vectors:

1. Draw a diagram of the vectors on a coordinate system.

2. Establish the x and y-axes.

3. Resolve each vector into x and y components.

4. Calculate each component using sines and cosines.

5. Add the components in each direction to determine the resultant vector.

To find the magnitude and direction of the resultant vector, use:

$$\vec{v} = \sqrt{v_x^2 + v_y^2} \qquad\qquad \tan\theta = \frac{v_y}{v_x}$$

Speed, Velocity

Speed is the quantity of how far an object travels in a given time interval. Since speed is the rate of change in *distance*, it does not include a direction and is, therefore, a scalar quantity. Average speed is the distance traveled divided by the time elapsed during that travel:

$$\text{Average speed: } speed_{average} = v_{avg} = \frac{d}{t} = \frac{distance\ traveled}{time\ elapsed}$$

Meanwhile, *velocity* quantifies the speed of an object in a particular direction, or rather the rate of change in *displacement*. Since velocity includes direction, it is a vector quantity.

Average velocity is the displacement divided by the elapsed time:

$$velocity_{average} = \vec{v}_{avg} = \frac{s}{t} = \frac{displacement}{time\ elapsed} = \frac{final\ position - initial\ position}{time\ elapsed}$$

Likewise, instantaneous speed is the speed at a point in time (infinitesimal time interval), while instantaneous velocity is the velocity at a point in time (infinitesimal time interval).

Mathematically, instantaneous velocity is the limit, as time becomes infinitesimally small, of the displacement over that infinitesimally short time interval:

$$\vec{v}_{inst} = \lim_{\Delta t \to 0} \frac{\Delta x}{\Delta t}$$

As with other measurements of velocity, instantaneous velocity has a direction, while instantaneous speed does not. The direction of instantaneous velocity is tangent to the path at that point, and its magnitude is equal to that of the instantaneous speed at that point.

These graphs show (a) constant velocity and (b) varying velocity:

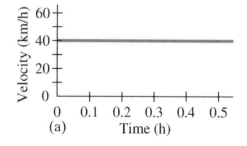 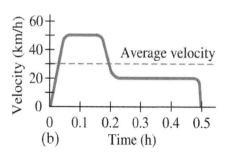

Relative Velocity

Relative speed in one dimension was discussed. It is similar in two dimensions, but velocities must be added and subtracted as vectors.

Each velocity is labeled first with the object and second with the reference frame in which it has this velocity.

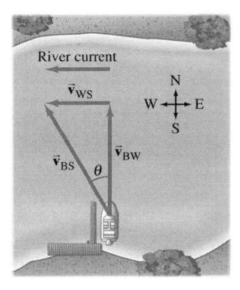

In the following example, $\vec{v}_{BS}$ is the velocity of the boat in the shore frame, $\vec{v}_{BW}$ is the velocity of the boat in the water frame and $\vec{v}_{WS}$ is the velocity of the water in the shore frame.

In this case, the relationship between the three velocities is:

$$\vec{v}_{BS} = \vec{v}_{BW} + \vec{v}_{WS}$$

Acceleration

Acceleration is the rate of change in the velocity of an object. Average acceleration is expressed as:

$$average\ acceleration = \vec{a}_{avg} = \frac{\Delta \vec{v}}{\Delta t} = \frac{\vec{v}_f - \vec{v}_i}{t} = \frac{change\ in\ velocity}{time\ elapsed}$$

From this, the instantaneous acceleration of an object can be determined. The instantaneous acceleration is the average velocity over the limit of the time interval as it becomes infinitesimally small:

$$\vec{a}_{inst} = \lim_{\Delta t \to 0} \frac{\Delta \vec{v}}{\Delta t}$$

Like velocity, acceleration is a vector. However, in one-dimensional motion, only a positive or negative sign is needed.

If acceleration is constant and there is no change in direction, the values speed and velocity are interchangeable, as are the values of distance and displacement.

Keep in mind the direction of the acceleration.

There is a slight difference between negative acceleration and deceleration:

- Negative acceleration is an acceleration in the negative direction as defined by the coordinate system.

  The direction of the acceleration is independent of velocity.

- Deceleration is relative to the object's velocity; it occurs when the acceleration is opposite in direction to the velocity.

  If the object is traveling in a positive direction (i.e., the velocity is positive), then deceleration and negative acceleration are the same.

The image below depicts an example of positive acceleration:

Acceleration

$t_1 = 0$
$v_1 = 0$

$a = 15 \dfrac{km/h}{s}$

at $t = 1.0$ s
$v = 15$ km/h

at $t = 2.0$ s
$v = 30$ km/h

at $t = t_2 = 5.0$ s
$v = v_2 = 75$ km/h

This image provides an example of negative acceleration:

Acceleration

at $t_1 = 0$
$v_1 = 15.0$ m/s

$a = -2.0$ m/s^2

at $t_2 = 5.0$ s
$v_2 = 5.0$ m/s

Motion at Constant Acceleration

The average velocity of an object during a time interval *t* is:

$$\bar{v} = \frac{\Delta x}{\Delta t} = \frac{x - x_0}{t - t_0} = \frac{x - x_0}{t}$$

The acceleration, assumed constant, is:

$$\vec{a} = \frac{v - v_0}{t}$$

Additionally, as the velocity increases at a constant rate, it is known that:

$$\bar{v} = \frac{v_0 + v}{2}$$

Combine the last three equations:

$$x = x_0 + \bar{v}t = x_0 + \left(\frac{v_0 + v}{2}\right)t = x_0 + \left(\frac{v_0 + v_0 + at}{2}\right)t$$

Or

$$x = x_0 + v_0 t + \frac{1}{2}at^2$$

Combine these equations to eliminate t:

$$v^2 = v_0{}^2 + 2a(x - x_0)$$

Here are the equations needed to solve constant acceleration problems:

- $v = v_0 + at$

- $x = x_0 + v_0 t + \frac{1}{2}at^2$

- $v^2 = v_0{}^2 + 2a(x - x_0)$

- $\bar{v} = \frac{v_0 + v}{2}$

- $s = v_{avg}t$

- $v_{avg} = \frac{v_f + v_i}{2}$

- $a = \frac{\Delta v}{\Delta t} = \frac{v_f - v_i}{t}$

- $v_f^2 = v_i^2 + 2as$

- $s = \frac{1}{2}at^2 + v_i t$

- $l_f = l_i + s$

Memorize these equations and be able to rearrange them, combine them and apply them appropriately.

When solving a problem involving these equations, assign one direction as positive and the opposite as negative, and keep this scheme for all calculations.

In Cartesian (horizontal x and vertical y-axes) coordinates, take upward and rightward motion as positive, and downward and leftward motion as negative.

For free falls, taking downward (gravitational acceleration) as positive is helpful.

Ultimately, the directions can be assigned in any fashion, provided that the opposite direction has the opposite sign.

Graphical Analysis of Linear Motion

Here is an example of a graph of x vs. t for an object moving with constant velocity. The velocity is the slope of the x-t curve.

Note that the slope is positive.

Therefore the velocity is positive.

Velocity is constant because the graph is linear:

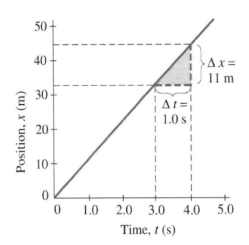

Freely Falling Bodies

One of the common examples of motion with constant acceleration is an object in *free fall*. Near the surface of the Earth, all objects experience approximately the same acceleration due to gravity ($g = 9.8$ m/s^2, sometimes given as 10 m/s^2 for ease of calculation). Differences in acceleration due to gravity between objects can be attributed to air resistance in the atmosphere. In a vacuum such as outer space, gravity causes all objects to fall with the same acceleration. Acceleration g is constant because the mass of the object and the gravitational force acting on the object are constant.

Whenever an object is in the air, it is in free fall, regardless of whether it is being tossed upwards, downward or at an angle. For objects that are dropped, it is easier to label the downward direction as positive, since that will make g positive. Likewise, if the object is thrown downward, both initial velocity and g will be positive. For objects thrown upward, the initial velocity will have an opposite sign to g. Label either the upward or downward direction as positive depending on what is most convenient for the question. Regardless, if an object is thrown upward, the initial velocity will have the opposite sign as g.

Projectiles

A projectile is an object moving in two dimensions under the influence of Earth's gravity; its path is a parabola. The object's motion along this path is *projectile motion*, which can be understood and described through its vertical and horizontal components. The speed in the horizontal, or *x*-direction, is constant; in the vertical, or *y*-direction, the object moves with constant acceleration g.

Projectiles are freely falling bodies, so the vertical component of the projectile motion is always accelerating toward the Earth at a rate of g. Even when the projectile is traveling upward, the downward acceleration of gravity causes the projectile to decelerate when traveling upward. There is no acceleration in the horizontal component. Therefore the horizontal component of velocity is constant. The time that elapses while the projectile is in motion is dependent only on the vertical component of the projectile motion. The horizontal distance covered by the projectile is determined from the elapsed time during the projectile's path multiplied by its horizontal speed. When an object is tossed straight up, and it comes down to where it started, the displacement s for the entire trip is zero, and initial velocity and final velocity are equal and opposite ($\vec{v}_{final} + \vec{v}_{initial} = 0$). The acceleration is opposite in sign to the initial velocity.

This photograph shows two balls that start to fall at the same time. The one on the right has an initial velocity in the *x*-direction, while the ball on the left was dropped straight downward. The vertical positions of the two balls are identical at identical times, while the horizontal position of the ball on the right increases linearly.

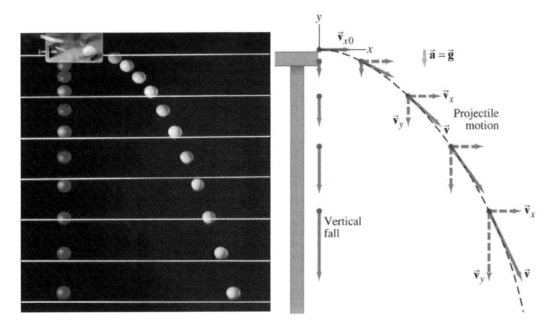

If an object is launched at an initial angle of θ_0 with the horizontal, the analysis is similar except that the initial velocity has a vertical component.

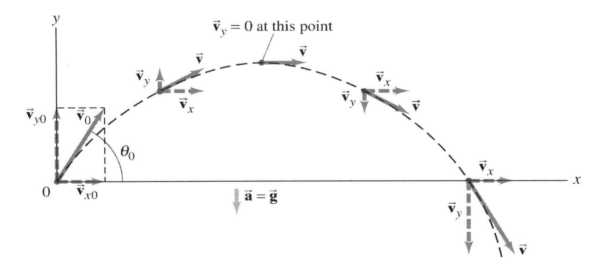

Projectile Motion Is Parabolic

To demonstrate that projectile motion is parabolic, write y as a function of x:

$$y = Ax^2 - Bx + C$$

This is the equation for a parabola, where A, B, and C are constants. Think of A as a scalar multiplier of the object's acceleration, B as a scalar multiplier of the velocity and C as a scalar multiplier of the object's initial position.

The signs associated with these constants determine the direction of the object's acceleration, velocity and initial displacement from the origin.

Solving Projectile Motion Problems

Projectile motion is motion with constant acceleration in one dimension, where the acceleration is due to gravity and therefore in a downward direction.

Kinematic Equations for Projectile Motion (y positive downward; $a_x = 0$, $a_y = g = 9.8$ m/s^2)	
Horizontal Motion ($a_x = 0$, v_x = constant)	Vertical Motion ($a_y = g$ = constant)
$v_x = v_{x0}$	$v_y = v_{y0} - gt$
$x = x_0 + v_{x0}t$	$y = y_0 + v_{y0}t - (1/2)gt^2$
	$v_y^2 = v_{y0}^2 - 2g(y - y_0)$

When solving projectile motion problems, follow these steps as a guideline:

1. Read the problem carefully, and choose the object(s) that should be analyzed.

2. Draw a diagram.

3. Choose an origin and a coordinate system.

4. Determine the time interval; this is the same in both directions and includes only the time the object is moving, with constant acceleration g.

5. Examine the x and y-components of the motion separately.

6. List known and unknown quantities.

   The v_x never changes and $v_y = 0$ at the highest point.

7. Use the appropriate equations; some of them may have to be combined.

Free Fall versus Non-Free Fall

In free fall, the only force acting on the object is that of gravity. Assuming there is no air resistance, the only resistance to change is the object's inertia and all objects fall at a constant acceleration of 9.8 m/s² downward. Since Earth is not a vacuum, air resistance is generally accounted for when objects are falling. This is a *non-free fall*.

In non-free fall, the upward force due to air resistance counteracts the downward force due to gravity. The net force of this interaction is the difference between the force due to gravity and air resistance. Therefore, the total force on an object in non-free fall is less than that of the same object in free fall, where the force from air resistance is zero.

As an object falls, the force from air resistance increases with the increased speed of the object, and the force downward decreases until the two opposing forces are equal in magnitude and the acceleration of the object is zero.

At this point, the object is traveling at a constant velocity downward in *terminal velocity*.

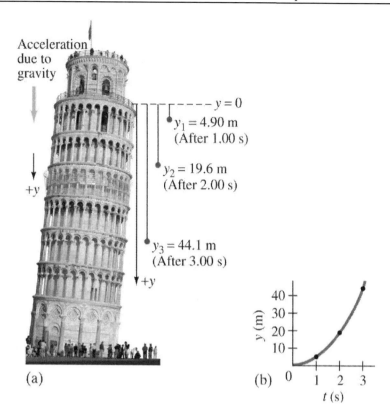

(a)

(b)

Satellites and "Weightlessness"

Satellites are routinely put into orbit around the Earth. The tangential speed must be enough so that the satellite does not fall to Earth, but not so much that it escapes Earth's gravity altogether.

Satellites orbiting the Earth are in continuous free fall, and their centripetal acceleration equals the acceleration from the Earth's gravity.

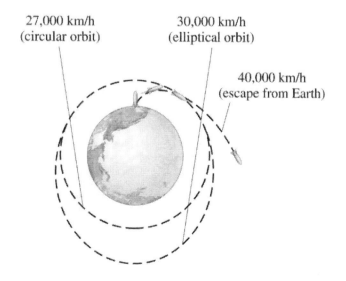

The satellite is kept in orbit by its speed. It is continually falling and accelerating toward the Earth, but it never crashes into the Earth's surface because the Earth curves from underneath it (the surface curves away from the satellite at the same rate as the satellite falls).

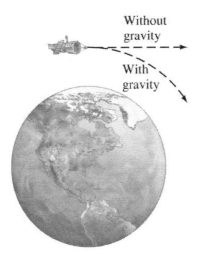

Objects in orbit are said to experience weightlessness, even though they do have a gravitational force acting on them. The satellite and all its contents are in free fall, so there is no normal force, leading to the experience of weightlessness. This effect is *apparent weightlessness* because the gravitational force still exists. It can be experienced on Earth as well, but only briefly.

For example, when a roller coaster drops down a hill, the normal force temporarily goes to zero and the person riding it experiences apparent weightlessness.

Real weightlessness occurs when there is no net gravitational force acting on an object. Either the object is so far out in space that there are no objects within light-years of it, or the object is between two other objects with equal gravitational forces that cancel.

Chapter Summary

Graphs are very useful tools to help visualize the motion of an object. They can also help solve problems once you learn how to translate from one graph to another. When working with graphs, keep in mind the following:

- Always look at a graph's axes first. This sounds obvious, but one of the most common mistakes students make when looking at the velocity vs. time graph is thinking about it as if it is a position vs. time graph.

- Don't assume one box is one unit; observe the numbers on the axis.

- Lining up position vs. time graphs *directly above* velocity vs. time graphs and *directly above* acceleration vs. time graphs is a must. This way, the key points from one graph to the next can be matched.

- The slope of an *x* vs. *t* graph gives velocity. The slope of a *v* vs. *t* graph gives acceleration.

- The area under an *a* vs. *t* graph gives the change in velocity. The area under a *v* vs. *t* graph gives the displacement.

- The motion of an object in one dimension can be described using the Big Five Equations. Look for what is given, determine what must be calculated, and use the equation that has those variables in them. Remember that sometimes there is hidden (assumed) information in the problem such as $g = -10$ m/s^2

		Missing variable
Big Five #1*	$\Delta x = vt$	a
Big Five #2	$v = v_0 + at$	x
Big Five #3	$x = x_0 + v_0 t + \frac{1}{2} at^2$	v
Big Five #4	$x = x_0 + vt - \frac{1}{2} at^2$	v_0
Big Five #5	$v^2 = v_0^2 + 2a(x - x_0)$	T

*Because the acceleration is uniform: $\Delta x = \frac{1}{2}(v_0 + v)t$

- For projectiles, it is important to separate the horizontal and vertical components.

Horizontal Motion:	Vertical Motion:
$x = v_x t$	$y = y_0 + v_0 t + \dfrac{1}{2}gt^2$
$v_x = v_{0x}$ = constant	$v_y = v_{0y} + gt$
$a_x = 0$	$a = g = -10\dfrac{m}{s^2}$

At any given moment the relationship between v, v_x and v_y is given by:

$$v^2 = v_x{}^2 + v_y{}^2$$

$$v_x = v \cos \theta$$

$$v_y = \sin \theta$$

$$\theta = \tan^{-1}(\frac{v_y}{v_x})$$

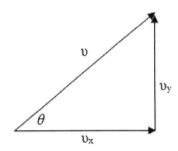

Practice Questions

1. Which graph represents a constant non-zero velocity?

   A. I only   B. II only   C. III only   D. I and II only   E. II and III only

2. A train starts from rest and accelerates uniformly until it has traveled 5.6 km and has acquired a velocity of 42 m/s. The train then moves at a constant velocity of 42 m/s for 420 s. The train then slows down uniformly at 0.065 m/s^2, until it stops moving. What is the acceleration during the first 5.6 km of travel?

   A. 0.29 m/s^2 B. 0.23 m/s^2 C. 0.16 m/s^2 D. 0.12 m/s^2 E. 0.20 m/s^2

3. A cannonball is fired straight up at 50 m/s. Ignoring air resistance, what is the velocity at the highest point it reaches before starting to return towards Earth?

   A. 0 m/s   B. 25 m/s   C. $\sqrt{50}$ m/s   D. 50 m/s   E. 100 m/s

4. The tendency of a moving object to remain in unchanging motion in the absence of an unbalanced force is:

   A. impulse   B. acceleration   C. free fall   D. inertia   E. momentum

5. Which statement is correct when an object that is moving in the $+x$ direction undergoes an acceleration of 2 m/s^2?

   A. It travels at 2 m/s   C. It decreases its velocity by 2 m/s every second
   B. It travels at 2 m/s^2 D. It decreases its velocity by 2 m/s^2 every second
                           E. It increases its velocity by 2 m/s every second

6. What is the increase in speed each second for a freely falling object?

   A. 0 m/s   C. 9.8 m/s
   B. 9.8 m/s^2 D. 19.6 m/s   E. 4.8 m/s

7. A marble is initially rolling up a slight incline at 0.2 m/s and starting at $t = 0$ s, decelerates uniformly at 0.05 m/s^2. At what time does the marble come to a stop?

   A. 2 s   B. 4 s   C. 8 s   D. 12 s   E. 6 s

8. An 8.7-hour trip is made at an average speed of 73 km/h. If the first third of the journey was driven at 96.5 km/h, what was the average speed for the rest of the trip?

A. 54 km/hr

C. 28 km/hr

B. 46 km/hr

D. 62 km/hr   **E.** 37 km/hr

9. The lightning flash and the thunder are not observed simultaneously because light travels much faster than sound. Therefore it can be assumed as instantaneous when the lightning occurs. What is the distance from the lightning bolt to the observer, if the delay between the sound and the lightning flash is 6 s? (Use speed of sound in air $v = 340$ m/s)

A. 2,040 m   **B.** 880 m   **C.** 2,360 m   **D.** 2,820 m   **E.** 1,460 m

10. If a cat jumps at a 60° angle off the ground with an initial velocity of 2.74 m/s, what is the highest point of the cat's trajectory? (Use the acceleration due to gravity $g = 9.8$ m/s^2)

A. 9.46 m   **B.** 0.69 m   **C.** 5.75 m   **D.** 1.55 m   **E.** 0.29 m

11. What is the resultant vector AB when vector A = 6 m and points 30° North of East, while vector B = 4 m and points 30° South of West?

A. 8 m at an angle 45° East of North

B. 8 m at an angle 30° North of East

C. 2 m at an angle 30° North of East

D. 2 m at an angle 45° North of East

E. 8 m at an angle 45° North of East

12. How much farther would an intoxicated driver's car travel before he hits the brakes than a sober driver's car if both cars are initially traveling at 49 mi/h, and the sober driver takes 0.33 s to hit the brakes while the intoxicated driver takes 1 s to hit the brakes?

A. 38 ft   **B.** 52 ft   **C.** 32 ft   **D.** 48 ft   **E.** 60 ft

13. A projectile is fired at time $t = 0$ s from point 0 at the edge of a cliff with initial velocity components of $v_{0x} = 80$ m/s and v_{0y} = 800 m/s. The projectile rises, then falls into the sea at point P. The time of flight of the projectile is 200 s. What is the height of the cliff? (Use the acceleration due to gravity $g = 10$ m/s^2)

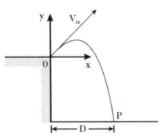

A. 30,000 m

C. 47,500 m

B. 45,000 m

D. 35,000 m

E. 40,000 m

14. Which of the following is a unit that can be used for a measure of weight?

    A. kilogram   **B.** kg·m/s   **C.** Newton   **D.** milligram   **E.** liter

15. Which of the following statements about the direction of the velocity and acceleration is correct for a ball that is thrown straight up, reaches a maximum height, and falls to its initial height?

    A. Its velocity changes from upward to downward and its acceleration points downward
    B. Its velocity points downward, and its acceleration points upward
    C. Both its velocity and its acceleration point downward
    D. Both its velocity and its acceleration point upward
    E. Its velocity points downward and its acceleration changes from upward to downward

Solutions

1. B is correct. Graph I depicts a constant zero velocity process.

Graph II depicts a constant non-zero velocity.

Graph III depicts non- constant velocity.

2. C is correct.

$$v_f^2 = v_i^2 + 2ad$$

$$a = (v_f^2 - v_i^2) / 2d$$

$$a = [(42 \text{ m/s})^2 - (0 \text{ m/s})^2] / [2(5,600 \text{ m})]$$

$$a = (1,764 \text{ m}^2/\text{s}^2) / 11,200 \text{ m}$$

$$a = 0.16 \text{ m/s}^2$$

3. A is correct.

At the maximum height, the velocity = 0 and the cannonball stops moving up and begins to come back.

4. D is correct.

An object's inertia is its resistance to change in motion.

5. E is correct.

$$v = v_0 + at$$

If $a = 2 \text{ m/s}^2$ then the object has a 2 m/s increase in velocity every second.

Example:

$$v_0 = 0 \text{ m/s}, a = 2 \text{ m/s}^2, t = 1 \text{ s}$$

$$v = 0 \text{ m/s} + (2 \text{ m/s}^2){\cdot}(1 \text{ s})$$

$$v = 2 \text{ m/s}$$

6. C is correct.

The acceleration due to gravity is 9.8 m/s^2.

If an object is in freefall, then every second it increases velocity by 9.8 m/s.

$$v = v_0 + at$$

$$v = v_0 + (9.8 \text{ m/s}^2){\cdot}(1 \text{ s})$$

$$v = v_0 + 9.8 \text{ m/s}$$

7. B is correct.

To determine the time at which the marble stops:

$v_2 - v_1 = a\Delta t$

where $v_1 = 0.2$ m/s and $a = -0.05$ m/s^2

$\Delta t = (v_2 - v_1) / a$

$\Delta t = (0$ m/s $- 0.2$ m/s$) / (-0.05$ m/s$^2)$

$\Delta t = (-0.2$ m/s$) / (-0.05$ m/s$^2)$

$\Delta t = 4$ s

8. D is correct.

$v_{avg} = (1/3)v_1 + (2/3)v_2$

73 km/h $= (1/3) \cdot (96.5$ km/h$) + (2/3)v_2$

73 km/h $= (32$ km/h$) + (2/3)v_2$

$(2/3)v_2 = 41$ km/h

$v_2 = (41$ km/h$) \cdot (3/2)$

$v_2 = 62$ km/h

9. A is correct. The distance to the lightning bolt is calculated by determining the distance traveled by the sound.

Distance = velocity × time

$d = vt$

$d = (340$ m/s$) \cdot (6$ s$)$

$d = 2{,}040$ m

10. E is correct.

Calculate the vertical component of the initial velocity:

$v_{up} = v(\sin \theta)$

$v_{up} = (2.74$ m/s$) \sin 60°$

$v_{up} = 2.37$ m/s

Then solve for the upward displacement given the initial upward velocity:

$d = (v_f^2 - v_i^2) / 2a$

$d = [(0 \text{ m/s})^2 - (2.37 \text{ m/s})^2] / 2(-9.8 \text{ m/s}^2)$

$d = (-5.62 \text{ m}^2/\text{s}^2) / (-19.6 \text{ m/s}^2)$

$d = 0.29 \text{ m}$

11. C is correct.

30° North of East is the exact opposite direction of 30° South of West, so set one vector as negative, and the direction of the resultant vector will be in the direction of the larger vector between A and B.

Since the magnitude of A is greater than the magnitude of B and vectors were added "tip to tail," the resultant vector is:

$AB = A + B$

$AB = 6 \text{ m} + (-4 \text{ m})$

$AB = 2 \text{ m at } 30° \text{ North of East}$

12. D is correct.

The solution is measured in feet, so first convert the car velocity into feet per second:

$v = (49 \text{ mi/h}) \cdot (5{,}280 \text{ ft/mi}) \cdot (1 \text{ h/3600 s})$

$v = 72 \text{ ft/s}$

The sober driver's distance:

$d = vt$

$d_{sober} = (72 \text{ ft/s}) \cdot (0.33 \text{ s})$

$d_{sober} = 24 \text{ ft}$

The intoxicated driver's distance:

$d = vt$

$d_{drunk} = (72 \text{ ft/s}) \cdot (1 \text{ s})$

$d_{drunk} = 72 \text{ ft}$

The differences between the distances:

$\Delta d = 72 \text{ ft} - 24 \text{ ft}$

$\Delta d = 48 \text{ ft}$

13. E is correct.

$$d = v_0 t + \tfrac{1}{2}gt^2$$

Set g as negative because it is in the opposite direction as +800 m/s:

$$d = (800 \text{ m/s}) \cdot (200 \text{ s}) + \tfrac{1}{2}(-10 \text{ m/s}^2) \cdot (200 \text{ s})^2$$

$$d = (160,000 \text{ m}) - (200,000 \text{ m})$$

$$d = -40,000 \text{ m}$$

The projectile traveled –40,000 m from the top of the cliff to the sea at point P, which means the cliff is 40,000 m from the base to the top.

14. C is correct.

1 Newton is the force needed to accelerate 1 kg of mass at a rate of 1 m/s^2.

$$F = ma$$

$$W = mg$$

$$N = \text{kg} \cdot \text{m/s}^2$$

15. A is correct.

When the ball is thrown upwards, its velocity is initially upwards but as it falls back down the velocity direction points downward.

The acceleration due to gravity always points down and does not change.

Please, leave your Customer Review on Amazon

Notes

Chapter 2

Force, Motion, Gravitation

- **Newton's First Law: Inertia**

- **Newton's Second Law: $F = ma$**

- **Newton's Third Law: Forces Equal and Opposite**

- **Weight**

- **Center of Mass**

- **Friction: Static and Kinetic**

- **Motion on an Inclined Plane**

- **Uniform Circular Motion and Centripetal Force**

- **Law of Gravitation**

- **Concept of a field**

Notes

Newton's First Law: Inertia

Newton's First Law states that an object at rest will remain at rest and an object in motion (with constant velocity) will remain in motion (with that same constant velocity) unless acted on by an external force.

In other terms, nothing will change about an object's motion regarding speed and direction, unless it is acted on by an outside force.

The key to this is the fact that all objects resist changes in their state of motion (even if that motion is zero) until an outside force manipulates them into a new state of motion. This is because all objects have *inertia*.

Inertia is an inherent property of all objects and is the tendency for objects to resist changes in their current state motion. Inertia cannot be calculated, but it can be measured by an object's *mass*; the more massive the object, the more inertia it will have.

In the SI system, mass is measured in kilograms (kg). Mass is not weight (remember: $w = mg$); weight depends on gravity (and can, therefore, change depending on location), while the mass of an object is always the same.

It is important to note that Newton's First Law is only valid in an inertial reference frame, which is any frame of reference that moves with constant velocity relative to the inertial system in question (no acceleration).

Newton's Second Law: *F = ma*

Newton's Second Law states that force is the vector product of mass and acceleration and it is expressed as:

$$\Sigma \vec{F} = m\vec{a}$$

(Net force equals mass times acceleration)

The unit for force in the SI system is the Newton, which is the product of the units of mass and acceleration (N = kg·m/s^2).

When dealing with force, it is important to note the units in question. The pound is a unit of force, not of mass, and can be equated to the Newton, but not to kilograms.

Conventionally, kilograms are often used as a measurement of weight (e.g., a person weighs 186 lbs or 80 kg). This usage can be misleading, as it is not technically correct; a kilogram is a unit of mass, and the weight of an object is a measurement of force. Remember that this common use of kilogram is incorrect and not to mistake kilograms for weight when solving problems.

Units for Mass and Force		
System	**Mass**	**Force**
SI	kilogram (kg)	Newton (N = kg·m/s^2)
CGS	gram (g)	dyne (= g·cm/s^2)
Imperial	slug	pound (lb)
Conversion factors: 1 dyne = 10^{-5} N; 1 lb ≈ 4.45 N; 1 slug ≈ 14.6 kg		

Like the equations of motion, Newton's Second Law can be split into *x* and *y* and *z*-components because the force is a vector:

$$\Sigma F_x = ma_x$$

$$\Sigma F_y = ma_y$$

$$\Sigma F_z = ma_z$$

Looking at the above equations, force is directly proportional to the mass of the object. This further explains Newton's First Law. For example, it requires much more force to push a boulder up a hill than to push a pebble up a hill, because the mass of the boulder is much greater than that of the pebble. If this situation is applied to Newton's First Law, the boulder has greater inertia than the pebble and will, therefore, be more resistant to changes in motion.

By applying Newton's Second Law, it can be said that the force needed to move (accelerate) the boulder is directly proportional to its mass and thus greater than the force needed to move (accelerate) the pebble.

Rearranging Newton's Second Law shows that acceleration is directly proportional to force and inversely proportional to mass:

$$a = \frac{F}{m}$$

For example, the force on an object with a mass of 2 kg is 4 N, therefore:

$$a = \frac{F}{m} \qquad a = \frac{4\ \text{N}}{2\ \text{kg}} \qquad a = 2\ \text{m/s}^2$$

If the force is now 8 N and the mass of the object is still 2 kg, then:

$$a = \frac{F}{m} \qquad a = \frac{8\ \text{N}}{2\ \text{kg}} \qquad a = 4\ \text{m/s}^2$$

Acceleration is directly proportional to force, so by doubling the force, the acceleration of the object is also doubled. The opposite holds when doubling the mass. Since mass is inversely proportional to acceleration, doubling the mass will halve the acceleration. This intuitively makes sense considering the mass of the boulder and pebble in the previous example. Exerting the same force on both will not give the same acceleration because the mass (which represents inertia, or the resistance to change) of each object is vastly different.

If the pebble has a mass of 5 kg and its acceleration is 20 m/s², what force was exerted on it?

$$a = \frac{F}{m} \qquad 20\ \text{m/s}^2 = \frac{F}{5\ \text{kg}} \qquad F = 100\ \text{N}$$

If the boulder has a mass of 20 kg and the same force of 100 N is exerted, what is the acceleration? The boulder has four times the mass of the pebble, so the acceleration must be one-fourth that of the pebble: 5 m/s² as compared to 20 m/s² for the pebble.

Both force and acceleration are vectors because they have a direction. Many test questions omit the directional attribute because it is usually assumed. For example, when an apple falls to the ground, the force of gravity acts downwards and the apple, of course, falls downwards. Many such questions are cases of substituting values into the appropriate formula.

However, more difficult questions have directional attributes associated with them. For example, when a bar of soap slides down an inclined plane, the force of gravity acts downwards, but the acceleration is not completely downwards; rather, it is slanted. Therefore, vector analysis is needed.

Solving problems involving Newton's Second Law

- Visualize the scenario. Draw a sketch and always use a free body diagram.

- Clearly define an appropriate coordinate system. This is particularly important when dealing with inclined planes because the angle between the normal force and the gravitational force that is acting on the object is altered.

- Always apply Newton's Second Law to each mass separately, and when there are forces in two or more directions, apply Newton's Second Law to each direction separately.

- The term "translational equilibrium" implies two equations: $\Sigma F_x = 0$ and $\Sigma F_y = 0$.

- When $\Sigma F = 0$, $a = 0$ and vice versa.

- Solve the component equations. If the acceleration of x and/or y is known, or the object is moving at constant velocity ($a = 0$), then the component equations can be used to solve for unknown forces.

- Remember the unit circle to calculate trigonometric functions, and make certain to use degrees if the angles are given in degrees, or radians if they are given in radians.

Newton's Third Law: Forces Equal and Opposite

To understand Newton's Third Law, it is essential to understand how forces work. A force must have a source object (i.e., any force exerted on one object is caused by another object). When a person interacts with an object by exerting a force on it, that object exerts the same amount, or magnitude, of force back on them. This is often simplified into the common dogma:

Every action has an equal and opposite reaction.

In other words, if a body A exerts a force F_A on body B, then B exerts a force F_B back on body A in the form:

$$F_B = -F_A$$

To correctly apply the Newton's Third Law, it is important to understand that the forces are exerted on different objects, and they should not be treated as if they were acting on the same object. These matched forces are *action and reaction pairs*.

Here is a helpful notation: the first subscript is the object that the force is being exerted on and the second is the source object. For example, a person (P) walking forward exerts a force on the ground (G) which exerts an equal and opposite force to move them forward. This can be expressed as:

$$\vec{F}_{GP} = -\vec{F}_{PG}$$

Horizontal force exerted on the ground by person's foot

$\vec{\mathbf{F}}_{GP}$

Horizontal force exerted on the person's foot by the ground

$\vec{\mathbf{F}}_{PG}$

Another good example of Newton's Third Law is rocket propulsion. When a rocket is in flight, hot gases from combustion spew out of the tail of the rocket at high speeds (*action force*). The *reaction force* is what propels the rocket forward. It is important to note that the rocket does not need anything to "push" against. Regardless if it is traveling within Earth's atmosphere or in the vacuum of space, the rocket can propel itself forward because of the action-reaction forces from combustion.

To summarize, all three of Newton's Laws of Motion can be extrapolated and observed in just about any situation. A cannon and cannonball provide an example:

- A cannon is initially at rest. It has a large mass and therefore large inertia. It will remain at rest until a force is applied (Newton's First Law).

- When the cannon is fired, a large force is applied by the cannon to the cannonball to overcome the inertia of the cannonball and cause it to accelerate (Newton's Second Law).

- The large force applied by the cannon is reciprocated by the cannonball back onto the cannon, causing the cannon to recoil (Newton's Third Law).

Why does the cannonball accelerate faster than the recoiling cannon?

Consider all three laws, but the most important component to consider is inertia.

The Third Law states that the forces being exerted on the cannon and cannonball must be the same.

The Second Law states that force and mass (inertia) determine acceleration; since the forces are equal, but the masses are considerably different, the accelerations are considerably different. The cannonball will accelerate faster because its mass (i.e., inertia) is less than the mass of the cannon: $a = \frac{F}{m}$.

Once the cannonball is airborne, it will remain in flight (according to the first law) unless a force acts upon it to change its motion. In this case, air resistance and gravity will eventually cause the cannonball to slow down and fall to the ground.

Solving Problems with Newton's Laws – Free-Body Diagrams

1. Draw a sketch.

2. For every object, draw a free-body diagram showing all the forces acting *on* the object.

   Make the magnitudes and directions as accurate as possible.

   Label each force.

   If there are multiple objects, draw a separate diagram for each.

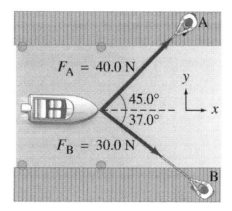

3. Resolve vectors into components.

4. Apply Newton's Second Law to each component.

5. Solve for the net force in each component direction and combine each component to determine the total net force.

Weight

Weight is the gravitational force (i.e., the force of gravity) that acts on a mass when an object is close to the Earth's surface (the gravitational force changes with large increases or decreases in altitude). It is a force and is, therefore, a vector quantity. The gravitational force is:

$$\vec{F_g} = m\vec{g}$$

where g is the acceleration due to gravity at 9.8 m/s^2 (sometimes rounded to 10 m/s^2).

An object weighs more on an elevator accelerating up because $F = mg + ma$, where a is the acceleration of the elevator. An elevator accelerating up has the same force as an elevator decelerating on its way down, only the direction of the acceleration changes.

An object weighs less when it is further away from the Earth because the force of gravity decreases with distance. However, when an object orbits in space (such as an astronaut in a spacecraft), it is not truly weightless in space. An astronaut is falling toward the Earth at the same rate as the spacecraft he resides. If the astronaut's spacecraft were to fall from space to the surface of the Earth, their weight would increase during the fall due to the increase of gravitational acceleration as they get closer to the Earth's surface.

For a given mass, its weight on Earth is different than it is on the Moon. If a person stands on the Moon, which has a gravitational acceleration of about 1/6 g, that person is 1/6 of their normal weight on Earth. Their mass, however, is the same in both locations.

From Newton's Second Law, an object at rest must have no net force on it. It is also true that an object always has a gravitational force acting upon it.

To adhere to both Newton's Second and Third Laws, there must be an equal but opposite force. If the object is resting on a flat surface, then the force of the surface pushing up on the object is the normal force.

This force is always perpendicular to the plane of the object.

When an object is lying still on a horizontal surface, the normal force is equal and opposite to the weight (i.e., the force of gravity). It is exactly as large as needed to balance the downward force from the object (if the required force gets too big, something breaks).

For example, if a statue is placed on a table, the normal force from the table is equal and opposite to the force of gravity.

As a result, the statue experiences no net force and does not move.

$$-\vec{F}_G = \vec{F}_N$$

Center of Mass

Every object has a center of mass. This is a single, approximate point at which all an object's mass is concentrated. It is also at this point that external forces can be considered to act on the object. If an object is balanced on its center of mass, it will spin uniformly about this axis. If an object is uniform along its entire length, the center of mass is the center of the object. If the object is not uniform, the center of mass is the point obtained by taking an average of all the positions weighted by their respective masses:

$$x_{cm} = \frac{\sum x_i m_i}{\sum m_i} \qquad y_{cm} = \frac{\sum y_i m_i}{\sum m_i} \qquad z_{cm} = \frac{\sum z_i m_i}{\sum m_i}$$

It is not necessary to have absolute coordinates when calculating the center of mass. Set the point of reference for a convenient location and use relative coordinates. It is important to understand that the center of mass need not be within the object. For example, a doughnut's center of mass is in the center of its hole. For two objects, the center of mass lies closer to the one with the most mass.

Imagine two balls of an unequal mass attached to a massless stick. The equation and image below describe the situation and the center of mass calculation:

$$m_A > m_B$$

$$x_{CM} = \frac{m_A x_A + m_B x_B}{m_A + m_B} = \frac{m_A x_A + m_B x_B}{\sum M}$$

If the difference in mass between two objects is extremely large, then the center of mass can be assumed to be that of the more massive object.

For example, the center of mass of the Earth and a man in space is going to be almost at the Earth's center because the man is comparatively tiny, and therefore his coordinate, weighted with respect to his mass, is almost negligible.

Translational Motion using Center of Mass

When problems involve directional forces on an object and the subsequent path that the object takes, these directions and paths are based on the object's center of mass.

The object is treated as a point or particle that has the same mass as the object but is located at the object's center of mass. The sum of all the forces acting on a system is equal to the total mass of the system multiplied by the acceleration of the center of mass:

$$ma_{\text{CM}} = F_{\text{net}}$$

This simplifies calculations because calculating the motion of an irregularly-shaped object as a whole involves much complex mathematics.

Center of Gravity

The center of gravity is the average location of the weight of an object, and it is the point at which the gravitational force can be considered to act. It is the same as the center of mass only if the gravitational force does not vary between different parts of the object.

The center of gravity can be found experimentally by suspending an object from different points. To perform this experiment, a piece of string about the length of the object is securely attached to a point near the object's edge. The object is then held by the string near the point of connection, and a line is traced along the hanging string. The string will hang straight down, perpendicular to the ground because gravitational force acts purely in the *y*-direction. The object is then rotated, and the steps are repeated. The point at which the drawn lines cross is the center of gravity. If hundreds of lines were drawn onto the object, all of them would intersect at this point. Similar to the center of mass, an object will rotate perfectly around its center of gravity.

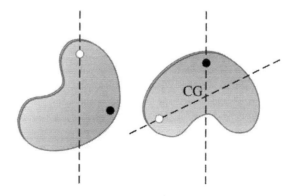

Friction: Static and Kinetic

Friction is a force that always opposes the direction of motion. Like all other forces, friction is a vector. A dog can walk, and cars can drive because of friction. Lubricants reduce friction because they change surface properties and decrease the coefficient of friction. Heat is produced as a by-product from the force of friction.

What is friction? Friction has to do with multiple factors, and it changes depending on the surface of contact. On a microscopic scale, most surfaces are rough. As one surface moves over the other, the crevices of the two surfaces catch and release. This is where the force resisting motion (i.e., friction) comes from.

In the figure below, the block is moving to the right, and as its ragged surface moves over the ragged surface of the table, a force of friction acts to the left, in the direction opposing motion.

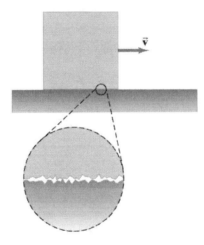

The frictional force is calculated as the product of the normal force of an object and a dimensionless value of the *coefficient of friction*. The coefficient of friction is determined empirically and is intrinsic to the material properties of the surface and the object. Friction occurs in two types: static and kinetic.

Static friction pertains to objects sitting still (an object can remain stationary on an inclined plane because of static friction).

Kinetic friction pertains to objects in motion (a vase sliding across a table has its motion resisted by a force of kinetic friction).

Both the force and the coefficient of static friction are always greater than the force and coefficient of kinetic friction. This is why it takes a greater force to start an object moving on a rough surface than it does to keep the object moving on the same surface.

Equations to find friction:

$$\text{Static friction: } F_s = \mu_s F_N$$

$$\text{Kinetic friction: } F_k = \mu_k F_N$$

where μ is the coefficient of friction and F_N is the normal force.

Note:

$$F_s > F_k$$

$$\mu_s > \mu_k$$

This table lists the measured values of some coefficients of friction. Note that the coefficient depends on both surfaces.

Coefficients of Friction		
Surfaces	**Coefficient of Static Friction μ_s**	**Coefficient of Kinetic Friction μ_k**
Wood on wood	0.4	0.2
Ice on ice	0.1	0.03
Steel on steel (unlubricated)	0.7	0.6
Rubber on dry concrete	1.0	0.8
Rubber on wet concrete	0.7	0.5
Rubber on other solid surfaces	1 – 4	1
Teflon® on Teflon® in air	0.04	0.04
Teflon® on steel in air	0.04	0.04
Lubricated ball bearings	<0.01	<0.01
Synovial joints (in human limbs)	0.01	0.01
Values are approximate and intended only as a guide.		

An object at rest on a frictional surface will have the force of static friction acting on it. The force of this friction is $F_s \leq \mu_s F_N$, and it is only equal when the object is just about to move, meaning that the static friction is on the verge of changing over to kinetic friction.

For an object that starts at rest and then has a force applied to it, the force of static friction increases as the applied force increases, until the applied force is enough to overcome the maximum value of static friction.

Then the object starts to move, and the force of kinetic friction takes over.

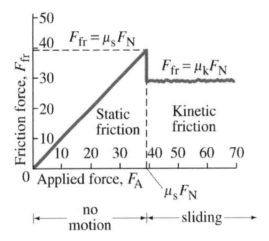

Note: the normal force of an object on a horizontal surface is equal to the weight ($w = mg$) of the object.

However, on an inclined plane, the normal force is perpendicular to the inclined plane, and its magnitude is equal to the weight of the object times the cosine of the incline angle ($F_N = w \cos \theta$; see the chapter on inclined planes).

Motion on an Inclined Plane

When an object is on an inclined plane, the force of gravity is divided into two components: one component is normal (i.e., perpendicular) to the plane surface and the other component is parallel to the plane surface.

The image and equations below describe the situation:

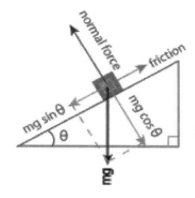

Parallel Force: $F_\parallel = mg \sin \theta$

Perpendicular Force: $F_\perp = F_N$

$$F_N = mg \cos \theta$$

where θ is the angle between the horizontal axis and the surface on which the object rests.

How does the force of gravity affect the force of friction? An object on an incline has three forces acting on it: the normal force, the gravitational force and the frictional force:

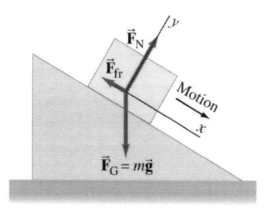

However, the gravitational force is split into parallel and perpendicular components concerning the incline. In the case of an object moving down the inclined plane at a constant velocity, the parallel component of gravity is equal and opposite to the force of kinetic friction:

$$F_\parallel = F_k$$

$$F_\parallel = \mu_k F_N$$

$$mg \sin \theta = \mu_k mg \cos \theta$$

If the object is not moving, the parallel component of gravity is instead equal and opposite to the force of static friction:

$$F_\parallel = F_s$$

$$F_\parallel = \mu_s F_N$$

$$mg \sin \theta = \mu_s mg \cos \theta$$

Note: frictional forces are always less than or equal to the forces causing an object to move; they are never greater than the forces causing movement.

If a frictional force exceeds the other forces involved, it causes the object to move in the opposite direction.

Friction does not produce movement; it only inhibits it.

When an object is pushed or pulled up an inclined plane, the parallel component of gravity and the force of friction must be overcome; these forces need to be broken up into their x and y components to perform calculations.

Only the component parallel to the plane contributes to the motion.

For example, if a block of mass m is accelerating down an inclined plane of angle θ with friction present, what is its acceleration along the x-axis?

$$F_\parallel = mg \sin \theta$$

$$F_N = mg \cos \theta$$

$$F_{fr} = \mu_k F_N$$

$$F_x = F_\parallel - F_{fr}$$

$$ma_x = mg \sin \theta - \mu_k mg \cos \theta$$

$$a_x = g \sin \theta - \mu_k g \cos \theta$$

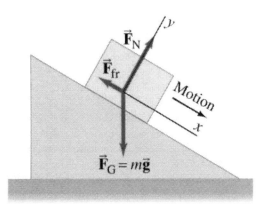

Uniform Circular Motion and Centripetal Force

An object moving in a circle at constant speed is in *uniform circular motion*; this is an example of simple harmonic motion.

The instantaneous velocity is always tangent to the circle, and the *centripetal* (or radial) acceleration points inward along the radius.

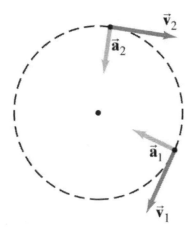

The equation for centripetal (radial) acceleration for uniform circular motion is:

$$a_c = \frac{v^2}{r}$$

Distinguishing between velocity and speed is important.

Velocity is displacement over time, while speed is the distance over time. In the case of uniform circular motion, displacement is the shortest straight-line distance between two points on the perimeter of a circle (this is a *chord*).

However, distance is the path that the object travels and can be calculated as the product of the radius and arc angle:

$$s = \theta r$$

When working with circular motion problems, the instantaneous velocity is almost always given and is equal to the speed.

Some typical cases:

- For displacements and distances that approach zero, the instantaneous velocity equals the speed.

- For a quarter of the circle ($\pi/2$ radians or 90°), the displacement is the hypotenuse of a right-angled triangle with the radius as the other two sides. Using the Pythagorean Theorem, the displacement is $\sqrt{2r^2}$. The distance is the length of the arc, or ¼ of the circumference.

- For halfway around the circle, the displacement is the diameter, and the distance is half the circumference.

- For three-quarters around the circle, the displacement is again obtained by the Pythagorean Theorem. The magnitude of the displacement here is the same as that for a quarter of a circle ($\sqrt{2r^2}$), but the direction is different. The distance is ¾ of the circumference.

- Going around the circle completely means the displacement is zero, which makes the average velocity zero as well. The distance is equal to the circumference.

- The velocity is always less than or equal to the speed, and the displacement is always less than or equal to the distance. Displacement and velocity are vectors, while distance and speed are scalars.

Frequency (*f*) is the number of times an object makes a revolution in one second, measured in Hertz (Hz = s^{-1}). The *period* (*T*) of an object in circular motion is the time it takes the object to make one revolution, measured in seconds (s). The frequency and period of an object are inversely related:

$$f = 1/T$$

Formulas to know:

Centripetal Acceleration: $\quad a_c = \dfrac{v^2}{r}$

Circumference: $\quad C = 2\pi r$

Arc: $\quad arc = \dfrac{\theta}{2\pi} \times C = r\theta$

Area of a Circle: $\quad A = \pi r^2$

Note that theta (θ) is in radians, and that 2π radians = 360 degrees.

Centripetal Force ($F = \frac{mv^2}{r}$)

In some situations, more forces are acting on an object than in others.

For example, a puck gliding across an air table experiences almost no frictional force and no pushing force.

However, a block being pulled up a rough incline experiences both a frictional force and a force of tension. Both objects experience a normal force and a gravitational force. In regards to circular motion, the number of forces (and whether they are changing or constant) differs depending on the situation.

The following principle is useful when considering the qualities of circular motion: centripetal force is due to centripetal acceleration.

Centripetal acceleration is due to changes in velocity when going around a circle.

The changes in velocity are due to a constant change in direction.

The diagrams demonstrate a change in velocity due to change in direction, and the resulting centripetal acceleration.

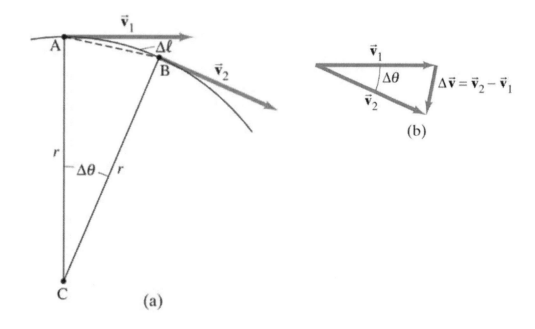

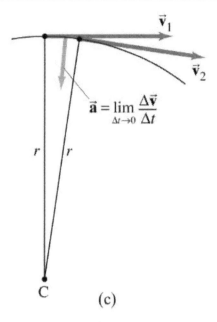

(c)

The centripetal force is found when the mass is multiplied by the centripetal acceleration. The centripetal force may be provided by friction, gravity, tension, the normal force or other forces.

Centripetal force: $F = ma_c = \dfrac{mv^2}{r}$ Centripetal acceleration: $a_c = \dfrac{v^2}{r}$

Sometimes a negative sign is used for centripetal force to indicate that the direction of the force is toward the center of the circle.

In centripetal motion, the acceleration is always inward.

Since the force is always in the same direction as the acceleration, the direction of both the acceleration and the force is toward the center of the circle.

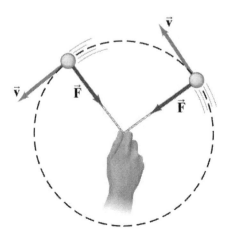

For example, suppose a ball attached to a string is spun around in the air, and suddenly the string breaks. The ball flies off, following a line of motion tangent to its previous circular path. For an object to be in uniform circular motion, there must be a net force acting on it in the same direction as the acceleration. If gravity is ignored, the centripetal force is the only force acting on the ball and keeping it the same distance away from the center.

If the centripetal force vanishes (the string breaks), the object will retain its instantaneous velocity at the point in time at which the string broke (following Newton's Laws) and flew off, tangent to the circle.

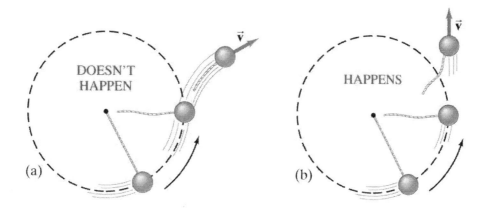

Banked curves (sloped inwards) provide another example of centripetal force. When a car goes around a curve, there must be a net force pointing toward the center of the circle, of which the curve is an arc. If the road is flat, that force is supplied by friction. If the frictional force is insufficient, the car will tend to move more closely in a straight line.

If the tires do not slip, the friction is static. If the tires do start to slip, the friction is kinetic. This is bad in two ways:

1. The kinetic frictional force is smaller than the static, and the tires will have less grip on the road.

2. The static frictional force can point toward the center of the circle, but the kinetic frictional force opposes the direction of motion, making it very difficult to regain control of the car and continue around the curve.

Banking the curve on the road can help keep cars from skidding. In fact, for every banked curve, there is one speed where the entire centripetal force is supplied by the horizontal component of the normal force, and no friction is required.

This occurs when:

$$F_N \sin \theta = \frac{mv^2}{r} = ma_c$$

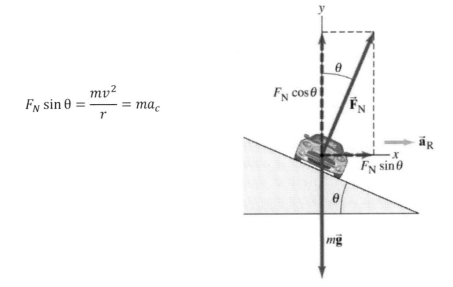

Non-uniform Circular Motion

It is important to note that uniform circular motion is usually an idealized scenario and most systems exhibit some degree of non-uniform circular motion. An object experiencing non-uniform circular motion will have varying speed. It will still have an instantaneous velocity tangent to its circular motion, but the acceleration will not point inward along the radius. Because its speed is changing, it must have a tangential component to its acceleration (and to its force) as well as a radial one.

The direction of net acceleration, and thus net force, depends on the combination of these two components.

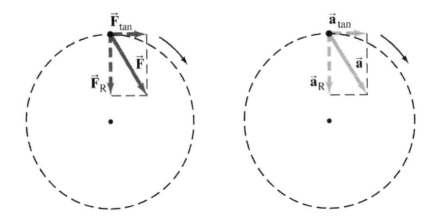

Law of Gravitation

Newton's Third Law of Motion states that every force has an equal and opposite reaction force, indicating that every object pulls on every other object.

If the force of gravity is being exerted on objects on Earth, what is the origin of that force? Newton realized that the force must come from the Earth itself. He further realized that this force must be what keeps the Moon in its orbit.

Newton derived another law that explains this relationship, the Law of Gravitation. It states that any two bodies in the universe attract each other with force related to the square of the distance between them, the product of their two masses, and the gravitational constant *G*. Force, in this case, is defined as:

$$F_G = G \times \frac{m_1 m_2}{r^2}$$

Remember, the force of gravity on an object acts through its center of gravity.

How did Newton come up with this equation?

The gravitational force is one half of an action-reaction pair: Earth exerts a downward force on a person, and they exert an upward force on the Earth. The reaction force that they exert on the Earth is undetectable because the mass of a person is negligible compared to that of the Earth.

However, for bodies with less disparity in mass (such as the Earth and the Moon), the reaction force can be significant.

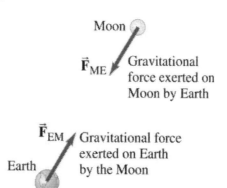

Therefore, the gravitational force must be proportional to both masses. By observing planetary orbits, Newton also concluded that the gravitational force must decrease as the inverse of the square of the distance between the masses.

Where does the constant G come from?

Earlier in this chapter, the acceleration of an object toward the Earth's surface due to the force of Earth's gravity equaled 9.8 m/s² and was represented by the variable *g*.

Here, the variable used is *G*, which is different. *G* is a constant of proportionality, the *universal gravitational constant*. Note the term "universal;" everything in the universe is pulling on everything else. Observe the value of *G* and how it affects the equation.

Since Newton could measure force, he was able to assign a value for *G* by rearranging the equation and using known values. In this case, he used two 1 kg masses, 1 m apart, of known force:

$$G = 0.000000000067 \ N \cdot m^2/kg^2$$

$$G = 6.67 \times 10^{-11} \ N \cdot m^2/kg^2$$

The magnitude of the gravitational constant *G* can also be measured in the laboratory through the Cavendish experiment, pictured below:

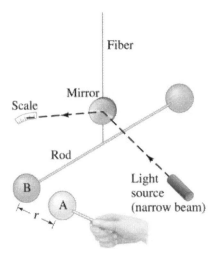

Since *G* is a very small value, it can dilute the value of $\dfrac{m_1 m_2}{r^2}$

For example, in the case of a person pulling on the stars and vice versa, the sheer fact that the stars are a huge distance away is enough to make $\frac{m_1 m_2}{r^2}$ a small value (especially since the distance is squared in this equation). Multiplying it by G makes it infinitely small, to the point of approaching zero. Even when considering a person's pull on their neighbor's house, where the value of "r" is relatively small, G still dilutes the value.

If that person weighs 0.7 kg, the house weighs 700 kg, and the distance between them is 70 m, then:

$$\frac{m_1 m_2}{r^2} = \frac{(0.7 \text{ kg})(700 \text{ kg})}{(70 \text{ m})^2} = 0.1 \text{ kg}^2/\text{m}^2$$

If that is multiplied by $6.67 \times 10^{-11} \text{ N} \cdot \text{m}^2/\text{kg}^2$, the resulting force is $6.67 \times 10^{-12} \text{ N}$, an undetectable value.

As shown in the previous examples, the only real gravitational force felt on Earth is that which is caused by the Earth. The concept of G was used to determine the mass of the Earth mathematically. Since the force of gravity at the Earth's surface was known (9.8 N) and the radius of the Earth was known (which approximates the distance between the center of the Earth and the center of a person standing on the surface), an object can be substituted for m and solved for the Earth's mass as m_E:

On the surface of the Earth, F = ma, so:

$$F_G = mg = G\frac{m m_E}{r_E^2}$$

Solving for g gives:

$$g = G\frac{m_E}{r_E^2}$$

Knowing g and the radius of the Earth, the mass of the Earth can be calculated ($r_E = 6.38 \times 10^6$ m):

$$m_E = \frac{g r_E^2}{G} = \frac{(9.8 \text{ m/s}^2)(6.38 \times 10^6 \text{ m})^2}{6.67 \times 10^{-11} \text{ N} \cdot \text{m}^2/\text{kg}^2} = 5.98 \times 10^{24} \text{kg}$$

The Earth has a mass of about 6×10^{24} kg. Since this is a huge number, multiplying it by G will not decrease it to a negligible amount. The resulting value is the force felt by those on Earth.

Like the value of G, the value of r has a great impact on the result of this equation. There are two important things to note about the distance component, r, of this equation:

$$F_G = G \frac{m_1 m_1}{r^2}$$

First of all, it refers to the distance between the centers of mass of the two objects (this becomes critical in the discussion of the Earth's pull on objects). In this regard, the two objects are treated as *point masses*; that is, as if they were the size of one-dimensional points at the locations of their centers of mass, but with the same amount of mass.

Secondly, the distance is squared, which means that subtle changes in distance result in large changes in F, as will be demonstrated with the *inverse square law*.

According to the equation above, the force is inversely proportional to the square of the distance, which means that by increasing the distance between two objects, the force between those two objects is decreased by the inverse square. For example, if the distance increases by a factor of two, the force of gravity decreases by a factor of $2^2 = 4$.

This is the reason why the gravitational forces of other planets are not felt on Earth, even though they have large masses which are equal to or greater than that of Earth. Since the distance between Earth and any given planet is so great, and because that distance is squared in the calculation for gravitational force, the force felt on Earth due to these other planets is negligible and essentially eliminated.

For example, Mars is 2.25×10^{11} m away, and it has a mass of 6.4×10^{23} kg. For a 1 kg mass on Earth, how much force is it exerting on Mars?

$$F = (6.67 \times 10^{-11}\ \text{Nm}^2/\text{kg}^2) \times \frac{(1\ \text{kg})(6.4 \times 10^{23}\ \text{kg})}{(2.25 \times 10^{11}\text{m})^2}$$

$$F = 6.83 \times 10^{-10}\ \text{N}$$

In most calculations thus far, a gravitational acceleration value of 9.8 m/s² has been used. For most calculations, this is acceptable.

However, in reality, the acceleration due to gravity varies over the Earth's surface as a result of altitude, local geology, and the shape of the Earth, which is not quite spherical.

Acceleration Due to Gravity at Various Locations		
Location	Elevation (m)	g (m/s²)
New York	0	9.803
San Francisco	0	9.800
Denver	1,650	9.796
Mount Everest	8,800	9.770
Sydney	0	9.798
Equator	0	9.780
North Pole (calculated)	0	9.832

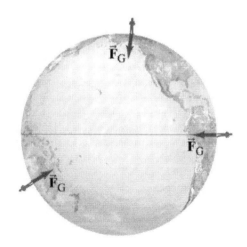

Concept of a Field

Often, forces which act on a body act in a single direction, like a car that accelerates in a straight line path. Other times, however, they can act in a multitude of directions, either from a singular point outward or all directions inward towards a point. One common example of this is the gravitational force.

On Earth, people experience gravity in a single direction (downward) because people are so small relative to the size of the Earth that the Earth is always a flat surface below them. In actuality, since the Earth is an approximate sphere, its gravitational pull comes from all directions towards its center of mass.

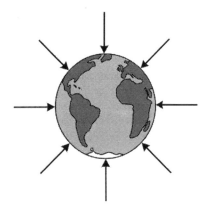

These are field lines, or more specifically to this scenario, gravitational field lines. Field lines are often used to depict situations in which multiple vectors are acting in a plane or 3D space.

Notice above that only eight arrows are used to depict the gravitational field around the Earth, even though gravity acts continuously all around the Earth. It would be impossible to draw enough field lines to represent the continuity of Earth's gravitational pull accurately, so it suffices to draw enough lines to show that Earth's gravity acts from all directions.

Notice that the arrows are closer to each other the closer they are to the Earth, and farther apart the farther away they are from the Earth.

Field lines that are drawn close together represent a stronger field, and field lines drawn farther apart represent a weaker field.

From the figure above, the field lines are closer together nearer to Earth, signifying the stronger gravitational force closer to the surface of the Earth. This supports the Law of Gravitation, which was discussed in the previous section.

In general, field lines represent a field of vectors, typically force vectors. The force vectors used in calculations, such as projectile motion, a mass-pulley system or a mass on a pendulum, are usually single arrows that indicate the direction of a single force. This is because the masses involved in these problems are treated as point masses or masses that have an infinitesimally small size, which reduces the complexity of the calculations.

In actuality, a boulder-sized projectile or car-sized object on a pendulum would have a force vector field acting on its entire volume, with all of the vectors pointing in the same direction.

For example, when a car accelerates in a straight line path, typically this action is represented by a single force vector originating from the center of the car's mass in the direction of motion. To depict it more accurately, a force vector would be drawn from every single point in the car in the direction of motion, creating a force vector field.

Since this creates a far more complex calculation to determine a negligibly more accurate value of the force involved, the vector field is simplified to a single vector originating from the object's center of mass.

Chapter Summary

- Newton's First Law: An object at rest will remain at rest, and an object in motion (with constant velocity) will remain in motion (with that same constant velocity) unless acted upon by an external force.

- Newton's Second Law: Force is the vector product of mass and acceleration, expressed as:

$$F = ma$$

- Newton's Third Law: When a person interacts with an object by exerting a force on it, that object exerts the same amount, or magnitude, of force back on them.

- Solving Problems with Newton's Laws – Free-Body Diagrams

    1. Draw a sketch.

    2. For every object, draw a free-body diagram showing all the forces acting *on* the object.

        Make the magnitudes and directions as accurate as possible.

        Label each force. If there are multiple objects, draw a separate diagram for each.

    3. Resolve vectors into components.

    4. Apply Newton's Second Law to each component.

    5. Solve for the net force in each component direction and combine each component to determine the total net force.

- Gravitational force: $F_g = mg$, where g is the acceleration due to gravity at 9.8 m/s^2.

- Equations to find friction, the force that always opposes the direction of motion:

Static friction: $F_s = \mu_s F_N$

Kinetic friction: $F_k = \mu_k F_N$

where μ is the coefficient of friction and F_N is the normal force.

Motion on an Inclined Plane:

Parallel Force: $F_\| = mg \sin \theta$

Perpendicular Force: $F_\perp = F_N$

$F_N = mg \cos \theta$

where θ is the angle between the horizontal axis and the surface on which the object rests.

- An object moving in a circle at constant speed is in *uniform circular motion*; this is an example of simple harmonic motion.

The instantaneous velocity is always tangent to the circle, and the *centripetal* (or radial) acceleration points inward along the radius.

- Centripetal acceleration for uniform circular motion:

$a_c = v^2/r$

- Centripetal force:

$$F = ma_c = \frac{mv^2}{r}$$

- Law of Gravitation:

$$F_G = G \times \frac{m_1 m_2}{r^2}$$

Notes

Practice Questions

1. Two bodies of different masses are subjected to identical forces. Compared to the body with a smaller mass, the body with a greater mass experiences:

   A. less acceleration, because the ratio of force to mass is smaller

   B. greater acceleration, because the ratio of force to mass is greater

   C. less acceleration, because the product of mass and acceleration is smaller

   D. greater acceleration, because the product of mass and acceleration is greater

   E. equal acceleration, because the forces are identical

2. An object is propelled along a straight-line path by force. If the net force were doubled, the object's acceleration would:

   A. halve   **C.** double

   B. stay the same   **D.** quadruple   **E.** none of the above

3. A 500 kg rocket ship is firing two jets at once. The two jets are at right angles with one firing with a force of 500 N and the other with a force of 1,200 N. What is the magnitude of the acceleration of the rocket ship?

   A. 1.4 m/s^2 **B.** 2.6 m/s^2 **C.** 3.4 m/s^2 **D.** 5.6 m/s^2 **E.** 4.2 m/s^2

4. Assume the strings and pulleys in the diagram below have negligible masses and the coefficient of kinetic friction between the 2 kg block and the table is 0.25. What is the acceleration of the 2 kg block? (Use acceleration due to gravity g = 9.8 m/s^2)

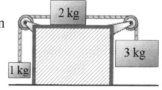

   A. 3.2 m/s^2 **B.** 4 m/s^2 **C.** 0.3 m/s^2 **D.** 1.7 m/s^2 **E.** 2.5 m/s^2

5. Which of the following statements must be true for an object moving with constant velocity in a straight line?

   A. The net force on the object is zero

   B. No forces are acting on the object

   C. A constant force is being applied in the direction opposite of motion

   D. A constant force is being applied in the direction of motion

   E. There is no frictional force acting on the object

6. A person gives a shopping cart an initial push along a horizontal floor to get it moving and then releases the cart. The cart travels forward along the floor, gradually slowing as it moves. Consider the horizontal force on the cart while it is moving forward and slowing. Which of the following statements is correct?

    A. Only a forward force is acting, which diminishes with time
    B. Only a backward force is acting; no forward force is acting
    C. Both a forward and a backward force are acting on the cart, but the forward force is larger
    D. Both a forward and a backward force are acting on the cart, but the backward force is larger
    E. No forces are acting because it has been released

7. A truck is using a hook to tow a car whose mass is one quarter that of the truck. If the force exerted by the truck on the car is 6,000 N, then the force exerted by the car on the truck is:

    A. 1,500 N   **B.** 24,000 N   **C.** 6,000 N   **D.** 12,000 N
    E. Need to know if the car is accelerating

8. How large is the force of friction impeding the motion of a bureau when the 120 N bureau is being pulled across the sidewalk at a constant speed by a force of 30 N?

    A. 0 N   **B.** 30 N   **C.** 120 N   **D.** 3 N   **E.** 15 N

9. An object maintains its state of motion because it has:

    A. mass   **B.** acceleration   **C.** speed   **D.** weight   **E.** all of the above

10. The Earth and the Moon attract each other with the force of gravity. The Earth's radius is 3.7 times that of the Moon, and the Earth's mass is 80 times greater than the Moon's. The acceleration due to gravity on the surface of the Moon is 1/6 the acceleration due to gravity on the Earth's surface. If the distance between the Earth and the Moon decreases by a factor of 4, how would the force of gravity between the Earth and the Moon change?

    A. Remain the same   **C.** Decrease by a factor of 16
    B. Increase by a factor of 16   **D.** Decrease by a factor of 4
                                E. Increase by a factor of $1/\sqrt{4}$

11. Two forces acting on an object have magnitudes $F_1 = -6.6$ N and $F_2 = 2.2$ N. Which third force causes the object to be in equilibrium?

    A. 4.4 N at 162° counterclockwise from F_1
    B. 4.4 N at 108° counterclockwise from F_1
    C. 7 N at 162° counterclockwise from F_1
    D. 7 N at 108° counterclockwise from F_1
    E. 3.3 N at 162° counterclockwise from F_1

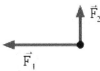

12. What are the readings on the spring scales when a 17 kg fish is weighed with two spring scales if each scale has negligible weight?

A. The top scale reads 17 kg, and the bottom scale reads 0 kg

B. Each scale reads greater than 0 kg and less than 17 kg, but the sum of the scales is 17 kg

C. The bottom scale reads 17 kg, and the top scale reads 0 kg

D. The sum of the two scales is 34 kg

E. Each scale reads 8.5 kg

13. Two forces of equal magnitude are acting on an object as shown. If the magnitude of each force is 2.3 N and the angle between them is 40°, which third force causes the object to be in equilibrium?

A. 1.8 N pointing to the right   C. 3.5 N pointing to the right

B. 2.2 N pointing to the right   D. 6.6 N pointing to the right

                                       E. 4.3 N pointing to the right

14. An object at rest on an inclined plane starts to slide when the incline is increased to 17°. What is the coefficient of static friction between the object and the plane? (Use the acceleration due to gravity $g = 9.8$ m/s^2)

A. 0.37   B. 0.43   C. 0.24   D. 0.31   E. 0.17

15. What is the force exerted by the table on a 2 kg book resting on it? (Use acceleration due to gravity $g = 10$ m/s^2)

A. 100 N   B. 20 N   C. 10 N   D. 0 N   E. 40 N

Solutions

1. A is correct.

Newton's Second Law ($F = ma$) is rearranged:

$a = F / m$

If F is constant, then a is inversely proportional to m.

A larger mass implies a smaller F / m ratio; the ratio is the acceleration.

2. C is correct.

$F = ma$, so doubling the force doubles the acceleration.

3. B is correct.

Pythagorean Theorem ($a^2 + b^2 = c^2$) to calculate the net force:

$F_1^2 + F_2^2 = F_{net}^2$

$(500 \text{ N})^2 + (1{,}200 \text{ N})^2 = F_{net}^2$

$250{,}000 \text{ N}^2 + 1{,}440{,}000 \text{ N}^2 = F_{net}^2$

$F_{net}^2 = 1{,}690{,}000 \text{ N}^2$

$F_{net} = 1{,}300 \text{ N}$

Newton's Second Law:

$F = ma$

$a = F_{net} / m$

$a = 1{,}300 \text{ N} / 500 \text{ kg}$

$a = 2.6 \text{ m/s}^2$

4. E is correct. The acceleration of the 2 kg block is the acceleration of the system because the blocks are linked together. Balance forces and solve for acceleration:

$F_{net} = m_3 g - m_2 g \mu_k - m_1 g$

$(m_3 + m_2 + m_1)a = m_3 g - m_2 g \mu_k - m_1 g$

$a = (m_3 - m_2 \mu_k - m_1)g / (m_3 + m_2 + m_1)$

$a = [3 \text{ kg} - (2 \text{ kg}) \cdot (0.25) - 1 \text{ kg}] \cdot (9.8 \text{ m/s}^2) / (3 \text{ kg} + 2 \text{ kg} + 1 \text{ kg})$

$a = 2.5 \text{ m/s}^2$

5. A is correct.

Objects moving at a constant velocity experience no acceleration and no net force.

6. B is correct.

The cart decelerates, which is an acceleration in the opposite direction caused by the force of friction in the opposite direction.

7. C is correct.

Newton's Third Law states that when two objects interact by a mutual force, the force of the first on the second is equal in magnitude to the force of the second on the first.

8. B is correct.

If the bureau moves in a straight line at a constant speed, its velocity is constant. Therefore, the bureau is experiencing zero acceleration and zero net force. The force of kinetic friction equals the 30 N force that pulls the bureau.

9. A is correct.

Newton's First Law states that an object at rest tends to stay at rest, and an object in motion tends to maintain that motion unless acted upon by an unbalanced force. This law depends on a property of an object called inertia, which is inherently linked to the object's mass. More massive objects are more difficult to move and manipulate than less massive objects.

10. B is correct.

$$F_g = Gm_{Earth}m_{moon} / d^2$$

d is the distance between the Earth and the Moon. If d decreases by a factor of 4, F_g increases by a factor of $4^2 = 16$

11. C is correct.

Find equal and opposite forces:

$$F_{Rx} = -F_1$$

$$F_{Rx} = -(-6.6 \text{ N})$$

$$F_{Rx} = 6.6 \text{ N}$$

$$F_{Ry} = -F_2$$

$$F_{Ry} = -2.2 \text{ N}$$

Pythagorean Theorem ($a^2 + b^2 = c^2$) to calculate the magnitude of the resultant force:

The magnitude of F_R:

$$F_R{}^2 = F_{Rx}{}^2 + F_{Ry}{}^2$$

$$F_R{}^2 = (6.6 \text{ N})^2 + (-2.2 \text{ N})^2$$

$$F_R{}^2 = 43.6 \text{ N}^2 + 4.8 \text{ N}^2$$

$$F_R{}^2 = 48.4 \text{ N}^2$$

$$F_R = 7 \text{ N}$$

The direction of F_R:

$$\theta = \tan^{-1} (-2.2 \text{ N} / 6.6 \text{ N})$$

$$\theta = \tan^{-1} (-1 / 3)$$

$$\theta = 342°$$

The direction of F_R with respect to F_1:

$$\theta = 342° - 180°$$

$$\theta = 162° \text{ counterclockwise of } F_1$$

12. D is correct.

Each scale weighs the fish at 17 kg, so the sum of the two scales is:

$$17 \text{ kg} + 17 \text{ kg} = 34 \text{ kg}$$

13. E is correct.

If θ is the angle with respect to a horizontal line, then:

$$\theta = \tfrac{1}{2}(40°)$$

$$\theta = 20°$$

Therefore, in order for the third force to cause equilibrium, the sum of all three forces' components must equal zero. Since F_1 and F_2 mirror each other in the y direction:

$$F_{1y} + F_{2y} = 0$$

Therefore, in order for F_3 to balance the forces in the y direction, its y component must also equal zero:

$$F_{1y} + F_{2y} + F_{3y} = 0$$

$$0 + F_{3y} = 0$$

$$F_{3y} = 0$$

Since the y component of F_3 is zero, the angle that F_3 makes with the horizontal is zero:

$\theta_3 = 0°$

The x component of F_3:

$F_{1x} + F_{2x} + F_{3x} = 0$

$F_1 \cos \theta + F_2 \cos \theta + F_3 \cos \theta = 0$

$F_3 = -(F_2 \cos \theta_2 + F_3 \cos \theta_3)$

$F_3 = -[(2.3 \text{ N}) \cos 20° + (2.3 \text{ N}) \cos 20°]$

$F_3 = -4.3 \text{ N}$

$F_3 = 4.3 \text{ N to the right}$

14. D is correct.

At $\theta = 17°$, the force of static friction is equal to the force due to gravity:

$F_f = F_g$

$\mu_s mg \cos \theta = mg \sin \theta$

$\mu_s = \sin \theta / \cos \theta$

$\mu_s = \tan \theta$

$\mu_s = \tan 17°$

$\mu_s = 0.31$

15. B is correct.

The force of the table on the book, the normal force (F_N), is a result of Newton's Third Law of Motion, which states for every action there is an equal and opposite reaction.

A book sitting on the table experiences a force from the table equal to the book's weight:

$W = mg$

$F_N = W$

$F_N = mg$

$F_N = (2 \text{ kg}) \cdot (10 \text{ m/s}^2)$

$F_N = 20 \text{ N}$

Notes

Chapter 3

Equilibrium and Momentum

EQUILIBRIUM

- **Concept of Equilibrium****

- **Concept of Force and Linear Acceleration, Units**

- **Translational Equilibrium** ($Fi = 0$) Σ

- **Torques, Lever Arms**

- **Rotational Equilibrium**

- **Analysis of Forces Acting on an Object**

MOMENTUM

- **Momentum**

- **Conservation of Linear Momentum**

- **Elastic Collisions**

- **Inelastic Collisions**

- **Impulse**

Notes

Concept of Equilibrium

The concept of equilibrium is directly related to Newton's First Law. As discussed in Chapter 2, Newton's First Law states that an object at rest tends to stay at rest, and an object in motion will remain in motion at a constant velocity, unless acted upon by an external force. In either case, the object in question is in equilibrium until an outside force is applied, upon which the object begins to accelerate.

Thus, the concept of equilibrium is linked to acceleration; objects undergoing acceleration are not in equilibrium, while those with zero acceleration are in equilibrium.

It is important to distinguish here that two forms of equilibrium exist: translational equilibrium and rotational equilibrium.

Objects in *translational equilibrium* have no linear acceleration.

Objects in *rotational equilibrium* have no angular acceleration.

These two forms of equilibrium may exist concurrently or separately.

For example, an object with zero linear acceleration and zero angular acceleration is in both translational and rotational equilibrium, but an object with zero linear acceleration but non-zero angular acceleration is only in translational equilibrium.

Both types of equilibrium can be separated into static and dynamic equilibrium.

Static equilibrium refers to objects with zero velocity (linear or angular).

Dynamic equilibrium refers to objects with constant non-zero velocity (linear or angular). These concepts are discussed in the following pages.

Concept of Force and Linear Acceleration, Units

Force causes objects to accelerate (i.e., change speed), change direction, or both. This can be explained by Newton's Second Law of Motion, which states that the acceleration of an object is directly proportional to the applied force and inversely proportional to the mass of the object:

$$\vec{a} = \frac{F}{m} \quad \text{or} \quad F = m\vec{a}$$

In physics questions, a force is indicated by an arrow with the arrowhead pointing in the direction of the force. The magnitude of the force is often labeled beside the arrow and is measured in units of the Newton (N). Below is an example of how a force vector is typically labeled:

F = 20 N

The concept of force is important when discussing equilibrium, as it imparts linear or angular acceleration to an object.

Linear acceleration is measured in units of m/s^2 and is the rate of change of the linear velocity of an object over time:

$$\vec{a} = \frac{\Delta\vec{v}}{\Delta t}$$

Angular acceleration is measured in units of rad/s^2 and is the rate of change of the angular velocity of an object over time:

$$\vec{\alpha} = \frac{\Delta\vec{\omega}}{\Delta t}$$

Translational Equilibrium

Translational equilibrium refers to an object undergoing zero linear acceleration. Therefore, in translational equilibrium either no forces are acting upon the object and linear acceleration is zero, or all the forces acting upon the object cancel and the object experiences no linear acceleration in any direction. Most situations refer to the latter scenario, and thus translational equilibrium is achieved when the sum of all forces along each coordinate axis add up to zero. This is expressed mathematically by:

$$\sum \vec{F} = 0 \text{ N}$$

In the example below, a book lies at rest on a table in translational equilibrium. The force due to gravity is canceled by the equal and opposite normal force provided by the table. Thus, the book experiences a net linear acceleration of zero.

Additionally, the book has zero velocity and is an example of a static system.

$$\Sigma F_y = F_N + F_G = 0 \text{ N}$$

$$\vec{v} = 0 \text{ m/s}$$

The example below presents another system in static translational equilibrium.

In this example, a two-coordinate axis (x and y) is presented, and the forces along each axis sum to zero.

Like the previous example, no velocity vector is labeled; therefore, the system is static and has no velocity.

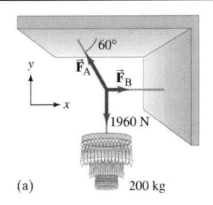

$$F_{Ax} = F_A \cos 60$$

$$F_{Ay} = F_A \sin 60$$

$$\Sigma F_x = F_{Ax} + F_B = 0 \text{ N}$$

$$\Sigma F_y = F_{Ay} + 1960 \text{ N} = 0 \text{ N}$$

$$\vec{v} = 0 \text{ m/s} \qquad \text{(a)}$$

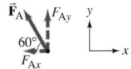

(b)

The picture below presents an example of a dynamic translational equilibrium. A skydiver has achieved terminal velocity. Therefore the force of gravity (weight) is balanced by the equal and opposite force from air resistance. Unlike the previous two examples, the skydiver has a constant non-zero velocity and is therefore considered a dynamic translational system.

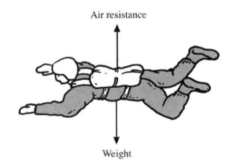

$$\Sigma F_y = F_G + F_{Air\ Resistance} = 0 \text{ N}$$

$$\vec{v} = constant$$

The following are examples of translational equilibrium vs. non-equilibrium:

Scenario	Type of Equilibrium	Translational non-equilibrium
An apple at rest	Static Translational	An apple falling toward the Earth with an acceleration of g
A car moving at constant velocity	Dynamic Translational	A car either accelerating or decelerating
A skydiver falling at terminal velocity	Dynamic Translational	A skydiver before reaching terminal velocity

Torques, Lever Arms

Force applied to an object or system that induces rotation is *torque*. Torque is the angular equivalent of force; it causes objects to rotate, have angular acceleration and change angular velocity. The position and direction of the force applied to the rotating body, concerning the axis of rotation, determines the amount of torque on that object. Mathematically, torque is the product of the applied force and the lever arm and is thus directly proportional to the magnitude of the applied force and the length of the lever arm. Torque can, therefore, be expressed as:

$$\vec{\tau} = r_{\perp}\vec{F} = r \sin \theta \vec{F}$$

The lever arm is the distance from the axis of rotation, to the line along which the perpendicular component of the force acts. The diagram below shows the calculation of the lever arm from the angle between the applied force and the distance to the axis of rotation:

$r_{\perp} = r \sin \theta$

$\theta \leq 90$

$r_{\perp} \leq r$

(c)

The unit of torque is the Newton-meter (N·m). Maximum torque on an object always occurs when the force is applied completely perpendicular to the radius (i.e., when the angle $\theta = 90°$ between the force vector and the radius $\vec{\tau}_{max} = r\sin(90)\vec{F} = r_{\perp}\vec{F}$). Minimum torque occurs when the force applied to the rotational body is directed toward the center of that body (i.e. when $\theta = 0°$, $\vec{\tau}_{min} = r \sin (0)\vec{F} = 0 \text{ N} \cdot \text{m}$). As an example, imagine a door with two forces applied at different points along its length:

$\vec{F}_A = \vec{F}_B$

$\theta_A = \theta_B = 90°$

$\vec{\tau} = r_{\perp}\vec{F}$

$r_{\perp A} > r_{\perp B}$

$\vec{\tau}_A > \vec{\tau}_B$

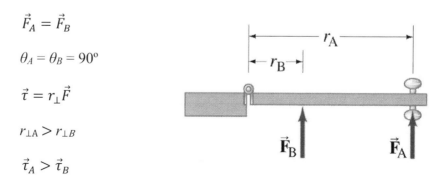

In the diagram above, both F_A and F_B are equal in magnitude and applied perpendicularly to the door. However, moving the door using F_A will be easier than using F_B because the lever arm for F_A is much longer than the lever arm for F_B. Accordingly, the torque produced by F_A will be larger than the torque produced by F_B, and the door can be opened more easily with its larger torque. Now, imagine a door with force applied at various angles with respect to the doorknob:

$$\vec{F}_A = \vec{F}_C = \vec{F}_D$$

$$90° = \theta_A > \theta_C > \theta_D$$

$$\vec{\tau} = r_\perp \vec{F} = r \sin \theta \vec{F}$$

(a)

$$r_{\perp A} > r_{\perp C} > r_{\perp D}$$

$$\vec{\tau}_A > \vec{\tau}_C > \vec{\tau}_D$$

As seen above, forces A, C, and D are all equal in magnitude and are applied at the same point from the axis of rotation (the length from the doorknob to the hinge).

However, the torques produced by forces A, C and D are different because the forces are applied at different angles.

Force A produces the maximum torque because it is applied perpendicular to the door, and thus will have the largest lever arm.

Force C is applied at a non-perpendicular angle to the door; therefore, it has a smaller lever arm and will produce a smaller torque.

Force D will produce no torque because the force is applied parallel to the door and its lever arm is equal to zero *(r sin (θ) = 0)*.

Rotational Equilibrium

The Conditions for Rotational Equilibrium

When objects are in rotational equilibrium, they have zero angular acceleration. Therefore, either no torques are applied, or the sum of all torques around every rotational axis equals zero. This is expressed mathematically by:

$$\sum \vec{\tau} = 0 \, \text{N} \cdot \text{m}$$

Additionally, the object either does not rotate (static rotational equilibrium), or it rotates at a constant rate (dynamic rotational equilibrium). Conventionally, positive torques act counterclockwise, while negative torques act clockwise.

Positive Convention +   Negative Convention -

In the example below, a pulley demonstrates static rotational equilibrium. Forces 1 and 2 are equal and applied at opposite ends tangent to the pulley. The resulting torques 1 and 2 are therefore equal and opposite, and the sum of all torques along the pulley's rotational axis is zero. Also, the pulley experiences no angular velocity and is considered to be a static system.

$$\vec{F}_1 = \vec{F}_2 \text{ and } \theta_1 = \theta_2 = 90°$$

$$r_\perp = d$$

$$\vec{\tau}_1 = \vec{F}_1 (d \sin \theta_1)$$

$$\vec{\tau}_2 = \vec{F}_2 (d \sin \theta_2)$$

$$\sum \vec{\tau} = \vec{\tau}_1 + \vec{\tau}_2 = 0 \, \text{N} \cdot \text{m}$$

$$\vec{\omega} = 0 \, \text{rad/s}$$

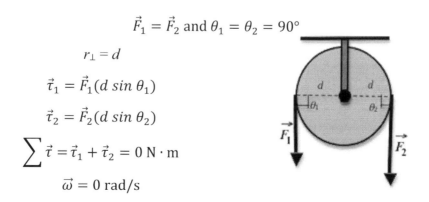

A mass attached to a cable-supported beam provides another example of a system in static rotational equilibrium. The mass hangs perpendicularly from the beam at distance *L*, creating a clockwise torque from the gravitational force.

However, the cable attached at a distance *d* produces its torque from the tension force and cancels the torque from the mass.

The sum of all torques about the axis of rotation is zero, and the system is considered static because it has no angular velocity.

$$\vec{F}_G \neq \vec{F}_T$$

$$\vec{\tau}_G = \vec{F}_1 (L \sin 90°)$$

$$\vec{\tau}_T = \vec{F}_T (d \sin \theta)$$

$$\sum \vec{\tau} = \vec{\tau}_G + \vec{\tau}_T = 0 \text{ N} \cdot \text{m}$$

$$\vec{\omega} = 0 \text{ rad/s}$$

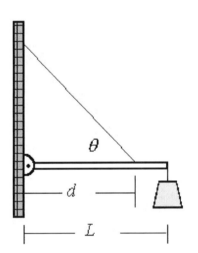

The following are examples of rotational equilibrium vs. non-equilibrium:

Scenario	Type of Equilibrium	Rotational Non-Equilibrium:
Equal masses on a balance	Static rotational	Unequal masses on a balance causing an angular acceleration
Propeller spinning at a fixed frequency	Dynamic rotational	Propeller spinning faster and faster
Asteroid rotating at a constant velocity	Dynamic rotational	Asteroid rotation slowing down

Analysis of Forces Acting on an Object

Solving Problems

1. Identify objects and draw free-body diagrams of all forces acting on them and where they act.

2. Choose a coordinate system and determine the negative and positive directions for each axis.

3. Resolve forces into components (normal and parallel components for inclined planes).

4. Add up all the force components. The resulting x, y and z components make up the net force acting on the object.

5. Choose any axis perpendicular to the plane of the forces and write equilibrium equations for the forces and torques. A clever choice here can simplify the problem enormously.

6. What type of equilibrium is it? Consult the table below for reference.

7. Solve. Use the Pythagorean Theorem to determine the magnitude of the net force from its components and use trigonometry to solve for the angles. Angles are measured in radians, with a whole circle equaling 2π radians.

Acceleration	Velocity	Equilibrium Type
$a = 0$ m/s^2	$v = 0$ m/s	Static Translational
	$v \neq 0$ m/s	Dynamic Translational
$\alpha = 0$ rad/s^2	$\omega = 0$ rad/s	Static Rotational
	$\omega \neq 0$ rad/s	Dynamic Rotational

The following are several solved examples of typical static equilibrium systems:

Example 1.

A 15,000 kg printing press is set upon a 1,500 kg table as shown in the diagram. Assuming the center of gravity of the table contains all its mass, what are the reaction forces from the table legs A and B?

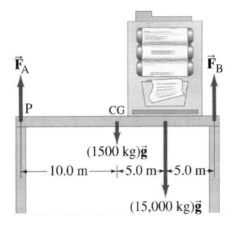

Sum all forces in y-axis:

$$\Sigma F_y = F_A + F_B - (1,500 \text{ kg}) \cdot (9.8 \text{m/s}^2) - (15,000 \text{ kg}) \cdot (9.8 \text{m/s}^2) = 0$$

$$F_A + F_B = 161,700 \text{ N}$$

Sum all torques about point P:

$$\Sigma \tau_P = - (1,500 \text{ kg}) \cdot (9.8 \text{m/s}^2) \cdot (10 \text{ m}) - (15,000 \text{ kg}) \cdot (9.8 \text{m/s}^2) \cdot (15 \text{ m}) + F_B (20 \text{ m}) = 0$$

$$F_B (20 \text{m}) = 2,352,000 \text{ N} \cdot \text{m}$$

$$F_B = 117,600 \text{ N}$$

Solve for remaining forces:

$$F_A + 117,600 \text{ N} = 161,700 \text{ N}$$

$$F_A = 44,100 \text{ N}$$

Note: if a force in the solution comes out negative, it just means that it is in the opposite direction of the direction chosen to be positive.

There is no "correct" way to choose which direction should be positive; either direction is fine, if it is kept consistent throughout the problem.

Example 2.

A beam with a mass of 500 kg located at the center of gravity is attached to two supporting legs. According to the diagram, what are the reaction forces from legs A and B?

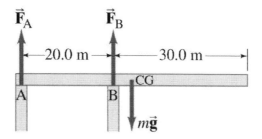

Sum all forces in y-axis:

$$\Sigma F_y = F_A + F_B - (500 \text{ kg}) \cdot (9.8 \text{ m/s}^2) = 0$$

$$F_A + F_B = 4{,}900 \text{ N}$$

Sum all torques about point A (center of gravity is at the midpoint of the beam):

$$\Sigma \tau_A = -(500 \text{ kg}) \cdot (9.8 \text{m/s}^2) \cdot (25 \text{ m}) + F_B(20 \text{ m}) = 0$$

$$F_B(20 \text{ m}) = 122{,}500 \text{ N} \cdot \text{m}$$

$$F_B = 6{,}125 \text{ N}$$

Solve for remaining forces:

$$F_A + 6{,}125 \text{ N} = 4{,}900 \text{ N}$$

$$F_A = -1{,}225 \text{ N}$$

If there is a cable or cord in the problem, it can support tension forces (F_T) only along its length.

Forces perpendicular to that would cause it to bend.

Example 3.

A sign support consists of a beam attached to a hinge with a sign attached at the opposite end and a cable to support the load. The beam has a length of 10 m and mass of 500 kg (located at the center of gravity 5 m), and the sign has a mass of 1,000 kg and is located at 10 m from the hinge. If the support cable forms an angle of 45 degrees with the beam, what are the reaction forces labeled in the diagram?

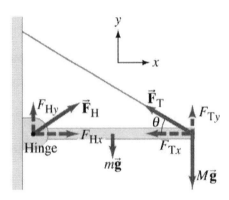

Sum all forces in y-axis:

$$\Sigma F_v = F_{Hy} + F_{Ty} - (500 \text{ kg}) \cdot (9.8 \text{ m/s}^2) - (1,000 \text{ kg}) \cdot (9.8 \text{ m/s}^2) = 0$$

$$F_{Hy} + F_{Ty} = 14,700 \text{ N}$$

Sum all forces in x-axis:

$$\Sigma F_x = F_{Hx} - F_{Tx} = 0$$

$$F_{Hx} = F_{Tx}$$

Sum all torques about hinge H (center of gravity is at the midpoint of the beam):

$$\Sigma \tau_H = -(1,000 \text{ kg}) \cdot (9.8 \text{ m/s}^2) \cdot (10 \text{ m}) - (500 \text{ kg}) \cdot (9.8 \text{ m/s}^2) \cdot (5 \text{ m}) + F_T (10 \text{ m}) \sin (45^\circ) = 0$$

$$F_T (10 \text{ m}) \sin (45^\circ) = 122,500 \text{ N} \cdot \text{m}$$

$$F_T = 17,324 \text{ N}$$

Solve for remaining forces:

$$F_{Ty} = F_T \sin(45°) \text{ N and } F_{Hx} = F_{Tx} = F_T \cos(45°)\text{N}$$

$$F_{Ty} = (17{,}327 \text{ N}) \sin(45°) \text{ and } F_{Hx} = F_{Tx} = (17{,}327 \text{ N}) \cos(45°)$$

$$F_{Ty} = 12{,}250 \text{ N and } F_{Hx} = F_{Tx} = 12{,}250 \text{ N}$$

$$F_{Hy} + 12{,}250 \text{ N} = 14{,}700 \text{ N}$$

$$F_{Hy} = 2{,}450 \text{ N}$$

These same principles can be used to understand forces within the human body. In the diagram of the arm below, the elbow is acting as a fulcrum, and the forearm is acting as the lever arm. The biceps in this example can be modeled as a cable containing tension.

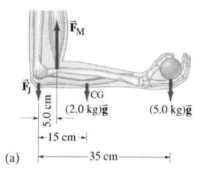

Sum all forces in *y*-axis:

$$\Sigma F_y = F_M - F_J - (2 \text{ kg}) \cdot (9.8 \text{ m/s}^2) - (5 \text{ kg}) \cdot (9.8 \text{ m/s}^2) = 0$$

$$F_M - F_J = 69 \text{ N}$$

Sum all torques about point J:

$$\Sigma \tau_J = F_M(0.05 \text{ m}) - (2 \text{ kg}) \cdot (9.8 \text{ m/s}^2) \cdot (0.15 \text{ m}) - (5 \text{ kg}) \cdot (9.8 \text{ m/s}^2) \cdot (0.35 \text{ m}) = 0$$

$$F_M = 402 \text{ N}$$

Solve for remaining forces:

$$402 \text{ N} - F_J = 69 \text{ N}$$

$$F_J = 333 \text{ N}$$

Stability and Balance

If the forces on an object tend to return the object to its equilibrium position, it is said to be in stable equilibrium. A hanging ball connected to a string is a good example of a stable equilibrium. If the ball were to be disturbed, the net force would ultimately return the ball to its original equilibrium position.

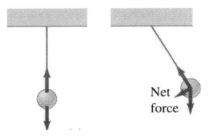

If, however, the forces tend to move an object away from its equilibrium point, it is said to be in unstable equilibrium. A pencil balanced on its tip is in unstable equilibrium. When disturbed from its equilibrium position, the net force will not return it to its original equilibrium position, but rather cause it to settle in a new equilibrium position (on its side).

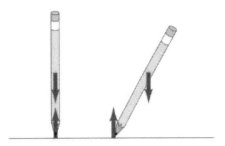

An object in stable equilibrium may become unstable if it is disturbed in such a way that its center of gravity is outside the pivot point. A leaning refrigerator provides an example. When disturbed, the refrigerator is in stable equilibrium, until its center of gravity is vertically positioned over the pivot point. If the refrigerator's center of gravity were to surpass the pivot point, it transitions to unstable equilibrium, and the net force will cause it to settle in a new equilibrium position (on its side).

Concept of Momentum

Recall Newton's First Law of Motion, which states that an object at rest tends to stay at rest, and an object in motion will remain in motion at a constant velocity unless acted upon by an external force. This is due to the object's *inertia*, or resistance to change. Inertia is directly correlated to an object's mass, so the more massive an object is, the more resistant it is to change.

When an object is in motion (i.e., it has a non-zero velocity), this inertia translates into the object's momentum.

Momentum (*p*) is the vector product of mass and velocity, represented by the equation:

$$\vec{p} = m\vec{v}$$

where *m* is mass measured in kg, $\vec{v}$ is velocity measured in m/s and $\vec{p}$ is measured in units of kg·m/s or N·s (Newton·seconds)

Total momentum is the vector sum of individual momenta (note the velocity directions of individual momenta).

According to the Law of Conservation of Momentum, in an isolated system of objects, total momentum is always conserved. This has very important implications in understanding the world and predicting the behavior of natural phenomena.

One classic scenario in which to consider the Law of Conservation of Momentum is in the collision of objects.

Conservation of Linear Momentum

In an isolated system, the total momentum in any collision is conserved. The concepts of an isolated system and conservation must first be defined and understood to apply this.

An isolated system is a collection of two or more objects free from any net external force. The only force present within the system is those supplied by the objects themselves.

If two balls were to collide on a frictionless surface, it is an isolated system since no external forces are present, and conservation of momentum would apply.

If, however, friction was present and not negligible, then the balls experience an external force, and their momentum changes according to the force supplied by friction. In this case, the Law of Conservation of Momentum does not apply because an external force is supplied and the collision is no longer considered to be within an isolated system.

The next concept, conservation of momentum in a collision (within isolated systems), is the phenomenon where momentum before any collisions always equals the total momentum after the collision, or rather:

$$\vec{p}_{initial} = \vec{p}_{final}$$

Momentum is a vector, so be sure to assign one direction as positive and the opposite direction as negative when adding component momenta.

For example, the momentum of a bomb at rest equals the vector sum of the momenta of all the shrapnel from the explosion. Because shrapnel tends to travel in all directions, the momenta of individual pieces cancel, and total momentum is conserved.

Conservation of momentum applies to a rocket in flight as well, provided the rocket and its fuel are considered to be one system and account for the mass loss of the rocket.

When a rocket fires in space, it does not need air to push against, because the momentum of the combustion gasses must be conserved. Thus, the rocket moves in the opposite direction.

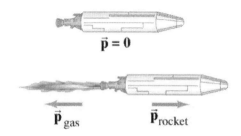

Momentum before = Momentum after = 0 N·s

$$m_{Gas}\vec{v}_{Gas} = m_{Rocket}\vec{v}_{Rocket}$$

In collision problems, it is important to understand that two types of collisions exist: *elastic collisions* and *inelastic collisions*.

Within both types of collisions, momentum is always conserved.

However, kinetic energy is only conserved within elastic collisions, not inelastic collisions. The characteristics of each collision type will be discussed below.

Elastic Collisions

Perfectly elastic collisions conserve both kinetic energy and momentum so that the initial total kinetic energy equals the final total kinetic energy ($KE_{Before} = KE_{After}$). Kinetic energy is a scalar, calculated by:

$$KE = \frac{1}{2}mv^2$$

The unit for energy is the Joule (J), and since energy is scalar, there are no positive or negative signs associated with kinetic energy. In a perfectly elastic collision, a dropped ball will bounce back to its original height.

Similarly, a ball thrown at a wall will bounce back at the same speed with which it was thrown. When solving problems regarding elastic collisions, use conservation of kinetic energy and conservation of momentum.

The example below has two objects, with known masses and initial speeds, colliding elastically.

Since both momentum and kinetic energy are conserved, both equations can be written to solve for the two unknown final speeds via the method of substitution:

$$\vec{p}_A + \vec{p}_B = \vec{p}'_B + \vec{p}'_A$$

$$m_A\vec{v}_A + m_B\vec{v}_B = m_A\vec{v}'_A + m_B\vec{v}'_B$$

$$KE_{Before} = KE_{After}$$

$$KE = \frac{1}{2}mv^2$$

$$\frac{1}{2}m_A\vec{v}_A{}^2 + \frac{1}{2}m_B\vec{v}_B{}^2 = \frac{1}{2}m_A\vec{v}'_A{}^2 + \frac{1}{2}m_B\vec{v}'_B{}^2$$

When objects collide while traveling in opposite directions, the procedure remains the same.

The initial momentum equals final momentum, and the initial kinetic energy equals final kinetic energy; only the signs of the velocity changes, depending upon the given coordinate axis.

$$\vec{p}_A + \vec{p}_B = \vec{p}'_B + \vec{p}'_A$$

$$m_A \vec{v}_A + m_B \vec{v}_B = m_A \vec{v}'_A + m_B \vec{v}'_B$$

$$KE_{Before} = KE_{After}$$

$$KE = \frac{1}{2} m v^2$$

$$\frac{1}{2} m_A \vec{v}_A{}^2 + \frac{1}{2} m_B \vec{v}_B{}^2 = \frac{1}{2} m_A \vec{v}'_A{}^2 + \frac{1}{2} m_B \vec{v}'_B{}^2$$

Inelastic Collisions

Inelastic collisions only conserve momentum and do not conserve kinetic energy ($KE_{initial} > KE_{final}$). This does not violate the Law of Conservation of Energy because the lost kinetic energy is converted into another form of energy during the collision.

Collisions in everyday life are typically inelastic, to varying extents.

For example, if a ball is dropped from a person's hand, it is known from experience that the ball will never reach the same height after bouncing off the ground. This is because the collision was not elastic, but inelastic. Momentum was conserved, but the kinetic energy was not, because some of the ball's energy was converted to other forms (acoustic, thermal, vibrational, etc.). The diagram illustrates what is expected if two objects collide elastically and inelastically.

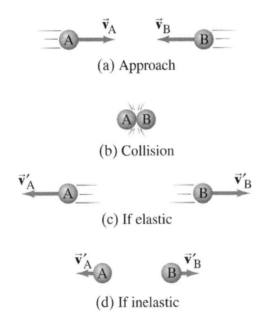

(a) Approach

(b) Collision

(c) If elastic

(d) If inelastic

Objects that stick after a collision are typically involved in an inelastic collision.

Below, a bullet with a known velocity and mass is shot into a hanging block of known mass. To solve for the height attained by the block + bullet, apply the conservation of momentum to find the velocity after the collision.

After the collision, all the kinetic energy of the system will be converted to potential energy. Conservation of energy can be applied, and the height can then be calculated.

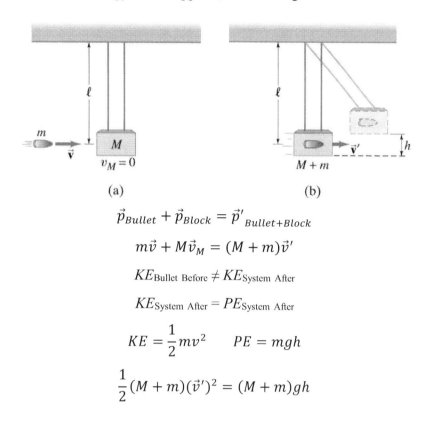

(a)   (b)

$$\vec{p}_{Bullet} + \vec{p}_{Block} = \vec{p}'_{Bullet+Block}$$

$$m\vec{v} + M\vec{v}_M = (M + m)\vec{v}'$$

$$KE_{Bullet\ Before} \neq KE_{System\ After}$$

$$KE_{System\ After} = PE_{System\ After}$$

$$KE = \frac{1}{2}mv^2 \qquad PE = mgh$$

$$\frac{1}{2}(M + m)(\vec{v}')^2 = (M + m)gh$$

Collisions in Two or Three Dimensions

Conservation of kinetic energy and momentum can also be used to analyze collisions in two or three dimensions. Here, a moving object m_A collides with an object m_B initially at rest. Knowing the masses and initial velocities are not enough; the angles of the objects post-collision are also needed to determine the final velocities.

$$\sum \vec{p}_x = \vec{p}_{Ax} + \vec{p}_{Bx} = \vec{p}'_{Bx} + \vec{p}'_{Ax}$$

$$m_A \vec{v}_A = m_A \vec{v}'_A \cos \theta'_A$$
$$+ m_B \vec{v}'_B \cos \theta'_B$$

$$\sum \vec{p}_y = \vec{p}_{Ay} + \vec{p}_{By} = \vec{p}'_{By} + \vec{p}'_{Ay}$$

$$0 = m_A \vec{v}'_A \sin \theta'_A + m_B \vec{v}'_B \sin \theta'_A$$

Solving Collision Problems:

1. Choose the system. If it is a complex system, such as one that involves both elastic and inelastic collisions, subsystems may be chosen where one or more conservation laws apply.

2. If there are external forces, choose a different system, so no external forces are present.

3. Draw diagrams of the initial and final situations, with momentum vectors labeled.

4. Choose a coordinate system. If an object's momentum is at an angle to the axis, split it into x and y components. That is, $p_x = \vec{p} \cos \theta$ and $p_y = \vec{p} \sin \theta$ for any given object.

5. Apply momentum conservation; there is one equation for each dimension.

    The total initial momentum in the x direction must equal the total final momentum in the x-direction ($\sum p_{xi} = \sum p_{xf}$).

    The total initial momentum in the y-direction must equal the total final momentum in the y-direction ($\sum p_{yi} = \sum p_{yf}$).

6. Is the collision elastic or inelastic? Do not assume the type of collision if it is not known. Sometimes the type is given; however, if it is not clear, check if kinetic energy is conserved.

7. Solve. In problems concerning elastic collisions, use the method of substitution between conservation of kinetic energy and conservation of momentum; for inelastic collisions, only use momentum conservation.

    $$\vec{p} = \sqrt{p_x^2 + p_y^2} \text{ , and the angle is given by } \theta = \tan^{-1}\left(\frac{p_y}{p_x}\right).$$

8. Check units and magnitudes of the result to see if they make sense.

Typical Inelastic Collision Example

Train car A (m = 1,000 kg) collides inelastically with train car B of equal mass. After the collision, the train cars stick. What is the final velocity of the attached train cars?

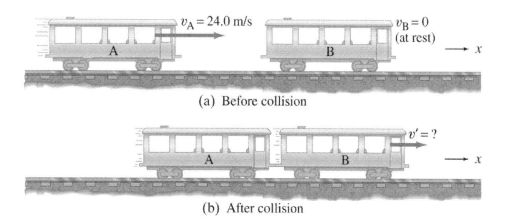

(a) Before collision

(b) After collision

Apply the Law of Conservation of Momentum:

$$\vec{p}_A + \vec{p}_B = \vec{p}\,'_{A+B}$$

$$m_A \vec{v}_A + m_B \vec{v}_B = (m_A + m_B)\vec{v}\,'$$

Solve for final velocity:

$$(1{,}000 \text{ kg}) \cdot (24 \text{ m/s}) + (1{,}000 \text{ kg}) \cdot (0 \text{ m/s}) = (1{,}000 \text{ kg} + 1{,}000 \text{ kg})\vec{v}\,'$$

$$\vec{v}\,' = 12 \text{ m/s}$$

Check the difference in kinetic energy:

$$KE = \frac{1}{2}mv^2$$

$$KE_{\text{Before}} = \frac{1}{2}(1{,}000 \text{ kg})(24 \text{ m/s})^2 = 288 \text{ kJ}$$

$$KE_{\text{After}} = \frac{1}{2}(2{,}000 \text{ kg})(12 \text{ m/s})^2 = 144 \text{ kJ}$$

$$KE_{\text{Before}} \neq KE_{\text{After}}$$

Impulse

During a collision, objects are deformed to varying degrees due to the large forces involved. Softer objects, such as pillows, are deformed more dramatically over a larger time frame than objects made of harder materials such as metal. The extent to which an object deforms due to an impact, regarding the time the object spends in contact with another mass, is related to that object's *impulse* (J).

Impulse, or the change in momentum, is represented as $F\Delta t$, where F is a force, and Δt is the time interval during which the force acts:

$$\sum \vec{F} = \frac{\Delta \vec{p}}{\Delta t}$$

Force is equal to the change in momentum divided by the time interval:

$$\vec{F}\Delta t = \Delta \vec{p}$$

The definition of impulse, $\vec{J} = \vec{F}\Delta t$, can be derived using the equation $\vec{F} = m\vec{a}$:

$$\vec{F} = m\vec{a} = m\frac{\Delta \vec{v}}{\Delta t} \quad \rightarrow \quad \vec{F}\Delta t = m\Delta \vec{v} = \Delta \vec{p} = \vec{J}$$

The impulse is important because it determines if a change in momentum occurs with either a large force acting for a short time or a small force acting for a long time.

For example, automobile airbags are effective because they increase the length of time between the initial impact of the two objects (the airbag and the person) and the moment both objects come to rest. Without an airbag, this time interval would be much briefer, and therefore the impact more damaging.

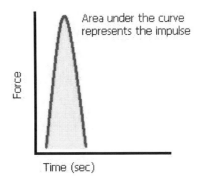

Area under the curve represents the impulse

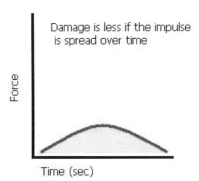

Damage is less if the impulse is spread over time

From the example force vs. time diagrams above, it is apparent that the force changes with time.

However, the time of the collision is often very short, and the exact time dependence of the force does not matter.

Since the time interval is relatively short, the average force, rather than the time-dependent force, can be used when calculating impulse.

This is seen in the force vs. time diagrams below.

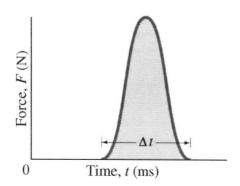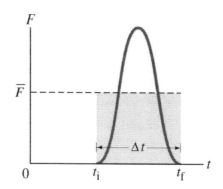

Chapter Summary

- Objects in *translational equilibrium* have no linear acceleration, while objects in *rotational equilibrium* have no angular acceleration. These two forms of equilibrium may exist concurrently or separately.

- *Static equilibrium* refers to objects with zero velocity (linear or angular).

  Dynamic equilibrium refers to objects with constant non-zero velocity (linear or angular).

- In translational equilibrium either no forces are acting upon the object and linear acceleration is zero, or all the forces acting upon the object cancel and the object experiences no linear acceleration in any direction.

- Force applied to an object or system that induces rotation is *torque*. Torque can be expressed as:

$$\vec{\tau} = r_{\perp}\vec{F} = r\,sin\,\theta\vec{F}$$

- When objects are in rotational equilibrium, they have zero angular acceleration. Therefore, either no torques are applied, or the sum of all torques around every rotational axis equals zero.

Acceleration	Velocity	Equilibrium Type
$a = 0$ m/s^2	$v = 0$ m/s	Static Translational
	$v \neq 0$ m/s	Dynamic Translational
$\alpha = 0$ rad/s^2	$\omega = 0$ rad/s	Static Rotational
	$\omega \neq 0$ rad/s	Dynamic Rotational

- Momentum (p) is the vector product of mass and velocity, represented by the equation:

$$\vec{p} = m\vec{v}$$

- According to the Law of Conservation of Momentum, in an isolated system of objects, total momentum is always conserved.

$$\vec{p}_{initial} = \vec{p}_{final}$$

- For elastic collisions, momentum and total kinetic energy are conserved:

$$\frac{1}{2}m_A\vec{v}_A{}^2 + \frac{1}{2}m_B\vec{v}_B{}^2 = \frac{1}{2}m_A\vec{v}_A'{}^2 + \frac{1}{2}m_B\vec{v}_B'{}^2$$

- Inelastic collisions only conserve momentum and do not conserve kinetic energy ($KE_{initial} > KE_{final}$).

- This does not violate the Law of Conservation of Energy because the lost kinetic energy is converted into another form of energy during the collision.

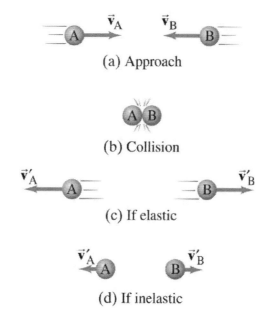

(a) Approach

(b) Collision

(c) If elastic

(d) If inelastic

- The extent to which an object deforms due to an impact, regarding the time the object spends in contact with another mass, is related to that object's *impulse* (*J*). Impulse, or the change in momentum, is represented as *F*Δ*t*, where *F* is a force, and Δ*t* is the time interval during which the force acts:

$$\sum \vec{F} = \frac{\Delta\vec{p}}{\Delta t}$$

Notes

Practice Questions

1. A 1.2-kg asteroid is traveling toward the Orion Nebula at a speed of 2.8 m/s. Another 4.1 kg asteroid is traveling at 2.3 m/s in a perpendicular direction. The two asteroids collide and stick. What is the change in momentum from before to after the collision?

   A. 0 kg·m/s   **C.** 9.4 kg·m/s

   B. 2.1 kg·m/s   **D.** 12 kg·m/s   **E.** 19.7 kg·m/s

2. A 1,120 kg car experiences an impulse of 30,000 N·s during a collision with a wall. If the collision takes 0.43 s, what was the speed of the car just before the collision?

   A. 12 m/s   **B.** 64 m/s   **C.** 42 m/s   **D.** 27 m/s   **E.** 18 m/s

3. Does the centripetal force acting on an object do work on the object?

   A. No, because the force and the displacement of the object are perpendicular

   B. Yes, since a force acts and the object moves, and work is force times distance

   C. Yes, since it takes energy to turn an object

   D. No, because the object has a constant speed

   E. Yes, because the force and the displacement of the object are perpendicular

4. Cars with padded dashboards are safer in an accident than cars without padded dashboards, because a passenger hitting the dashboard has:

      I. increased time of impact

      II. decreased impulse

      III. decreased impact force

   A. I only   **B.** II only   **C.** III only   **D.** I and III only   **E.** I and II only

5. The acceleration due to gravity on the Moon is only one-sixth of that on Earth, and the Moon has no atmosphere. If a person hit a baseball on the Moon with the same effort (and therefore at the same speed and angle) as on Earth, how far would the ball travel on the Moon compared to on Earth? (Ignore air resistance on Earth)

   A. The same distance as on Earth   **C.** 1/6 as far as on Earth

   B. 6 times as far as on Earth   **D.** 36 times as far as on Earth

                                         E. √6 times as far as on Earth

6. A uniform meter stick weighing 20 N has a weight of 50 N attached to its left end and a weight of 30 N attached to its right end. The meter stick is hung from a rope. What is the tension in the rope and how far from the left end of the meter stick should the rope be attached so that the meter stick remains level?

  A. 100 N placed 37.5 cm from the left end of the meter stick
  B. 50 N placed 40 cm from the left end of the meter stick
  C. 80 N placed 37.5 cm from the left end of the meter stick
  D. 80 N placed 40 cm from the left end of the meter stick
  E. 100 N placed 40 cm from the left end of the meter stick

7. To catch a ball, a baseball player extends her hand forward before impact with the ball and then lets it ride backward in the direction of the ball's motion upon impact. Doing this reduces the force of impact on the player's hand principally because the:

  A. time of impact is decreased
  B. time of impact is increased
  C. relative velocity is less
  D. force of impact is reduced by $\sqrt{2}$
  E. none of the above

8. A 1,200 kg car, moving at 15.6 m/s, collides with a stationary 1,500 kg car. If the two vehicles lock together, what is their combined velocity immediately after the collision?

  A. 12.4 m/s   **B.** 5.4 m/s   **C.** 6.9 m/s   **D.** 7.6 m/s   **E.** 11.8 m/s

9. A 0.05 kg golf ball, initially at rest, has a velocity of 100 m/s immediately after being struck by a golf club. If the club and ball were in contact for 0.8 ms, what is the average force exerted on the ball?

  A. 5.5 kN   **B.** 4.9 kN   **C.** 11.8 kN   **D.** 7.1 kN   **E.** 6.3 kN

10. Which of the following is an accurate statement for a rigid body that is rotating?

  A. All points on the body are moving with the same angular velocity
  B. Its center of rotation is its center of gravity
  C. Its center of rotation is at rest and therefore not moving
  D. Its center of rotation must be moving with a constant velocity
  E. All points on the body are moving with the same linear velocity

11. Cart 1 (2 kg) and Cart 2 (2.5 kg) run along a frictionless, level, one-dimensional track. Cart 2 is initially at rest, and Cart 1 is traveling 0.6 m/s toward the right when it encounters Cart 2. After the collision, Cart 1 is at rest. Which of the following is true concerning the collision?

A. The collision is completely elastic

B. Kinetic energy is conserved

C. Momentum is conserved

D. Total momentum is decreased

E. Potential energy is conserved

12. What is the reason for using a long barrel in a gun?

A. Allows the force of the expanding gases from the gunpowder to act for a longer time

B. Increases the force exerted on the bullet due to the expanding gases from the gunpowder

C. Exerts a larger force on the shells

D. Reduces frictional losses

E. Reduces the force exerted on the bullet due to the expanding gases from the gunpowder

Questions **13-15** are based on the following:

A 5-gram bullet is fired horizontally into a 2 kg block of wood suspended from the ceiling by 1.5 m strings. The bullet becomes embedded within the block of wood, and they move together at a speed of 1.5 m/s. Gravity can be ignored during the time of the bullet's impact with the block. Then, the wood block with the bullet swings upward by height h.

13. What best describes the energy flow as the bullet impacts the block of wood?

A. Kinetic to heat and kinetic

B. Potential and kinetic to heat

C. Kinetic to potential

D. Potential to heat

E. Kinetic to heat and potential

14. What is the velocity of the bullet just before it enters the block?

A. 30 m/s   **B.** 60 m/s   **C.** 600 m/s   **D.** 90 m/s   **E.** 180 m/s

15. Immediately after the bullet embeds itself in the wood, what is the kinetic energy of the block and bullet?

A. 2.26 J   **B.** 4.5 J   **C.** 9 J   **D.** 18 J   **E.** 36 J

Solutions

1. A is correct.

Since the momentum is conserved during the collision, the change is $p = 0$.

$$p_{initial} = p_{final}$$

$$m_1v_1 + m_2v_2 = (m_1 + m_2)v_3$$

2. D is correct.

$$J = \Delta p = m\Delta v$$

$$\Delta v = J / m$$

$$\Delta v = (30,000 \text{ N·s}) / (1,120 \text{ kg})$$

$$\Delta v = 27 \text{ m/s}$$

$$\Delta v = v_f - v_i$$

$$27 \text{ m/s} = 0 - v_i$$

$$v_i = 27 \text{ m/s}$$

3. A is correct. In uniform circular motion, the centripetal force does no work because the force and displacement vectors are at right angles.

$$W = Fd$$

The work equation is only applicable if force and displacement direction are the same.

4. D is correct.

$$J = F\Delta t$$

Impulse remains constant, so the time of impact increases and the impact force decreases.

5. B is correct. Consider a dropped baseball on Earth:

$$d_E = -\tfrac{1}{2}gt^2$$

On the Moon:

$$d_M = -\tfrac{1}{2}(g / 6)t^2$$

$$d_E / d_M = (-\tfrac{1}{2}gt^2) / (-\tfrac{1}{2}(g / 6)t^2)$$

$$d_E / d_M = 1/6, \text{ so the distance is 6 times greater on the Moon}$$

6. E is correct.

The total downward force on the meter stick is:

$$20 \text{ N} + 50 \text{ N} + 30 \text{ N} = 100 \text{ N}$$

The total upward force on the meter stick – which is provided by the tension in the supporting rope – must also be 100 N to keep the meter stick in static equilibrium.

Let x be the distance from the left end of the meter stick to the suspension point.

From the pivot point, balance the torques.

The counterclockwise (CCW) torque due to the 50 N weight at the left end is $50\,x$.

The total clockwise (CW) torque due to the weight of the meter stick and the 30 N weight at the right end is:

$$(50 \text{ N})x = (20 \text{ N}) \cdot (50 \text{ cm} - x) + (30 \text{ N}) \cdot (100 \text{ cm} - x)$$

$$(50 \text{ N})x = [1{,}000 \text{ cm} - (20 \text{ N})x] + [3{,}000 \text{ cm} - (30 \text{ N})x]$$

$$(50 \text{ N})x = 4{,}000 \text{ cm} - (50 \text{ N})x$$

$$(100 \text{ N})x = 4{,}000 \text{ cm}$$

$$x = 40 \text{ cm}$$

7. B is correct.

$$J = F\Delta t \text{ is constant}$$

$$\text{increased } t = \text{decreased } F$$

8. C is correct.

$$m_1 v_1 = (m_1 + m_2)v_2$$

$$v_2 = (m_1 v_1) / (m_1 + m_2)$$

$$v_2 = (1{,}200 \text{ kg}) \cdot (15.6 \text{ m/s}) / (1{,}200 \text{ kg} + 1{,}500 \text{ kg})$$

$$v_2 = (18{,}720 \text{ kg·m/s}) / (2{,}700 \text{ kg})$$

$$v_2 = 6.9 \text{ m/s}$$

9. E is correct.

$$F\Delta t = m\Delta v$$

$$F = (m\Delta v) \,/\, \Delta t$$

$$F = [(0.05 \text{ kg})\cdot(100 \text{ m/s} - 0 \text{ m/s})] \,/\, (0.0008 \text{ s})$$

$$F = (5 \text{ kg·m/s}) \,/\, (0.0008 \text{ s})$$

$$F = 6{,}250 \text{ N} = 6.3 \text{ kN}$$

10. A is correct.

In circular motion, all points along the rotational body have the same angular velocity regardless of their radial distance from the center of rotation.

11. C is correct. In both elastic and inelastic collisions, momentum is conserved.

However, in an ideal elastic collision, *KE* is also conserved, but not in an inelastic collision. To determine if the collision is elastic or inelastic, compare the *KE* before and after the collision.

Initial *KE*:

$$KE_i = \tfrac{1}{2}m_1v_1{}^2$$

$$KE_i = \tfrac{1}{2}(2 \text{ kg})\cdot(0.6 \text{ m/s})^2$$

$$KE_i = 0.36 \text{ J}$$

Conservation of momentum:

$$m_1v_1 + m_2v_2 = m_1u_1 + m_2u_2$$

$$m_1v_1 = m_2u_2$$

$$(m_1 \,/\, m_2)v_1 = u_2$$

$$u_2 = (2 \text{ kg} \,/\, 2.5 \text{ kg})\cdot(0.6 \text{ m/s})$$

$$u_2 = 0.48 \text{ m/s}$$

Final the *KE*:

$$KE_f = \tfrac{1}{2}m_2u_2{}^2$$

$$KE_f = \tfrac{1}{2}(2.5 \text{ kg})\cdot(0.48 \text{ m/s})^2$$

$$KE_f = 0.29 \text{ J}$$

KE_i does not equal KE_f and thus *KE* is not conserved.

The collision is therefore inelastic, and only momentum is conserved.

12. A is correct.

A longer barrel gives the expanding gas more time to impart a force upon the bullet and thus increase the impulse upon the bullet.

$$J = F\Delta t$$

13. A is correct.

The energy starts as kinetic. Initially, there is no change in the potential energy.

Upon impact, most of the bullet's kinetic energy is converted into heat, some are transferred into kinetic energy of the block, and a small amount remains as kinetic energy for the bullet.

Since gravity is being ignored, the increase in the height of the block does not lead to potential energy.

14. C is correct.

Conservation of momentum:

$$m_1 v_1 = (m_1 + m_2) v_2$$

$$(0.005 \text{ kg}) v_1 = (0.005 \text{ kg} + 2 \text{ kg}) \cdot (1.5 \text{ m/s})$$

$$v_1 = 600 \text{ m/s}$$

15. A is correct.

$$KE = \frac{1}{2} m v^2$$

$$KE = \frac{1}{2} (m_1 + m_2) v^2$$

$$KE = \frac{1}{2} (2.005 \text{ kg}) \cdot (1.5 \text{ m/s})^2$$

$$KE = 2.2556 \text{ J} \approx 2.26 \text{ J}$$

Please, leave your Customer Review on Amazon

Notes

Chapter 4

Work and Energy

WORK

- **Concept of Work**

- **Derived Units, Sign Conventions**

- **Work Done by a Constant Force**

- **Mechanical Advantage**

- **Conservative Forces**

- **Path Independence of Work Done in Gravitational Field**

ENERGY

- **Concept of Energy**

- **Kinetic Energy**

- **Work-Kinetic Energy Theorem**

- **Potential Energy**

- **Conservation of Energy**

- **Power, Units**

Notes

Concept of Work

Work is the relationship between a force and the distance traveled by an object acted upon by force, in a direction parallel to the force.

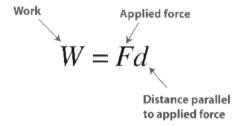

The above equation is for an applied force and a displacement parallel to the force. However, sometimes the distance traveled is not parallel to the force, but at an angle. In this case, the angle in question must be accounted for by applying the following formula:

$$W = \vec{F}d \cos \theta$$

Where $\vec{F}$ is force, d is the distance over which the force is applied, and θ is the angle between the force and distance.

Essentially, this formula divides the forces into components, and the only value used in the work calculation is the force parallel to displacement.

There are some instances in which the work will be zero:

• When the displacement is zero ($W = \vec{F} \cdot 0 = 0$)

• When the displacement is perpendicular to the applied force (the object moves at 90° to the applied force):

$$W = \vec{F}d \cos (90) = \vec{F} \cdot 0 = 0$$

• When an object is moving at constant velocity, with no forces acting in its direction of movement:

$$(W = 0 \cdot d = 0)$$

Derived Units, Sign Conventions

The units of work are:

$$W = \vec{F}\vec{d}$$

$$W = m\vec{a}\vec{d} = (\text{kg}) \cdot \left(\frac{\text{m}}{\text{s}^2}\right) \cdot (\text{m})$$

$$W = \frac{\text{kg} \times \text{m}^2}{\text{s}^2} = \text{N} \cdot \text{m} = J$$

Although this is sometimes a Newton-meter, which represents the combined units of force and distance, work is generally in Joules (J) since the Newton-meter is the unit of measurement for torque. Joules, named after English physicist James Prescott Joule, are also used as the unit of measurement for energy.

If the force and the displacement are in the same direction, work is positive.

For example, pushing a crate across a rough terrain involves doing positive work (pushing forward as the crate moves forward).

Conversely, if the force opposes the direction of motion (such as friction), work will be negative.

Work Done by a Constant Force

As noted earlier, the work done by a constant force is defined as the distance moved multiplied by the component of the force in the direction of displacement:

$$W = \vec{F}\vec{d}\cos\theta$$

For example, a crate on the ground has a rope attached to the side, which a woman pulls to move the crate a distance *d*.

If she pulls with a constant force, and the rope forms an angle θ with the crate, how much work did she perform?

$$W = \vec{F_{\parallel}}\vec{d}$$

$$\vec{F_{\parallel}} = \vec{F}\cos\theta$$

$$W = \vec{F}\vec{d}\cos\theta$$

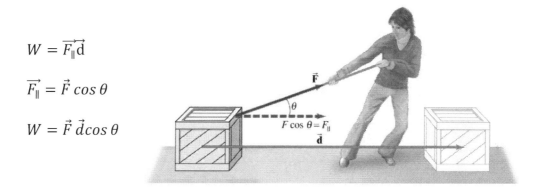

The following steps can be useful in solving work problems:

1. Draw a free-body diagram.

2. Choose a coordinate system.

3. Apply Newton's laws to determine any unknown forces.

4. Find the work done by a specific force.

5. To find the net work, either find the net force and then find the work it does, or find the work done by each force and add them.

If the force and displacement are perpendicular, the work done is zero. This means that centripetal forces do no work.

Although in uniform circular motion the centripetal force is constant, it is always directed toward the center of a circular path and is therefore perpendicular to the linear movement of the object.

For example, if a ball attached to a string is spun around in a circle how much work is performed?

$$W = \vec{F}_\parallel \vec{d}$$
$$\overrightarrow{F_\parallel} = \vec{F} \cos (90°) = 0 \text{ N}$$
$$W = 0 \text{ J}$$

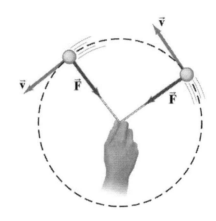

Mechanical Advantage

A mechanical advantage takes an input force of little effort and outputs a much larger force. Using a *lever arm* or a *pulley* achieves such an advantage. Mechanical advantages are useful in the construction and movement of large objects, which are otherwise too heavy to manipulate.

Simple machines are any basic mechanical devices used to apply a force. The basic premise of a simple machine is that the work put in is equal to the work put out. This refers to the amount of force, multiplied by a ratio of distances. Some examples of simple machines are:

- Pulleys

- Inclined planes

- Wedges

- Screws

- Levers

- Wheels and axles

Pulley systems are a simple machine encountered on the test. Like all simple machines, a pulley system does not reduce the amount of work upon an object, but it does reduce the amount of force needed to manipulate it. This is possible because the distance over which the force acts is increased. The work equation below shows that force and distance are inversely related and that the distance of pulling increases by the same factor the force decreases by.

$$\frac{W}{\vec{d}} = \vec{F}$$

A method for solving pulley problems is to realize that the ropes on either side of a moving pulley contribute to pulling the load. A stationary pulley, however, does not contribute to the load. The test will focus on simple pulleys where the above rule is applicable. Complex pulleys have additional ropes that contribute to pulling the load and are not likely to be tested.

In the scenario below, a pulley is attached to the ceiling and is used to lift a box. The pulley is stationary, so no mechanical advantage is imparted to the system.

Therefore, if the weight of the box is 100 N, the force needed to pull the box up is 100 N, and for every 1 m pulled, the box will move up 1 m.

$$W = \vec{F}\vec{d}$$

$$W = (100\ \text{N}) \cdot (1\ \text{m})$$

$$W = 100\ \text{Joules}$$

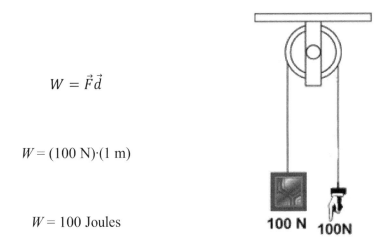

100 N   **100N**

As stated earlier, moving pulleys will impart a mechanical advantage to the system.

For example, in the diagrams below, there is one moving pulley in each system. When there is one moving pulley, the force needed to pull is halved because the rope on each side of the pulley contributes equally. The 50 N force is transmitted to the right-hand rope, while the left-hand rope contributes the other 50 N.

However, the distance required to pull the rope is not the same. If the box is to be pulled up one meter (as in the previous example), the distance of rope required to pull the box is doubled because the force is halved.

Observe that in the diagram below, the pulley system on the right is an equivalent system to the pulley system on the left. Although there are two pulleys on the right, only the mobile pulley halves the force needed to pull the box.

For any system, the work required to lift the box one meter is always be the same regardless of the force reduction.

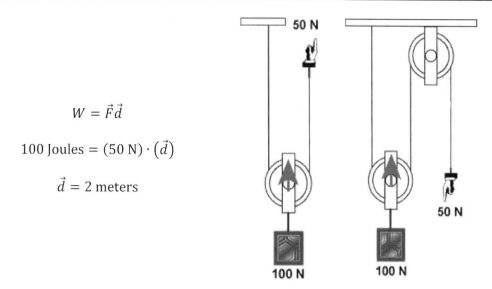

$$W = \vec{F}\vec{d}$$

$$100 \text{ Joules} = (50 \text{ N}) \cdot (\vec{d})$$

$$\vec{d} = 2 \text{ meters}$$

In the diagrams below, two equivalent systems are shown. Although the pulley arrangement is different, each system has two mobile pulleys, which reduce the force needed to lift the box. If each mobile pulley reduces the force by half, then the total force needed to lift the box will be reduced to a quarter of the original value.

Thus, the 100 N box can be lifted with only 25 N. Again, the work required to lift the box one meter must always be the same, so for every 1 m the box moves, 4 m of rope must be pulled.

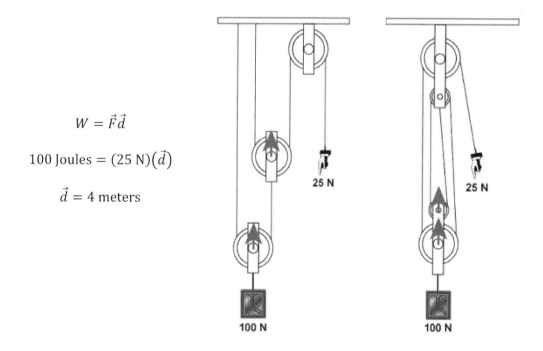

$$W = \vec{F}\vec{d}$$

$$100 \text{ Joules} = (25 \text{ N})(\vec{d})$$

$$\vec{d} = 4 \text{ meters}$$

The example below is a complex pulley system.

Just like with the simple pulleys, the ropes on both sides of the moving pulley contribute.

Here, however, the left-most rope also contributes. This makes three contributing ropes, which reduces the effort required by a factor of three.

The distance needed to pull is three times the distance the box travels.

$$W = \vec{F}\vec{d}$$

$$100 \text{ Joules} = (33 \text{ N})(\vec{d})$$

$$\vec{d} \cong 3 \text{ meters}$$

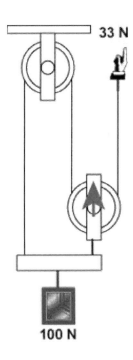

Conservative Forces

A force can be either conservative or non-conservative. Determining which label a certain force falls under can be slightly confusing, but there are a few qualifications that can be checked to determine what conservation a certain force follows.

If a force does not dissipate heat, sound or light, then it is a *conservative force*. Furthermore, if the work done by a force is path independent, then that force is conservative. Conservative forces are associated with potential energy; as potential energy can only be defined for conservative forces.

For example, the force from a spring can be stored as spring potential energy, and gravitational force can be stored as gravitational potential energy.

Electromagnetic forces are also conservative.

If only conservative forces are acting, mechanical energy is conserved.

A few things to keep in mind when a particle is moving along a certain path:

- If the work done to move a particle in any round-trip path is zero, the force is conservative.

- If the work needed to move a particle between two points is the same regardless of the path taken, then the force is conservative.

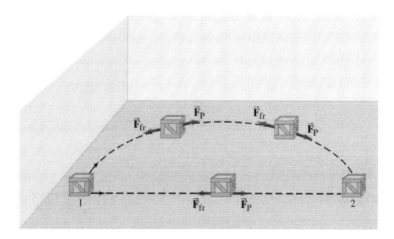

Most forces are conservative, but some non-conservative forces include friction and human exertion. If friction is present, the work done depends not only on the starting and ending points but also on the path taken, as frictional forces directly oppose the course of motion of an object.

As an object encounters friction, heat and sound energy are released, and the total energy is not conserved. Heat energy is also lost in human exertion.

For example, when a muscle is flexed in an activity, the heat from those muscles rises off the skin and cannot be recovered or reabsorbed.

Conservative Forces	Non-conservative Forces
Gravitational	Friction
	Air resistance
Elastic	Tension in a cord
	Motor or rocket propulsion
Electric	Push or pull by a person

Above, potential energy is defined for conservative forces. Therefore, the work done by conservative forces must be distinguished from the work done by non-conservative forces.

The work done by non-conservative forces is equal to the total change in kinetic and potential energies:

$$W_{NC} = \Delta KE + \Delta PE$$

Accounting for all forms of energy, the total energy neither increases nor decreases; energy as a whole is conserved.

The concept of conservation of energy with mechanical forces is discussed in subsequent chapters.

Path Independence of Work Done in Gravitational Field

The amount of work done in a gravitational field is path-independent since gravitational forces always act downward. Sideward motion, which is perpendicular to the gravitational force, involves no work.

For example, a man lifting a bag of groceries is a form of positive work in a gravitational field. The act of lifting a bag of groceries is positive work because a force is exerted (to overcome the force of gravity) and the distance the bag is lifted is in the direction of the force.

However, once the bag is being held up, it is at rest (as in, no longer traveling) and no work is being done on the bag. If the man does not lift or lower the bag, he is doing no work on it because there is no vertical displacement. Walking home with the bag of groceries also does no work on the bag. This is because the displacement (horizontal) is perpendicular to the force of gravity, and the resulting work must be zero.

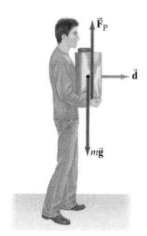

$$\vec{F}_P = m\vec{g}$$

Work to lift the bag: $W = \vec{F}_P \vec{d}_y > 0 \text{ J}$

Work to walk home: $W = \vec{F}_P \vec{d}_x = 0 \text{ J}$

Another example of work in a gravitational field is pushing an object at constant speed up a frictionless, inclined plane. This uses the same amount of work as directly lifting the object to the same height at a constant speed because the displacement perpendicular to the force of gravity contributes no work.

Similarly, sliding an object down a frictionless, inclined plane involves the same gravitational work as the object undergoing a free fall from the same height. Since the only forces involved in these motions are acting on a vertical plane, the work done is only dependent on the height of the ramp.

Concept of Energy

Work and energy are closely related concepts. *Energy* is traditionally defined as the ability to do work, and, like work, the unit of energy is Joules.

However, although work and energy have the same units, the two concepts are not always interchangeable. Energy takes many different forms, while mechanical work is limited to the definition presented above.

For example, energy may be exerted in an attempt to move a heavy box, but if the box does not budge, then no work has been done.

Another important concept of energy is that the sum of the energy of the universe in its current state is the same amount of energy that was present at the inception of the universe.

There is an infinite amount of space for it to go, but it never disappears. This is the Law of Conservation of Energy and will be discussed in the chapter.

Energy forms

All energy that was created from the beginning of the universe is divided into types.

Mechanical energy—The energy associated with motion and position. It is equal to kinetic plus potential energy.

Electrical energy—The energy made up of the current and potential provided by a circuit. Any charged particle within an electrical field contains electrical energy.

Chemical energy—The energy involved in all chemical reactions. This is the potential of a certain substance to undergo a transformation or reaction.

Radiant energy—Consists of all the energy from electromagnetic waves. It can be viewed as the energy stored in a photon, or in the motion of an electromagnetic wave.

Visible light is a small part of the full spectrum of electromagnetic waves—there are many other sources of radiant energy that cannot be seen with the naked eye.

Nuclear energy—The energy that is released during reactions involving the fusion or fission of the nucleus. Examples include nuclear bombs and nuclear power plants.

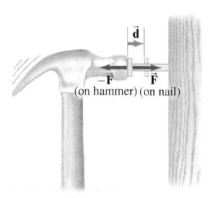

Although energy can take different forms, there are two main types of energy within mechanical physics problems:

- *Kinetic energy*: the energy of motion (energy that is being consumed/released at a given time)

- *Potential energy*: stored energy (energy that could be released for a certain body)

Kinetic Energy

Kinetic energy (*KE*) is the energy associated with the motion of an object and results from work or a change in potential energy.

Kinetic energy is only dependent on the mass of an object as well as its speed. As with every energy, the unit of kinetic energy is a Joule (kg·m^2/s^2).

Below is the equation for kinetic energy:

$$KE = \frac{1}{2}mv^2$$

An important feature of kinetic energy is its relation to the mass and speed of an object. From the equation above, *KE* is directly proportional to mass, and *KE* is proportional to the square of the velocity.

So if the mass (*m*) of an object is doubled, *KE* is also doubled.

If the velocity (*v*) is doubled, the *KE* is quadrupled (because velocity is squared).

For example, two cars are on the road, but one is twice as heavy as the other. If both cars are traveling at the same speed, the car with twice the mass has twice as much *KE* as that of the other car.

If two cars of equal mass are on the road, and one is traveling twice as fast as the other, the faster car has a *KE* four times that of, the slower car.

The importance of this is that a change in velocity is more significant, regarding kinetic energy than a change in mass because the velocity is squared.

For objects of the same mass, the object with the greater velocity has greater *KE*.

For objects with the same velocity, the object with a greater mass has greater *KE*.

Work-Kinetic Energy Theorem

Work on an object can be transformed into kinetic energy. If the net work on the object is positive, the kinetic energy increases; if the net work is negative, the kinetic energy decreases.

Thus, work and kinetic energy (*KE*) are directly related by the equation:

$$|W| = |\Delta KE| \quad \text{(change in kinetic energy)}$$

Given that the definition of kinetic energy is:

$$KE = \frac{1}{2}mv^2$$

Work can be written, regarding a change in the kinetic energy, as:

$$W = \Delta KE = \frac{1}{2}mv_2^2 - \frac{1}{2}mv_1^2$$

For example, the force *F* provided by a car's engine moves the car a distance *d*, and thus performs positive work on the car. This work is transformed into kinetic energy and increases the total kinetic energy of the car.

As a result, the car has a higher final velocity than before the work was performed.

$$+W = +\Delta KE$$

$$v_2 > v_1$$

Conversely, if the same car applied its brakes at a stop sign, the force provided by friction in the car's brakes would do negative work on the car. In this case, the negative work on the car would reduce its kinetic energy and the change in kinetic energy would be negative.

As a result, the final velocity of the car would be less than its initial velocity.

$$-W = -\Delta KE$$

$$v_2 < v_1$$

The kinetic energy of an object can also do work when forces are involved.

For example, a moving object on a frictionless surface can convert all of its kinetic energy to work if it slides up an inclined plane before coming to a complete stop.

Here, the kinetic energy of the object is converted to work to lift the object a distance against the force of gravity.

$$-\Delta KE = +W$$

In summary, energy can perform work against:

- inertia

- gravity

- friction

- deformation of shape

- combinations of the above

Potential Energy

Potential energy is the energy stored in an object. Regardless if an object is in motion, an object always retains energy. This energy can be stored in many different forms, such as the chemical potential energy of food. The reason living things eat is because food is full of chemically-bonded substances. Organisms' bodies store these substances in cells until they are needed. Then the cells will break the bonded substances down into individual parts. This process of breaking bonds releases the potential energy.

Unlike chemical potential energy, potential energy in mechanical physics problems depends solely upon the position or configuration of objects. By this definition, an object has potential energy by its surroundings. Here are some examples:

- An object at some height above the ground

- A wound-up spring

- A stretched elastic band

There are a few types of potential energy: gravitational potential energy (local and general) and spring (elastic) potential energy.

Gravitational, local ($PE = mgh$)

Local gravitational potential energy is the energy stored in an object due to its position (height) above the ground. It only depends upon the mass of the object, its height above the ground and the acceleration of gravity:

$$PE = mgh$$

From the equation above, potential energy is directly proportional to mass and height. If two objects of equal mass are at different heights above the ground, then the higher object has more potential energy.

Likewise, if two objects of unequal mass are at the same height than the object with a larger mass has greater potential energy. On Earth, g is 9.8 m/s^2 and is assumed constant regardless of location or height (unless stated otherwise).

Another important feature of gravitational potential energy is that measuring h requires a reference height. Usually, the reference height is obvious in a problem (i.e., the ground), but if not, a reference height can be established at any arbitrary location, as long as at the reference height $h = 0$ and thus the potential energy is zero.

For example, if a rock of mass m is held a height h_1 above a table, its potential energy concerning the table (reference height) is:

$$PE = mgh_1$$

If the surface of the table is a height h_2 above the ground, then the rock's potential energy concerning the ground (reference height) is:

$$PE = mg(h_2 + h_1)$$

Like kinetic energy, work can be performed to increase or decrease potential energy. If all the work is transformed into potential energy (or vice versa), then work, and potential energy can be related by the equation:

$$|W| = |\Delta PE|$$

Which can be written, regarding a change in the potential energy, as:

$$W = \Delta PE = mgh_2 - mgh_1$$

For example, the diagram below shows a block of mass m that is raised a height h from position y_1 to position y_2. The work performed results in a positive change in potential energy because the new position of the block is at a greater height than its original position.

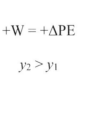

$+W = +\Delta PE$

$y_2 > y_1$

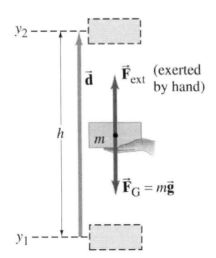

Gravitational, general ($PE = -GmM/r$)

The general formula for gravitational potential energy is found by using Newton's Law of Universal Gravitation. This formula was discussed in depth in the previous chapter, but it defines g as being:

$$g = \frac{GM}{r^2}$$

Where G is the universal gravitation constant, M is the mass of the attracting object, and r is the distance between the two objects in question. The gravitational constant G has a value of 6.67×10^{-11} N·m^2/kg^2.

To find the general form of gravitational potential energy g is substituted into the equation for local gravitational energy, and the results in the equation:

$$PE = m \cdot \frac{GM}{r^2} \cdot h$$

The height h is essentially another measurement of the distance between two objects and is equal to the radius r. This cancels an r in the denominator, and results in the equation for the general gravitational potential energy:

$$PE = \frac{GmM}{r}$$

Spring ($PE = \frac{1}{2}kx^2$)

Springs can also store potential energy. The potential energy of a spring is dependent upon the spring material and the stretch or compression of the spring:

$$PE = \frac{1}{2}kx^2$$

The spring constant k is a measure of the stiffness of the spring; stiffer springs have a larger k because they require more energy for them to stretch or compress. The compression of the spring from its original equilibrium position is represented as x.

The PE of a spring is the elastic potential energy and is sometimes notated as PE_{el}.

The force required to compress a spring is described by the equation:

$$F_s = -kx$$

Notice the negative sign in front of the constant; this is to indicate that the spring force is a restoring force and acts opposite to the direction of the stretch.

This can be observed in the diagram below:

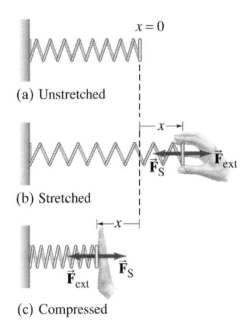

Initially, the spring is at equilibrium as seen in figure (a).

In figure (b), if stretched a distance x from the equilibrium length, then the spring force acts opposite to the direction of the stretch.

In figure (c), if the spring is compressed a distance x from the equilibrium length, then the spring force acts opposite to the compression.

Conservation of Energy

Remember that conservative forces include gravity, spring forces, and the electrostatic force. Non-conservative forces include friction and human exertion. Mechanical energy, like all energy, must be conserved. If there are no non-conservative forces, the sum of the changes in the kinetic energy and the potential energy is zero. The kinetic and potential energy changes are equal but opposite in sign.

The total mechanical energy can then be defined as:

$$\sum E = KE + PE$$

Moreover, its conservation is:

$$E_2 = E_1 = \text{constant}$$

The total amount of initial energy equals the total amount of final energy. Gravitational potential energy is converted to kinetic energy as an object falls, but the total amount of energy stays the same. When a crate slides to a stop on a rough surface, its kinetic energy is converted into heat and sound energy.

Take the following example of a man dropping a rock some distance y. By conservation of energy, the total mechanical energy of the rock at any given instant is:

$$\Sigma E = KE + PE = \tfrac{1}{2} mv^2 + mgh$$

all potential energy $\quad y_1 = h$

half PE, half KE $\quad h$

$\quad y$

all kinetic energy $\quad y_2 = 0$

PE KE

PE KE

PE KE

Initially, the rock is held stationary above the ground a distance y, and all of its energy is potential energy. When the rock is released, it drops down the ground; at exactly the halfway point of the rock's descent, half of its potential energy has been converted to kinetic energy. Finally, right before impact with the ground, all the initial potential energy has been converted to kinetic energy. The energy bar graphs next to the figure show how the energy moves from all potential to all kinetic.

Another example of energy conservation is a rollercoaster. The speed of a roller coaster only depends on its current height compared to its starting height.

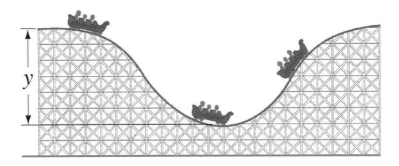

$$PE_{1st\ hill} = KE = PE_{2nd\ hill}$$

At the top of the drop, all of the rollercoaster's energy will exist as potential energy. At the bottom, the rollercoaster will have converted all its energy to kinetic energy. If there is no friction present, then all of the kinetic energy at the bottom could be converted back to potential energy to bring the roller coaster up the second hill of equal height to the first.

A final example of conservation of energy can be seen in the spring. The diagram below depicts a ball shot using a spring:

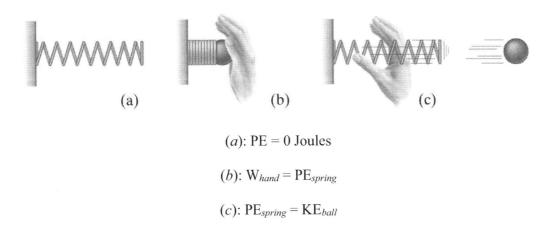

(a): $PE = 0$ Joules

(b): $W_{hand} = PE_{spring}$

(c): $PE_{spring} = KE_{ball}$

In figure (a) the spring is at its equilibrium length and has no potential energy.

Figure (b) shows that work has been performed against the restoring force of the spring. Assuming an ideal system, the work performed is converted entirely into spring potential energy.

In figure (c), the ball is released, and all of the spring's potential energy is converted into the kinetic energy of the ball.

However, if there is a non-conservative force, such as friction, where does the kinetic and potential energy go? Energy cannot be destroyed, only converted into different forms.

In this case, friction performs work, which transforms the initial energy into heat.

In the presence of friction:

$$PE_{initial} > PE_{final}$$

$$KE_{initial} > KE_{final}$$

Tips for Problem Solving:

1. Draw a picture

2. Determine the system for which energy will be conserved

3. Figure out what to look for, and decide on the initial and final positions

4. Choose a logical reference frame

5. Apply conservation of energy

6. Solve

Power, Units

Often, problems do not give total energy or input work, but instead, give the power a system consumes. *Power* is the work performed over time, and can be written as:

Power can be derived as the product of the force on an object times its velocity:

$$P = \vec{F}\vec{v}$$

The SI unit for power is the *watt* (Joules/second). Another unit for power, commonly used for highly-powered objects such as engines, is *horsepower* (hp). One hp is equal to ~745.7 Watts. A key concept of power is the time at which work is performed. For example, lifting an object of mass *m* one meter off the ground will always require the same amount of work.

However, lifting the object in one minute requires more power than lifting the object in an hour. The longer the time interval, the less power is required. The difference between walking and running upstairs is power—the change in gravitational potential energy is the same.

$$P = average\ power\ = \frac{work}{time} = \frac{energy\ transformed}{time}$$

Power is a useful tool in predicting the amount of work that can be performed over a given time.

For example, if there are two engines, the more powerful engine can do the same amount of work in less time than the less powerful engine. This is why sports cars are often described by their engine's horsepower and are compared by how they accelerate from 0 mph to 60 mph. Sports cars have powerful engines that can perform work, which is, in turn, converted into kinetic energy.

Electric companies use power because it describes energy (work done) over time.

Chapter Summary

- Work is a force applied across a displacement. Work can cause a change in energy.

  Positive work puts energy into a system.

  Negative work takes energy out of a system.

  Basic equations for work include:

$$W = \vec{F}\vec{d}\cos\theta \qquad W = \Delta KE \qquad W = \text{area under an } F \text{ vs. } d \text{ graph}$$

Conservative Forces	Non-conservative Forces
Gravitational	Friction
	Air resistance
Elastic	Tension in a cord
	Motor or rocket propulsion
Electric	Push or pull by a person

- Energy is the ability to do work and is a conserved quantity. This means that the total initial energy is equal to the total final energy.

  Basic equations for energy include:

$$KE = \frac{1}{2}mv^2 \qquad PE_g = mgh \qquad PE_s = \frac{1}{2}kx^2$$

- *Kinetic energy*: the energy of motion (energy that is being consumed/released at a given time)

- *Potential energy*: stored energy (energy that could be released for a certain body)

- Types of energy:

  Mechanical energy—The energy associated with motion and position. It is equal to kinetic plus potential energy.

  Electrical energy—The energy made up of the current and potential provided by a circuit. Any charged particle within an electrical field contains electrical energy.

  Chemical energy—The energy involved in all chemical reactions. This is the potential of a certain substance to undergo a transformation or reaction.

  Radiant energy—Consists of all the energy from electromagnetic waves. It can be viewed as the energy stored in a photon, or in the motion of an electromagnetic wave. Visible light is only a small part of the full spectrum of electromagnetic waves—there are many other sources of radiant energy that cannot be seen with the naked eye.

  Nuclear energy—The energy that is released during reactions involving the fusion or fission of the nucleus. Examples include nuclear bombs and nuclear power plants.

- Gravitational energy: $PE = \frac{GmM}{r}$

- Spring energy: $PE = \frac{1}{2}kx^2$

- The Law of Conservation of Energy states that the total amount of initial energy equals the total amount of final energy,

- Often, interactions are limited to mechanical energy with no heat lost or gained.

  In this case:

  $$KE_i + PE_i \pm W = KE_f + PE_f$$

- Power is the rate at which one does work, and is given by:

  $$P = \frac{W}{t} \quad \text{or} \quad P = \vec{F}\vec{v}$$

Practice Questions

1. When a pebble is dropped from height h, it reaches the ground with kinetic energy. Ignoring air resistance, from what height should the pebble be dropped to reach the ground with twice the *KE*?

A. $\sqrt{2}h$ **B.** $2h$ **C.** $4h$ **D.** $8h$ **E.** $16h$

2. Which of the following situations requires the greatest power?

A. 50 J of work in 20 minutes   **C.** 10 J of work in 5 minutes

B. 200 J of work in 30 minutes   **D.** 100 J of work in 20 minutes

     E. 100 J of work in 10 minutes

3. A kilowatt-hour is a unit of:

     I. work   II. force   III. power

A. I only   **B.** II only   **C.** III only   **D.** I and II only   **E.** I and III only

4. A hydraulic press (like a simple lever), properly arranged, is capable of:

     I. multiplying energy input

     II. multiplying output force

     III. exerting force only vertically

A. I only   **B.** II only   **C.** III only   **D.** I and II only   **E.** I and III only

5. 4.5×10^5 J of work are done on a 1,150 kg car while it accelerates from 10 m/s to some final velocity. What is this final velocity? (Use the acceleration due to gravity $g = 10$ m/s^2)

A. 30 m/s   **B.** 37 m/s   **C.** 12 m/s   **D.** 19 m/s   **E.** 43 m/s

6. Which of the following is not a unit of work?

A. N·m   **B.** kw·h   **C.** J   **D.** kg·m/s   **E.** W·s

7. The law of conservation of energy states that:

     I. the energy of an isolated system is constant

     II. energy cannot be used faster than it is created

     III. energy cannot change forms

A. I only   **B.** II only   **C.** III only   **D.** I and II only   **E.** I and III only

8. A crane lifts a 300 kg steel beam vertically upward a distance of 110 m. Ignoring frictional forces, how much work does the crane do on the beam if the beam accelerates upward at 1.4 m/s^2? (Use the acceleration due to gravity $g = 9.8$ m/s^2)

A. 2.4×10^3 J

B. 4.6×10^4 J

C. 3.7×10^5 J

D. 6.2×10^5 J

E. 8.8×10^2 J

9. Steve pushes twice as hard against a stationary brick wall as Charles. Which of the following statements is correct?

A. Both do the same amount of positive work

B. Both do positive work, but Steve does one-half the work of Charles

C. Both do positive work, but Steve does four times the work of Charles

D. Both do positive work, but Steve does twice the work of Charles

E. Both do zero work

10. What is the change in the gravitational potential energy of an object if the height of the object above the Earth is doubled? (Assume that the object remains near the surface)

A. Quadruple

B. Doubled

C. Unchanged

D. Halved

E. Tripled

11. If 1 N is exerted for a distance of 1 m in 1 s, the amount of power delivered is:

A. 3 W

B. 1/3 W

C. 2 W

D. 1 W

E. ½ W

12. A brick is dropped from a roof and falls a distance h to the ground. If h were doubled, how does the maximal KE of the brick, just before it hits the ground, change?

A. It doubles

B. It increases by $\sqrt{2}$

C. It remains the same

D. It increases by 200

E. Requires more information

13. A helicopter with single landing gear descends vertically to land with a speed of 4.5 m/s. The helicopter's shock absorbers have an initial length of 0.6 m. They compress to 77% of their original length and the air in the tires absorbs 23% of the initial energy as heat. What is the ratio of the spring constant to the helicopter's mass?

A. 0.11 kN/kg·m

B. 1.1 N/kg·m

C. 0.8 kN/kg·m

D. 11 N/kg·m

E. 0.11 N/kg·m

14. A 21 metric ton airplane is observed to be a vertical distance of 2.6 km from its takeoff point. What is the gravitational potential energy of the plane with respect to the ground? (Use the acceleration due to gravity $g = 9.8$ m/s^2, the metric ton = 1,000 kg)

   A. 582 J   **B.** 384 J   **C.** 535 MJ   **D.** 414 MJ   **E.** 773 J

15. A tennis ball bounces on the floor. During each bounce, it loses 31% of its energy due to heating. How high does the ball reach after the third bounce, if it is initially released 4 m from the floor?

   A. 55 cm   **B.** 171 mm   **C.** 106 cm   **D.** 131 cm   **E.** 87 cm

Solutions

1. B is correct.

When the pebble falls, *KE* at impact = *PE* before impact.

$PE = KE$

$mgh = KE$

$mg(2h) = 2KE$

$2PE = 2KE$

If the mass and gravity are constant, then the height must be doubled.

2. E is correct.

Power = Work / time

A: Power = 50 J / 20 min = 2.5 J/min

B: power = 200 J / 30 min = 6.67 J/min

C: power = 10 J / 5 min = 2 J/min

D: power = 100 J / 20 min = 5 J/min

E: power = 100 J / 10 min = 10 J/min

Typically, power is measured in watts or J/s.

3. A is correct.

kilowatt = unit of power

hour = unit of time

kW·h = power × time

power = work / time

kW·h = (work / time) × time

kW·h = work

4. B is correct. Mechanical advantage:

d_1 / d_2

where d_1 and d_2 are the effort arm and load arm, respectively.

If d_1 is greater than d_2, force output is increased.

5. A is correct.

Find the final speed using the conservation of energy.

Let the energy added as work be represented by W. Then, conservation of energy requires:

$E_f = E_i + W$

$\frac{1}{2}mv^2_f = \frac{1}{2}mv^2_i + W$

Solving for v_f:

$v_f = \sqrt{v^2_i + (2W)/m}$

$v_f = \sqrt{[(10 \text{ m/s})^2 + (2) \cdot (4.5 \times 10^5 \text{ J})/(1150 \text{ kg})]}$

$v_f = 29.7 \text{ m/s} \approx 30 \text{ m/s}$

6. D is correct.

Work = Force × distance

$W = Fd$

The unit kg·m/s cannot be manipulated to achieve this.

7. A is correct. The Law of Conservation of Energy states that for an isolated system (no heat or work transferred), the energy of the system is constant. Energy can only transform from one form to another.

8. C is correct. The work done by this force is:

$W = Fd,$

where F = force applied by the crane and d = distance over which the force is active.

Solve for F using Newton's Second Law.

There are two forces on the beam – the applied force due to tension in the crane's cable and gravity.

$F_{net} = ma$

$F - mg = ma$

Therefore:

$W = m(a + g)d$

$W = (300 \text{ kg}) \cdot (1.4 \text{ m/s}^2 + 9.8 \text{ m/s}^2) \cdot (110 \text{ m})$

$W = 3.7 \times 10^5 \text{ J}$

9. E is correct.

Work = Force × displacement × cos θ

$W = Fd \cos \theta$

If $d = 0$, then work = 0

10. B is correct.

Relative to the ground, an object's gravitational $PE = mgh$, where h is the altitude.

PE is proportional to h; doubling h doubles PE.

11. D is correct.

$W = Fd$

$P = W / t$

$P = Fd / t$

$P = (1 \text{ N}) \cdot (1 \text{ m}) / 1 \text{ s}$

$P = 1 \text{ W}$

12. A is correct.

$KE = PE$

$KE = mgh$

h is directly proportional to the KE. If h doubles, then the KE doubles.

13. C is correct.

The initial kinetic energy of the helicopter is entirely converted to the potential energy of the landing gear and heat. By conversation of energy:

$\Delta KE = \Delta PE + Q$

Let the equilibrium length of the landing gear's spring be L_0 and the compressed length be L. The change in potential energy of the landing gear is:

$\Delta PE = \frac{1}{2}k(\Delta x)^2$

$\Delta PE = \frac{1}{2}k(L_0 - L)^2$

$\Delta PE = \frac{1}{2}k(L_0 - (0.23)L_0)^2$

$\Delta PE = \frac{1}{2}k(0.77)L_0^2$

The energy lost to heat is 23% of the initial kinetic energy. The final kinetic energy is zero, therefore:

$$Q = (0.23) \, \Delta KE$$

$$Q = (0.23) \, \tfrac{1}{2}mv^2$$

Conservation of energy becomes:

$$\tfrac{1}{2}mv^2 = (0.77)\tfrac{1}{2}kL_0^2 + (0.23)\tfrac{1}{2}mv^2$$

Solving for k/m:

$$k/m = [(0.77)\,v^2]\,/\,[(0.23)^2 L_0^2]$$

$$k/m = 819 \text{ s}^{-2}$$

$$k/m = 0.8 \text{ kN m}^{-1}\text{ s}^{-1}$$

14. C is correct.

$$PE = mgh$$

$$PE = (21 \times 10^3 \text{ kg}) \cdot (9.8 \text{ m/s}^2) \cdot (2.6 \times 10^3 \text{ m})$$

$$PE = 535 \text{ MJ}$$

15. D is correct.

$$h_0 = 3.5 \text{ m}$$

$$PE_0 = mgh$$

$$PE_1 = mgh(0.69) \rightarrow \text{after first bounce}$$

$$PE_2 = mgh(0.69)^2 \rightarrow \text{after second bounce}$$

$$PE_3 = mgh(0.69)^3 \rightarrow \text{after third bounce}$$

Because mass and gravity are constant, the final height is:

$$\text{final height} = h(0.69)^3$$

$$\text{final height} = (4 \text{ m}) \cdot (0.69)^3$$

$$\text{final height} = 1.31 \text{ m} = 131 \text{ cm}$$

Notes

Chapter 5

Waves and Periodic Motion

PERIODIC MOTION

- **Amplitude, Period, Frequency**

- **Simple Harmonic Motion, Displacement as a Sinusoidal Function of Time**

- **Hooke's Law ($F = -kx$)**

- **Energy of a Mass-Spring System**

- **Motion of a Pendulum**

WAVE CHARACTERISTICS

- **Transverse and Longitudinal Waves**

- **Phase, Interference and Wave Addition**

- **Reflection and Transmission**

- **Refraction and Diffraction**

- **Amplitude and Intensity**

Notes

Amplitude, Period, Frequency

Periodic motion, sinusoidal motion, is a motion that repeats itself. If an object moves back and forth over the same path at constant speed, each cycle will take the same amount of time; the resulting motion is periodic.

In periodic motion, this back-and-forth activity is an *oscillation* or vibration. Many different systems can display oscillatory/vibratory motion; there are several types of periodic motion as well. Periodic motion can be damped (friction is present) or undamped, driven (an outside force is acting upon the system) or free.

Regardless of the motion, an oscillatory system has several inherent characteristics that define its periodic motion. These characteristics are the amplitude, frequency, and period.

In general, most questions will refer to several types of oscillatory systems, but only one motion: undamped and free periodic motion (simple harmonic motion).

Amplitude (*A*): In periodic motion, the *amplitude* expresses the displacement of the system about its equilibrium (center) position. Amplitude can have several different units depending on the system.

Frequency (*f*): is the rate of oscillation, or the number of cycles per second, where a cycle is one complete vibration (when the displacement is zero). This value is usually measured in Hertz (Hz) and can be calculated by:

$$f = \frac{\# \, of \, cycles}{time}$$

In some situations, the frequency is expressed as angular frequency (ω). This value is related to frequency; however, angular frequency is measured in radians per second (rad/s).

The equation for angular frequency is:

$$\omega = 2\pi f$$

Period (*T*): is the time required to complete one cycle or one oscillation. The period is often measured in seconds and can be calculated by:

$$T = \frac{time}{\# \ of \ cycles}$$

The period is sometimes measured in degrees or radians. One trip around a circle requires 360° or 2π radians and is analogous to one complete cycle of an oscillating system.

Additionally, as seen from the above equation, period and frequency are inversely related.

The inverse relationship between period and frequency is expressed as:

$$T = \frac{1}{f}$$

Simple Harmonic Motion, Displacement as a Sinusoidal Function of Time

An object or system exhibiting *simple harmonic motion* is a special case of periodic motion that is undamped and free. This means there is no force of friction present and no external, time-dependent force acting upon it. It also means that the system requires a restoring force (not a driving force), which must be proportional to the displacement (amplitude). This proportionality allows the system to oscillate about its equilibrium position while retaining the same amplitude.

Simple harmonic motion is usually depicted as a sine or cosine graph, as seen in the diagram below:

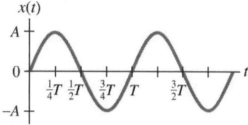

Notice that the system oscillates about its equilibrium position with the same amplitude and a constant period (and thus constant frequency). Another important distinction is that, regardless of the magnitude of the amplitude, the period and frequency do not change. In simple harmonic motion, frequency and period are independent of amplitude. Any object's simple harmonic motion is found by the equation:

$$x = A \sin (\omega t)$$

$$x = A \sin (2\pi f t)$$

where x is displacement, A is amplitude, t is time, ω is angular frequency, and f is frequency.

Sometimes the equation is written as:

$$x = A \cos (\omega t)$$

$$x = A \cos (2\pi f t)$$

Sine or cosine may be used interchangeably, if the translation of these graphs is accounted for. A cosine graph has a y-intercept of A (maximum amplitude), whereas a sine graph has a y-intercept of 0 (equilibrium). These are translations of each other, but the translations must be accounted for in the equation. Otherwise, it will be incorrect.

Hooke's Law

One classic example of simple harmonic motion is the oscillatory motion of a mass-spring system. When a mass is attached to a spring, the only forces acting upon it are tension and weight of the mass. In such systems, there is no driving force, and it is assumed to be completely undamped.

An important characteristic of a mass-spring system is the *spring constant*. Robert Hooke discovered that, given a certain spring, there is a constant that can be found when different masses are attached, and the equilibrium position is measured. This constant is an inherent constant of all springs and relates displacement of the spring (change in length) to the restoring force the spring exerts. This relationship is Hooke's Law and is expressed as:

$$F = -k\Delta x$$

where k is the spring constant measured in (N/m), Δx is the displacement, and F is the restoring force (N).

The minus sign in Hooke's Law is by convention and means that the restoring force is in the opposite direction to the displacement (because force and displacement are vectors).

For example, in diagram (a), a spring is attached to a wall, and the other side is attached to a mass.

If the scenario is considered ideal (no friction present), then when the mass is displaced, and the spring is stretched, the direction of the restoring force is opposite to the displacement and act left (b).

Conversely, if the spring were compressed the same distance, then the restoring force would be of equal magnitude but in the opposite direction (c).

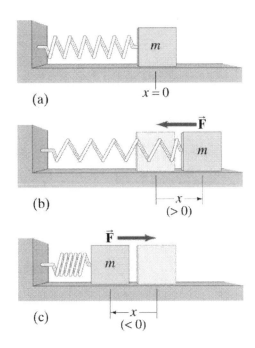

Additionally, if the spring is hung vertically, the only change is in the equilibrium position, which is now at a point where the restoring spring force is equal and opposite the weight of the mass.

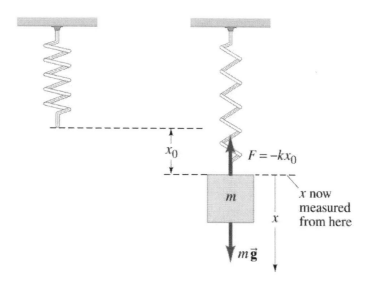

Hooke's Law can also be used to find the acceleration of the mass attached to the spring. Regardless if the mass-spring system is horizontally- or vertically-positioned, forces always follow Newton's Second Law, therefore (assuming no friction):

$$|ma| = |k\Delta x|$$

$$|a| = \left| \frac{k\Delta x}{m} \right|$$

More importantly, Hooke's Law demonstrates that mass-spring systems are good examples of simple harmonic motion. When disturbed from the equilibrium position, a restoring force acts to bring the spring towards equilibrium.

The restoring force (F) is proportional to the stretched or compressed distance, which makes the system a simple harmonic. The amplitude (A) of this oscillation is the maximum displacement (Δx):

$$A = \Delta x$$

For example, if a mass-spring system is oriented vertically, and the mass is displaced a certain distance, the resulting motion will follow that of a simple harmonic oscillator. This can be seen if a pen is attached to the mass and a roll of paper is moved across the surface of the pen during the motion of the mass:

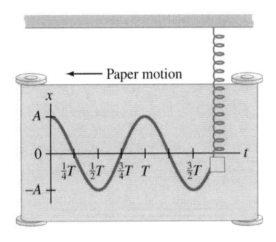

$$x = A \cos (\omega t)$$
$$F = -kA$$

In simple harmonic motion of a mass-spring system, the frequency and angular frequency of the system can be calculated by:

$$\omega = \sqrt{\frac{k}{m}}$$

$$f = \frac{\sqrt{k/m}}{2\pi} = 2\pi \sqrt{\frac{m}{k}}$$

The period can then be calculated as:

$$T = \frac{2\pi}{\sqrt{k/m}} = 2\pi \sqrt{\frac{m}{k}}$$

Notice that the frequency and period of a mass-spring system are only based upon the mass and spring constant. This is important to note because a vertically-angled mass-spring system will always have the same frequency and period, regardless of the value for gravitational acceleration. As such, the frequency and period would not change, even if the system were on the moon, in space or on Earth.

Energy of a Mass-Spring System

By definition, an oscillating mass accelerates, decelerates, changes direction and repeats. This means it contains motion energy and stationary energy (its velocity is zero at the peaks and troughs of its movement). Therefore, the equations for the potential and kinetic energy of a mass on a spring can be written as:

$$Potential\ energy = PE = \frac{1}{2}kx^2$$

$$Kinetic\ energy = KE = \frac{1}{2}mv^2$$

When the mass is in motion and passes through the equilibrium position, the displacement will be zero, as will the potential energy. However, the kinetic energy will be at its maximum because the mass is at its maximum velocity. This occurs at the point where the net force is zero.

At the maximum displacement, the value of x will equal the amplitude (A). The potential energy will be at its maximum, and the kinetic energy is zero (because the velocity is zero as the object changes its direction of motion). This occurs at the moment of maximum force, which is also the point of maximum acceleration of an oscillating particle.

At any point along its motion, the potential energy plus the kinetic energy of the particle will always be the same value. This value will be constant, and it will always be the same as the total energy present in the system:

$$Total\ Energy = E = PE + KE$$

$$E = \frac{1}{2}kx^2 + \frac{1}{2}mv^2$$

When potential energy is at its maximum (at the amplitude), kinetic energy is zero. This means that all of the energy in the system must be equal to only the potential energy. The same relationship applies when kinetic energy is at its maximum:

$$PE_{max} = KE_{max} = E = Total\ Energy$$

The equations for maximum potential and kinetic energy are summed by:

$$PE_{max} = \frac{1}{2}kA^2$$

$$KE_{max} = \frac{1}{2}mv^2 \text{ at } x = 0$$

For example, a spring has been compressed, but it is not currently in motion. This means all energy is stored in potential energy, as in diagram (a):

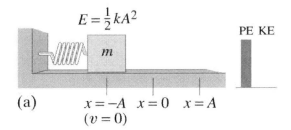

If the mass is allowed to move, the spring will expand towards its equilibrium position. Once it has reached its equilibrium position, all of its potential energy is transformed into kinetic energy, as in diagram (b):

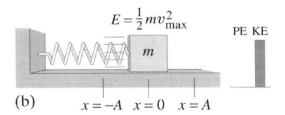

As the mass reaches the maximum stretched amplitude, its kinetic energy is converted to potential energy, as in diagram (c):

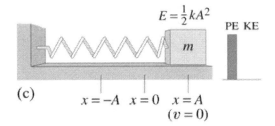

The object then moves toward equilibrium but does not yet reach the equilibrium position. Therefore, most of the energy is kinetic, but some energy is still stored as potential. As it gets closer to the equilibrium position, the amount of potential energy will decrease, and the amount of kinetic energy will increase, as in diagram (d):

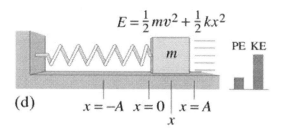

The velocity of the mass can also be calculated at various points during its motion.

By setting the maximum potential energy and kinetic energy are equal, the maximum velocity of mass can be calculated as:

$$v_{max} = \sqrt{\frac{k}{m}} * A$$

This can be solved for the velocity as a function of position:

$$v = \pm v_{max}\sqrt{1 - \frac{x^2}{A^2}},$$

Motion of a Pendulum

Thus far, the examples have been oscillating masses attached to springs. In this chapter, the simple harmonic motion of a pendulum will be discussed. A pendulum undergoing simple harmonic motion (i.e., a simple pendulum) consists of a mass at the end of an assumed massless cord or rod. To be in simple harmonic motion, the restoring force on the pendulum must be proportional to the negative of the displacement.

For example, in the diagram below:

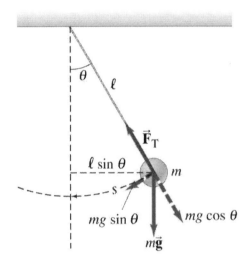

The diagram shows that the angle θ measures the displacement of the pendulum and thus the restoring force is given as:

$$F = -mg \sin \theta$$

$$|a| = |g \sin \theta|$$

For small displacement angles $\sin \theta \approx \theta$, and thus the restoring force becomes:

$$F = -mg\theta$$

$$|a| = |g\theta|$$

Unlike mass-spring systems, the frequency of a simple pendulum is dependent upon the acceleration due to gravity. It is also dependent upon the length of the cord or rod attached to the mass, and is expressed as:

$$\omega = \sqrt{\frac{g}{l}}$$

$$f = 2\pi\sqrt{\frac{g}{l}}$$

where g is the acceleration of gravity (9.8 m/s^2) and l is the length of the cord or rod.

The period of a simple pendulum's oscillation can then be given by the equation:

$$T = 2\pi\sqrt{\frac{l}{g}}$$

Like mass-spring systems, simple pendulums conserve energy, and the total energy is the sum of potential and kinetic energy.

Unlike mass-spring systems, the *PE* is dependent upon gravity and is found by:

$$PE = mgh$$

where h is the height above the equilibrium position.

Given that *PE* is at its maximum when the height (or x) is equal to the amplitude, this equation can be rewritten as:

$$PE_{max} = mgl(1 - \cos\theta)$$

Maximum *KE* is the same for simple pendulums as it is for mass-spring systems:

$$KE_{max} = \frac{1}{2}mv^2$$

Wave Characteristics

Waves are periodic disturbances that transport energy through a medium but do not transport matter. Many examples of waves exist; including the light one sees, the sound one hears and ocean waves breaking on the beach. While all these examples may seem very different, they share characteristics intrinsic to all waves. Like periodic motion, the motion of a wave can be defined by a few characteristics, which are:

- Amplitude, *A*

- Frequency *f* and period *T*

- Wavelength, *λ*

- Wave velocity

Amplitude, frequency, and period were discussed earlier. Wavelength and wave velocity are new terms but are easily understood.

Observe the diagram of a sine wave shown below:

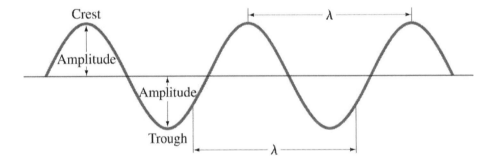

The amplitude is a representation of energy, and its magnitude is not dependent upon frequency or period. The *wavelength* is the distance of one cycle of the wave and is measured in meters (m). The *wave velocity* is the speed and direction of the wave. These two characteristics are related to the frequency and period by the equations:

$$f = \frac{v}{\lambda}$$

$$T = \frac{1}{f} = \frac{\lambda}{v}$$

where *v* is the wave velocity (m/s), and *λ* is the wavelength (m).

Transverse and Longitudinal Waves

There are three main types of wave motion: transverse, longitudinal and surface. These types can be described by the characteristics above but differ in the motion of particles within the wave. Remember, the wave is not transporting the particles; rather, as the wave passes through a particle in a medium, the particle will undergo a specific periodic motion. Two wave types are transverse and longitudinal waves.

For example, imagine a hand moving a slinky, as seen in the figures below.

A *transverse wave*, seen in diagram (a), oscillates particles with motion perpendicular to the wave direction.

A *longitudinal wave*, seen in diagram (b), oscillates particles with motion parallel to the wave direction.

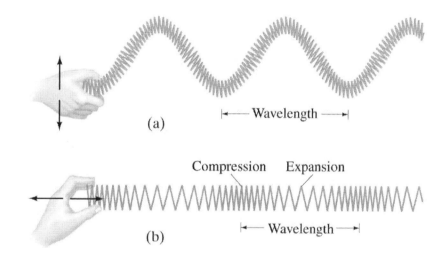

Another way to think about these types of waves is to ask, "What is oscillating, and in what direction?" Imagine there is a red mark on one of the crests in the diagram (a). The mark would move up and down, even though the energy is traveling through the medium from left to right. The wave displacement is perpendicular to the direction of the wave motion, meaning the mark is experiencing a transverse wave.

For diagram (b), imagine a mark on the top of a crest. As the hand pushes the slinky through the medium from left to right and back again, the red mark would travel left-to-right along with it. There is no vertical motion anywhere. This means the wave displacement is parallel to the direction of motion, and the mark is experiencing a longitudinal wave. Notice in diagram (b) how the particles in this medium move closer together and then farther apart.

This is compression and expansion and only occurs in longitudinal waves.

Transverse waves have crests and troughs.

Longitudinal waves have compressions and expansions.

Surface waves are waves in which particles oscillate in a circular motion, rather than vertically or horizontally. These types of waves only occur at the interface of two different mediums, where the wave is traveling in only one of the mediums.

An example of surface waves is the waves seen on the ocean.

For example, the diagram below is a wave propagating through the ocean with a velocity *v*.

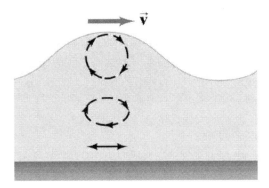

At the interface of the two mediums (air and water), the particles are moved in a circular pattern, which is seen in the diagram above. Deeper in the ocean, the particles are further from the interface, and the motion begins to resemble that of an ellipse.

At greater depths, the particle motion is only horizontal, and the wave becomes a longitudinal wave.

This is a characteristic of surface waves; the further from the interface of the two mediums, the more longitudinal the wave becomes.

Phase, Interference and Wave Addition

Phases occur when two waves interact. A phase difference between two waves means that the crests (or troughs) do not occur at the same points in space. For example, the diagrams below have two waves: in-phase and out-of-phase:

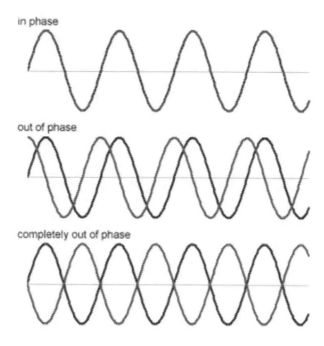

The phase of two or more waves, with respect to each, is important because it gives rise to interference effects. Interacting waves will combine to create a combination wave, the amplitude of which can be determined depending on the interaction between the two component waves. The interference depends upon the phase of the waves: *constructive interference* (if the waves are in-phase) and *destructive interference* (if the waves are out-of-phase).

For example, in the diagram (a) below, two transverse waves of equal magnitude travel across a rope until they meet. At the moment the two waves overlap, they are completely out-of-phase and destructively interfere to produce no wave.

In diagram (b), two waves of equal magnitude overlap and are completely in-phase. This produces constructive interference and results in a wave with double the magnitude of the two incoming waves.

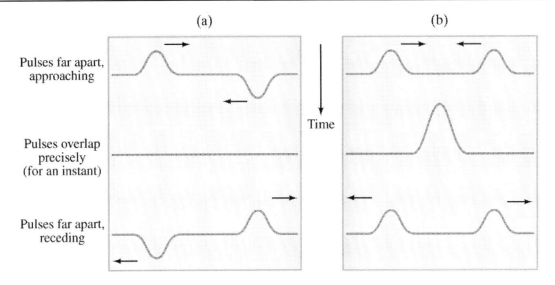

In-phase: This occurs when the waves are 0 or 2π radians (0 or 360°) apart in their oscillations. This means the peaks and troughs of one wave are aligned with the peaks and troughs of another. When two waves are in-phase and interfere, they combine, and the amplitude of the resulting wave is the sum of the amplitudes of the interfering waves.

This is constructive interference.

$$A_1 + A_2 = A_{net}$$

Out-of-phase: All out-of-phase waves are destructive interference. This means that the resulting amplitude of the combined waves will be less than that of the sum of the waves.

$$0 < A_{net} < A_1 + A_2$$

Completely out-of-phase: The waves are completely out-of-phase if the waves are π radians (180°) apart in their oscillations, and the crests of one are aligned with the troughs of the other. When two waves are completely out-of-phase, the amplitude of the resulting wave is the absolute value of the difference between the two separate amplitudes.

If the waves have the same amplitude, then the waves will completely destructively interfere, and no wave will exist (amplitude = 0).

$$A_{net} = | A_1 - A_2 |$$

The following figures show all three cases of wave interference discussed above.

In diagram (a), two waves are in-phase, and therefore exhibit constructive interference. The resulting amplitude will be the sum of the two individual amplitudes.

Diagram (b) demonstrates two waves that are completely out-of-phase thus will exhibit destructive interference. In this particular case, the two individual amplitudes are equal, and the result is no wave at all.

The final diagram, (c), illustrates two waves out-of-phase (not completely out-of-phase). Here, the resulting waves destructively interfere to produce a wave with an amplitude less than that of the wave with the larger amplitude.

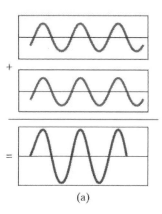

(a)

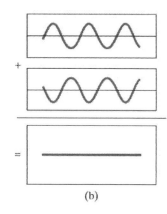

(b)

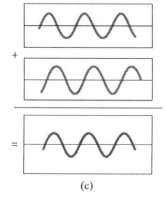

(c)

Reflection and Transmission

Reflection

Reflection occurs when waves bounce off the surface of an object or medium. All waves exhibit reflection and several examples of reflection are: the reflection of light off a mirror to see a person's image, echoes produced by reflection of sound waves, and the glare from sunlight reflecting off the water. These all occur because when a wave encounters an obstacle or an interface between two different mediums, it will be forced to change direction.

Reflections of waves depend upon the object or medium the wave reflects off of.

For example, imagine a wave traveling down a string, as seen in the figure below.

If the wave hits an immobile object, as in diagram (a), it will be reflected in the other direction, but its reflection will be inverted.

In diagram (b), the end of the string is connected to a point where it is free to move. The wave on the string is reflected in the opposite direction, but upright instead of inverted.

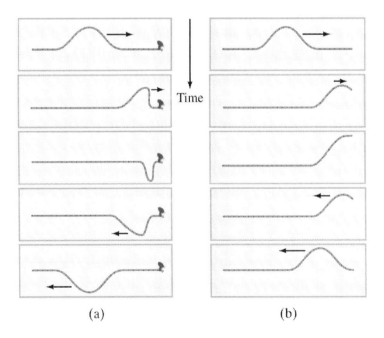

(a)   (b)

Law of Reflection

The Law of Reflection governs the reflection of light off surfaces and interfaces of two different mediums. It states that the angle of incidence of the incoming light ray will be equal to the angle of reflection of the outgoing light ray, concerning the normal line of the reflecting surface.

$$\theta_{incident} = \theta_{reflected}$$

The game of pool is an example of this, in which the balls are waves and the edges of the table surface off of which they reflect. A good pool player understands the reflection angle of the ball off an edge will equal the incoming angle of the ball, concerning the normal of the surface.

The diagram below is an incident light ray on a reflecting surface:

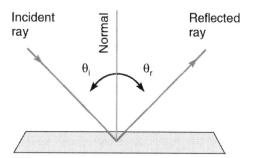

From the diagram, it is clear that the incident angle is equal to the reflected angle. It is important to note that the Law of Reflection only applies to smooth surfaces, which are assumed to be ideal reflectors (mirrors are approximated as ideal reflectors).

If the surface is rough and not smooth, the angle of reflection of one wave would not be equal to the angle of reflection of another wave, even if they left the same place with the same angle. This is because the rough surface would scatter incoming waves.

Observe the figure below of an ideal reflector and a rough surface. The ideal reflector obeys the Law of Reflection, and thus the angle of reflection is equal to the angle of incidence, allowing an observer to see the source of the light (like a mirror). The rough surface scatters the incoming light rays, and the angle of reflection is not equal to the angle of incidence.

In this case, the observer would not be able to see the source of light but instead see only the surface of the rough reflector.

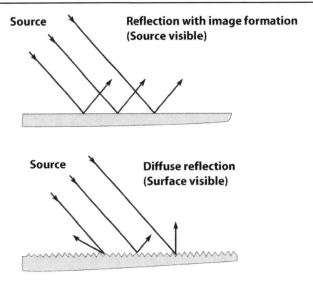

Transmission

   Transmission occurs when a wave encounters a different medium. Unlike reflection, transmission is the phenomenon where some or all of the wave is energy is transmitted through the different medium. An important aspect of transmission is that it is usually not total. An incoming wave is usually partially reflected from an interface of two different mediums, and the rest is transmitted through the new medium.

   The transmission and reflection of water is an example. When light travels through the atmosphere and encounters the surface of a lake, some of the light is reflected, but some are transmitted through the water. This is known to be true because often there is a glare on lakes, ponds, and oceans, indicating reflection. However, when a person jumps into the body of water, it becomes see-through, indicating transmission of light.

   Another example is that of two strings of different densities attached. The figure below represents this scenario. If a wave is traveling down the lower-density section, it will both reflect off and transmit some of its energy to the higher-density section.

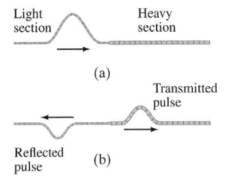

Refraction and Diffraction

Refraction

When a wave encounters a boundary between two different mediums or enters a medium where the wave speed is different, it will be refracted. Specifically, when waves are transmitted from one medium to another, the different physical properties cause the light to bend and therefore change direction within the new medium. This phenomenon is *refraction* and is commonly observed in light waves (although it is possible with any wave).

When dealing with light, the speed is *light propagation speed.* This speed depends upon the medium through which the light propagates: in a vacuum, light travels at a constant 3×10^8 m/s, and in different mediums, such as glass or water, the light propagating speed is less.

Which direction the light bends during refraction depends on the light speed in the different mediums.

This is expressed mathematically by Snell's Law, which relates the speed and angle of the incoming wave to that of the refracted wave:

$$n_1 \sin (\theta_1) = n_2 \sin (\theta_2)$$

Where n is the index of refraction and θ is the angle of the wave, concerning the normal of the medium interface.

The index of refraction is a relation of the light propagation speed in a medium, to that of the speed of light in a vacuum (n is always greater than 1 because light cannot travel faster than when in a vacuum).

$$n = \frac{c}{v}$$

Below is a list of indices of refraction for some common materials:

Substance	Index of refraction	Light speed
Air	Approx. 1	~c
Water	1.333	0.75c
Glass	1.5	0.67c
Diamond	2.4	0.42c

Observe the figures below, which depict the refraction of light from water to air and vice versa. When a wave moves to a denser medium (with a greater refractive index), it bends toward the normal.

When it moves to a less dense medium (with a smaller refractive index), it bends away from the normal.

When the light is refracted from water into the air (left diagram), it is refracted away from the normal.

If the light is refracted from air to water (right diagram), it bends toward the normal.

Given the angle of incidence, the angle of refraction is computed by Snell's Law.

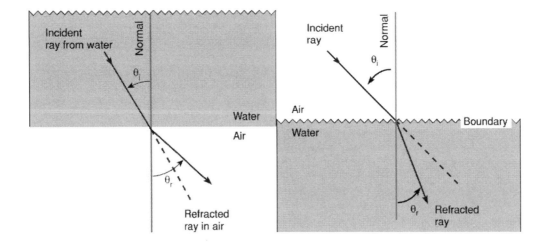

A well-known example of refraction is white light through a prism. The prism is an interesting example of refraction because it separates the mixture of colors in sunlight (white light) into a rainbow. This is only possible because the index of refraction varies with speed (and therefore with wavelength), meaning different wavelengths refract at different angles. This produces an assortment of colored light, like a rainbow, where the refraction takes place in water droplets instead of a prism. Violet is refracted the most (which is why the sky is blue), whereas red is refracted least (when the angle of refraction is greater, red sunsets happen).

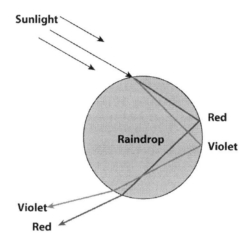

An important aspect of refraction is the *critical angle*. The critical angle is the greatest angle a wave can make with the boundary between two mediums and not be refracted into the second medium. At the critical angle, a wave is refracted parallel to the surface of the interface boundary. Angles greater than the critical angle will cause the incident wave to reflect off the boundary completely. Thus, at angles greater or equal to the critical angle, none of the waves will pass through the boundary, meaning there is "total internal reflection." Some examples of this are fiber optics and gemstone brilliance.

$$n_1 \sin(\theta_{critical}) = n_2 \sin(90°)$$

Diffraction

Diffraction is refraction that occurs when a wave encounters an obstacle in a medium within which it is traveling. A wave then spreads out (dissipate), to move around the obstacle or through an opening in the obstacle (an *aperture*), leaving a "shadow region."

The figure below demonstrates diffraction around an obstacle and through an aperture:

Diffraction around obstacle

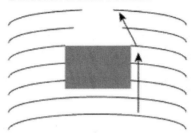

Diffraction through aperture

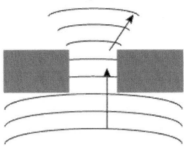

Some types of waves diffract more efficiently than others. Take a sound wave as opposed to a light wave, for example. Music can be heard from around the corner of a building, but the speaker that is emitting it cannot be seen. Conversely, shining light through a hole does not produce a dot of light, but a diffused circle of light. The amount of diffraction depends on how the wavelength and the size of the obstacle or aperture compare. If the opening is larger than the wavelength, diffraction will be minimal, and for the most part, the wave will continue as before. If the opening is much smaller than the wavelength, the diffraction will be noticeable, and the wave will bend into a circular orientation.

If the wave encounters an obstacle, its reaction is the opposite. For example, take the figure below depicting different waves diffracting off different objects. If the obstacle is much smaller than the wavelength, the wave barely diffracts, as seen in diagram (a). If the object is comparable to or larger than the wavelength, diffraction is much more significant, as seen in diagrams (b), (c), (d).

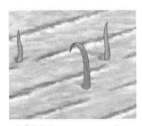   

| (a) Water waves passing blades of grass | (b) Stick in water | (c) Short-wavelength waves passing log | (d) Long-wavelength waves passing log |

Amplitude and Intensity

Just as with the oscillation that starts it, the energy transported by a wave is proportional to the square of the amplitude.

The amplitude is the maximum height of a crest or the maximum displacement from the equilibrium position.

Amplitude is correlated with the energy of the wave.

A greater amplitude means the wave has greater energy.

Intensity is the energy per area per time, which translates to power (Watts) per area (m^2).

$$I = \frac{P}{A}$$

Thus, amplitude and intensity are correlated similarly as amplitude and energy.

A greater amplitude (and therefore greater energy) leads to a higher intensity.

Chapter Summary

Periodic Motion Summary

- Periodic motion is a motion that repeats itself.
- Amplitude relates displacement and potential energy
- Frequency gives cycles per second
- Period is the time to complete one cycle
- At the equilibrium position, $PE = 0$, KE = maximum.
- At the maximum displacement (amplitude) $x = $ A, PE = maximum, $KE = 0$.
- At any point, $PE + KE$ = maximum PE = maximum KE = constant.
- From the velocity at the equilibrium position, the amplitude can be calculated by setting maximum KE = maximum PE
- From the amplitude, the velocity at the equilibrium position can be calculated by setting maximum PE = maximum KE

Wave Characteristics Summary

- The speed of a wave depends on the medium through which it travels.

  Speed can be determined by $v = f\lambda$ where f is the frequency ($f = \frac{\# \, cycles}{time}$) and λ is the wavelength.

  Because $f = \frac{1}{T}$, the speed can be written as $v = \frac{\lambda}{T}$.

- Changing the period, the frequency, or the wavelength of a wave will affect the other two quantities but will not affect the speed if the wave stays in the same medium.

- Superimposition is when parts of waves interact so that so that they constructively or destructively interfere (e.g., create larger or smaller amplitudes, respectively).

- Waves will reflect and transmit through different mediums.

- Waves transmitted through two different mediums with different indices of refraction bends according to Snell's Law:

$$n_1 \sin (\theta_1) = n_2 \sin (\theta_2)$$

- Angles equal to or greater than the critical angle will exhibit total internal reflection:

$$n_1 \sin (\theta_{critical}) = n_2 \sin (90°)$$

- Diffraction occurs for all waves around objects or through apertures.

- Standing waves on a string that are fixed at both ends can form with wavelengths of $\lambda_n = \frac{2L}{n}$ and frequencies of $f_n = \frac{nv}{2L}$,

where L is the length of the string, v is the speed of the wave, and n is a whole positive number.

Notes

Practice Questions

1. Considering a vibrating mass on a spring, what effect on the system's mechanical energy is caused by doubling of the amplitude only?

A. Increases by a factor of two

B. Increases by a factor of four

C. Increases by a factor of three

D. Produces no change

E. Increases by a factor of $\sqrt{2}$

2. Which of the following is an accurate statement?

A. Tensile stress is measured in N·m

B. Stress is a measure of external forces on a body

C. Stress is inversely proportional to strain

D. Tensile strain is measured in meters

E. The ratio stress/strain is called the elastic modulus

3. The efficient transfer of energy taking place at a natural frequency occurs in a phenomenon called:

A. reverberation

B. the Doppler effect

C. beats

D. resonance

E. the standing wave phenomenon

4. A simple pendulum and a mass oscillating on an ideal spring both have period T in an elevator at rest. If the elevator now accelerates downward uniformly at 2 m/s², what is true about the periods of these two systems?

A. The period of the pendulum increases, but the period of the spring remains the same

B. The period of the pendulum increases and the period of the spring decreases

C. The period of the pendulum decreases, but the period of the spring remains the same

D. The periods of the pendulum and the spring both increase

E. The periods of the pendulum and the spring both decrease

5. All of the following is true of a pendulum that has swung to the top of its arc and has not yet reversed its direction, EXCEPT:

A. The PE of the pendulum is at a maximum

B. The displacement of the pendulum from its equilibrium position is at a maximum

C. The KE of the pendulum equals zero

D. The velocity of the pendulum equals zero

E. The acceleration of the pendulum equals zero

6. The explanation for refraction must involve a change in:

I. frequency   II. speed   III. wavelength

A. I only   **B.** II only   **C.** III only   **D.** I and II only   **E.** I and III only

7. Consider the wave shown in the figure. The amplitude is:

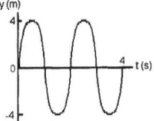

A. 1 m
B. 2 m
C. 4 m
D. 8 m
E. $\sqrt{2}$ m

8. Increasing the mass m of a mass-and-spring system causes what kind of change on the resonant frequency f of the system?

A. The f decreases
B. There is no change in the f
C. The f decreases only if the ratio k / m is < 1
D. The f increases
E. The f decreases only if the ratio k / m is > 1

9. A simple pendulum that has a bob of mass M has a period T. What is the effect on the period if M is doubled while all other factors remain unchanged?

A. T/2   **B.** T/$\sqrt{2}$ **C.** 2T   **D.** $\sqrt{2}$T   **E.** T

10. A skipper on a boat notices wave crests passing the anchor chain every 5 s. The skipper estimates that the distance between crests is 15 m. What is the speed of the water waves?

A. 3 m/s   **B.** 5 m/s   **C.** 12 m/s   **D.** 9 m/s   **E.** Requires more information

11. For an object undergoing simple harmonic motion, the:

A. maximum potential energy is larger than the maximum kinetic energy
B. acceleration is greatest when the displacement is greatest
C. displacement is greatest when the speed is greatest
D. acceleration is greatest when the speed is greatest
E. total object energy oscillates at frequency $f = \frac{1}{2}\pi(\sqrt{k / m})$

12. As the frequency of a wave increases, which of the following must decrease?

A. The speed of the wave   **C.** The amplitude of the wave

B. The velocity of the wave   **D.** The cycles per second

                                         E. The period of the wave

13. What is the period for a weight on the end of a spring that bobs up and down one complete cycle every 2 s?

A. 0.5 s   **B.** 1 s   **C.** 2 s   **D.** 3 s   **E.** 2.5 s

14. After rain, one sometimes sees brightly colored oil slicks on the road. These are due to:

A. selective absorption of different λ by oil   **C.** polarization effects

B. diffraction effects   **D.** interference effects

                                         E. birefringence

15. If two traveling waves with amplitudes of 3 cm and 8 cm interfere, which of the following best describes the possible amplitudes of the resultant wave?

A. Between 5 and 11 cm   **C.** Between 3 and 5 cm

B. Between 3 and 8 cm   **D.** Between 8 and 11 cm

                                         E. Less than 8 cm

Solutions

1. B is correct.

$$PE = \frac{1}{2}kx^2$$

Doubling the amplitude x increases PE by a factor of 4.

2. E is correct.

The elastic modulus is given by:

E = tensional strength / extensional strain

$E = \sigma / \varepsilon$

3. D is correct.

Resonance is the phenomenon where one system transfers its energy to another at that system's resonant frequency (natural frequency). It is a forced vibration that produces the highest amplitude response for a given force amplitude.

4. A is correct.

Period of a pendulum:

$T_P = 2\pi\sqrt{(L / g)}$

Period of a spring:

$T_S = 2\pi\sqrt{(m / k)}$

The period of a spring does not depend on gravity and is unaffected.

5. E is correct.

At the top of its arc, the pendulum comes to rest momentarily; the KE and the velocity equal zero.

Since its height above the bottom of its arc is at a maximum at this point, its (angular) displacement from the vertical equilibrium position is at a maximum also.

The pendulum constantly experiences the forces of gravity and tension and is therefore continuously accelerating.

6. B is correct.

Refraction is the bending of a wave when it enters a medium where its speed is different. Refraction occurs in sound waves and light waves.

7. C is correct.

The amplitude of a wave is the magnitude of its oscillation from its equilibrium point.

8. A is correct.

$$f = (1/2\pi)\sqrt{(k/m)}$$

An increase in m causes a decrease in f.

9. E is correct.

$$T = 2\pi[\sqrt{(L/g)}]$$

No effect on the period because T is independent of mass.

10. A is correct.

speed = wavelength × frequency

period = 1 / frequency

$v = \lambda f$

$v = \lambda / T$

$v = 15$ m / 5 s

$v = 3$ m/s

11. B is correct.

When the displacement is greatest, the force on the object is greatest. When force is maximized, then acceleration is maximum.

12. E is correct.

$\lambda = vf$

$f = v / \lambda$

$f = 1 / T$

The period is the reciprocal of the frequency.

If f increases, then T decreases.

13. C is correct.

The definition of the period is the time required to complete one cycle.

Period = time / # cycles

$T = 2$ s / 1 cycle

$T = 2$ s

14. D is correct.

When it rains the brightly colored oil slicks on the road are due to thin film interference effects.

This is when light reflects from the upper and lower boundaries of the oil layer and form a new wave due to interference effects.

These new waves are perceived as different colors.

15. A is correct.

Constructive interference: the maximal magnitude of the amplitude of the resultant wave is the sum of the individual amplitudes:

3 cm + 8 cm = 11 cm

Destructive interference: the minimal magnitude of the amplitude of the resultant wave is the difference between the individual amplitudes:

8 cm – 3 cm = 5 cm

The magnitude of the amplitude of the resultant wave is between 5 and 11 cm.

Please, leave your Customer Review on Amazon

Chapter 6

Sound

- **Production of Sound**

- **Relative Speed of Sound in Solids, Liquids, and Gases**

- **Intensity of Sound**

- **Attenuation: Damping**

- **Doppler Effect**

- **Pitch**

- **Ultrasound**

- **Resonance in Pipes and Strings**

- **Beats**

- **Shock Waves**

Notes

Production of Sound

Sound is a wave that is experienced by nearly everyone in their everyday life. Everything that is being heard is the result of the sound wave, from the noise of traffic to the wind through trees, to a jet flying by overhead.

However, many sounds are not audible. Like other waves, the sound is produced by vibrations in a medium.

Specifically, the sound is a mechanical longitudinal wave that travels through a medium as vibrations. This means that vibrations produce pressure waves, which oscillate parallel to the direction of propagation.

If the vibrations have a frequency too low to hear, they are *infrasound*.

Comparatively, if the frequency is too high to hear, they are *ultrasound*.

Musical instruments produce sounds through vibrations in various ways— strings, membranes, metal or wood shapes, or air columns. Vibrations may be started by plucking, striking, bowing or blowing. They are transmitted to the air and then to the perceivers' ears.

For example, a drum produces sound by vibrating a thin membrane when struck. The vibrating membrane creates a longitudinal wave through the air to a person's ears, which results in the perception of sound.

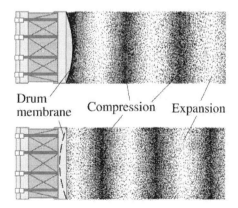

The strings on a guitar can be effectively shortened by fingering, which raises the fundamental pitch.

The pitch of a string at a given length can be altered by using a string of different density.

The strings on stringed instruments produce a fundamental tone whose wavelength is twice the length of the string. There are also various harmonics present.

A piano uses both methods to cover its more than seven-octave range—the lower notes are produced by strings that are much longer and much thicker than the strings that produce the higher notes.

Wind instruments create sound through standing waves in a tube, and they have a vibrating column of air when played.

During a storm, lightning is seen before thunder is heard, even though they occur at the same time because the speed of light (300,000,000 m/s) is much faster than the speed of sound (300 m/s).

Relative Speed of Sound in Solids, Liquids, and Gases

Like all waves, sound waves do not transport matter. Even though a sound wave travels, the medium through which the sound wave propagates does not travel. The particles within the medium vibrate around their initial position (horizontally, because the wave is longitudinal) and return to their initial position after the wave has propagated. It is important to remember that waves carry energy, not matter.

Two essential values affect the speed of sound: the elasticity and the density of the medium. Sound travels through a medium by transferring energy from one particle to the other. A rigid medium, or one with little elasticity, will have strong attractions between its molecules.

Therefore, the molecules can vibrate at a much higher speed and transfer energy faster than a more elastic material. For this reason, the speed of sound is faster through solids than through liquids, and faster through liquids than through gases. This also means that sound cannot travel in a vacuum; sound requires a medium, and in a vacuum, there are no particles to vibrate and transmit the wave.

As previously stated, the speed of sound depends upon the density and elasticity of the medium. The speed of sound is given by the equation:

$$v = \sqrt{\frac{\beta}{\rho}}$$

where β is the bulk modulus, which indicates how the medium responds to compression (how elastic or inelastic it is), and ρ is the density of the medium.

Generally, a substance with a large density is made of larger molecules. Larger molecules mean more mass, thus requiring more kinetic energy to vibrate them.

Since waves are made of kinetic energy, they will travel slower through a medium with larger molecules and a higher mass and faster through a medium with smaller molecules and a lower mass.

If the medium is a gas, the temperature can also change the speed of sound. Say two equally sized jars contain the same gas but with different densities. Since there is so much space between particles in a gas, the ideal gas laws play a much larger role than individual particle characteristics, such as mass.

A higher density at the same volume means an increase in temperature. An increase in temperature means the addition of heat energy, or kinetic energy, to the system. More kinetic energy means the gas molecules will bounce around faster than at cooler temperatures, and transfer energy at a quicker rate.

This allows the sound wave to travel faster through the warmer medium.

$$v = \sqrt{\frac{\gamma RT}{M}}$$

Where γ is the adiabatic constant of the gas, R is the ideal gas constant (8.314 J/mol K), T is the temperature in Kelvin (K) and M is the molecular mass of the gas (kg/mol).

The following are some examples of speed comparison through different media:

- Sound will travel faster through wood than it will through the air. Wood is very inelastic, whereas air is extremely compressible.

- Sound travels faster through American Redwood, which has a density of 28 lb/ft^3, than through African Teak, which has a density of about 45 lb/ft^3. Notice that their elasticities will be very similar, which is why density matters.

- Even though gases are less dense than solids, sound travels slower in a gas (e.g., helium) because it is too compressible.

- Sound travels much faster over a hot desert than it does over a cold tundra; the temperature is higher. Therefore the speed of sound is higher.

At room temperature and normal atmospheric pressure, the speed of sound is approximately 343 m/s.

Below is a table of sound speed through various mediums, at constant temperature and pressure, unless otherwise noted:

Speed of Sound in Various Materials (20 °C and 1 atm)

Material	Speed (m/s)
Air	343
Air (0 °C)	331
Helium	1,005
Hydrogen	1,300
Water	1,440
Seawater	1,560
Concrete	≈3000
Hardwood	≈4,000
Glass	≈4,500
Iron and steel	≈5,000
Aluminum	≈5,100

Intensity of Sound

The *intensity* of a wave is equal to the energy transported per unit time across a unit area. The human ear can detect sounds with intensity as low as 10^{-12} W/m^2 and as high as 1 W/m^2.

However, perceived loudness is not proportional to the intensity; the two are related, though, as in the table below.

Intensity of Various Sounds

Source of the Sound	Sound Level (dB)	Intensity (W/m^2)
Jet plane at 30m	140	100
Threshold of pain	120	1
Siren at 30m	100	1×10^{-2}
Busy street traffic	80	1×10^{-4}
Noisy restaurant	70	1×10^{-5}
Talk, at 50cm	65	3×10^{-6}
Quiet radio	40	1×10^{-8}
Whisper	30	1×10^{-9}
Rustle of leaves	10	1×10^{-11}
Threshold of hearing	0	1×10^{-12}

The loudness of a sound is much more closely related to the logarithm of the intensity.

Sound level is measured in decibels (dB) and is defined as:

$$\beta = 10 log \left(\frac{I}{I_0}\right)$$

β is the sound level in decibels (dB), and I is the intensity in power per area, or energy per unit time per unit area, given in Watts per meters squared (W/m^2).

I_0 is the threshold of hearing at 10^{-12} W/m^2.

The intensity follows an inverse square law $I \propto 1/r^2$, where r is the distance between the source and detector (observer). From the above equation, as the distance increases, the decibels decrease.

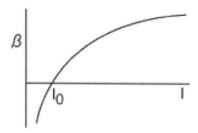

Intensity	Decibels
I_0	0
$10\ I_0$	10
$100\ I_0$	20
$1{,}000\ I_0$	30

An increase in sound level of 3 dB, which is a doubling in intensity, is a very small change in loudness. In a large area (large value of r), this change in intensity is insignificant. However, in a smaller space (smaller value of r) any change in intensity will be extremely noticeable.

The decibel system is based on human perception. The decibel value for sound with an intensity of I_0 is zero - below this intensity, the sound is not audible. As intensity increases, our perception of its loudness increases as well, but to a much lesser degree.

Pitch

Pitch is the human perception of the frequency of sound. A high pitch is the result of high vibrations and a shorter wavelength; therefore, a higher frequency. A low pitch is the result of low vibrations and a longer wavelength; therefore, a lower frequency. Humans can hear sound waves with frequencies of 20-20,000 Hz. The upper limit of this range will decrease with age. Waves with frequencies above 20,000 Hz are ultrasonic. Waves with frequencies below 20 Hz are infrasonic.

Attenuation: Damping

Sound attenuation is the gradual loss of intensity as sound travels through a medium, and is the greatest for soft, elastic, viscous, and/or less dense material.

A vibration causes the sound, and the characteristics of this vibration determine how the sound wave acts as it travels through the medium.

A wave can oscillate in free harmonic motion, in which the amplitude remains unchanged throughout the duration of the vibration.

A wave can also exhibit damped harmonic motion, in which a frictional or dragging force inhibits the vibrations oscillation.

If the damping is small, it can be treated as an "envelope" that modifies the undamped oscillation:

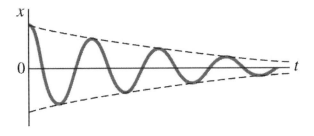

However, if the damping is large, it no longer resembles a general oscillation (Simple Harmonic Motion, or SHM) at all:

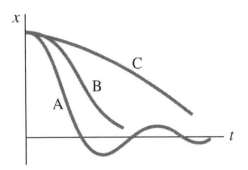

There are a few different shapes a graph can take if there is a large damping force acting on the system.

Underdamping, as in graph A above, is when there are a few small oscillations before the oscillator comes to rest.

Critical damping, shown in graph B above, is the fastest way to get to equilibrium. Over-damping, pictured in graph C, occurs when the system is slowed so much that it takes a long time to get to equilibrium.

There are systems where damping is unwanted, such as clocks and watches. Moreover, then there are systems in which it is wanted, and often needs to be as close to critical damping as possible.

Such systems include earthquake protection for buildings and automobile shock absorbers, as pictured below.

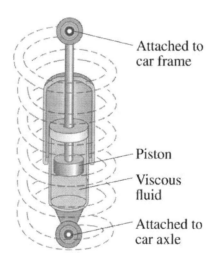

Doppler Effect

The Doppler shift describes the relationship between the frequency detected and the frequency emitted by the source when the source and detector are in relative motion.

$$f_d = f_e[(v_s \pm v_d) / (v_s \mp v_e)]$$

where f_d is the frequency detected by the observer, f_e is the frequency emitted by the source v_d is the velocity of the detector, v_e is the velocity of the source and v_s is the speed of the wave.

When the source and a detector are moving with respect to each other, the f of the detected wave is shifted from the f of the emitted wave (Doppler shift). The effect is that the f_d is increased when the source and detector are approaching and decreased when the source and detector are receding.

When calculating the Doppler shift between a source and detector, the individual velocities are with respect to each other. For example, if the source and detector are moving away at equal speeds, this is equivalent to the source moving at double its speed away from a stationary detector. This allows for one of the velocities to be set to zero in the calculation.

The Doppler Effect says the frequency of the sounds will vary if there is relative motion between the source of the sound and the observer or detector of the sound. If the relative motion between the sound source and observer is towards each other, the frequency will be perceived as higher.

If the relative motion between the sound source and observer is away, the frequency will be perceived as lower. This is why oncoming sirens seem to sound louder than when they have already passed.

This is expressed by the equation:

$$f' = \frac{v \pm v_o}{v \mp v_s} \times f$$

Where f' is the perceived frequency, f is the wave frequency, v_o is the velocity of the observer or detector, v_s is the velocity of the source and v is a reference value equal to the velocity of sound through the given medium.

To solve this equation, it must first be decided whether to add or subtract the velocities from the speed of sound through the medium. The best way to decide is to think about the problem logically.

If the observer is walking away from the source, the wavelengths will get longer, and the perceived pitch will decrease. This means the velocity of the observer must be subtracted in the numerator.

If the source is getting closer to the observer, the wavelengths are getting shorter, and the perceived frequency is increasing. This means the denominator must get smaller, and the velocity of the source must be subtracted in the denominator as well.

Take care when analyzing the movement of the source and remember how fractions react as their denominator is either increased or decreased.

Situations where the observed frequency is higher than the actual:

- Source moving toward stationary observer: $f' = \dfrac{v}{v - v_s} \times f$

- Observer moving toward stationary source: $f' = \dfrac{v + v_o}{v} \times f$

- Source and observer both moving toward each other: $f' = \dfrac{v + v_o}{v - v_s} \times f$

Situations where the observed frequency is lower than the actual:

- Source moving away from stationary observer: $f' = \dfrac{v}{v + v_s} \times f$

- Observer moving away from stationary source: $f' = \dfrac{v - v_o}{v} \times f$

- Source and observer both moving away from each other:

$$f' = \dfrac{v - v_o}{v + v_s} \times f$$

Situations where the observed frequency is either higher or lower than the actual:

- Source is moving toward the observer; observer is moving away from the source:

$$f' = \frac{v - v_o}{v - v_s} \times f$$

- Source is moving away from the observer; observer is moving toward the source:

$$f' = \frac{v + v_o}{v + v_s} \times f$$

When the source and observer are moving at the same speed, and in the same direction, there is no frequency shift. This is because their relative motion is zero. This instance shows that reference frames are very important.

When the source of waves and a detector are moving with respect to each other, the frequency of the detected wave is shifted from the frequency of the emitted wave (*Doppler shift*). The effect of this is an increase in the detected frequency when the source and detector are approaching, and an increase in the detected frequency when they are receding. f_{det} is the detected frequency, v_s is the speed of the wave in the medium, v_{det} is the speed of the detector, v_{em} is the speed of the emitter and f_{em} is the emitted frequency.

Choose the sign in the numerator to reflect the direction the detector is going (positive if approaching, negative if moving away), and choose the sign in the denominator to reflect the direction the source is going (positive if moving away, negative if approaching).

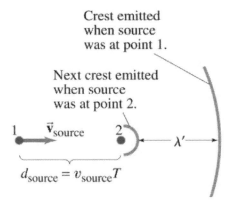

The change in the wavelength is given by:

$$\lambda' = d - d_{source}$$

$$= \lambda - v_{source}T$$

$$= \lambda - v_{source} \times \frac{\lambda}{v_{snd}}$$

$$= \lambda(1 - \frac{v_{source}}{v_{snd}})$$

If the observer is moving with respect to the source, the wavelength remains the same, but the wave speed is different for the observer:

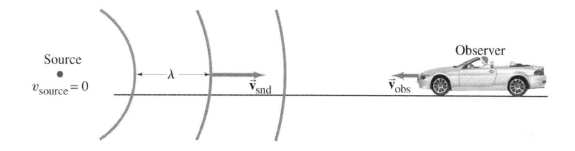

Ultrasound

Sound has three fundamental properties: reflection, refraction, and diffraction.

Ultrasound imaging is based on the reflective property of sound. A source emits a sound wave with an ultrasonic frequency, which reflects off a surface and travels back into the detector to form an image.

Ultrasound is sound with frequencies of 20,000 Hz or greater.

Ultrasound is also used for medical imaging.

Repeated traces are made as the transducer is moved, and a complete picture is built.

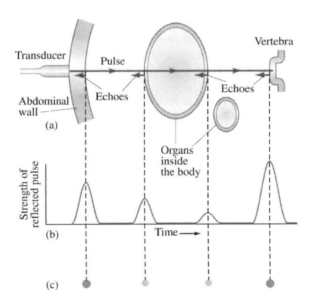

Sonar is used to locate objects underwater by measuring the time it takes a sound pulse to reflect to the receiver.

Similar techniques can be used to learn about the internal structure of the Earth. Sonar usually uses ultrasound waves, as the shorter wavelengths are less likely to be diffracted by obstacles.

Resonance in Pipes and Strings

In every standing wave pattern, there are points along the medium that appear to be standing still. These points are *nodes* and are described as points of no displacement.

There are other points along the medium that undergo the maximum displacement during each vibrational cycle. These points are *antinodes,* and they are opposite of nodes.

A standing wave pattern always consists of an alternating pattern of nodes and antinodes.

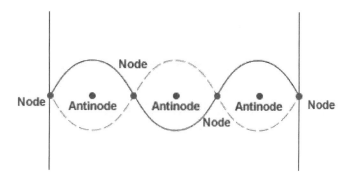

If a tube is open at both ends, like most wind instruments, and a wave of sound passes through it, the characteristics of the wave can be analyzed if the number of nodes or antinodes the wave has can be determined.

In a tube, an open end always has a displacement antinode, and a closed end always has a displacement node. The pressure in the air varies in the same way air displacement does but shifted. This means everywhere there is a displacement antinode, there will be a pressure node, and everywhere there is a displacement node, there will be a pressure antinode.

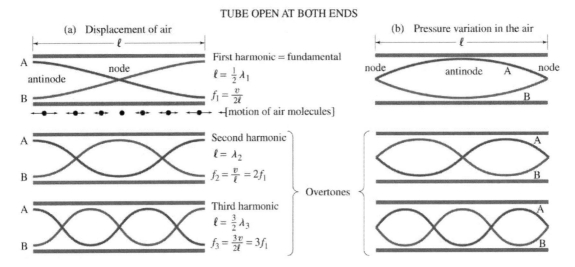

A tube closed at one end, like some organ pipes, has a displacement node and a pressure antinode at the closed end. The number of each node and antinode contained within the pipe depends on the harmonic level (e.g., first harmonic, second harmonic, etc.).

The *fundamental frequency*, also the fundamental, is the first harmonic ($n = 1$).

The next frequency is the second harmonic ($n = 2$).

This continues to the nth harmonic.

Higher harmonics in pipes, either open or closed, have shorter wavelengths and higher frequencies, but the same wave speed.

For the nth harmonic on a string, an n number of half wavelengths fit exactly along the length of the string.

The frequency of a wave can be obtained by:

$$f = \frac{v}{\lambda}$$

If a pipe is open at both ends, or if a string is unfixed at both ends, its length can be found by:

$$L = \frac{n}{2} \times \lambda$$

If a pipe has one closed end, or if a string has one fixed end, its length can be found instead by:

$$L = \frac{2n - 1}{4\lambda}$$

For an open-ended tube, resonance occurs when:

$$f_n = n \times \frac{v}{2L}$$ where n can be any integer

Resonance occurs when an outside force acts at a frequency very close to the normal frequency of some component of the system. This depends on whether the tube is closed on one end or open at both ends. For a tube with one closed end, resonance occurs when:

$$f_n = n\frac{v}{4L} \quad \text{and} \quad \lambda = \frac{4L}{n}$$ where n must be an *odd* integer

An instrument never plays just one sound. They are known for their overtones, which combine with other instruments' overtones to create music, as opposed to simply much noise. A trumpet sounds different from a flute, and the reason is overtones—which ones are present and how strong they are. The plots below show the frequency spectra for a clarinet, a piano, and a violin.

The differences in overtone strength are apparent.

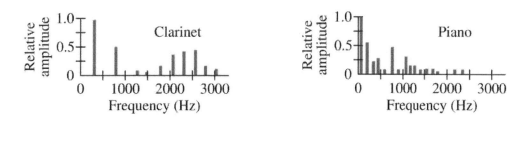

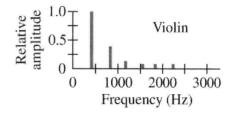

Beats

Sound waves interfere in the same way that other waves do, causing a phenomenon of *beats*. Beats are the slow "envelope" around two waves that are relatively close in frequency, as the two speakers exhibit below.

The region of overlapping sound waves is what produces a beat.

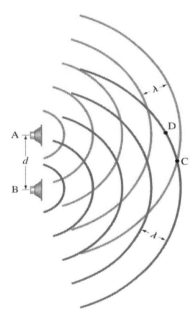

If the two frequencies are graphed on a linear axis (graph a), it can be seen that, although they start in the same place, one frequency is higher than the other.

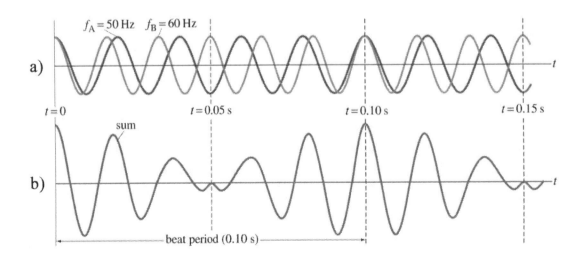

The combination, or interference, of these two results in the wave is shown lower in graph b. This is an out-of-phase interference, meaning the amplitude of this combined wave is equal to the addition of the two individual amplitudes of the two waves shown in graph a.

A beat period is the length of time it takes for the beat to start all over again.

Even though the wave in graph b does not oscillate with a constant amplitude as the two above, it will repeat itself over and over as long as the component waves stay constant.

The beat frequency is given by the equation:

$$f_{beat} = |f_1 - f_2|$$

where f_1 and f_2 are the frequencies of the interfering waves.

If two notes are played at the same time that are close in pitch but not the same, one can hear a pulse, or "wobble."

This is the beat, and its frequency is f_{beat}.

When musicians are tuning their instruments, they listen for this beat and try to eliminate it, thereby matching the frequency of their instrument with the frequency of the reference pitch.

Shock Waves

If a source is moving faster than the speed of the waves that it is producing in a given medium, then a *shock wave* is formed.

The diagram shows an object with a velocity of zero (a), a velocity less than the speed of sound (b), a velocity equal to the speed of sound (c), and a velocity greater than the speed of sound (d). The only situation in which a shock wave occurs is (d). The object in (c) creates a shock wave front, but the waves do not pile up as in (d).

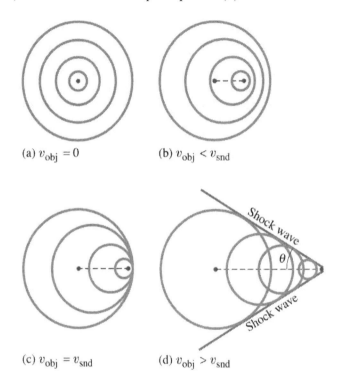

(a) $v_{obj} = 0$ (b) $v_{obj} < v_{snd}$

(c) $v_{obj} = v_{snd}$ (d) $v_{obj} > v_{snd}$

Shock waves are analogous to the bow waves produced by a boat going faster than the wave speed in water. An aircraft exceeding the speed of sound in air produces two sonic booms, one from the nose of the plane and one from the tail.

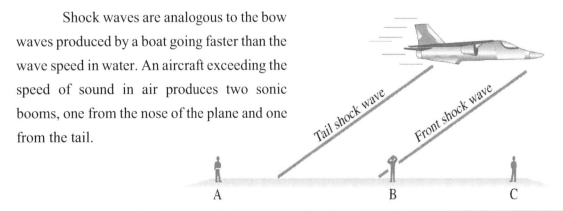

Chapter Summary

- Sound is a mechanical longitudinal wave that travels through a medium as vibrations. This means that vibrations produce pressure waves, which oscillate parallel to the direction of propagation.

    Two essential values affect the speed of sound: the elasticity and the density of the medium.

    $$v = \sqrt{\frac{\beta}{\rho}}$$

    where β is the bulk modulus, which indicates how the medium responds to compression (how elastic or inelastic it is), and ρ is the density of the medium.

- The *intensity* of a wave is equal to the energy transported per unit time across a unit area.

- The loudness of a sound is much more closely related to the logarithm of the intensity. Sound level is measured in decibels (dB) and is defined as:

    $$\beta = 10log\left(\frac{I}{I_0}\right)$$

    where β is the sound level in decibels (dB), and I is the intensity in power per area, or energy per unit time per unit area, given in Watts per meters squared (W/m^2).

- The Doppler shift describes the relationship between the frequency detected and the frequency emitted by the source when the source and detector are in relative motion.

    $$f_d = f_e[(v_s \pm v_d) / (v_s \mp v_e)]$$

    where f_d is the frequency detected by the observer, f_e is the frequency emitted by the source v_d is the velocity of the detector, v_e is the velocity of the source and v_s is the speed of the wave.

- In every standing wave pattern, there are points along the medium that appear to be standing still. These points are *nodes* and are described as points of no displacement.

There are other points along the medium that undergo the maximum displacement during each vibrational cycle. These points are *antinodes,* and they are opposite of nodes.

- The frequency of a wave can be obtained by:

$$f = \frac{v}{\lambda}$$

- If a pipe is open at both ends, or if a string is unfixed at both ends, its length is found by:

$$L = \frac{n}{2} \times \lambda$$

- If a pipe has one closed end, or if a string has one fixed end, its length is found by:

$$L = \frac{2n - 1}{4\lambda}$$

- For an open-ended tube, resonance occurs when:

$$f_n = n \times \frac{v}{2L} \qquad \text{where n can be any integer}$$

- Sound waves interfere in the same way that other waves do, causing a phenomenon of *beats*. The beat frequency is given by the equation:

$$f_{beat} = |f_1 - f_2|$$

where f_1 and f_2 are the frequencies of the interfering waves.

- If a source is moving faster than the speed of the waves that it is producing in a given medium, then a *shock wave* is formed.

Practice Questions

1. Two tuning forks have frequencies of 460 Hz and 524 Hz. What is the beat frequency if both are sounding simultaneously and resonating?

A. 52 Hz   C. 396 Hz

B. 64 Hz   D. 524 Hz   E. 588 Hz

2. Which of the of the following is true of the properties of a light wave as it moves from a medium of the lower refractive index to a medium of the higher refractive index?

A. Speed decreases   C. Frequency decreases

B. Speed increases   D. Frequency increases   E. None of the above

3. Resonance can be looked at as forced vibration with the:

A. matching of constructive and destructive interference

B. matching of wave amplitudes

C. maximum amount of energy input

D. least amount of energy input

E. minimum beat frequency

4. The Doppler effect occurs when a source of sound moves:

     I. toward the observer

     II. away from the observer

     III. with the observer

A. I only   B. II only   C. III only   D. I and II only   E. I and III only

5. Which of the following increases when a sound becomes louder?

A. Amplitude   C. Frequency

B. Period   D. Wavelength   E. Velocity

6. Sound intensity is defined as the:

A. sound power per unit volume   C. sound energy passing through a unit of area

B. sound power per unit time   D. loudness of a sound

                                     E. sound energy passing an area per unit time

7. A violin with string length 36 cm and string density 3.8 g/cm resonates with the first overtone of an organ pipe with one end closed. The pipe length is 3 m. What is the tension in the string so that the sound wave resonates at its fundamental frequency? (Use the speed of sound $v = 340$ m/s)

    A. 1,390 N   **B.** 1,946 N   **C.** 1,414 N   **D.** 987 N   **E.** 1,216 N

8. A speaker is producing a total of 10 W of sound, and Rahul hears the music at 20 dB. His roommate turns up the power to 100 W. What level of sound does Rahul now hear?

    A. 15 dB   **B.** 30 dB   **C.** 40 dB   **D.** 100 dB   **E.** 120 dB

9. Seven seconds after a flash of lightning, thunder shakes a house. Approximately how far was the lightning strike from the house? (Use the speed of sound $v = 340$ m/s)

    A. Requires more information   **C.** About one kilometer away

    B. About five kilometers away   **D.** About ten kilometers away

                                        E. About two kilometers away

10. The natural frequencies for a stretched string of length L and wave speed v are $nv / (2L)$, where n equals:

    A. 0, 1, 3, 5, ...   **C.** 2, 4, 6, 8, ...

    B. 1, 2, 3, 4, ...   **D.** 0, 1, 2, 3, ...   **E.** 1, 3, 4, 5, ...

11. What is the source of all electromagnetic waves?

    A. electric fields   **C.** heat

    B. vibrating charges   **D.** magnetic fields

                                         E. none of the above

12. When a radio is tuned to a certain station, the frequency of the internal electrical circuit is matched to the frequency of that radio station. In tuning the radio, what is being affected?

    A. Beats   **C.** Forced vibrations

    B. Reverberation   **D.** Resonance

                                        E. Wave interference

13. A standing wave is oscillating at 670 Hz on a string, as shown in the figure. What is the wave speed?

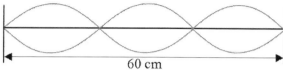

60 cm

A. 212 m/s

B. 178 m/s

C. 268 m/s

D. 404 m/s

E. 360 m/s

14. A 50 m/s train is moving directly toward Carlos, who is standing near the tracks. The train is emitting a whistling sound at 415 Hz. What frequency does Carlos hear? (Use the speed of sound $v = 340$ m/s)

A. 290 Hz

B. 476 Hz

C. 481 Hz

D. 487 Hz

E. 473 Hz

15. Two tuning forks are struck simultaneously, and beats are heard every 500 ms. What is the frequency of the sound wave produced by one tuning fork, if the other produces a sound wave of 490 Hz frequency?

A. 490 Hz

B. 498 Hz

C. 492 Hz

D. 506 Hz

E. 510 Hz

Solutions

1. B is correct.

Beat frequency equation:

$$f_{beat} = |f_2 - f_1|$$

$$f_{beat} = |524 \text{ Hz} - 460 \text{ Hz}|$$

$$f_{beat} = 64 \text{ Hz}$$

2. A is correct.

The frequency of a wave does not change when it enters a new medium.

$$v = (1 / n)c$$

where c = speed of light in a vacuum and n = refractive index.

The speed v decreases when light enters a medium with a higher refractive index.

3. D is correct. Resonance is the phenomenon where one system transfers its energy to another at that system's resonant frequency (natural frequency). It is forced vibrations with the least energy input.

4. D is correct.

The Doppler effect is the observed change in frequency when a sound source is in motion relative to an observer (away or towards). If the sound source moves with the observer, then there is no relative motion between the two and the Doppler effect does not occur.

5. A is correct.

When a sound becomes louder, the energy of the sound wave becomes higher.

Amplitude is directly related to the energy of the sound wave:

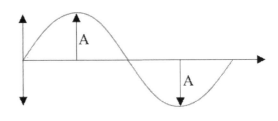

more energy = higher amplitude

less energy = lower amplitude

6. E is correct.

Intensity is the power per unit area:

$$I = W/m^2$$

Loudness is a subjective measurement of the strength of the ear's perception to sound.

7. C is correct.

An overtone is any frequency higher than the fundamental.

In a stopped pipe (i.e., open at one end and closed at the other):

Harmonic #	Tone
1	fundamental tone
3	1st overtone
5	2nd overtone
7	3rd overtone

The first overtone is the 3rd harmonic.

Find the wavelength:

$\lambda_n = (4L / n)$, for stopped pipe

where n = 1, 3, 5, 7…

$\lambda_3 = [(4) \cdot (3 \text{ m}) / 3)]$

$\lambda_3 = 4$ m

Find the frequency:

$f = v / \lambda$

$f = (340 \text{ m/s}) / (4 \text{ m})$

$f = 85$ Hz

Find the velocity of a standing wave on the violin:

$f = v / 2L$

$v = (2L) \cdot (f)$

$v = (2) \cdot (0.36 \text{ m}) \cdot (85 \text{ Hz})$

$v = 61$ m/s

Convert the linear density to kg/m:

$\mu = (3.8 \text{ g/cm}) \cdot (1 \text{ kg}/10^3 \text{ g}) \cdot (100 \text{ cm} / 1 \text{ m})$

$\mu = 0.38$ kg/m

Find the tension:

$$v = \sqrt{(T / \mu)}$$

$$T = v^2 \mu$$

$$T = (61 \text{ m/s})^2 \times (0.38 \text{ kg/m})$$

$$T = 1{,}414 \text{ N}$$

8. B is correct.

I = Power / area

The intensity I is proportional to the power, so an increase by a factor of 10 in power leads to an increase by a factor of 10 in intensity.

$$I \text{ (dB)} = 10\log_{10} (I / I_0)$$

dB is related to the logarithm of intensity.

If the original intensity was 20 dB then:

$$20 \text{ dB} = 10\log_{10} (I_1 / I_0)$$

$$2 = \log_{10} (I_1 / I_0)$$

$$100 = I_1 / I_0$$

The new intensity I is a factor of 10 higher than before:

$$I_2 = 10\, I_1$$

$$1{,}000 = I_2 / I_0$$

$$I \text{ (dB)} = 10\log_{10} (1{,}000)$$

$$I \text{ (dB)} = 30 \text{ dB}$$

9. E is correct.

velocity = distance / time

$$v = d / t$$

$$d = vt$$

$$d = (340 \text{ m/s}){\cdot}(7 \text{ s})$$

$$d = 2{,}380 \text{ m} \approx 2 \text{ km}$$

10. B is correct.

A stretched string has all harmonics of the fundamental.

11. B is correct.

All electromagnetic waves arise from accelerating charges. When a charge is vibrating it is accelerating (change in the direction of motion is acceleration).

12. D is correct.

When tuning a radio, the tuner picks up certain frequencies by resonating at those frequencies. This filters out the other radio signals, so only that specific frequency is amplified. By changing the tuner on the radio, a particular frequency is chosen that the tuner resonates at and the signal is amplified.

13. C is correct.

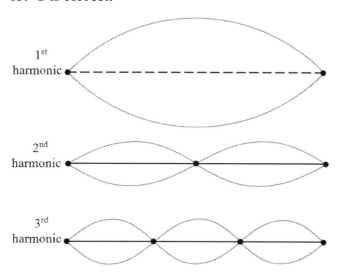

From the diagram, the wave is a 3rd harmonic standing wave.

Find the wavelength:

$\lambda_1 = 2L$

$\lambda_n = 2L / n$

where n = 1, 2, 3, 4…

$\lambda_n = (2 \times 0.6 \text{ m}) / 3$

$\lambda_n = 0.4 \text{ m}$

Find the speed:

$$\lambda = v / f$$

$$v = \lambda f$$

$$v = (0.4 \text{ m}) \cdot (670 \text{ Hz})$$

$$v = 268 \text{ m/s}$$

14. D is correct.

Doppler equation for an approaching sound source:

$$f_{observed} = [v_{sound} / (v_{sound} - v_{source})] f_{source}$$

$$f_{observed} = [(340 \text{ m/s}) / (340 \text{ m/s} - 50 \text{ m/s})] \cdot (415 \text{ Hz})$$

$$f_{observed} = 487 \text{ Hz}$$

The observed frequency is always higher when the source is approaching.

15. C is correct.

If beats are heard every 500 ms (i.e., ½ s), or 2 beats per second.

Since $f_{beat} = 2$ Hz, the frequencies of the two tuning forks differ by 2 Hz.

One tuning fork has an f of 490 Hz:

$$f \text{ is } (490 \text{ Hz} - 2 \text{ Hz}) = 488 \text{ Hz}$$

or

$$f \text{ is } (490 \text{ Hz} + 2 \text{ Hz}) = 492 \text{ Hz}$$

Chapter 7

Electrostatics and Electromagnetism

ELECTROSTATICS

- **Charges, Electrons, Protons, Conservation of Charge**
- **Conductors, Insulators**
- **Coulomb's Law**
- **Electric field *E***
- **Potential Difference, Electric Potential at Point in Space**
- **Equipotential Lines**
- **Electric Dipole**
- **Electrostatic Induction**
- **Gauss's Law**

MAGNETISM

- **Magnetic Fields and Poles**
- **Magnetic Field Force**
- **Faraday's Law**
- **Torque on Current-Carrying Wire**

ELECTROMAGNETIC RADIATION (LIGHT)

- **Properties of Electromagnetic Radiation**
- **Classification of Electromagnetic Spectrum, Photon Energy**

Notes

Charges, Electrons, and Protons, Conservation of Charge

What is charge?

Like mass, the *charge* is an innate property of all matter. Every particle in the universe has a mass and a charge, measured in coulombs (C).

Unlike mass, however, three distinct types of charges exist: positive charge, negative charge, and neutral charge. (Note: neutral charge DOES NOT mean the particle has no charge, the net charge is neutral.)

Where does charge come from?

Today, it is known that the basic unit of matter is the atom, which is made up of electrons orbiting a nucleus of protons and neutrons. These subatomic particles, specifically the electron and proton, are the basis of all macroscopically observed charge phenomenon. The electron is negatively charged and has a measured charge of -1.60×10^{-19} coulombs.

Conversely, the proton is positively charged and has an equal but opposite charge of $+1.60 \times 10^{-19}$ coulombs. When dealing with macroscopic objects that contain a charge, it is important to note that only the electrons contribute to the charge, because they are mobile. Protons are part of the nuclei of the atom and are not mobile.

Therefore any charge on an object is either due to an excess of electrons (if the observed charge is negative) or shortage of electrons (if the observed charge is positive).

Negative charge: # electrons > # protons

Positive charge: # electrons < # protons

Neutral charge: #electrons = # protons

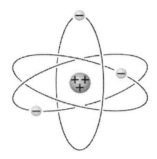

What are the properties of charge?

Charges have several unique properties that govern the laws of nature. Most importantly, charges exhibit force upon each other according to the charge. Same charges exhibit repulsive forces, and opposite charges exhibit attractive forces.

For example, the figure below shows a ruler that is negatively charged (excess of electrons) and a glass rod that is positively charged (shortage of electrons).

In diagram (a), two negatively charged rulers are brought close and repel due to their like charges.

Diagram (b) demonstrates the same effect with two positively charged glass rods.

However, in diagram (c), the charged ruler and glass rod attract due to their opposite charges.

(a) Two charged plastic rulers repel

(b) Two charged glass rods repel

(c) Charged glass rod attracts
charged plastic ruler

Additionally, the charge is always conserved. Like mass and energy, the charge cannot be created or destroyed, only transferred from one source to another.

Thus, if a charged object, such as the ruler in the above example, is placed on a table for some time, and later found to be neutrally charged, it can be concluded that the charge was not destroyed, but rather transferred to the surroundings (air and table).

Another unique property of charge is that all charge is quantized. The magnitude of the electron's charge (or proton), is the *fundamental charge* and is the smallest unit of charge that exists. This means that all macroscopically charged objects have a net charge equal to an integer multiple of the fundamental charge.

This can be expressed as:

$$q = ne$$

where q is the net charge (C), n is the integer multiple (i.e., excess electrons or protons), and e is the magnitude of the fundamental charge (1.60×10^{-19} C).

The quantization of charge enables one to calculate the excess or shortage of electrons in an object that contributes to its net charge.

For example, if the negatively charged ruler from the earlier example is measured to have one coulomb of charge, then the number of excess electrons in the ruler is:

$$n = \frac{q}{e}$$

$$n = \frac{1.00 \text{ Coulomb}}{1.60 \times 10^{-19} \text{Coulomb}} = 6.25 \times 10^{18} \text{ electrons}$$

Conductors, Insulators

Conductivity is a measure of a material's ability to transmit charge through itself. Materials which have a high conductivity are *conductors*. These types of materials allow electrical charge (electrons) to "flow" through the material.

An example of a good conductor is copper. Notice that in most wires for electrical equipment, the electricity is provided via copper wires, which allow the electrical charges to flow through it easily.

If a material does not transmit charge very well, then it is considered a poor conductor and is an *insulator*. Common insulators are wood, glass, and paper.

In the example below, there are two spheres. One has been charged positively (deficit of electrons), and the other has been left neutral (a).

In diagram (b), a metal nail is placed on top of both spheres. As a conductor, the metal nail allows electrons to flow through itself (from the neutral to the positive sphere) until the charges in each sphere are equal.

In diagram (c), a piece of wood is placed across the spheres instead of the nail. The piece of wood is an insulator and does not allow the free flow of electrons into the right sphere.

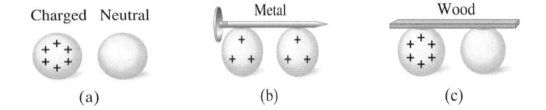

Charged   Neutral   Metal   Wood

(a)   (b)   (c)

Coulomb's Law

As mentioned earlier, charges will either repel or attract one another, depending if the charges are similar or opposite.

This force is the electrostatic force (Coulomb force) and can be found using *Coulomb's Law*, which describes the interaction between two charged particles:

$$F = \frac{1}{4\pi \, \epsilon_0} \frac{q_1 q_2}{r^2}$$

Which simplifies to:

$$F = k \frac{q_1 q_2}{r^2}$$

where F is the electrostatic force between the two charges (N), q is the magnitudes of the charges (C), r is the distance between them (m), ϵ_0 is the permittivity of free space ($8.854 \times 10^{-12} \frac{C^2}{N \cdot m^2}$) and k is Coulomb's constant, with a value of 9×10^9 N·m²/C².

Coulomb's Law strictly applies only to point charges. If two objects have a net charge, then they must be approximated as point charges to calculate the force they exert on each other.

Moreover, the electrostatic force is always along the line connecting the charges.

If the charges have the same sign, the force is repulsive.

If the charges have opposite signs, the force is attractive.

To find the electrostatic force on more than two point charges, use the superposition principle and sum the force from each charge in all axial directions.

For example, what is the net force on Q_3 in the example below?

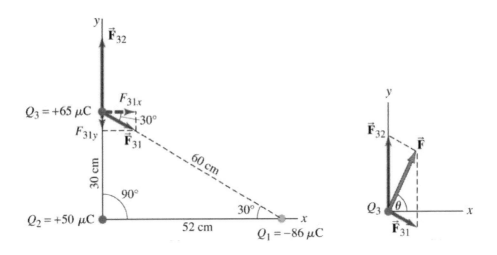

$$F_{32} = k\frac{q_1 q_2}{r^2} = \frac{(9 \times 10^9 \text{Nm}^2)(65 \times 10^{-6}\text{C})(50 \times 10^{-6}\text{C})}{(0.3 \text{ m})^2} = 325 \text{ N}$$

$$F_{31y} = \sin \theta\, k\frac{q_1 q_2}{r^2} = \left|\frac{\sin 30 \,(9 \times 10^9 \text{Nm}^2)(65 \times 10^{-6}\text{C})(-86 \times 10^{-6}\text{C})}{(0.6 \text{ m})^2}\right| = 70 \text{ N}$$

$$F_{31x} = \cos \theta\, k\frac{q_1 q_2}{r^2} = \left|\frac{\cos 30 \,(9 \times 10^9 \text{Nm}^2)(65 \times 10^{-6}\text{C})(-86 \times 10^{-6}\text{C})}{(0.6 \text{ m})^2}\right| = 121 \text{ N}$$

$$F_{net} = \sqrt{(121 \text{ N})^2 + (325\,N - 70\,N)^2} = 282 \text{ N}$$

Electric Field *E*

Every charge is surrounded by *electric fields* (*E*), which emanate in all directions around the charge. These fields are directional, vector fields. The orientation of any field is always in the direction that a positive charge would be pushed if placed in the field.

Consequently, for positive charges, the electric field points outward in every direction, and for negative charges, the electric field points inward in every direction.

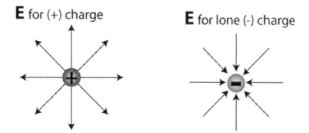

The electric field (*E*) can be expressed as the force (*F*) on a charge, divided by the magnitude of the charge (*q*):

$$\vec{E} = \frac{\vec{F}}{q}$$

where (E) is the electric field in the Newton/Coulombs (N/C).

Substituting in the electrostatic equation for force, the electric field from a single point charge (*Q*) will be:

$$\vec{E} = \frac{\vec{F}}{q} = \frac{kqQ/r^2}{q} = k\frac{Q}{r^2}$$

These equations can be rearranged to solve for the force on a point charge in an electric field (*E*):

$$\vec{F} = q\vec{E}$$

For example, in figure (a) below, an electric field points in an arbitrary direction. If a positive charge is placed in the electric field, as in diagram (b), then the force on charge will be in the direction of the electric field.

If a negative charge is placed in the same electric field, then the force is in the opposite direction, as in diagram (c).

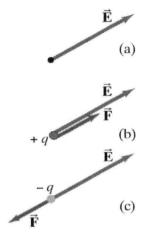

When solving problems in electrostatics, with electric forces and electric fields, make sure to draw a diagram of the entire situation. Show all charges with signs, electric fields, and force. Be sure to include the directions. Then calculate forces using Coulomb's Law, and add forces as vectors.

Like all vectors, the net strength of multiple electric fields on a point charge can be calculated by the superposition principle:

$$\vec{E} = \vec{E_1} + \vec{E_2} + \ ...$$

E as vector sum

Field lines

Like all field lines, the density of electric field lines denotes the strength of the field. If there are certain places where the field lines are closer together, the electric field is stronger.

If the lines are spread out, the field is weaker. The density of field lines can also be used to determine the magnitude of the charge emitting the field. If the density of field lines is high, then the charge must have a higher magnitude.

If the density is low, the charge must have a lower magnitude.

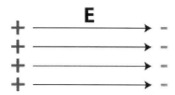

Field due to the charge distribution

When two charges are brought close, their electric fields will interact depending on the types of charge.

For example, if two positive charges are close, the field lines repel, not intersect.

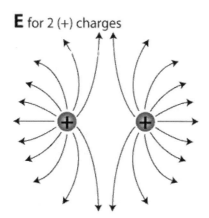

If the two charges were negative, the field lines would be the same as those for two positive charges, except that the direction of the field lines would be reversed.

When two opposite charges are brought near, an *electric dipole* is created.

In an electric dipole, the field lines will come out of the positive charge and go into the negative charge, as pictured below:

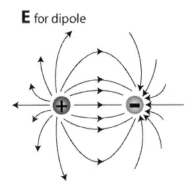

The net charge on a conductor is always on its surface, which radiates electric field lines. For a charged cylinder, the electric field runs radially perpendicular to the cylinder and is zero (nonexistent) inside the cylinder. This is true for all conducting objects; the net electric field is always from the surface and nonexistent within the object.

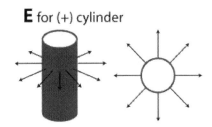

Summary of field lines:

1. Field lines indicate the direction of the field.

   The field is tangent to the line.

2. The magnitude of the field is proportional to the density of the lines.

3. Field lines start on positive charges and end on negative charges.

   The number of field lines is proportional to the magnitude of charge.

4. Net electric field within a conductor is zero

Potential Difference, Electric Potential at Point in Space

Because charges exert a force on each other in relation to the distance between the charges, charges must also have potential energy. The *electric potential energy* has units of joules (J) and is written as:

$$U = \frac{kQq}{r}$$

where U is the electric potential energy (J), Q and q are the point charges (C), r is the distance between the point charges (m) and k is Coulomb's constant, with a value of 9×10^9 N·m^2/C^2.

The electric potential energy of a single point charge is related but different from its electric potential. The *electric potential* is the amount of energy per charge that something possesses.

The unit for electric potential is joules per coulomb (J/C) or volts (V) and is a scalar field associated with potential energy.

An electric potential can be found using either of the two equations.

$$V = \frac{U}{q} \ \ or \ \ V = \frac{kQ}{r}$$

where V is the electric potential (V), Q is the charge that is causing the potential (C), q is the charge experiencing the potential (the magnitude of q is small), U is the electrical potential energy possessed by q (J), k is Coulomb's constant and r is the distance between the two charges (always positive).

If multiple charges are contributing to the electric potential, then the total electric potential is the sum of the potentials caused by the individual components.

Positive charges cause positive potentials.

Negative charges cause negative potentials.

These plots show the potential due to (a) positive and (b) negative charge.

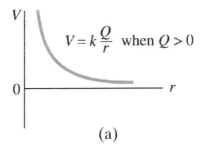

(a)

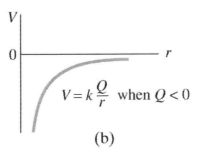

(b)

The potential difference is important in producing forces and moving charges. The process is analogous to moving masses in gravitational fields. The potential difference is given by ΔV and is the difference between the two potentials.

$$\Delta V = V_B - V_A$$

The potential difference is used in scenarios such as the difference in potential between the two plates of a capacitor, or the positive and negative terminals of a battery. Using potentials instead of fields can make solving problems much easier— the potential is a scalar quantity, whereas a field is a vector. For example, the Coulomb force is conservative.

Therefore the work in an electric field is conservative. As such, the work required to move a point charge in an electric field is only dependent upon the displacement of the charge, not the path taken by it. An easy way to calculate this work is to use electric potential difference, which can be written in a way that relates it to work involved in positioning charges.

$$\Delta V = \frac{W}{q}$$

where ΔV is the electric potential difference (V), W is the work needed to move the charge (J), and q is the magnitude of the moving charge (C).

Equipotential Lines

Equipotential lines are placed around a charge and mark where the electric potential is the same. Equipotential lines are always perpendicular to electric field lines.

In 3D, equipotential lines form a "surface" as an equipotential surface. Any movement along an equipotential surface requires no work because the movement is perpendicular to the electric field.

The figure below depicts equipotential lines under different circumstances.

On the left is a single charge, along with its electric field and corresponding equipotential lines.

On the right, there is a dipole with its bent electric field lines and mirrored equipotential lines.

Notice that in both instances, the equipotential lines are perpendicular to the electric field lines at every point.

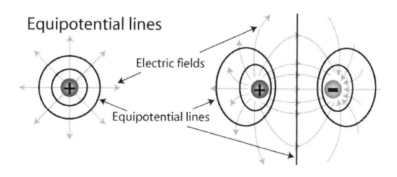

Electric Dipole

Definition of dipole

A dipole is an interaction between a positive charge and a negative charge that are separated by some distance.

Behavior in an electric field

Dipole in an electric field

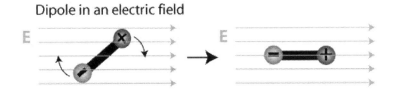

A dipole in an electric field will want to align itself with the electric field, such that the positive end of the dipole is in the direction of the electric field (furthest from the source of the electric field). It will spin or rotate until it reaches such a position.

Many molecules exhibit electric dipoles and are *polar molecules*.

The water molecule below is a good example of a polar molecule.

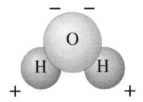

In this water molecule, the dipole moment arises from the negative charge near the location of the oxygen atom, and two positive charges near the hydrogen atoms. The asymmetric distribution of charge creates an electric dipole, which plays an important role in the physical and chemical properties of water.

For example, a microwave heats food by heating the water in the food. This occurs because the oscillating electric field of a microwave (see the next chapter on electromagnetic waves) rotates the water molecule such that the electric dipole is in line with the electric field.

The movement of the water molecule creates heat, which increases the temperature of the food.

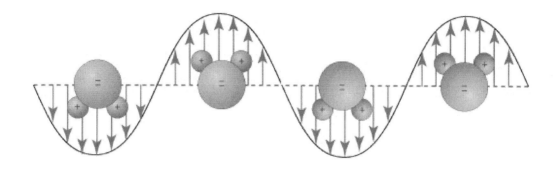

Electrostatic Induction

Electrostatic energy is a charge more or less fixed in a single place. However, this charge can be transferred to other objects in two ways. Energy can be transferred through *conduction*, which means there is a point of direct contact between two objects (as discussed earlier), or through *induction*, which is a transfer of energy across an open space between two objects.

Electrostatic induction is where a charged object induces the movement or redistribution of charges in another object. This occurs whenever an object is placed in or near an electric field.

Metal objects can be charged by conduction.

In diagram (a) below, the metal rod B is initially neutral. When the neutral rod B touches a charged rod A, negatively charged electrons flow from B to A.

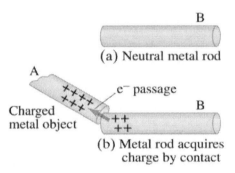

(a) Neutral metal rod

(b) Metal rod acquires charge by contact

The rods can also be charged by induction. In the figure below, the two rods never touch, and the neutral rod is grounded. This means that electrons from the neutral rod can be transferred to the ground and leave the surface of their object.

In diagram (b) below, when the negatively charged rod is brought near the neutral rod, the electric field will attract positive charge and cause the negatively charged electrons to be repelled and go into the ground.

In diagram (c), if the connection to ground is cut (such that electrons cannot flow back into the system) and the negatively charged rod is removed, the neutral rod will now have a positive charge evenly distributed across its surface.

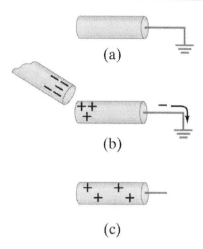

Insulators will not become charged by conduction or induction but will experience a charge separation as *polarization*.

Unlike conductors, insulators do not have electrons that can move freely about the material. Instead, when a strong charge is brought near the insulator, the molecules become polarized and orient themselves such that charges on the molecule align themselves with the electric field (like electric dipoles in an electric field). This is seen in the figure below.

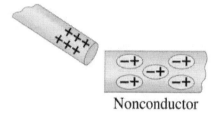

Nonconductor

An electroscope is a device that can be used for detecting charge in an object.

Below is a picture of a gold leaf electroscope. The gold arms in the middle will hang together if there is no charge and spread apart when there is a charge present.

As seen below, if an object is held near to (a) or touching (b) the metal knob on top.

If electrons flow one way or the other due to induction or conduction (diagrams (a) and (b) below, respectively), the gold leaves become similarly charged and repel.

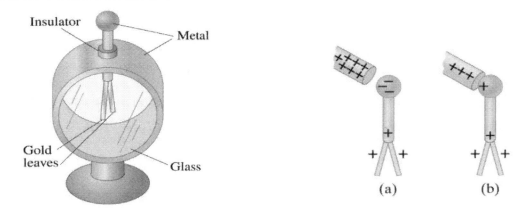

(a)   (b)

The charged electroscope can also be used to determine the sign of an unknown charge. If a negatively charged object is held near the knob and the leaves expand wider still, it means that even more electrons are trying to get away from the like-charged object, causing an even stronger negative charge in both of the two leaves.

If a positively charged object is held near the knob and the leaves swing in toward each other, it means electrons are cramming into the knob to be close to the presence of the opposite charge; the leaves will not be as negatively charged as before, and there will be less of a force driving them apart.

(a)   (b)   (c)

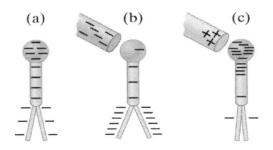

Gauss's Law

Gauss's Law relates the flow of a vector field through a surface to the behavior of the vector field inside the surface. In this case, the vector field in question will be an electric field:

$$\Phi_E = EA \cos (\theta)$$

where Φ_E is the electric flux (V·m), E is the electric field (N/C), A is the area that the field covers and θ is the angle between the field and plane that runs perpendicular to the direction of field flow.

For an enclosed surface, the electric flux is equal to the charge inside the enclosure (q), over the permittivity of free space (ε_0).

$$\Phi_E = \frac{q}{\varepsilon_0}$$

The net electric flux through any enclosed surface is dependent on the charge inside. If there is no charge inside, then the net electric flux through the enclosure is zero.

Electric flux through an area is proportional to the total number of field lines crossing the area.

In diagram (a) below, an electric field passes through an area A that is at an angle concerning the electric field.

In diagram (b), the electric flux is either proportional to the electric field that is perpendicular to that area.

In diagram (c), the electric field passing through the projection of the area perpendicular to the electric field

Regardless of the method, the two values will be equal.

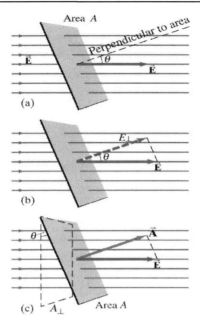

The flux through a closed surface of multiple electrical fields can be found using the total:

$$\Phi_E = E_1 \Delta A_1 \cos(\theta_1) + E_2 \Delta A_2 \cos(\theta_2) + \ldots = \sum E \Delta A \cos(\theta) = \sum E \perp \Delta A$$

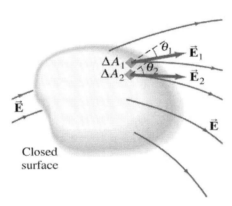

Closed surface

The net number of field lines through the surface is proportional both to the charge enclosed and the flux, giving Gauss's Law:

$$\sum_{\substack{closed \\ surface}} E_\perp \Delta A = \frac{Q_{encl}}{\epsilon_0}$$

This can be used to find the electric field in situations with a high degree of symmetry.

Magnetic Fields and Poles

Magnetism is a natural phenomenon that has very important applications in the modern world. For example, navigation with a compass, memory storage on a computer and high-speed trains all require magnetism and the understanding of the properties of magnets.

The earliest assumption about magnetism was that it was associated with naturally occurring magnetic materials such as iron, cobalt or nickel. Now, it is known that there are a few ways in which magnetism can be produced. On the atomic level, the electrons of material can produce magnetism due to their motion (the electron spin and revolution). Electric currents can also create magnets. This is the basis behind electromagnetism.

All magnetic objects emit magnetic fields, which can be visualized using magnetic field lines. These lines are very similar to electric field lines in their behavior and always start from the north pole (think positive charge) and go toward the south pole (think negative charge).

Unlike the electric field, magnetic fields always form closed loops because all magnets have a north pole and south pole. The figure below is a bar magnet showing the closed loop and the magnetic field created from north to south pole.

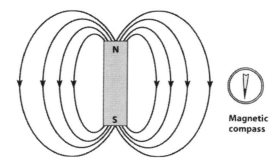

Magnetic compass

Another example is Earth's magnetic field. Earth's magnetic field originates deep beneath the surface layer and is caused by currents of conductive elements in the molten core. The magnetic field lines originate at the geographic south pole (magnetic north pole) and terminate at the geographic north pole (magnetic south pole).

A compass operates by aligning itself with the magnetic field of Earth (because magnetic fields will always form complete loops), allowing the user to navigate relative to a known axis.

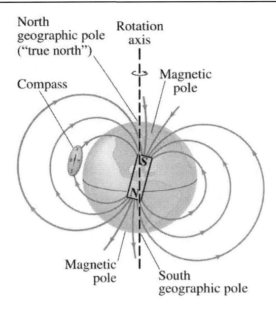

Another important aspect of magnets is that they can never have only one pole, all magnets must have a north and south pole. If a large magnet is broken into two halves, it will not produce two single polarity magnets. Instead, the two fragments will each have their north and south pole.

If these pieces are broken again, the process will repeat itself.

Magnets also have some other similar behaviors to electrically-charged particles. Most importantly, the poles of two different magnets exert a force on each other according to their polarity. Opposite poles attract, while like poles repel.

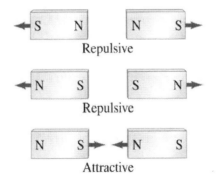

Magnetic fields around a current-carrying wire

As discussed previously, the charge can be made to travel across a conductor if an electric potential difference exists. When this occurs, the traveling charge is *electric current*, and is the rate of flow of charge through a conductor over time:

$$I = \frac{\Delta q}{\Delta t}$$

where I is the electric current given in amperes (A), and Δt is time (s).

Current is conventionally considered to be the movement of positive charge through a conductor. Although this is technically wrong (protons are immobile, only electrons can "flow"), all diagrams and calculations of current follow this convention. Remember that the movement of electrons is opposite to that shown.

When a current flows through a wire, a magnetic field is formed that circulates the wire.

The direction of the magnetic field can be found via the *right-hand rule*. Observe the diagram below.

According to the right-hand rule, the thumb goes in the direction of positive charge (i.e., the direction of current by convention), and the direction the fingers curl around in the direction of the magnetic field.

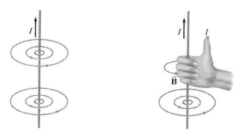

To understand the flow of electrons through the conductor, see the figure below. Notice the direction of the magnetic field. The magnetic field is clockwise because current flows down the wire from top to bottom.

However, the electron flow is opposite to the conventional current flow. Thus electrons flow from bottom to top.

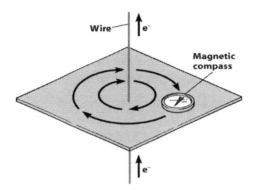

When a current induces a magnetic field in a straight wire, the magnetic field strength can be calculated via *Ampère's Law*:

$$B = \frac{\mu_0 I}{2\pi r}$$

where μ_0 is the constant of permeability of free space ($4\pi \times 10^{-7}$ T·m/A), I is the current (A), and r is the distance away from the wire (m).

Magnetic fields in solenoids

When a current-carrying wire is wrapped around, such that it forms a loop, it is a *solenoid*. Solenoids have many applications and are the basis for common electromagnets.

The primary importance of a solenoid is that the magnetic field can be manipulated, as seen in the diagrams:

In this configuration, the net magnetic field created by the loop can be imagined as:

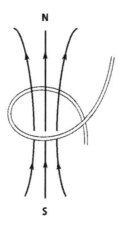

If the number of loops is increased in the solenoid, the magnetic field will increase proportionally with the number of loops.

Additionally, if a piece of iron is inserted in the solenoid, the magnetic field greatly increases.

Using the equation for the magnetic field strength of a wire, the magnetic field strength through a solenoid (not outside of) can be expressed as:

$$B = \frac{\mu_0 \mu_r n I}{l}$$

where n is the number of loops, μ_r is the relative permeability of core material ($\mu_r = 1$ in air) and l is the length of the solenoid (m).

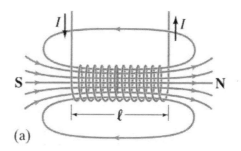

(a)

Magnetic Field Force

Particles

When a charged particle passes through a magnetic field with a specific velocity, which must be perpendicular to the magnetic field) it will experience a force from the magnetic field. This only occurs if the charge has a velocity perpendicular to the magnetic field. If its speed is zero or its direction is parallel to the field, then no force will be exerted:

$$F = qvB \sin (\theta)$$

where q is the electric charge (C), v is the velocity of the charge (m/s), B is the strength of the magnetic field given in the Tesla (T), and θ is the angle between the charge velocity and the magnetic field (degrees). Sometimes the sin (θ) is omitted, as θ is assumed to be 90°.

The magnetic force is always perpendicular to both the magnetic field and the velocity of the charge:

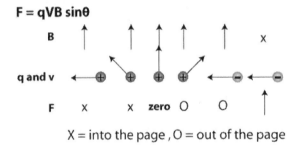

X = into the page , O = out of the page

Again, an easy way to remember this is the right-hand rule. The thumb of the right-hand goes in the direction of a positive charge, the middle finger is the direction of the magnetic field, and the palm faces the direction of the force.

If the charge is negative, then the direction of the force is opposite.

Right –hand rules (RHR)

Physical Situation	Example	How to Orient Right Hand	Result
1. Magnetic field produced by current (RHR-1)		Wrap fingers around wire with thumb pointing in direction of current I	Fingers curl in direction of $\vec{B}$
2. Force on electric current I due to magnetic field (RHR-2)		Fingers first point straight along current I, then bend along magnetic field $\vec{B}$	Thumb points in direction of the force $\vec{F}$
3. Force on electric charge $+q$ due to magnetic field (RHR-3)		Fingers point along particle's velocity $\vec{v}$, then along $\vec{B}$	Thumb points in direction of the force $\vec{F}$

Motion of charged particles in magnetic fields

When a charged particle travels through a magnetic field, it will be deflected according to the magnitude and direction of the field. The deflection of the particle has important applications, such as mass spectrometers, because it can be related to the centripetal force to solve for the mass of the particle.

For example, the equations for centripetal force and magnetic field force on a charged particle are:

$$F_C = \frac{mv^2}{r} \qquad F_M = qvB \sin(\theta)$$

If the particle is assumed to be traveling perpendicular to the magnetic field, then the magnetic field force becomes:

$$F_M = qvB$$

Thus, if a particle with some velocity perpendicular to a magnetic field travels in a circular orbit, the mass can be solved for by:

$$\frac{mv^2}{r} = qvB$$

$$m = \frac{qBr}{v}$$

When $qvB < mv^2/r$, there is not enough centripetal force, and the charged particle will fly out of orbit.

When $qvB > mv^2/r$, there is too much centripetal force, and the charged particle spirals inward.

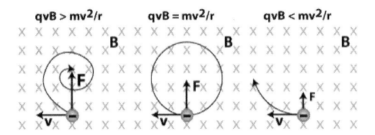

Current-carrying wires

Wires carrying current have charged particles in motion through them.

Consequently, a magnetic field exerts a calculable force on a current-carrying wire. This can be expressed as:

$$F = I\ell B \sin (\theta)$$

where I is the current through the wire (A) and l is the length of wire exposed to the magnetic field (m).

Again, the direction of the force is given by the right-hand rule.

For example, in the diagrams below a length of current-carrying wire is exposed to a magnetic field.

In diagram (a), the current flows in such a manner that the magnetic field exerts a downward force.

In diagram (b), if the current is reversed, then the magnetic force is opposite its original direction and point upwards.

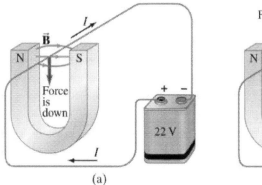 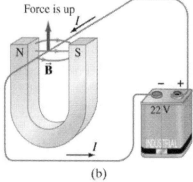

Parallel current-carrying wires

When two current-carrying wires are parallel and close enough such that their magnetic field can interact, they exert a force on each other according to the magnitude and direction of their respective currents.

The magnitude of the force per unit length of the parallel wire section is given by:

$$\frac{F}{l} = \frac{\mu_0}{2\pi}\frac{I_1 I_2}{d}$$

The direction of the force between the wires depends upon the direction of the currents in the wires with respect to each other.

In the diagram below on the left, parallel currents (currents moving in the same direction) create an attractive force.

In the diagram below on the right, anti-parallel currents (currents moving in opposite directions) create repulsive forces.

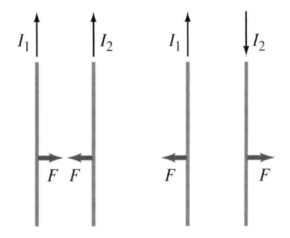

Faraday's Law

Michael Faraday came up with a relationship that linked the induced electromotive force (EMF) in a wire loop proportionally to the rate of change of magnetic flux through the loop. He called this the law of induction. To understand the full meaning of this law, magnetic flux must first be investigated.

The magnetic flux (Φ_B) is similar to the electric flux and is defined as the amount of magnetic field passing through an area of a surface. The Weber (Wb) is the SI unit of magnetic flux, which is equal to volt-seconds. It may also be given in tesla-meters-squared ($T \cdot m^2$). The equation for computing magnetic flux is:

$$\Phi_B = B_{\perp}A = BA \cos(\theta)$$

where $B_{\perp}$ is the magnitude of the magnetic field that is perpendicular to the area (A). If the field lines are not perpendicular to the area, then the right-hand equation must be used where θ is the angle between the field lines and the vector normal to the surface.

The diagrams below demonstrate the varying amounts of magnetic flux through the coiled wire as it is rotated with respect to the magnetic field.

In diagram (a) below, the magnetic flux is equal to zero because the coil area is perpendicular to the applied field.

Diagram (b) below has some magnetic flux because the area of the coil is at an angle to the field.

Diagram (c) below has the maximum flux because its area is fully parallel to the magnetic field.

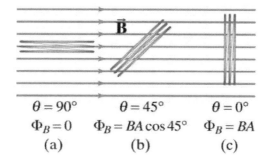

$$
\begin{array}{ccc}
\theta = 90° & \theta = 45° & \theta = 0° \\
\Phi_B = 0 & \Phi_B = BA \cos 45° & \Phi_B = BA \\
\text{(a)} & \text{(b)} & \text{(c)}
\end{array}
$$

Using an equation for magnetic flux, one can investigate how *Faraday's Law* pertains to the voltage induced in a coiled wire under certain situations. This law states that the induced voltage in a coil is proportional to the number of loops it contains, multiplied by the rate at which the magnetic field changes within those loops.

The magnitude of the current is related to the resistance of the coil, its circuit and the voltage induced. The more coils a wire has, the greater the induced voltage.

However, the higher the voltage, the greater the current that pushes back against the magnet. The rapid motion of the magnet also induces a greater voltage.

This relationship is explained in the equation of Faraday's Law of Induction (sometimes Lenz's Law, named after the scientist who, after more experimentation, added the negative sign):

$$EMF = -N\frac{\Delta \Phi_B}{\Delta t}$$

For example, the diagrams below show a loop of wire exposed to a magnetic field.

In diagram (b) below, the loop is stretched such that the area exposed to the flux changes. According to Faraday's Law, an EMF is induced and current results through the loop.

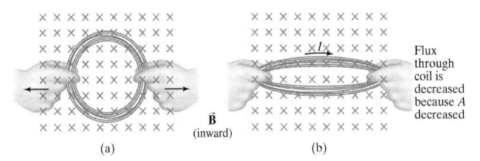

Flux through coil is decreased because *A* decreased

(a)   (b)

An EMF can also be formed by a moving conductor.

In diagram (a) below, the rectangle represents a conductor with a movable slide. If the slide is moved outward, then the magnetic flux will change.

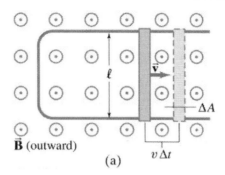

(a)

In the diagram below, the induced current from the movement of the sliding bar causes a current to form.

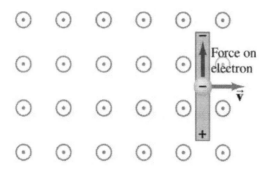

The induced EMF in such a situation has a magnitude of the form:

$$EMF = \frac{\Delta \Phi_B}{\Delta t} = \frac{B\Delta A}{\Delta t} = \frac{B\ell v\Delta t}{\Delta t} = B\ell v$$

Solving problems with Faraday's Law:

1. Determine if the magnetic flux is increasing, decreasing or unchanged.

2. The magnetic field due to the induced current points is in the opposite direction to the original field if the flux is increasing, in the same direction if it is decreasing and is zero if the flux is not changing.

3. Use the right-hand rule to determine the direction of the resulting current. To do so, point the thumb in the direction of a vector normal to the area on the side the flux is exiting. The direction curled by the fingers as they close toward the palm is the direction of the current.

4. Remember that the external field and the field due to the induced current are different.

Torque on Current-Carrying Wire

When a wire carrying a current forms a loop, the current will reverse directions (concerning the *x* and *y*-axes) as it travels in the loop and out of the loop. If the loop is exposed to a magnetic field, a torque will be generated about the axis of the loop, due to the opposing forces on each side of the loop. This concept has many applications and is used in equipment such as galvanometers, motors, and loudspeakers.

For example, a galvanometer takes advantage of the torque on a current loop to measure current. Observe the figure below of a galvanometer:

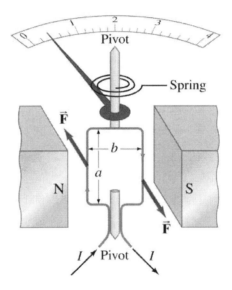

If the current increases in the loop, the force from the magnetic field will increase in proportion, and the dial will twist more because of increased torque. The magnitude of the produced torque can be calculated by:

$$\tau = nIAB \sin (\theta)$$

where the quantity *nIA* is the magnetic dipole moment, *n* is the number of loops (this equation also works for a solenoid), *I* is the current (A), *A* is the area of the enclosed space (m²) and θ is the angle of the loop area with respect to the magnetic field (degrees).

Properties of Electromagnetic Radiation

What is electromagnetic radiation?

Electromagnetic radiation is a form of energy that propagates through space as an oscillating electric and magnetic field. Classically, electromagnetic radiation is considered to be a wave; however, in quantum mechanics, electromagnetic radiation can be considered as packets of energy of *photons*.

Below is a figure of the wave nature of electromagnetic radiation.

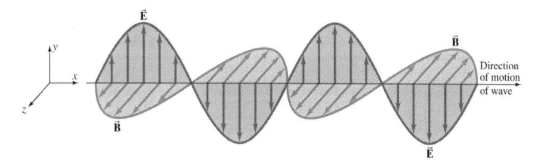

Radiation velocity equals constant *c* in a vacuum

Unlike sound and mechanical waves, electromagnetic radiation does not need a medium in which to propagate. In a vacuum, it has a constant speed of:

$$c = 2.99792458 \times 10^8 \text{ m/s} \approx 3 \times 10^8 \text{ m/s}$$

This is the standard value of the *speed of light*. Nothing in the universe can travel faster than light in a vacuum. Electromagnetic radiation will travel slower than this speed in other mediums, according to the value of the mediums' refractive index.

The speed in these mediums can be calculated by:

$$v = \frac{c}{n}$$

where *v* is the speed of light in the medium and *n* is the refractive index of that medium.

Production, energy, and momentum of electromagnetic waves

Electromagnetic waves are produced by accelerating charges. The acceleration produces oscillations of electric and magnetic fields (electromagnetic radiation), which propagate through space indefinitely until absorbed. Like all waves, electromagnetic waves can be related by their speed, frequency, and wavelength by:

$$c = \lambda f$$

where c is the speed of light, λ is the wavelength (m), and f is the frequency of the electromagnetic radiation (Hz).

Additionally, when considering electromagnetic radiation from the quantum mechanical viewpoint, the photons have discrete, quantifiable energies related to their frequency. This can be found via:

$$E = hf = \frac{hc}{\lambda}$$

where E is the energy per photon (J or eV), and h is Planck's constant (6.626×10^{-34} J·s or 4.135×10^{-15} eV).

Electromagnetic radiation also carries momentum. Although the wave has no mass, it still can exert a force of *radiation pressure.*

When the radiation is fully absorbed, the radiation pressure is at a minimum, and is expressed as:

$$P_{minimum} = \frac{\bar{I}}{c}$$

When the radiation is fully reflected, the radiation pressure is at a maximum, expressed as:

$$P_{maximum} = \frac{2\bar{I}}{c}$$

where P is the radiation pressure (N/m^2) and I is the intensity of the electromagnetic radiation (W/m^2).

Classification of Electromagnetic Spectrum, Photon Energy

Electromagnetic radiation varies significantly in properties and energies depending on the frequency of the radiation. The figure below shows the spectrum of electromagnetic radiation according to wavelength and frequency. Notice that as frequency increases, the wavelength decreases due to the inverse proportionality of the wavelength vs. frequency. The higher frequency forms of electromagnetic radiation (ultraviolet, X-rays, gamma rays) are carcinogens and harmful to one's health. This is because these high frequency forms of radiation gives them very high energies, which can cause damage to cells and DNA.

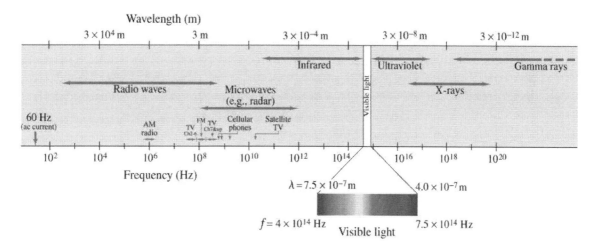

Lower frequency = longer wavelength = less energy	
Radio	Causes electronic oscillations in the antenna
Microwave	Causes molecular rotation
Infrared	Causes molecular vibration
Visible	Can excite electrons to orbits of higher energy. Visible light ranges from 400-700 nm. 400 being violet, 700 is red.
Ultraviolet	Can break bonds and excite electrons so much as to eject them, which is why UV is considered ionizing radiation.
X-rays	Ionizing radiation, the photoelectric effect
Gamma rays	Even more energetic than X-rays
Higher frequency = shorter wavelength = more energy	

Chapter Summary

Charge

- There are two kinds of electric charge—positive and negative.

- Charge is always conserved.

- The charge on an electron is: $e = 1.602 \times 10^{-19}$ C

- Charge is quantized in units of e (how many times greater than the charge on an electron).

- Conductors are materials in which electrons are free to move.

- Insulators are nonconductors, and thus do not allow electrons to move freely.

- Objects can be charged by conduction or induction.

Electric Fields

- Coulomb's Law gives magnitude of the electrostatic force: $F = k \times \frac{Q_1 Q_2}{r^2}$

- Electric field is force per unit charge: $\vec{E} = \frac{\vec{F}}{q}$

- Electric field is given by a single point charge: $E = \frac{F}{q} = \frac{kqQ/r^2}{q} = k \times \frac{Q}{r^2}$

- Electric field lines can represent electric fields.

- Static electric field inside a conductor is zero; the surface field is perpendicular to the surface.

- Electric flux (flow of a field through a closed surface): $\Phi_E = E_\perp A = E A_\perp = E A \cos(\theta)$

- Gauss's Law (electric flux through a closed surface): $\sum_{\substack{closed \\ surface}} E_\perp \Delta A = \frac{Q_{encl}}{\epsilon_0}$

Electromagnetic Waves

- Maxwell's equations are the basic equations of electromagnetism.

- Electromagnetic waves are produced by accelerating charges.

- The propagation speed of electromagnetic waves is given by $c = \frac{1}{\sqrt{\epsilon_0 \mu_0}}$

- The fields are perpendicular to the direction of propagation.

- The wavelength and frequency of EM waves are related: $c = \lambda f$

- The electromagnetic spectrum includes all wavelengths, from radio waves through visible light to gamma rays.

Magnets

- Magnets have north and south poles.

- Like poles repel, unlike attract.

- Electric currents produce magnetic fields.

Magnetic Fields

- Given in units of Tesla (T).

- Parallel currents attract, anti-parallel currents repel.

- A magnetic field exerts a force on an electric current: $F = I\ell B \sin (\theta)$

- A magnetic field exerts a force on a moving charge: $F = qvB \sin (\theta)$

- Magnitude of the field of a long, straight current-carrying wire: $B = \frac{\mu_0}{2\pi} \times \frac{I}{r}$

- Ampère's Law (magnitude of a field): $\sum B_{\parallel} \Delta \ell = \mu_0 I_{encl}$

- Magnetic field inside a solenoid: $B = \frac{\mu_0 N I}{\ell}$

Torque

- Torque on a current loop: $\tau = NIAB \sin (\theta)$

Notes

Practice Questions

1. In the figure, $Q = 5.1$ nC. What is the magnitude of the electrical force on the charge Q? (Use Coulomb's constant $k = 9 \times 10^9$ N·m²/C²)

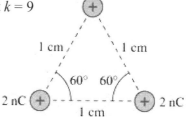

   A. 4.2×10^{-3} N   **C.** 1.6×10^{-3} N

   B. 0.4×10^{-3} N   **D.** 3.2×10^{-3} N

                                    E. 7.1×10^{-3} N

2. Which one of the following statements is correct?

   A. The north pole of a magnet points towards Earth's geographic North Pole
   B. The north pole of a magnet points towards Earth's geographic South Pole
   C. Earth's geographic North Pole is the north pole of Earth's magnetic field
   D. Earth's geographic South Pole is the south pole of Earth's magnetic field
   E. None of the above

3. Two uncharged metal spheres, A and B, are mounted on insulating support rods. A third metal sphere, C, carrying a positive charge, is then placed near B. A copper wire is momentarily connected between A and B, and then removed. Finally, sphere C is removed. In this final state:

   A. spheres A and B both carry equal positive charges
   B. sphere A carries a negative charge and B carries a positive charge
   C. sphere A carries a positive charge and B carries a negative charge
   D. spheres A and B both carry positive charges, but B's charge is greater
   E. sphere A remains uncharged, and B carries a positive charge

4. Two charges separated by 1 m exert a 1 N force on each other. What is the force on each charge when they are pulled to a separation distance of 3 m?

   A. 3 N   **B.** 0 N   **C.** 9 N   **D.** 0.33 N   **E.** 0.11 N

5. A balloon after being rubbed on a wool rug can stick to a wall. This illustrates that the balloon has:

   I. magnetism
   II. net charge
   III. capacitance

   A. I only   **B.** II only   **C.** III only   **D.** I, II and III   **E.** I and III only

6. The diagram shows two unequal charges $+q$ and $-Q$, of opposite sign. Charge Q has a greater magnitude than charge q. Point X is midway between the charges.

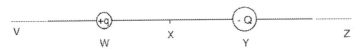

In what section of the line is the point where the resultant electric field could equal zero?

A. VW   **B.** WX   **C.** XY   **D.** YZ   **E.** VX

7. One coulomb of charge passes through a 6 V battery. Which of the following is the correct value for the increase of some property of the battery?

A. 6 watts   **B.** 6 ohms   **C.** 6 amps   **D.** 6 J   **E.** 6 N

8. What travels through a conductor at near the speed of light when a current is established?

A. Protons   **C.** An electric field
B. Photons   **D.** Electrons   **E.** Neutrons

9. Which statement is accurate for a proton that moves in a direction perpendicular to the electric field lines?

A. it is moving from high potential to low potential and gaining electric potential energy
B. it is moving from high potential to low potential and losing electric potential energy
C. it is moving from low potential to high potential and gaining electric potential energy
D. it is moving from low potential to high potential and losing electric potential energy
E. both its electric potential and electric potential energy remain constant

10. Light having a frequency in a vacuum of 3×10^{14} Hz enters a liquid with a refractive index of 2. What is the frequency of the light in this liquid?

A. 6×10^{14} Hz   **C.** 12×10^{14} Hz
B. 1.5×10^{14} Hz   **D.** 3×10^{14} Hz   **E.** 9×10^{14} Hz

11. With all other factors remaining constant, how does doubling the number of loops of wire in a coil affect the induced emf?

A. The induced emf increases by a factor of $\sqrt{2}$
B. The induced emf doubles
C. There is no change in the induced emf
D. The induced emf quadruples
E. The induced emf increases by a factor of 3

12. A proton is traveling to the right and encounters a region S which contains an electric field or a magnetic field or both. The proton is observed to bend up the page. Which of the statements is true regarding region S?

I. There is a magnetic field pointing into the page
II. There is a magnetic field pointing out of the page
III. There is an electric field pointing up the page
IV. There is an electric field pointing down the page.

A. I only   **B.** II only   **C.** I and III   **D.** II and IV   **E.** II and III

13. An object with a 6 μC charge is accelerating at 0.006 m/s^2 due to an electric field. If the object has a mass of 2 μg, what is the magnitude of the electric field?

A. 0.002 N/C   **B.** −0.005 N/C   **C.** 2 N/C   **D.** −2 N/C   **E.** −0.07 N/C

14. Two Gaussian surfaces, A and B, enclose the same positive charge +Q. The Gaussian surface A has an area two times greater than surface B. Compared to the flux of the electric field through Gaussian surface B, the flux of the electric field through surface A is:

A. two times smaller   **C.** two times larger
B. equal   **D.** four times larger   **E.** four times smaller

15. Which of these electromagnetic waves has the shortest wavelength?

A. γ rays   **B.** Visible light   **C.** Radio waves   **D.** Infrared   **E.** Microwaves

Solutions

1. C is correct.

$$F_e = kQ_1Q_2 \,/\, r^2$$

$$F_e = [(9 \times 10^9 \text{ N·m}^2/\text{C}^2){\cdot}(5.1 \times 10^{-9} \text{ C})(2 \times 10^{-9} \text{ C})] \,/\, (0.1 \text{ m})^2$$

$$F_e = 9.18 \times 10^{-4} \text{ N}$$

$F_e \sin (60°)$ represents the force from one of the positive 2 nC charges.

Double to find the total force:

$$F_{total} = 2F_e \sin (60°)$$

$$F_{total} = 2(9.18 \times 10^{-4} \text{ N}) \sin (60°)$$

$$F_{total} = 1.6 \times 10^{-3} \text{ N}$$

The sine of the angle is used since only the vertical forces are added because the horizontal forces are equal and opposite and therefore they cancel.

2. E is correct. None of the statements are true.

3. C is correct.

When the positively charged sphere C is near sphere B, it polarizes the sphere causing its negative charge to migrate towards C and a positive charge to build on the other side of sphere B.

The wire between sphere A and sphere B allows negative charge to flow to B and create a net positive charge on sphere A. Once the wire is removed and sphere C is removed, sphere A will have a net positive charge and B has a net negative charge.

4. E is correct.

Coulomb's Law:

$$F_e = kQ_1Q_2 \,/\, r^2$$

If r is increased by a factor of 3:

$$F_{new} = kQ_1Q_2 \,/\, (3r)^2$$

$$F_{new} = kQ_1Q_2 \,/\, (9r^2)$$

$$F_{new} = (1/9)kQ_1Q_2 \,/\, r^2$$

$$F_{new} = F_{original} \, (1/9)$$

$$F_{new} = (1 \text{ N}){\cdot}(1/9)$$

$$F_{new} = 0.11 \text{ N}$$

5. B is correct.

The balloon sticks to the wall because the rubbing on the wool has transferred charges to the balloon, leading to an electrostatic force.

6. A is correct.

If the charge Q is of a greater magnitude than charge q then the electric field points toward Q (because its negative) in section W to Z.

In section VW the electric field is the difference in magnitude between q and Q. If Q has a large enough charge, then the difference could equal zero, and there is no electric field.

7. D is correct.

A volt is defined as the potential difference that causes 1 C of charge to increase potential energy by 1 J. Therefore, moving 1 C through 6 V causes the potential energy of the battery to increase by 6 J.

8. C is correct.

A current is caused by a voltage (potential difference) across a conductor.

Whenever a voltage exists an electric field exists, and this travels at near the speed of light. Electrons do not travel quickly when a current is established and only travel at their drift speed which is proportional to voltage.

9. E is correct.

A proton moving perpendicular to electric field lines does not get close to the charges creating the electric field. Thus its electric potential and potential energy remain constant because these values are related to distance from other charges.

Electric Potential Energy:

$$U = kQq\,/\,r$$

Electric Potential:

$$V = kQ\,/\,r$$

10. D is correct.

Only the wavelength of light changes in different mediums, not the frequency.

11. B is correct.

Faraday's Law states that the electromotive force (emf) in a coil is:

emf $= N\Delta BA \cos \theta / \Delta t$

where $N =$ number of loops of wire.

If N doubles, the emf also doubles.

12. C is correct.

There is a force on the proton up the page. The electric field points in the direction of the force on positive particles, therefore it is pointed upwards.

The direction of the magnetic field is determined by the right-hand rule.

$F = qvB$, where q is a charge, v is velocity and B is a magnetic field

When F is oriented upwards, curling your fingers from the direction of velocity gives B into the page.

13. A is correct.

Convert all units to their correct form:

$F = ma$

$F = (2 \times 10^{-6} \text{ kg}) \cdot (0.006 \text{ m/s}^2)$

$F = 1.2 \times 10^{-8} \text{ N}$

Substituting into the equation for electric field:

$E = F / q$

$E = (1.2 \times 10^{-8} \text{ N}) / (6 \times 10^{-6} \text{ C})$

$E = 0.002 \text{ N/C}$

Note: 1 N $= 1 \text{ kg} \cdot \text{m/s}^2$, not 1 $\text{g} \cdot \text{m/s}^2$

14. B is correct.

$\Phi = Q / E_0$

For an enclosed charge, the area of the surface does not affect the flux.

15. A is correct.

γ rays are the electromagnetic waves that have the shortest wavelength.

Chapter 8

Circuit Elements and DC Circuits

CIRCUITS

- **Batteries, Electromotive Force, Voltage**

- **Current**

- **Resistance**

- **Power**

- **Kirchhoff's Laws**

- **Capacitance**

- **Inductors**

- **DC Circuits**

ALTERNATING CURRENTS AND REACTIVE CIRCUITS

- **LCR circuits**

- **Transformers and Transmission of Power Transformers**

- **Measuring Devices**

Notes

Electric Circuits

An *electric circuit* is a series of connections between a voltage source, circuit elements and conducting wires, which result in a flow of current. The voltage source is the energy input and is necessary for continuing the flow of energy.

The circuit elements can use some of the energy from the voltage source as heat or light. The current in a circuit will always flow from high potential to low potential through the external circuit.

A complete circuit is one where current can flow in a complete loop.

Below, the left image shows a complete circuit.

The battery provides a potential difference, which causes current to flow from its positive terminal, through the light bulb, then to its negative terminal, completing the loop.

The figure on the right is a schematic circuit drawing of the circuit on the left.

Note that the schematic drawing does not look much like the physical circuit.

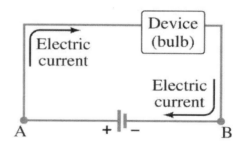

Batteries, Electromotive Force, Voltage

The electric potential difference is particularly important in solving circuit problems. The *electromotive force* (EMF) is used to describe the measure of energy that causes the flow of current in a circuit. It is defined as the potential difference between two points in a circuit and is the energy per unit of charge given by an energy source. This is the same as the amount of work done on one unit of electric charge, given in volts (V).

Batteries are physical devices that produce an electric potential difference and are often used to provide the EMF in electric circuits. These devices operate by transforming chemical energy into electrical energy.

Chemical reactions within the battery cell create a potential difference between two terminals. This potential difference can be maintained, even if a current is kept flowing until eventually the chemical reaction has exhausted itself and the battery can no longer maintain a potential difference.

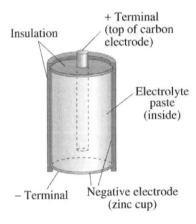

Internal resistance of a battery

Although batteries are often depicted as having no resistance, all non-ideal batteries will have some internal resistance.

The internal resistance of a battery is like a resistor right next to the battery, connected in series.

If the battery in a circuit has no internal resistance (ideal case), the potential difference across the battery equals the EMF.

If the battery does have an internal resistance, the potential difference across the battery equals the EMF, minus the voltage drop due to internal resistance. This is the *terminal voltage* and can be given by the equation:

$$V_{ab} = V_0 - IR_{battery}$$

where V_{ab} is the terminal voltage of the battery (V), V_0 is the voltage before internal resistance (V), I is the current through the battery (A) and $R_{battery}$ is the internal resistance of the battery (Ω).

The figure below depicts a non-ideal battery with internal resistance and resulting terminal voltage.

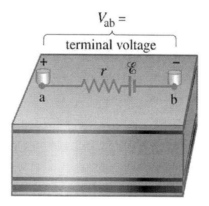

Batteries in series and parallel

When two or more batteries are in series, the total potential difference provided is the sum of the EMF provided by each battery. It is important to note that this is only the case if the terminals are aligned such that the batteries' terminals go from positive to negative, or vice versa. For example, the figure below shows two batteries in series (note that these batteries have internal resistance and the voltage shown is the terminal voltage). The total voltage provided by the two batteries is:

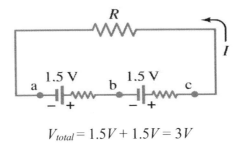

$$V_{total} = 1.5V + 1.5V = 3V$$

When the batteries are in series but aligned such that the positive terminal goes to positive or negative to negative, then the total voltage provided is the difference between the two batteries. In this case, however, the battery with less voltage is being charged:

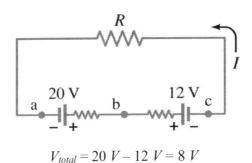

$$V_{total} = 20\ V - 12\ V = 8\ V$$

Batteries in parallel will produce the same voltage but can support larger current draws depending upon the resistance of the circuit.

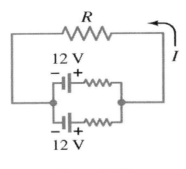

$$V_{total} = 12\ V$$

Current

Current is the result of electron flow through a conductor. Electrons in a conductor are loosely bound to the nuclei and have large, random speeds dependent upon the temperature of the conductor. For example, metals are well-known conductors because one electron from each atom is loosely bound and free to move through the metal lattice.

When an electric potential difference is applied across a metal or any conducting material, it creates an electrical field that passes through the conductor at near the speed of light.

Accordingly, the free electrons in the conductor are attracted against the line direction of the electric field due to Coulomb attraction forces. As they pass through the conduction material, these electrons acquire an average drift velocity, which although considerably smaller than the thermal velocity of the electrons, creates the electric current through the conductor.

Observe the diagram below of a conductor with an applied potential difference and subsequent electric field.

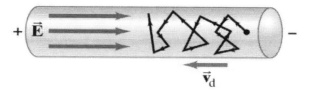

The current through the conductor can be calculated as the number of electrons drifting through a unit's volume at the drift velocity:

$$I = nq_eAv_d$$

where I is the current (A), n is the number of electrons per unit volume (electrons/m^3), A is the area of the conductor (m^2), v_d is the drift velocity (m/s) and q_e is the charge of an electron (1.6×10^{-19} C).

More generally, the electric current is defined as the rate at which charge flows through a conductor, and can also be expressed as:

$$I = \frac{\Delta q}{\Delta t}$$

There are two types of current: direct current (DC), and alternating current (AC).

A *direct current* is when a constant potential difference is applied to the circuit, and the current moves only in one direction. This is characteristic of electronic devices, batteries, and solar cells.

However, nearly all generated electricity is an *alternating current*, in which the potential difference is cycled between high and low, creating an oscillatory current flow. It is transmitted over high voltage lines and "stepped down" for use in homes and industry.

Resistance

Resistivity ($\rho = RA/l$)

Electrical resistance is the loss of current energy (electron flow) through a material. There are two sources of electrical resistance: collisions with other electrons in current, or collisions with other charges in the material. These factors are taken into account as the resistance, which is determined by the resistivity of a material (a measure of conductance) and several other factors, including geometry and temperature. For instance, in most electronic circuit applications, wires are used to transmit current from one point to another.

The resistance of a wire depends upon the length, the cross-sectional area, the temperature, and the material:

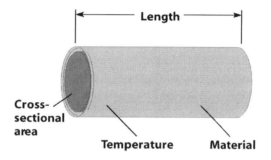

$$R = \rho \frac{\ell}{A}$$

where R is the resistance (Ohms or Ω), ρ is the resistivity ($\Omega \cdot$m), ℓ is the length of the wire (m) and A is the cross-sectional area of the wire (m^2).

Notice the resistivity is directly proportional to the resistance; therefore, the greater the resistivity, the greater the resistance of the material. Additionally, resistance is inversely proportional to the area (inverse square to the radius and diameter). Therefore, the greater the diameter, the less resistance there will be; there is a larger area for electrons to flow.

As shown mathematically in the equation above, a wire of low resistance will be short, of large diameter and made from a material that has low resistivity. For this reason, extension cords are made thicker to keep the resistance down.

The resistance of a wire is also dependent upon the temperature of the material. This is because, for any given material, the resistivity increases with temperature:

$$\rho_T = \rho_0[1 + \alpha(T - T_0)]$$

where ρ_T is the resistivity at a temperature T ($\Omega \cdot$m), ρ_0 is the standard resistivity at a standard temperature of T_0 ($\Omega \cdot$m), the α temperature coefficient of resistivity (K^{-1}) and T is temperature (K)

Ohm's Law (I = V/R)

Ohm's Law gives the relationship between the potential difference across a resistance and the current through the resistance. In electrical circuits, Ohm's Law states that the current through a conductor between two points is directly proportional to the potential difference, or voltage across, the two points, and inversely proportional to the resistance between them:

$$I = \frac{V}{R} \quad \text{or} \quad V = IR$$

where V is the potential difference (V), I is the current (A), and R is the resistance (Ω).

Resistors in series

In a circuit, *resistors* may be arranged in series or parallel.

In a series arrangement, the resistors have a current pass through the first resistor, then into the second, into the third and so on:

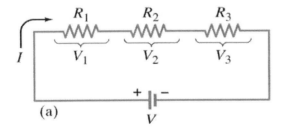

When in series, the total resistance of the circuit is the sum of all the resistances of the components, which means that as more elements are added to the circuit, the total resistance increases, and the total current drops.

The equivalent resistance of resistors in series is found by:

$$R_{equivalent} = R_1 + R_2 + R_3 + \ldots$$

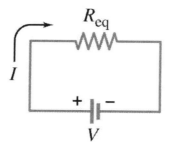

In a series circuit, the current through each resistor is the same ($I_{series} = I_1 = I_2 = I_3$); however, the voltage drops across each resistor. The voltage drop among resistors in series is split according to the resistance—a greater resistance equals a greater voltage drop ($V = IR$).

This can also be expanded for more than one resistor, by splitting it into components:

$$V = V_1 + V_2 + V_3 = IR_1 + IR_2 + IR_3$$

Resistors in parallel

Parallel resistors are arranged such that all resistors (in parallel) experience the same voltage drop across them, but have different currents through them according to their resistances.

In a parallel circuit, there is more than one available path for the current to take.

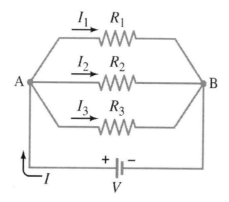

The equivalent resistance of resistors in parallel is found by:

$$\frac{1}{R_{equivalent}} = \frac{1}{R_1} + \frac{1}{R_2} + \frac{1}{R_3} + \cdots$$

As stated earlier, in an arrangement of parallel resistors, the voltage across each resistor is the same ($V_{parallel} = V_1 = V_2 = V_3$) however the current across each resistor is not. The total current can be found as the sum of the currents across each resistor:

$$\frac{V}{R_{eq}} = \frac{V}{R_1} + \frac{V}{R_2} + \frac{V}{R_3}$$

$$I = \frac{V}{R_{eq}}$$

Most common circuits are combinations of series and parallel circuits.

For example, household circuits are a combination of series and parallel circuits.

Generally, outlets in the same room are in series, but the separate rooms are in parallel. This is why a blown fuse may cut the power to an entire room, but not the entire house.

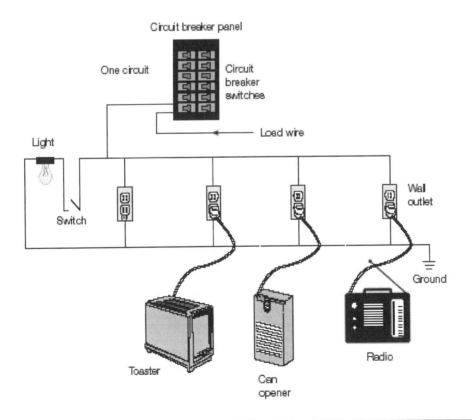

Power

The *power* (P) in a circuit is the rate at which energy is converted from electrical energy into another form, such as heat or mechanical energy.

The SI unit is the watt, which is equal to joules per second.

For a component in a DC circuit, the power is given by the equation:

$$P = IV$$

where P is the power (W), I is the current (A), and V is the voltage (V).

Using Ohm's Law, power in an electrical circuit can also be expressed as:

$$P = I^2R$$

Kirchhoff's Laws

Kirchhoff's Laws are an extremely useful tool to help solve for unknown components within a circuit.

Kirchhoff's Current Law

Kirchhoff's Current Law is an expression of the conservation of charge. By the Law of Conservation of Charge, a charge cannot be created or destroyed.

Therefore, in a circuit, the sum of all currents entering a junction must be equal to the sum of all currents exiting the junction.

$$I_{entering,total} = I_{exiting,total}$$

Kirchhoff's Voltage Law

Kirchhoff's Voltage Law is also an expression of the conservation of energy.

The voltage law states that the sum of all voltage drops, across any resistive elements within a closed circuit loop, must equal the EMF in the same loop.

$$\sum V_{drop} = EMF_{total}$$

When solving problems that require the use of Kirchhoff's rules, follow these steps:

1. Label each current.

2. Identify unknowns.

3. Apply junction and loop rules; as many independent equations will be needed as there are unknowns.

4. Solve the equations, being careful with signs.

For example, apply Kirchhoff's Circuit Laws to the circuit below:

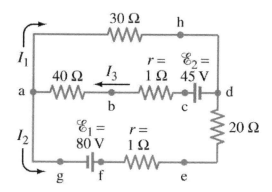

Apply Kirchhoff's Current Law:

$$I_1 + I_2 = I_3$$

Apply Kirchhoff's Voltage Law:

Loop CBAHD: $45V = I_3(1\Omega) + I_3(40\Omega) + I_1(30\Omega)$

Loop FEDCBAG: $80V = I_2(1\Omega) + I_2(20\Omega) + 45V + I_3(1\Omega) + I_3(40\Omega)$

Loop FEDHAG: $80V = I_2(1\Omega) + I_2(20\Omega) - I_1(30\Omega)$

Capacitance

A *capacitor* is a device used to store electrical charge. A basic capacitor usually consists of two conductors that are close but not touching. The two conducting plates can be separated by an insulator known as a dielectric, or simply by air.

In diagram (a) below, a parallel plate capacitor has no insulator, and only air is between the plates.

Diagram (b) depicts a variation of the parallel plate capacitor in which there is an insulating material.

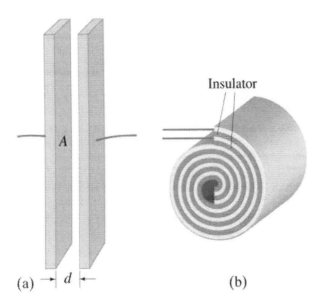

(a)   *d*   (b)

A capacitor's ability to store charge is *capacitance* and is measured in Farads (F).

The capacitance does not depend on the voltage; it is a function of the geometry and materials of the capacitor.

Capacitance is expressed by:

$$C = \frac{Q}{V}$$

where C is the capacitance (F), Q is the charge (J), and V is the voltage (V).

Parallel-plate capacitor

The simplest form of a capacitor is that of the parallel-plate capacitor. It consists, as its name implies, of two conductors in the form of plates, which are parallel and separated by air or a dielectric material.

In the diagrams below, a parallel-plate capacitor is connected to a battery, and the equivalent circuit diagram is on the right.

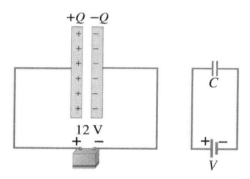

The capacitance of a parallel plate capacitor is expressed as:

$$C = \frac{Q}{V} = \frac{\epsilon_0\, A}{d}$$

where ϵ_0 is the permittivity of space (8.854×10^{-12} F/m), k is the relative permeability of the dielectric material; A is the area of the plates, not the sum of the areas (m^2) and d is the plate separation (m).

The voltage (V) across the capacitor can be found as the product of the electric field between the plates and the plate separation:

$$V = E \times d$$

where E is the electric field between the capacitor (V·m^{-1}).

Dielectrics

A *dielectric* is a non-conductive material that does not readily allow a current to pass through the material. Inserting a dielectric between the plates of a capacitor increases the capacitance by allowing more charge to be stored on the plates of the capacitor. For example, the diagrams below show an air-filled parallel plate capacitor and a dielectric-filled parallel plate capacitor.

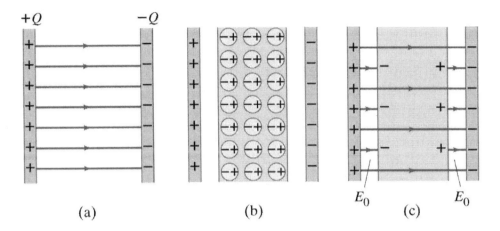

(a)   (b)   (c)

In an air-filled parallel plate capacitor (a), the amount of charge stored is limited by the strength of the electric field between the plates.

In diagram (b) above, if too much charge is stored between the plates, a strong electric field develops which ionizes the air and cause an arc of charge to jump across the plates.

In diagram (c) above, when a dielectric is placed between the plates, the dielectric material becomes polarized (insulator in an electric field) and inhibit the formation of a strong electric field between the plates.

Accordingly, more charge (and thus a higher capacitance) can be stored on the plates before the dielectric material breaks down and allows current to pass through it.

The capacitance of a parallel plate capacitor with a dielectric is expressed as:

$$C = \frac{Q}{V} = \frac{k \, \epsilon_0 \, A}{d}$$

where k is the relative permeability of the dielectric material (unitless).

Energy of charged capacitor

A charged capacitor stores electric energy; the energy stored is equal to the work done to charge the capacitor.

$$U = \frac{1}{2}QV = \frac{1}{2}CV^2 = \frac{1}{2}\frac{Q^2}{C}$$

where U is the potential energy of the charged capacitor (J), Q is the charge stored (magnitude of either $+Q$ or $-Q$ on one of the plates) (C), and C is capacitance (F).

The energy density of the capacitor is defined as the energy of the electric field per unit volume, and can be expressed as:

$$energy\ density = \frac{PE}{volume} = \frac{1}{2}k\,\epsilon_0\,E^2$$

Capacitors in series

Just like resistors, capacitors can be connected in series or parallel in a circuit.

For capacitors in series, the equivalent capacitance is found as the sum of the reciprocals of the individual capacitance:

$$\frac{1}{C_{eq}} = \frac{1}{C_1} + \frac{1}{C_2} + \frac{1}{C_3}$$

$$V = V_{ab}$$

Additionally, all capacitors in series will have the same charge, but the voltage across each capacitor will be different:

$$V_1 \neq V_2 \neq V_3$$

$$Q_1 = Q_2 = Q_3$$

Capacitors in parallel

Capacitors may also be connected in parallel, as depicted below:

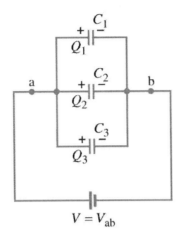

In this example, all the capacitors will have the same voltage, and the equivalent capacitance will be the sum of the individual capacitances.

$$V_1 = V_2 = V_3$$

$$C_{equivalent} = C_1 + C_2 + C_3$$

However, capacitors in parallel will hold different charges:

$$Q_1 \neq Q_2 \neq Q_3$$

Inductors

Inductors are circuit devices that resist changes in current, through the application of Faraday's Law.

Typical inductors consist of coils of wire wrapped around different types of the core material. They operate by producing a back EMF against a change in a current (according to Lenz's Law and Faraday's Law).

The unit for the inductor is the *Henry* (H), and the back EMF produced is:

$$EMF = -L\frac{\Delta I}{\Delta t}$$

where *EMF* is the opposing voltage produced (V), *L* is the inductance of the inductor (H) and $\frac{\Delta I}{\Delta t}$ is the change in current over the change in time (A/s).

The magnetic field produced by an inductor stores energy similar to the electric field of a capacitor.

The energy stored in this magnetic field is expressed as:

$$U = \frac{1}{2} \times \frac{B^2}{\mu_0}$$

where *U* is the stored energy (J), *B* is the magnetic field (T), and μ_0 is the permeability of free space (1.2566×10^{-6} m kg/s^2 A^2)

DC Circuits

RC Circuits

A simple RC circuit consists of a resistor and capacitor in series, connected to a potential difference; the capacitor will begin to charge when the switch is closed, and the circuit forms a complete loop. Below is a diagram of an RC circuit with the switch open.

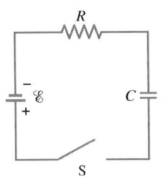

When the switch is closed, the capacitor will begin to charge over time. The voltage across the capacitor increases with time and can be expressed as:

$$V_C = V(1 - e^{-t/RC})$$

where V_C is the voltage across the capacitor (V), V is the potential difference across the circuit (V), t is time (s), R is resistance (Ω), and C is the capacitance (F).

The charge follows a similar curve:

$$Q_C = CV_b(1 - e^{-t/RC})$$

where $V_b = V_R + V_C$. V_R is the voltage across the resistor (V), and Q_C is the charge across the capacitor (C).

The current through the circuit is the same everywhere (series circuit) and is expressed as:

$$I = \frac{V_b}{R}(e)^{-t/RC}$$

where I is the current through the circuit (A).

This curve has a characteristic time constant:

$$\tau = RC$$

where τ is the time constant (s).

The graphs below display the voltage across the charging capacitor and current across the circuit. Diagram (b) illustrates the growth curve of voltage over time. Notice that the capacitor reaches 63% voltage in one time constant and is ~100% voltage after three-time constants. Diagram (c) displays the decay in current over time. Notice that after one time constant, the current is 37% of its original value (t = 0 seconds), and after three-time constants, the current is nearly zero amps.

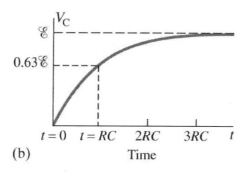

(b)

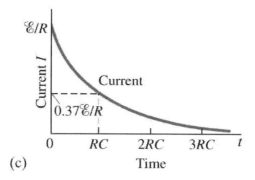

(c)

During the discharge of a capacitor, the capacitor acts as a battery and drives current flow, which decreases with time as the capacitor discharges. In this case, the capacitor voltage decays and is expressed as:

$$V_C = V_0(e)^{-t/RC}$$

where V_0 is the charged voltage across the capacitor (V).

The charge through the discharging capacitor follows a similar decay and is expressed as:

$$Q = CV_0(e)^{-t/RC}$$

The current in the circuit when the capacitor is discharging is expressed as:

$$I = \frac{V_0}{R}(e)^{-t/RC}$$

When the capacitor is discharging, the voltage, charge and current all follow a similar decay curve.

The figure below gives the voltage decay curve of a discharging capacitor. Although this curve represents the voltage, both the charge and current would have exponential decay curves that follow this pattern.

Also notice that by one time constant the voltage, charge, and current would be at 37% of the max value ($t = 0$ seconds), and by three-time constants, all three will have decayed to nearly zero.

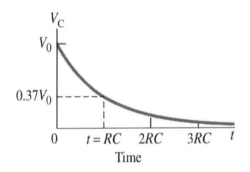

LR Circuits

A simple *LR circuit* consists of an inductor in series with a resistor, connected to a potential difference. In this configuration the inductor will resist change in current through the circuit, therefore causing a gradual, rather than abrupt, rise in current when the loop is closed. After a period, the current will remain steady and be equal to that if the circuit were a resistor alone (assuming ideal inductor with no resistance).

Below is a figure of an LR circuit with a switch that can either connect or disconnect the circuit to a potential difference.

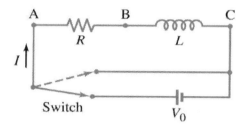

When the switch is initially open such that there is no potential difference, there will be no current through the circuit. When the switch is closed, the voltage across the capacitor is:

$$V_L = V_b e^{-tR/L}$$

where V_L is the voltage across the inductor (V), R is the resistance of the resistor (Ω), and L is the inductance of the inductor (H).

$V_b = V_L + V_R$ and V_R is the voltage across the resistor (V)

The current across the circuit is expressed as:

$$I = \left(\frac{V_b}{R}\right)(1 - e^{-tR/L})$$

where I is the current across the circuit (A).

The time constant of an LR circuit is:

$$\tau = \frac{L}{R}$$

where τ is the time constant (s).

The growth curve of the current through the circuit seen below.

Although it is not displayed, the maximum current is reached in approximately three-time constants (like the RC circuit), and after one time constant, the circuit has reached 63% of its maximum current.

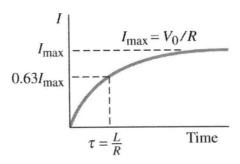

If the switch is opened, such that the potential difference is no longer across the circuit, but the circuit remains closed, the current will decay according to:

$$I = I_{max}e^{-t/\tau}$$

In this case, the current will decay from its maximum value, and after one time constant will be at 37% of its maximum; after three-time constants, the circuit will have approximately zero current through it.

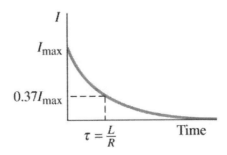

Alternating Currents and Reactive Circuits

As mentioned in the introduction to this chapter, the current provided by a battery flows steadily in one direction. This is where *direct current* (DC), gets its name. However, the power supplied by an electrical generation plant is always delivered in alternating current. The two figures below demonstrate DC vs. AC systems.

Diagram (a) shows a DC system in which the current is held steadily over time.

Conversely, in diagram (b) the current varies sinusoidally, and the result is *alternating current.*

An alternating current may vary as a function of a square wave or triangular wave. However, in the majority of applications, the current is supplied as a sinusoidal function.

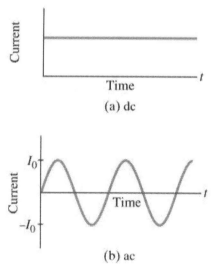

The sinusoidal variation in current can be expressed as a function of the frequency:

$$I = I_0 \sin \omega t = I_0 \sin 2\pi f t$$

where I_0 is the max current (amplitude) given in (A), ω is the frequency (rad/s) and f is the frequency (Hz).

Like current, the voltage varies in a sinusoidal motion when graphed against time:

$$V = V_0 \sin 2\pi f t = V_0 \sin \omega t$$

where V_0 is the max voltage (amplitude) given in (V).

The power delivered is the multiplication of the current squared and the voltage:

$$P = IV = I(IR) = I^2 R = I^2_0 R \sin^2 \omega t$$

Usually, the average power is of most interest, which can be found using:

$$\bar{P} = \frac{1}{2} I^2_0 R = \frac{1}{2} \frac{V^2_0}{R}$$

where $\bar{P}$ is the average power (W) and R is the resistance (Ω).

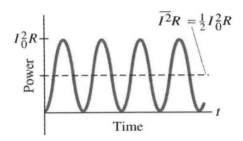

The current and voltage both have average values of zero. Thus they are expressed as root-mean-square values, which can be calculated by:

$$I_{rms} = \sqrt{I^2} = \frac{I_0}{\sqrt{2}} = 0.707 \, I_0$$

$$V_{rms} = \sqrt{V^2} = \frac{V_0}{\sqrt{2}} = 0.707 \, V_0$$

where I_{rms} is the root-mean-square current (A), and V_{rms} is root-mean-square voltage (V).

Ohm's Law can then be rewritten using the root-mean-square values:

$$V_{rms} = I_{rms} R$$

The average power can also be found using the root-mean-square values:

$$P_{avg} = I_{rms} V_{rms} = I^2_{rms} R$$

LRC Circuits

Resistors, capacitors, and inductors have different phase relationships between current and voltage when placed in an AC circuit instead of a DC circuit.

Below is a diagram of a simple AC circuit with an inductor, resistor, and capacitor (LRC circuit):

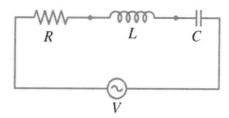

Unlike DC circuits, the current vs. voltage through the different elements of an LRC circuit is time-dependent. As such, the unique characteristics of each element must be known before the entire circuit can be analyzed.

For example, the current through a resistor in an AC circuit is in phase with the voltage, meaning both change sign at the same time.

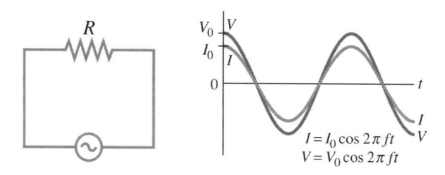

$$I = I_0 \cos 2\pi ft$$
$$V = V_0 \cos 2\pi ft$$

The phase relationship between current and voltage in inductors is different.

Inductors resist changes in current; the current lags behind the voltage by 90°.

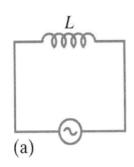

(a)

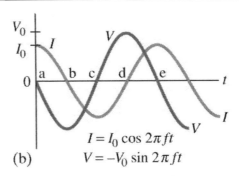

(b)

$I = I_0 \cos 2\pi ft$

$V = -V_0 \sin 2\pi ft$

Conversely, the capacitor's current leads the voltage by 90°.

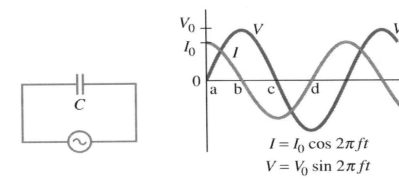

$I = I_0 \cos 2\pi ft$

$V = V_0 \sin 2\pi ft$

Because both the inductor and capacitor have phase differences concerning the voltage of their effective resistance (ratio of voltage to current), the root-mean-square current is calculated differently.

The *reactance* is the effective resistance of an inductor or capacitor and is given by:

$$X_L = \omega L = 2\pi f L$$

where X_L is the reactance of the inductor (Ω).

The reactance of the capacitor (X_C) is given by:

$$X_c = \frac{1}{\omega C} = \frac{1}{2\pi f C}$$

where X_c is the reactance of the capacitor (Ω).

Note that both of these equations depend on frequency. From the ratio of voltage to current, the effective resistance (the *impedance*) of the circuit is given by:

$$Z = \sqrt{R^2 + (X_L - X_C)^2}$$

where Z is the impedance (Ω).

The root-mean-square current in an AC circuit is:

$$I_{rms} = \frac{V_{rms}}{Z} = \frac{V_{rms}}{\sqrt{R^2 + (2\pi f L - \frac{1}{2\pi f C})^2}}$$

I_{rms} depends on the frequency.

I_{rms} is at a maximum when $X_c = X_L$; the frequency at which this occurs is:

$$f_0 = \frac{1}{2\pi} \sqrt{\frac{1}{LC}}$$

where f_0 is the resonant frequency of the circuit (Hz).

This is the *resonant frequency*.

The figure below illustrates the current peak at the resonant frequency for large resistances and small resistances:

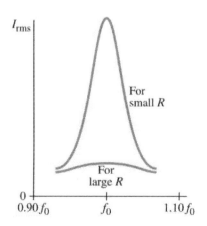

Transformers and Transmission of Power

Power is transmitted in alternating current for various reasons, but a significant factor is the reduced power losses through power lines when transporting the electricity. If electricity were transported at high current, the result would be large Ohmic power losses through the power lines themselves. These losses are reduced by transporting electricity at high voltages rather than higher currents. This is because according to the power loss equation:

$$P = I^2 R$$

However, how can the voltage be manipulated such that the electricity is transported at high voltage, and then reduced to lower voltages for the consumer? This is possible through an electrical device of a *transformer*. Transformers work only if the current is changing; this is an important reason why electricity is transmitted as AC.

A transformer operates according to Faraday's Law of electromagnetic induction and can step-up or step-down the voltage through a line, allowing power companies to reduce power loss during electricity delivery. The device consists of an iron core around which an input wire and output wire are wrapped around.

In a step-up transformer (increase voltage) the input wire will have a few primary coils around the iron core, whereas the output wire will have many secondary coils. When an AC runs through the input coil, the changing current (sinusoidal variation in current) will induce a magnetic field in the iron core.

The magnetic field will loop through the iron core and induce a voltage in the output wire wrapped around the core. The output voltage will be proportional to the number of coils it has wrapped around the core.

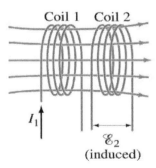

The figure below shows a basic power delivery system. The power station generates electricity, which it sends through a step-up transformer to reduce power loss in transit. The electricity runs the high voltage transmission line to a step-down transformer near the consumer.

The electricity is then sent to homes on low voltage lines, where a final step-down transformer lowers the voltage to 240 volts.

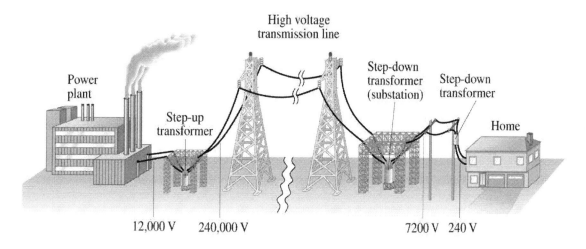

The ratio of the voltages in the primary and secondary coils of a transformer is equal to the ratio of the number of turns in each coil:

$$\frac{V_s}{V_P} = \frac{N_S}{N_P}$$

where V_s is the voltage through the secondary (V), V_P is the voltage through the primary (V), N_S is the number of turns in the secondary and N_P is the number of turns in the primary.

Given that power can be found by calculating the product of voltage (V) and current (I), the input power in the primary coil must equal the output power in the secondary coil; this can be found through the relationship:

$$V_p I_p = V_s I_s$$

where I_p is the current through the primary coils (A) and I_s is the current through the secondary coils (A).

Energy must be conserved; therefore, in an ideal system, the ratio of the currents must be the inverse of the ratio of turns:

$$\frac{I_P}{I_S} = \frac{N_S}{N_P}$$

For example, the diagram below is of a step-up transformer. These types of transformer are used at power-generating stations to increase the voltage of the power lines, to reduce Ohmic losses in the lines.

Notice that the primary coil has far fewer turns than the secondary coil.

Accordingly, the voltage through the secondary coil will be much higher, and the electricity can be sent down power lines at a higher voltage with less power loss.

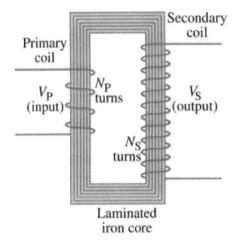

Measuring Devices

Electric meters are instruments used to measure various aspects of an electric circuit. There are many types; however, the ammeter and the voltmeter are two of the most commonly used.

Ammeters

An *ammeter* is a device used to measure the current through a circuit. Ammeters usually have two connecting electrodes that are placed alongside the point in the circuit where current is to be measured. A current passes through the ammeter and is recorded and displayed. It is important that an ammeter should have almost no resistance within it. This is because the current in the circuit passes through the ammeter, so the ammeter needs to have low resistance as not to affect the current.

An older but accurate ammeter is the galvanometer. The figure below displays a typical galvanometer setup. The two electrodes are placed at a point in the circuit, and current flows through them. As the current passes through the coil, it creates a magnetic field whose direction depends upon the direction of the flow of current.

The permanent magnets on the side of the coil produce a torque about the coil, which then rotates to display the measured current against a calibrated dial.

The symbol for an ammeter in a circuit diagram is below:

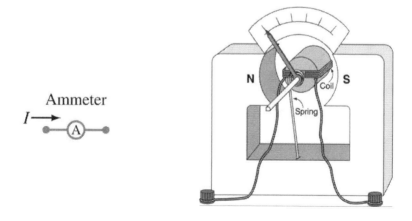

Ammeter

Voltmeters

Voltmeters measure the voltage through two points within a circuit.

Like ammeters, they have two connecting electrodes, which are placed on either side of the element to be measured.

However, voltmeters are designed such that they have infinitely high resistance, theoretically pushing all the current through the circuit element and not letting any flow through the voltmeter.

The figure below depicts a voltmeter connected across opposite sides of a resistor to measure the voltage through it.

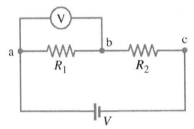

Ohmmeter

An *ohmmeter* is a device used to measure electrical resistance.

Unlike ammeters and voltmeters, it has a battery that allows it to pass current through resistive elements to measure their resistance.

The figure below depicts an ohmmeter symbol:

Chapter Summary

Electric Potential

- Electric potential is potential energy per unit charge: $V_a = \frac{PE_a}{q}$

- A source of EMF transforms energy from some other form to electrical energy.

- A battery is a source of constant potential difference.

- Electric potential of a point charge: $V = k\frac{Q}{r}$ [single point charge V=0 at r=∞] $= \frac{1}{4\pi\epsilon_0}\frac{Q}{r}$

- Kirchhoff's rules:

  - sum of currents entering a junction equals the sum of currents leaving.

  - total potential difference around a closed loop is zero.

Magnetic Fields and Flux

- Magnetic flux: $\Phi_B = B_\perp A = BA\cos(\theta)$

- Changing magnetic flux induces EMF: $\mathcal{E} = -N\frac{\Delta\Phi_B}{\Delta t}$

- An induced EMF produces current that opposes original flux change.

- A changing magnetic field produces an electric field.

- Energy density stored in a magnetic field: $u = energy\ density = \frac{1}{2}\times\frac{B^2}{\mu_0}$

Transformers

- Transformers use induction to change voltage: $\frac{V_S}{V_P} = \frac{N_S}{N_P}$

- Mutual inductance: $\mathcal{E}_2 = -M\frac{\Delta I_1}{\Delta t},\ \mathcal{E}_1 = -M\frac{\Delta I_2}{\Delta t}$

Circuits

- Electric current is the rate of flow of electric charge.

- Conventional current is in the direction that positive charge would flow.

- A direct current is constant.

- An alternating current varies sinusoidally:

$$I = \frac{V}{R} = \frac{V_0}{R} \sin \omega t = I_0 \sin \omega t$$

- Power in an electric circuit: $P = IV$

- An RC circuit has a characteristic time constant: $\tau = RC$

Resistance

- Resistance is the ratio of voltage to current: $V = IR$

- Ohmic materials have constant resistance, independent of voltage.

- Resistance is determined by shape and material:

$$R = \rho l / A, \ (\rho \text{ is the resistivity})$$

- A battery is a source of EMF in parallel with an internal resistance.

- Resistors in series: $R_{eq} = R_1 + R_2 + R_3$

- Resistors in parallel: $\dfrac{1}{R_{eq}} = \dfrac{1}{R_1} + \dfrac{1}{R_2} + \dfrac{1}{R_3}$

Capacitance

- Capacitors are non-touching conductors carrying an equal and opposite charge.

- Capacitance is given by the equation: $Q = CV$

- The capacitance of a parallel-plate capacitor is $C = \epsilon_0 \frac{A}{d}$

- A dielectric is an insulator (usually used between the plates of a parallel-plate capacitor)

- Dielectric constant gives a ratio of total field to an external field.

- Energy density in electric field: $energy\ density = \frac{PE}{volume} = \frac{1}{2} \epsilon_0 E^2$

- Capacitors in parallel:

  o $V = C_{eq} V = C_1 V + C_2 V + C_3 V = (C_1 + C_2 + C_3)V$

  o $C_{eq} = C_1 + C_2 + C_3$

- Capacitors in series:

  o $\frac{Q}{C_{eq}} = \frac{Q}{C_1} + \frac{Q}{C_2} + \frac{Q}{C_3} = Q\left(\frac{1}{C_1} + \frac{1}{C_2} + \frac{1}{C_3}\right)$

  o $\frac{1}{C_{eq}} = \frac{1}{C_1} + \frac{1}{C_2} + \frac{1}{C_3}$

Average RMS

- Current: $I_{rms} = \sqrt{\overline{I^2}} = \frac{I_0}{\sqrt{2}} = 0.707\ I_0$

- Voltage: $V_{rms} = \sqrt{\overline{V^2}} = \frac{V_0}{\sqrt{2}} = 0.707\ V_0$

- $I = \frac{\Delta Q}{\Delta t} = neAv_{\text{d}}$

- LRC series circuit: $z = \sqrt{R^2 + (X_L - X_c)^2}$

Notes

Practice Questions

1. Two parallel circular plates with radii 7 mm carrying equal-magnitude surface charge densities of ± 3 $\mu C/m^2$ are separated by a distance of 1 mm. How much stored energy do the plates have? (Use dielectric constant $k = 1$ and electric permittivity $\varepsilon_0 = 8.854 \times 10^{-12}$ F/m)

    A. 226 nJ   **C.** 127 nJ

    B. 17 nJ   **D.** 78 nJ   **E.** 33 nJ

2. The potential difference between the plates of a parallel plate capacitor is 75 V. The magnitude of the charge on each plate is 3.5 μC. What is the capacitance of the capacitor?

    A. 116×10^{-6} F   **C.** 0.7×10^{-6} F

    B. 37×10^{-6} F   **D.** 478×10^{-6} F

                                      E. 4.7×10^{-8} F

3. An electron is released from rest at a distance of 5 cm from a proton. How fast will the electron be moving when it is 2 cm from the proton? (Use Coulomb's constant $k = 9 \times 10^9$ $N \cdot m^2/C^2$, the mass of an electron $= 9.1 \times 10^{-31}$ kg, the charge of an electron $= -1.6 \times 10^{-19}$ C and the charge of a proton $= 1.6 \times 10^{-19}$ C)

    A. 92 m/s   **C.** 147 m/s

    B. 123 m/s   **D.** 1.3×10^3 m/s

                                      E. 4.8×10^5 m/s

4. A current of 5 A flows through an electrical device for 12 seconds. How many electrons flow through this device during this time? (Use the charge of an electron $= -1.6 \times 10^{-19}$ C)

    A. 5.2×10^{18} electrons   **C.** 6.3×10^{19} electrons

    B. 3.8×10^{20} electrons   **D.** 1.2×10^{8} electrons

                                        E. 9.1×10^{14} electrons

5. 1 mm separates two parallel plates. If the potential difference between them is 3 V, what is the magnitude of their surface charge densities? (Use the electric permittivity $\varepsilon_0 = 8.854 \times 10^{-12}$ F/m)

    A. 64×10^{-9} C/m^2 **C.** 27×10^{-9} C/m^2

    B. 33×10^{-9} C/m^2 **D.** 16×10^{-9} C/m^2

                                        E. 76×10^{-9} C/m^2

6. A 3 Ω resistor is connected in parallel with a 6 Ω resistor; both resistors are connected in series with a 4 Ω resistor, and all three resistors are connected to an 18 V battery as shown. If 3 Ω resistor burnt out and exhibits infinite resistance, which of the following is true?

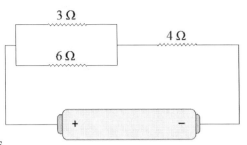

    A. The power dissipated in the circuit increases
    B. The current provided by the battery remains the same
    C. The current in the 6 Ω resistor decreases
    D. The current in the 4 Ω resistor decreases to zero
    E. The current in the 6 Ω resistor increases

7. Each plate of a parallel-plate air capacitor has an area of 0.005 m^2, and the separation of the plates is 0.08 mm. What is the potential difference across the capacitor when an electric field of 5.6×10^6 V/m is present between the plates?

    A. 367 V   **B.** 578 V   **C.** 448 V   **D.** 227 V   **E.** 834 V

8. What is the current in a wire if a total of 2.3×10^{13} electrons pass a given point in a wire in 15 s? (Use the charge of an electron $= -1.6 \times 10^{-19}$ C)

    A. 0.25 μA   **B.** 3.2 μA   **C.** 7.1 μA   **D.** 1.3 μA   **E.** 0.88 μA

9. The resistivity of gold is 2.44×10^{-8} Ω·m at a temperature of 20 °C. A gold wire, 0.6 mm in diameter and 48 cm long, carries a current of 340 mA. What is the number of electrons per second passing a given cross-section of the wire? (Use charge of an electron $= -1.6 \times 10^{-19}$ C)

    A. 2.1×10^{18} electrons   **C.** 1.2×10^{22} electrons
    B. 2.8×10^{14} electrons   **D.** 2.4×10^{17} electrons   **E.** 6.3×10^{15} electrons

10. When the frequency of the AC voltage across a capacitor is doubled, the capacitive reactance of that capacitor will:

    A. become zero   **C.** increase to 4 times its original value
    B. decrease to ½ its original value   **D.** decrease to ¼ its original value
                                           E. increase to 2 times its original value

11. A charged particle of mass 0.006 kg is subjected to a 6 T magnetic field, which acts at a right angle to its motion. If the particle moves in a circle of radius 0.1 m at a speed of 3 m/s, what is the magnitude of the charge on the particle?

    A. 3 C   **B.** 30 C   **C.** 3.6 C   **D.** 0.03 C   **E.** 1.8 C

12. When a current flows through a metal wire, the moving charges are:

    I. protons   II. neutrons   III. electrons

    A. I only   **B.** II only   **C.** III only   **D.** I and II only   **E.** I and III only

13. A kilowatt-hour is equivalent to:

    A. 3.6×10^6 J/s   **C.** 3.6×10^3 W

    B. 3.6×10^6 J   **D.** 3.6×10^3 J   **E.** 3.6×10^3 J/s

14. For the graph shown, what physical quantity does the slope of the graph represent?

    A. 1 / Voltage

    B. Resistance

    C. Power

    D. Charge

    E. 1 / Resistance

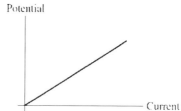

15. What is the voltage across a 15 Ω resistor that has 5 A current passing through it?

    A. 3 V   **B.** 5 V   **C.** 15 V   **D.** 30 V   **E.** 75 V

Solutions

1. D is correct. Find the area:

$$A = \pi r^2$$

$$A = \pi (7 \times 10^{-3} \text{ m})^2$$

$$A = 1.54 \times 10^{-4} \text{ m}^2$$

Find the capacitance:

$$C = A\mathcal{E}_o k / d$$

$$C = [(1.54 \times 10^{-4} \text{ m}^2){\cdot}(8.854 \times 10^{-12} \text{ F/m}){\cdot}(1)] / (1 \times 10^{-3} \text{ m})$$

$$C = 1.36 \times 10^{-12} \text{ F}$$

Find the charge:

$$\sigma = 3 \times 10^{-6} \text{ C/m}^2$$

$$\sigma = Q / A$$

$$Q = \sigma A$$

$$Q = (3 \times 10^{-6} \text{ C/m}^2){\cdot}(1.54 \times 10^{-4} \text{ m}^2)$$

$$Q = 4.6 \times 10^{-10} \text{ C}$$

Find the potential energy:

$$U = \tfrac{1}{2}Q^2 / C$$

$$U = \tfrac{1}{2}(4.6 \times 10^{-10} \text{ C})^2 / (1.36 \times 10^{-12} \text{ F})$$

$$U = 78 \times 10^{-9} \text{ J}$$

2. E is correct.

Use the relationship:

$$Q = CV$$

$$C = Q / V$$

$$C = (3.5 \times 10^{-6} \text{ C}) / (75 \text{ V})$$

$$C = 4.7 \times 10^{-8} \text{ F}$$

3. B is correct.

Use the energy relationship:

$$PE_{before} = PE_{after} + KE$$

Electrostatic Potential Energy:

$$PE = kQq / r$$

Solve:

$$kQq / r_1 = kQq / r_2 + \tfrac{1}{2}mv^2$$

$$\tfrac{1}{2}mv^2 = kQq(1 / r_1 - 1 / r_2)$$

$$v^2 = (2kQq / m)\cdot(1 / r_1 - 1 / r_2)$$

$$v = \sqrt{[(2kQq / m)\cdot(1 / r_1 - 1 / r_2)]}$$

$$v = \sqrt{[(2)\cdot(9 \times 10^9 \text{ N·m}^2/\text{C}^2)\cdot(1.6 \times 10^{-19} \text{ C})\cdot(1.6 \times 10^{-19} \text{ C}) /}$$

$$(9.1 \times 10^{-31} \text{ kg})]\cdot[(1 / 0.02 \text{ m}) - (1 / 0.05 \text{ m})]$$

$$v = 123 \text{ m/s}$$

Note: only the magnitude of the charge is used.

4. B is correct. 1 amp = 1 C/s

$\quad$ # of electrons = $(5 \text{ C/s})\cdot(12 \text{ s} / 1)\cdot(1 \text{ electron} / 1.6 \times 10^{-19} \text{ C})$

$\quad$ # of electrons = 3.8×10^{20} electrons

5. C is correct.

$$Q = A\mathcal{E}_0 V / d$$

$$Q / A = \mathcal{E}_0 V / d$$

$$Q / A = (8.854 \times 10^{-12} \text{ F/m})\cdot(3 \text{ V}) / (1 \times 10^3 \text{ m})$$

$$Q / A = 27 \times 10^{-9} \text{ C/m}^2$$

6. E is correct. The equivalent resistance of the 3 Ω and 6 Ω resistors is:

$$1 / R_{eq} = 1 / (3 \ \Omega) + 1 / (6 \ \Omega)$$

$$R_{eq} = 2 \ \Omega$$

The voltage across the equivalent resistor (i.e., the 6 Ω resistor) is given by the voltage divider relationship:

$$V_6 = 18 \ V \, (2 \ \Omega) / (2 \ \Omega + 4 \ \Omega) = 6 \ V$$

The current through the 6 Ω resistor is:

$$I_6 = V_6 / 6 \ \Omega = 1 \ A$$

After the 3 Ω resistor burns out, the voltage across the 6 Ω resistor is again found using the voltage divider relationship:

$$V_6' = 18 \ V \ (6 \ \Omega) \ / \ (6 \ \Omega \ + \ 4 \ \Omega) = 10.8 \ V$$

Now the current through the 6 Ω resistor is:

$$I_6' = V_6' \ / \ 6 \ \Omega = 1.8 \ A$$

The current has increased.

7. C is correct. Parallel-plate capacitor voltage:

$$V = Ed$$

$$V = (5.6 \times 10^6 \ \text{V/m}) \cdot (0.08 \times 10^{-3} \ \text{m})$$

$$V = 448 \ V$$

8. A is correct.

1 amp = 1 C/s

$$I = (2.3 \times 10^{13} \ \text{electrons} \ / \ 1) \cdot (1.6 \times 10^{-19} \ \text{C} \ / \ 1 \ \text{electron}) \cdot (1 \ / \ 15 \ \text{s})$$

$$I = 0.25 \times 10^{-6} \ \text{amps}$$

$$I = 0.25 \ \mu A$$

9. A is correct. Use the definition of one ampere:

1 amp = 1 C/s

Let the current expressed in electrons per second be denoted by I_e.

Solve:

$$I_e = (340 \times 10^{-3} \ \text{C} \ / \ 1 \ \text{s}) \cdot (1 \ \text{electron} \ / \ 1.6 \times 10^{-19} \ \text{C})$$

$$I_e = 2.1 \times 10^{18} \ \text{electrons/s}$$

10. B is correct. Capacitive Reactance formula: $X_c = 1 \ / \ (2\pi Cf)$

If f is doubled:

$$X_{c2} = 1 \ / \ [2\pi C(2f)]$$

$$X_{c2} = \tfrac{1}{2}[1 \ / \ (2\pi Cf)]$$

$$X_{c2} = \tfrac{1}{2}X_c$$

Capacitive reactance is halved.

11. D is correct.

Find forces acting on particle:

$$F_{centripetal} = F_{magnetic}$$

$$ma_{centripetal} = qvB$$

$$mv^2 / r = qvB$$

$$q = mv / Br$$

$$q = (0.006 \text{ kg}) \cdot (3 \text{ m/s}) / (6 \text{ T}) \cdot (0.1 \text{ m})$$

$$q = 0.03 \text{ C}$$

12. C is correct. In a solid, the locations of the nuclei are fixed; only the electrons move.

13. B is correct.

$$1 \text{ kW} = 1,000 \text{ W}$$

$$1,000 \text{ W} = 1,000 \text{ J/s}$$

$$1 \text{ hr} = (60 \text{ min}) \cdot (60 \text{ sec/min})$$

$$1 \text{ hr} = 3,600 \text{ s}$$

$$\text{kW} \cdot \text{hr} = (1,000 \text{ J/s}) \cdot (3,600 \text{ s})$$

$$\text{kW} \cdot \text{hr} = 3.6 \times 10^3 \text{ J}$$

14. B is correct.

$$V = IR$$

$$R = V / I$$

15. E is correct. Voltage = current × resistance

$$V = IR$$

$$V = (5 \text{ A}) \cdot (15 \text{ } \Omega)$$

$$V = 75 \text{ V}$$

Please, leave your Customer Review on Amazon

Notes

Chapter 9

Light and Optics

LIGHT

- Visual Spectrum
- Double Slit Diffraction
- Diffraction Grating
- Single Slit Diffraction
- Thin Films
- Other Diffraction Phenomena, X-Ray Diffraction
- Polarization of Light
- Doppler Effect

OPTICS

- Reflection from Plane Surface
- Refraction, Refractive Index N, Snell's Law
- Dispersion
- Conditions for Total Internal Reflection
- Mirrors
- Thin Lenses
- Combination of Lenses
- Lens Aberration
- Optical Instruments

Notes

Visual Spectrum

The visible light spectrum is an important topic within physics because it contributes extensively to the way humans perceive and interact with the world. For example, red stop signs, masterpiece paintings, and glasses are just a couple of objects that characterize the diverse range that visible light occupies in life.

As stated earlier, electromagnetic radiation is a form of energy that consists of oscillating electric and magnetic fields, without any need of a medium to propagate.

Visible light is a thin spectrum of electromagnetic radiation that humans can perceive as different colors. For perspective, the electromagnetic radiation spectrum spans from long radio waves to high energy gamma rays with wavelengths ranging from 10^4 m to 10^{-14} m, respectively. Out of this spectrum, the human eye can only perceive a narrow range of wavelengths between 400 nm to 750 nm. This range is the *visible light spectrum* and consists of all the different colors that humans can see.

Light of different frequencies is perceived as different colors. The figure below depicts the visible light range with respect to frequency, wavelength, and color. Lower frequency light consists of red, orange and yellow hues, while higher frequency light consists of greens, blues, and violets. Not only do different frequencies give different color, but the different frequencies of light give more or less energy (remember $E = hf$).

An easy way to remember the spectrum of visible light, with respect to increasing frequency (and thus energy), is by the mnemonic ROYGBIV. This stands for the lowest frequency light (red), through orange, yellow, green, blue, indigo and up to the highest frequency (highest energy) light – violet.

The sun, candles, and light bulbs are a few examples of objects that emit light. However, most objects absorb and reflect light, but do not emit light. When an object is perceived to be a certain color, it is usually not emitting light, but rather reflecting that specific frequency of light.

Likewise, if an object absorbs specific frequencies of light, those colors would not be visible at all. This is an important distinction because it determines the perceived colors of most objects.

For example, sunlight is considered white light, because it contains all the frequencies within the visible light spectrum. Therefore, it is perceived as white.

Similarly, a white tablecloth reflects all frequencies of the visible range and is perceived as white.

If the tablecloth were red, however, then that cloth reflects predominately red light.

A black tablecloth absorbs every color, and therefore, it is perceived as black.

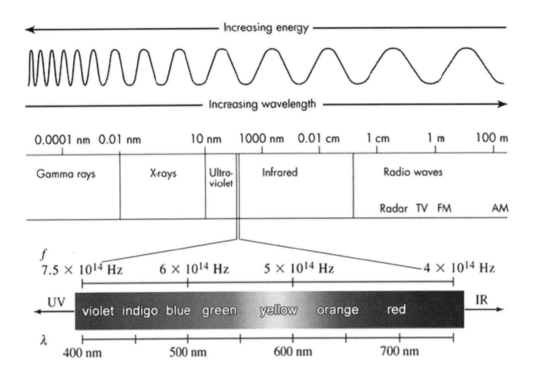

The sky is blue because of *Rayleigh scattering* (when the blue light gets scattered in the atmosphere). Sunlight hits the nitrogen and oxygen molecules and gets bounced around; it is reemitted at a high frequency.

Violet scatters the most, and then on down the spectrum to red. Because human eyes are not very violet-sensitive, the next color down on the spectrum (blue) is perceived.

This scattering process is affected by the composition of the atmosphere. In the Mediterranean areas where the air is dry, a deep blue is seen. When dust, water vapor or other large particles are present, the light of lower frequency is scattered, and the sky appears paler or hazier. In large cities, smog makes particles so large that they absorb light instead of scattering it, giving off a brownish haze.

Sunsets appear red because red, orange and yellow are transmitted better than colors at the other end of the visible light spectrum. When the sun is lower on the horizon, its light has to travel through the largest distance of the Earth's atmosphere.

The more atmosphere it travels through, the more that violet and blue are scattered, causing red to be perceived more intensely.

Primary Colors

Yellow, blue and green are considered the "primary" colors because they are detected by the eye independent of intensity but based instead on frequencies and the ocular receptors.

If any two of these colors are added together, all of the other colors can be made.

Red + blue = magenta

Red + green = yellow

Blue + green = cyan

If two secondary colors are added together, and they create white, they are complementary.

Magenta + green = white (magenta = red + blue)

Double Slit Diffraction

Like all waves, visible light can constructively and destructively interfere. This was famously observed in an iconic experiment of Young's *double slit diffraction experiment.* This experiment proved that light was indeed a wave, as it displayed the wave property of interference. Also, this helped establish the wave nature of light in the particle-wave duality disagreement of the time.

Observe the figure below of the double slit diffraction experiment. Two slits, S1 and S2, are positioned on an opaque wall, such that the distance between them is known. A viewing screen is also placed a known distance away from the wall with the slits. When a light source is shone at the wall with the slits, the expected behavior of light, according to particle theory, seen in diagram (b) below. In reality, the light that passes through the slits will constructively and destructively interfere, producing the pattern seen in diagram (c).

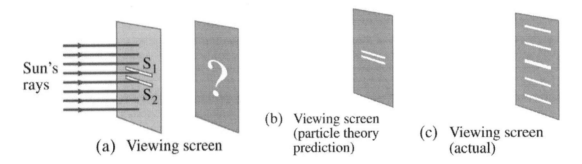

This result proves that light is indeed a wave because the resulting pattern is consistent with interference patterns seen in waves. The interference occurs because each point on the screen is not the same distance from both slits. Depending on the path length difference, the wave can interfere constructively (leaving a bright spot on the wall) or destructively (leaving a dark spot on the wall), as in the figure below.

Diagrams (a, b) below illustrate constructive interference spots on the viewing screen. At these points, the light waves coming through the screen are in phase and constructively interfere.

Notice in the diagram (b) that the wave from the lower slit traveled an extra wavelength compared to the upper wave. This is the path length difference and is important in identifying if a spot will be bright or dark (constructive or destructive).

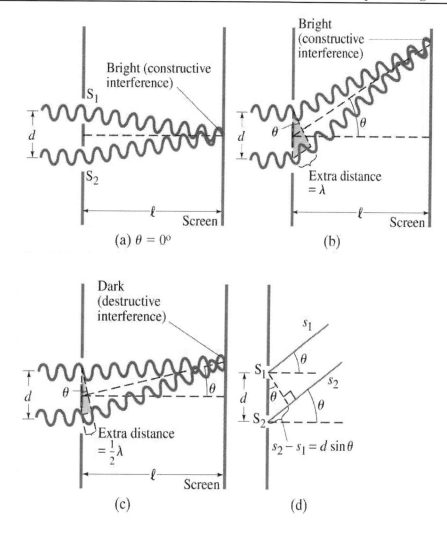

Geometry is used to find the conditions for constructive and destructive interference:

$$d \sin \theta \;=\; m\lambda, \qquad m \;=\; 0, 1, 2, \cdots. \qquad \left[\begin{array}{c} \text{constructive} \\ \text{interference} \\ \text{(bright)} \end{array}\right]$$

The occurrence of bright and dark spots can be predicted by the equation:

$$d \sin \theta = m\lambda$$

where d is the slit separation distance (m), θ is the angle of the bright or dark spot with respect to the center between the two slits (degrees), λ is the wavelength of the light passing through the slits (m), and m is the order value and determines whether or not the spot will be bright or dark (constructive or destructive interference).

If $m = 0,1,2,3\ldots$ then the interference will be constructive, and the spot will be bright.

If $m = \frac{1}{2}, \frac{3}{2}, \frac{5}{2} \dots$ then the interference will be destructive and the spot will be dark.

The figure below depicts the relation of the order number to constructive interference spots and destructive interference spots.

The maxima represent constructive interference.

The minima represent destructive interference.

Although only the order values for constructive interference are shown; the values for destructive interference occur between these.

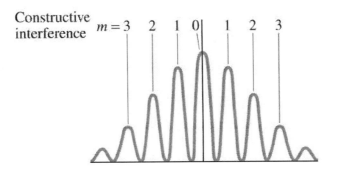

Diffraction Grating

A *diffraction grating* is similar to the double slit experiment except that instead of two slits, the grating has many slits close together. Diffraction gratings operate via the same principle as the double slit experiment, and the equation for a diffraction grating interference spots is the same as the double-slit experiment, including order values for destructive and constructive interference.

However, diffraction gratings are better able to separate wavelengths of incoming light than a double slit. Additionally, the peaks of the maxima from a diffraction grate will be much sharper and more pronounced than those of a double slit.

Observe the two figures below of a double slit maxima pattern and a diffraction grating maxima pattern.

The figure on the left is the maxima pattern produced by double slits.

The figure on the right is the maxima pattern for the diffraction grating.

Notice the sharper peaks of the maxima produced by the diffraction grating, and that the order values are the same as for the double slit.

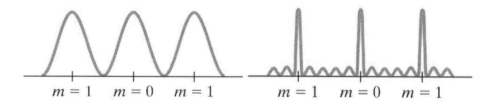

$m = 1 \quad m = 0 \quad m = 1 \qquad m = 1 \quad m = 0 \quad m = 1$

Single Slit Diffraction

Single slit diffraction is another method of diffraction where light is passed through a single slit, and the resulting diffraction pattern can be observed. Like other diffraction techniques, single slit diffraction is the result of interference of the incoming wave as it bends around the slit through which it passes.

Unlike double slit and diffraction grates, the maxima pattern produced by single slit diffraction does not follow the same order values or equation. This is because the light waves in single slit diffraction are in-phase (constructive) and out-of-phase (destructive) at different points than diffraction grates and double slit diffraction.

The maxima of the diffraction pattern are defined by:

$$a \sin (\theta) = m\lambda$$

where a is the width of the slit (m).

If $m = 0, \frac{3}{2}, \frac{5}{2} \dots$ then the interference will be constructive and the spot will be bright.

If $m = 1, 2, 3 \dots$ then the interference will be destructive, and the spot will be dark.

The diffraction pattern of single slit diffraction will also be slightly different.

The figure below compares the diffraction patterns produced by the three diffraction methods.

The single slit diffraction pattern produces the widest maxima; all subsequent maxima after the m = 0 value are substantially reduced.

The pattern produced by the diffraction grating and double slit are sharper and do not fade nearly as much after the m = 0 value.

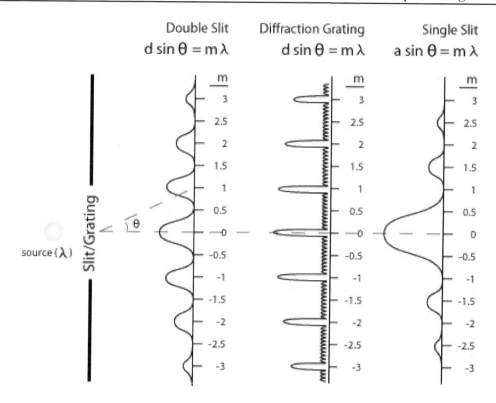

Thin Films

When observing an oil slick on water or the ground, one often sees various swirling colors on top of the slick. This phenomenon is *thin film interference* because the observed colors are not the color of the oil, but rather an effect of light interference when reflecting off the slick.

The figure below illustrates thin film interference. The interference of the light (both destructive and constructive) occurs because the incoming light partially reflects off the oil surface and partially transmits through the oil. The transmitted light is then reflected off the substance below the oil (water, in this case) and the observer sees both the oil-reflected light and the water-reflected light.

However, because the two reflected light rays traveled slightly different distances, according to the material they reflected off, they will have a path difference and therefore interfere. The most visible swirling colors are seen on top of the oil slick are a result of constructive interference, and the dim colors (or those not seen altogether) are a result of destructive interference.

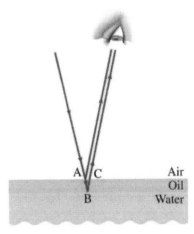

The wavelengths of light that will be displayed can be found via the equation:

$$(2) \cdot (n) \cdot (d) = m\lambda$$

where n is the index of refraction for the thin film, d is the thickness of the thin film (m), λ is the wavelength of the light source (m) and m is the order value dependent upon the material underneath the thin film.

Let $n_{thin\,film}$ be the index of refraction of the thin film material, and n_{under} be the index of refraction of the material underneath the thin film.

If $n_{thin\,film} > n_{under}$ then:

Destructive interference: $m = 1, 2, 3 \ldots$

Constructive interference: $m = \frac{1}{2}, \frac{3}{2}, \frac{5}{2} \ldots$

If $n_{thin\,film} < n_{under}$ then:

Destructive interference: $m = \frac{1}{2}, \frac{3}{2}, \frac{5}{2} \ldots$

Constructive interference: $m = 1, 2, 3 \ldots$

Other Diffraction Phenomena, X-Ray Diffraction

Another interesting form of diffraction is X-ray diffraction. Although X-rays are not visible light, they are waves which can have interference patterns caused by phase differences. This is particularly useful when investigating the structure of crystal lattices and molecular arrangements. X-rays have incredibly small wavelengths. Thus they can diffract off these objects at the molecular level, revealing the pattern of their structure.

For example, below is an illustration of an X-ray crystal diffraction experiment. When X-rays are shone upon a crystal structure, the wavelengths are small enough such that the waves reflect off individual atoms within the crystal structure.

If two or more waves reflect off the crystal surface, they will interfere due to their path length difference. The resulting diffraction pattern gives information into the crystal structure of the specimen being examined.

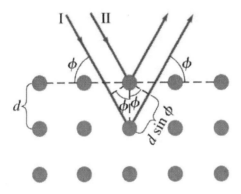

The pattern of maxima produced by X-ray diffraction can be calculated via Bragg's Law, which is expressed as:

$$n\lambda = 2d \sin \phi$$

where n is the order number (1, 2, 3…), λ is the wavelength of the X-ray (m), d is the lattice spacing of the crystal (m) and ϕ is the reflection angle (degrees).

Polarization of Light

Light from the sun and most sources is un-polarized. *Polarization* refers to the planes in which the electric field and magnetic field oscillate. When light is unpolarized, as it is from the sun, all the light waves oscillate randomly in different directions. If the light were to become polarized, then the oscillation of the electric and magnetic field would be uniform amongst all the light waves. For example, the diagram below shows when the light is emitted from the sun, it is unpolarized, and its electric field will oscillate in many directions, as indicated by the arrows of the unpolarized light. When the light strikes the surface of the water, it reflects and becomes horizontally polarized. The horizontally-polarized light only has its electric field oscillating in one direction, rather than all directions.

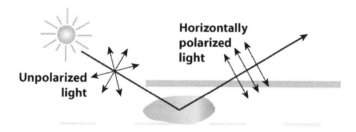

Polarized light and materials which polarize light have many applications. For example, the diagram (a) below shows a rope that represents a vertically polarized wave, which can be transmitted through a vertically polarized filter.

In diagram (b) the wave is horizontally polarized and cannot pass through the vertical polarizer. This is exactly how polarized glasses work to remove glare from the water. Light reflected off the water (glare) is usually horizontally-polarized and can be eliminated by a vertical polarizer.

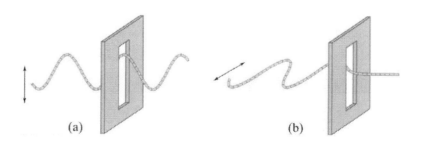

Polarized sunglasses allow the wearer to see through water because they have a vertical polarizer, and therefore reduce/eliminate the horizontally-polarized light reflecting off the water.

The intensity of light after passing through a polarizer filter is calculated by:

$$I = I_0 \cos^2(\theta)$$

where I_0 is the original intensity of the light (W/m^2), I is the intensity of the light after passing through the polarizer, and θ is the angle of the original light wave electric field concerning the axis of the polarizer, known as the transmission axis (degrees).

When unpolarized light is incident upon any polarizing filter, the intensity is reduced by half:

$$I = \frac{1}{2} I_0$$

If the light is incident upon crossed polarizers (90° angle between transmission axis) no light will pass through.

For example, the diagram below shows unpolarized light that is initially polarized such that its electric field oscillates only vertically after it passes through a filter with a vertical transmission axis. Next, it is passed through a polarizer with a horizontal transmission axis.

As a result, no light is transmitted because none of the light's electric field oscillates in the horizontal axis.

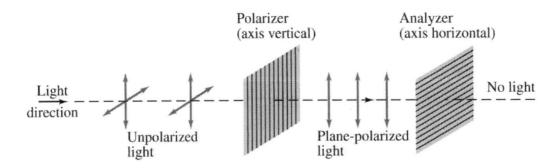

Doppler Effect

All electromagnetic radiation (light, in this case), can undergo the *Doppler effect*. The Doppler effect for light is commonly used in astronomy. When observing stars, galaxies, and other interstellar bodies, astronomers noted that sometimes the observed colors of these bodies shifted in regards to different periods of the year. This was found to be because of the Doppler effect.

When the Earth moves towards, and away from these stellar bodies during the year, the color would shift as a result of the Earth's speed about that of the observed body.

Specifically, two types of shifts were noted: the redshift and the blueshift.

A *redshift* occurs when the source of light and the observer are moving away. In this case, just like the Doppler effect for sound, the frequency of the observed wave decreases. Since lower frequencies of visible light are red, these sources appear to be redder than they are because the Doppler effect shifts the source frequency to a lower frequency for the observer.

The *blueshift* is the opposite of the redshift. When the source of light and the observer are moving towards each other, the observer sees a higher frequency than the source light itself.

Blues and violets are the higher frequency colors in the visible color spectrum. Thus the sources of light appear bluer than they are.

Reflection from Plane Surface

When light strikes various surfaces, it can be absorbed, transmitted or reflected. Mirrors are identifiable examples of surfaces that reflect all incoming light (ideal mirror). When someone looks in a mirror, he or she see his or her image because the light incident upon the mirror is completely reflected. Many other surfaces also provide reflection, such as shiny metal or calm water. However, these images are usually not nearly as clear as the mirror and tend to be somewhat blurry. All these effects, from the clear image presented in the mirror to the blurry image provided by other surfaces, are due to the law of reflection.

The law of reflection states that the angle of incidence of a light ray, concerning the normal of the surface, will be equal to the angle of reflection. When this occurs, it is a *specular reflection* and is what is observed in flat mirrors.

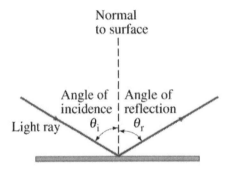

Blurry images are also formed according to the law of reflection. When the reflecting surface is irregular rather than smooth, the light rays reflect off the irregularities.

However, in this case, the reflected rays will not be parallel, but in every direction.

This is a *diffuse reflection* and results in a blurry image being formed.

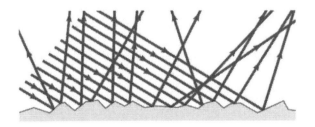

With diffuse reflection, a person's eye sees reflected light at all angles. With specular reflection (from a mirror), the eye must be in the correct position. Think about a person positioning themselves in the mirror to see something behind them—where they place themselves determines what they can see.

Diagram (a) below demonstrates diffuse reflection, in which the observer can see the reflected light from the source in multiple locations.

Diagram (b) below demonstrates specular reflection, in which the reflected light can only be seen in a specific location.

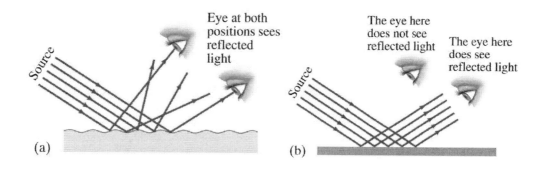

Refraction, Refractive Index N, Snell's Law

When light transmits from one medium to another, it changes direction slightly based upon the properties of the two mediums. This phenomenon is *refraction* and is commonly observed in many everyday experiences. The angle that the light ray bends, concerning the normal, depends upon the indices of refraction for each medium.

The angle of refraction is given by *Snell's Law*, where each n is the index of refraction for its respective medium:

$$n_1 \sin(\theta_1) = n_2 \sin(\theta_2)$$

where n is the index of refraction and θ is the angle of the wave concerning the normal of the medium interface.

The index of refraction is a relation of the light propagation speed in a medium to that of the speed of light in a vacuum (n is always greater than 1 because light cannot go faster than in a vacuum)

$$n = \frac{c}{v}$$

Observe the figures below, which depict the refraction of light from water to air and vice versa. When a wave moves to a denser medium (with a greater refractive index), it bends toward the normal. When it moves to a less dense medium (with a smaller refractive index), it bends away from the normal.

Accordingly, in the diagram (b), when the light is refracted from water into the air, it is refracted away from the normal.

In diagram (a), if the light is refracted from air to water, it bends toward the normal.

Given the angle of incidence, the angle of refraction is computed by Snell's Law.

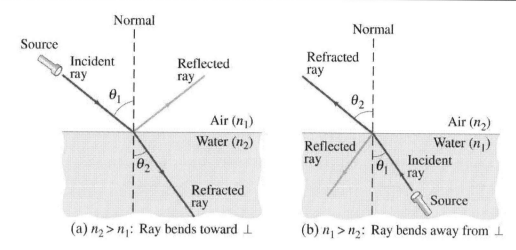

(a) $n_2 > n_1$: Ray bends toward $\perp$ (b) $n_1 > n_2$: Ray bends away from $\perp$

Mirages are also produced by refraction.

Hot surfaces warm up the air above them, producing air with a slightly lower index of refraction than the ambient air.

When a light ray passes through this air, it curves the light such that the observer sees an image that is a form of reflection off the ground.

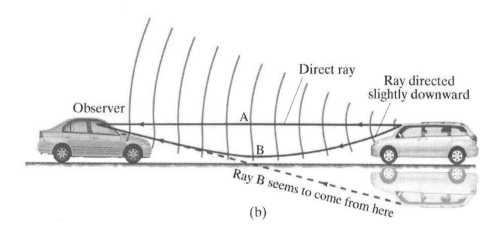

(b)

Dispersion

Dispersion is the phenomenon that separates light into its colors. All wavelengths of light will refract upon crossing a boundary between two different mediums, however different wavelengths of light refract at slightly different angles.

Lower wavelength light refracts the most; thus, the violet light refracts at a greater angle than blue light, which refracts at a greater angle than green light, etc.

An example of dispersion is when white light passes through a prism. The diagram below is of a prism producing the visible spectrum of colors.

White light is composed of the entire visible spectrum, which refract at slightly different angles.

If a screen is held a distance away from the prism, the visible spectrum can be seen because the white light is dispersed into all the wavelengths that compose it.

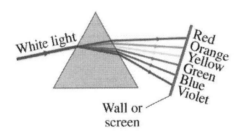

Atmospheric rainbows are created by dispersion as well.

Light passing through small raindrops or mist will refract and disperse into the visible spectrum, just like a prism.

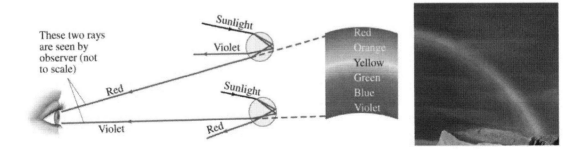

Conditions for Total Internal Reflection

The critical angle is defined as the angle of incidence for which an incident light ray will make an angle of refraction equal to 90°.

The critical angle can be found by using the equation:

$$n_1 \sin (\theta_c) = n_2 \sin (90°)$$

If the angle of incidence is larger than the critical angle, then no light will be transmitted between the two mediums and the light will only be reflected in the original medium. This is a *total internal reflection*.

The diagram below illustrates various angles of incidence and their corresponding angles of diffraction. At points, I and J, the angle of incidence are lower than the critical angle, and the light is refracted through the surface (along with a portion that is partially reflected).

At point K, the critical angle has been achieved, and the angle of refraction is exactly 90°. At point L, the angle of incidence is higher than the critical angle. Therefore, all the light will be reflected, resulting in total internal reflection.

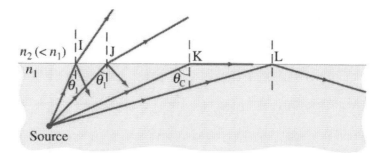

Total internal reflection is important because it is the principle behind the operation of fiber optics. In a fiber optic cable, light is transmitted along the fiber regardless of the loops or bends in the cable, because the indices of refraction of the cable and outer sheath are such that the light is always experiencing total internal reflection.

Mirrors

Spherical mirrors allow users to see different images than what is possible with only flat mirrors. For example, many parking garages have convex mirrors mounted near blind corners; they allow drivers to see a much wider image of what is around a corner than a flat mirror. Similarly, many beauty mirrors are slightly concave and present a magnified image to the user. Both of these examples are types of spherical mirrors, which have distinctive properties depending on the curvature of the reflective surface.

Mirror curvature, radius, focal length

Mirror curvature can be concave or convex. The figure below shows a concave and a convex mirror. The *convex mirror* (diagram a) disperses light rays such that they are diverging.

The *concave mirror* (diagram b) focuses light rays such that they converge.

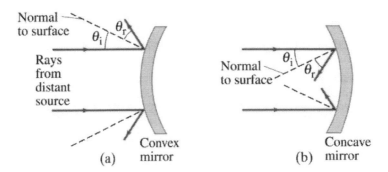

Regardless of the mirror, both convex and concave spherical mirrors have defined radii of curvature and foci. The *radius of curvature* is the radius of the curve of the mirror; in spherical mirrors, the radius of curvature is constant throughout the surface of the mirror. The *focal length* is the distance from the mirror surface to the where light rays converge (theoretically converge, in the case of a convex mirror). Concave mirrors have a positive focal length, while convex mirrors have a negative focal length. Both types have focal lengths that are equal to half the radius:

$$f = \frac{1}{2} R$$

where f is the focal length (m), and R is the radius of curvature (m).

The figure below displays the various features of a concave mirror. Point C is the *center of curvature* and is the point where the radius of curvature originates (center of a circle). Point F is the focus and demonstrates where all light rays would focus if reflected off the mirror. The distances *f* and *r* are the focal length and radius of curvature which are the distances to points F and C, respectively.

A convex mirror would have the same center of curvature, focal point, the radius of curvature and focal length; however, the light would be incident upon the outer edge of the mirror and disperse, rather than converge.

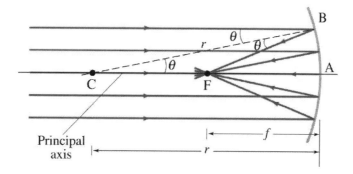

Mirror ray tracing

When looking at a mirror, it is important to know the relationship of the object held up to the mirror and the image formed by the mirror. Depending upon the object distance from the mirror, the mirror and the characteristics of the mirror, the formed image can be smaller, larger, virtual, real, erect or inverted.

The image formed by a mirror is classified by size about the original object, whether the image is inverted or not and if the formed image is real or virtual. The size of the image formed by a mirror can either be equal to, larger or smaller than the size of the object held up to the mirror. Additionally, the image may be erect like the object held up to the mirror, or the image may be inverted and appear to be upside down.

For example, a person's face reflected on the inside of a shiny spoon appears inverted and smaller than the face. The formed image may be real or virtual. Real images are images that are formed when light rays converge upon a point in a real location, whereas virtual images form from light rays that diverge. A virtual image is at the point where the light rays appear to diverge from (this point is not there, hence "virtual image").

An easy way to identify the image formed by a mirror is by using *ray diagrams*. Ray diagrams are tools that allow the user to visualize the image formed, depending upon object location with respect to the mirror. When drawing ray diagrams, three rays are typically drawn:

1. A ray from the top of the object height parallel to the axis—after reflection off the mirror, it passes through the focal point.

2. A ray from the top of the object height through the focal point—after reflection, it is parallel to the axis.

3. A ray perpendicular to the mirror, which passes through the object height and the center of curvature.

For example, the figure below is of a ray diagram drawn using a concave mirror. Diagrams (a, b, c) below show the paths of rays 1, 2 and 3 respectively. Notice that after the rays have been drawn in, the convergence point is the location of the image. The image height and orientation are then determined by drawing a line from the center axis to the convergence point. In this case, the image formed by the mirror is inverted, larger and real (the image is formed by the convergence of light rays on a real point).

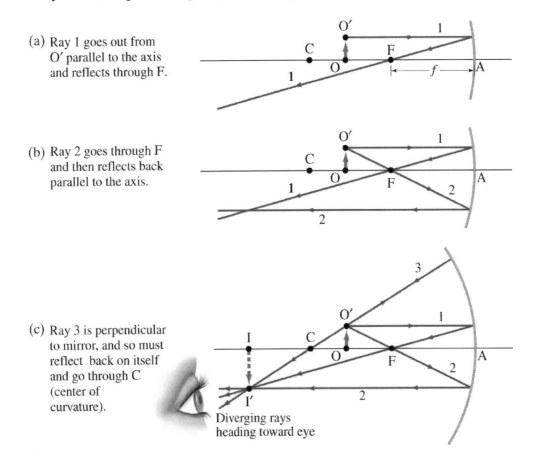

(a) Ray 1 goes out from O′ parallel to the axis and reflects through F.

(b) Ray 2 goes through F and then reflects back parallel to the axis.

(c) Ray 3 is perpendicular to mirror, and so must reflect back on itself and go through C (center of curvature).

Diverging rays heading toward eye

The location of the object determines the image.

The illustration below depicts the image formed by an object located in front of the focal point of a concave mirror.

In this case, the formed image is erect, larger and virtual (the image is formed by the convergence of light rays on a virtual point).

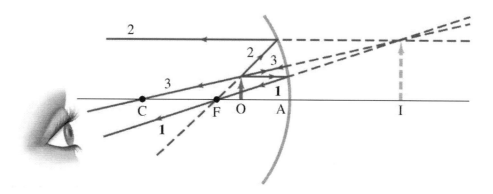

Concave mirrors can produce both real and virtual images, depending on where the object is located in relation to the mirror.

If the object is outside the radius of the sphere of the mirror, the image will be real. If it is inside the radius, the image will be virtual.

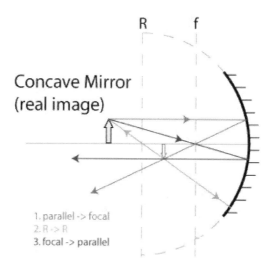

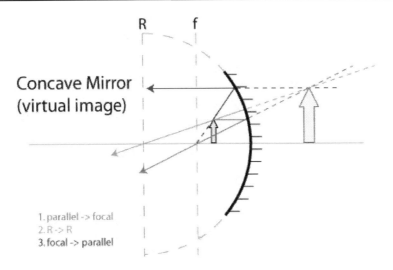

For convex mirrors, only a virtual image will be created, because the curve of the mirrors is different.

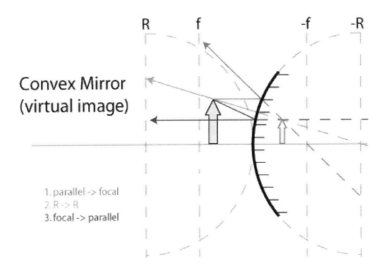

For mirrors:

1. First, draw a parallel line from the object; as it bounces off the mirror, it intersects the focal point. Which focal point (left or right) to intersect?

    For concave mirrors, it is going to focus the ray to the left focal point.

    For convex mirrors, which cannot focus, it is going to diverge the ray; this means extrapolation to the right focal point is needed.

2. Next, draw a line that intersects the R point on the principal axis. Which R? Left or right?

   The ray drawn should bounce right back its original path, and not be reflected elsewhere. By eye-balling the mirror, one can figure this out.

3. Now that two rays are drawn, an intersection can be made. Use this intersection as a guide to drawing the last ray. The last ray should first intersect the focal point, then bounce off the mirror parallel to the principal axis. Which focal point to intersect? Is extrapolation necessary?

   There is only one combination for the ray here to fit the intersection already made by the previous two rays.

   The trick to do this is to draw the parallel line first and force it to cross the intersection already made by the previous two rays.

The table gives the object-image relationship for both concave and convex mirrors:

Object Distance	Concave Mirror	Convex Mirror
Before C	inverted, smaller, real	erect, smaller, virtual
At C	inverted, equal size, real	erect, smaller, virtual
Between C and F	inverted, larger, real	erect, smaller, virtual
At F	no image	erect, smaller, virtual
Before F	erect, larger, virtual	erect, smaller, virtual

Thin Lenses

A lens is a device used to bend and focus light using the refractive properties of the lens material. For example, the lenses in a microscope bend and focus light such that objects become magnified. Eyeglasses correct vision problems by focusing the light in front of eyes so that those who wear glasses can see without blurry vision. Regardless of the application, lenses are an important tool in many day-to-day devices and scientific instruments.

Many similarities exist between lenses and mirrors in regards to image formation; however, there are a few differences to make a note of. Primarily, a convex lens is the same as a concave mirror (both are converging) except for the following instances:

- Real images are on the opposite side of the lens as the object, because light travels through the lens and can focus on a screen behind the lens.
- Virtual images are on the same side of the lens as the object, because light cannot focus in front of a lens and be cast on a screen.
- Concave lenses are the same as convex mirrors (both are diverging) except for in the following instance:
- The virtual images formed by the lens are on the same side of the lens as the object, because light cannot focus in front of a lens and be cast on a screen.

Converging and diverging lenses, focal length

Most lens problems approximate the lens as a *thin lens*. Thin lenses are those whose thickness is small compared to their radius of curvature. They may be either converging (convex) or diverging (concave). The figure below depicts a converging lens. Just like with mirrors, the light which passes through the lens will converge on the focal point of the lens (there are two focal points, one on each side).

The radius of curvature is the same as that of a spherical mirror, except that because the lens is double-sided, it has two radii of curvature (most of the time these are equal).

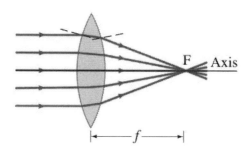

A diverging lens (concave) makes parallel light diverge; the focal point is the point where the diverging rays would converge if projected back.

Like the converging lens, the diverging lens has two radii of curvature (most of the time these are equal).

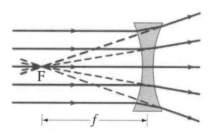

Ray tracing thin lens

Ray tracing for thin lenses is similar to that for mirrors. There are three key rays:

1. A ray from the top of the object height parallel to the axis—after transmission through the lens, it passes through the focal point.

2. A ray from the top of the object height through the focal point—after transmission, it is parallel to the axis.

3. A ray from the top of the object height through the center of the lens.

For example, the figure below demonstrates ray tracing through a converging lens.

Diagrams (a, b, c) below show the paths of rays 1, 2 and 3 respectively. Notice that after the rays have been drawn in, the convergence point is the location of the image.

The image height and orientation are then determined by drawing a line from the center axis to the convergence point. In this case, the image formed by the lens is inverted and real.

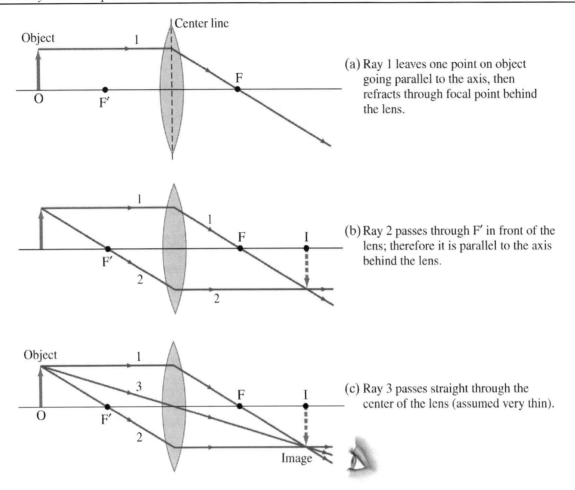

(a) Ray 1 leaves one point on object going parallel to the axis, then refracts through focal point behind the lens.

(b) Ray 2 passes through F′ in front of the lens; therefore it is parallel to the axis behind the lens.

(c) Ray 3 passes straight through the center of the lens (assumed very thin).

For a diverging lens, the same three rays can be used; the image is upright and virtual.

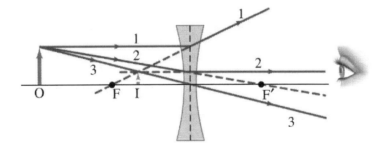

As stated previously, lenses are similar to mirrors.

This means a convex lens (like a concave mirror) can create either a real or a virtual image, depending on where the real object is positioned.

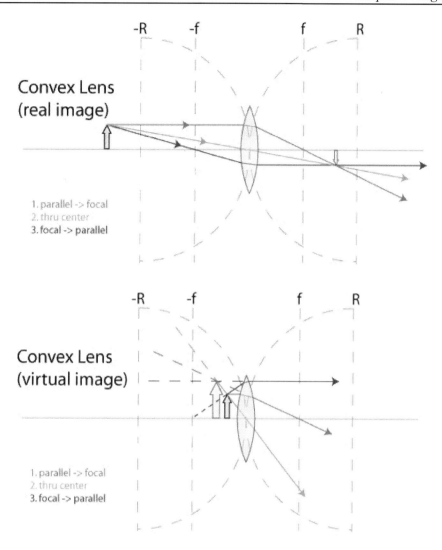

Convex Lens
(real image)

1. parallel -> focal
2. thru center
3. focal -> parallel

Convex Lens
(virtual image)

1. parallel -> focal
2. thru center
3. focal -> parallel

A concave lens, therefore, acts similar to a convex mirror, and only produce virtual images.

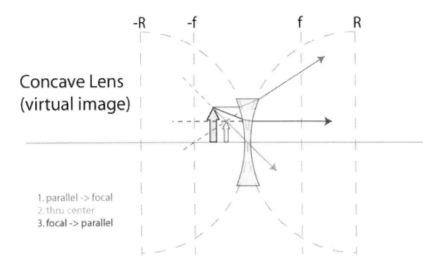

For lenses (similar to the method of drawing rays for mirrors):

1. First, draw the parallel → focal point ray. It should make sense which focal point the ray should hit/extrapolate, given the converging/diverging nature of the lens.
2. Next, draw a ray intersecting the center of the lens.
3. Lastly, using the intersection already made by the previous two rays as a guide, draw the focal point → parallel ray.
    Draw the parallel line first and force it to intersect the intersection already made by the previous two rays.

Use of formula $(1/p) + (1/q) = 1/f$ with sign conventions

To determine the distance from either the mirror or lens that an image forms, the thin lens equation can be used:

$$\frac{1}{d_o} + \frac{1}{d_i} = \frac{1}{f}$$

where d_o is the distance of the object away from the lens or mirror (m), d_i is the distance of the image away from the lens or mirror (m), and f is the focal length of the lens or mirror (m).

Although the thin lens equation is relatively simple, it is important that the proper sign conventions be followed for the types of mirrors and lenses. For a lens, several differences depend on whether the lens is converging or diverging. The focal length is written positive for converging lenses and negative for diverging. Also, the object distance is considered positive when the object is on the same side as the light entering the lens; otherwise it is negative. Finally, the image distance is positive if the image is on the opposite side from the light entering the lens; otherwise, it is negative.

For mirrors, the sign conventions are different. The focal length is written positive for concave mirrors and negative for convex mirrors. Also, the object distance is considered positive when the object is in front of the mirror, and negative if the object is behind the mirror (a virtual object, this is a rare case). Finally, the image distance is positive if the image is in front of the mirror (real image), and negative if the image is behind the mirror (virtual image).

When solving problems using the thin lens equation, be sure to perform as many steps as possible. Draw a ray diagram, and place the image where the key rays intersect. Solve for unknowns by following the sign conventions and check that the answers found are consistent with the ray diagram.

Magnification and lens power formula

The magnification of an object, in relation to image height, can also be obtained for lenses and mirrors. The magnification equation can find this, expressed as:

$$M = \frac{h_i}{h_0} = -\frac{d_i}{d_0}$$

where M is magnification, h_i is the height of the image (m), h_0 is the height of the object (m), d_o is the distance of the object away from the lens or mirror (m) and d_i is the distance of the image away from the lens or mirror (m).

Similar to the lens equation, the magnification equation has specific sign conventions for the types of mirrors and lenses.

The magnification should be expressed as positive for all types of lenses when the image is upright with respect to the object, and negative when the image is inverted.

Likewise, magnification should be expressed as positive for all types of mirrors when the image is upright with respect to the object, and negative when the image is inverted.

The power of a lens is not related to its magnification but rather is expressed as the inverse of its focal length, where the lens power has units of diopters (D), which are equal to m^{-1}.

The power of a lens is positive if it is converging, and negative if it is diverging:

$$P = \frac{1}{f}$$

where P is the lens power (D).

Lensmaker's equation

The relationship between the radii of curvature of a lens and the produced focal length can be related by the Lensmaker's equation:

$$\frac{1}{f} = (n-1)(\frac{1}{R_1} + \frac{1}{R_2})$$

where f is the focal length of the lens (m), n is the index of refraction of the lens material, R_1 is the radius of curvature of the first lens face (m), and R_2 is the radius of curvature of the second lens face (m).

Combination of Lenses

Combinations of lenses are used to multiply the magnification of objects. This is demonstrated in light microscopes and telescopes. These devices contain multiple lenses to allow the user to magnify objects beyond what a single lens can produce. This is possible because the real image formed by a lens can be used as the object for another lens.

The magnification by multiple lenses is the product of all of the individual magnifications and is expressed as:

$$M_{total} = M_1 M_2$$

where M_{total} is the total magnification, M_1 is the magnification of the first lens and M_2 is the magnification of the second lens.

The simplest form of a combination of lenses is when two lenses are placed in contact.

The total power of the combination of lenses is the sum of the two lens's powers:

$$P_{total} = P_1 + P_2$$

or

$$\frac{1}{f_{total}} = \frac{1}{f_1} + \frac{1}{f_2}$$

If some distance separates the two lenses, then total power of the combination is:

$$\frac{1}{f_{total}} = \frac{1}{f_1} + \frac{1}{f_2} - \frac{d}{f_1 f_2}$$

where d is the distance between the two lenses (m)

Lens Aberration

In real life, no lens is ideal, and the light rays will tend to converge in slightly different spots. This phenomenon is an aberration, and there are several types which can occur.

Spherical lenses and mirrors often suffer from *spherical aberration*. This occurs because the curvature of the lens/mirror is often quite large, and the rays striking the outer edges refract/reflect more and therefore bend more than the rays striking the center portion of the lens/mirror. This can be seen in the converging lens figure shown below. Spherical aberration can be reduced by utilizing only the center portion of the lens or mirror.

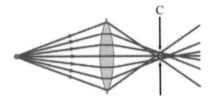

Chromatic aberration occurs in lenses and is when the light of different wavelengths focuses at different points. As stated earlier, different wavelengths of light will refract at slightly different angles in the phenomenon of dispersion. When light shines through a lens, this results in different focus points, depending upon the wavelength of light.

For instance, observe the figure below. The blue light gets refracted more than red light so that it will focus at an earlier point than the red light.

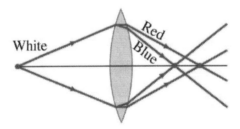

An *achromatic doublet* is a device that offers a solution for chromatic aberration. A second lens made of a different material is attached to the first lens.

When light passes, through the chromatic aberration will be corrected in the second lens, which focuses all wavelengths to one point.

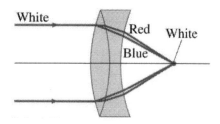

Distortion is an aberration caused when different parts of a lens have slightly different magnification factors. The two diagrams below illustrate two types of distortion.

Diagram (a) below represents *barrel distortion*, where the magnification of the image decreases with distance from the axis.

Diagram (b) represents *pincushion distortion*, where magnification increases with distance from the optical axis.

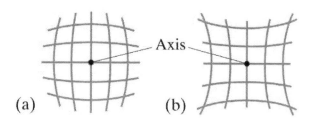

Optical Instruments

Like cameras, the human eye manipulates electromagnetic waves using an adjustable lens and an iris. The figure below shows a cross-section of an eye, with the iris and lens clearly labeled.

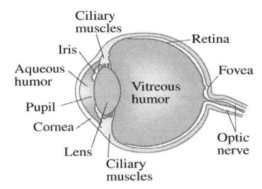

The eye works by making small adjustments of the lens shape to allow objects at different distances be focused against the retina. Most of the refraction of the light occurs at the surface of the cornea, while the lens only makes fine-tuned adjustments.

Observe the diagram below illustrating a lens adjusting to compensate for object distance. In diagram (a) below, the object is far away (far away objects have rays assumed to be parallel), and the lens adjusts itself such that its radius of curvature creates a focal point at the retina.

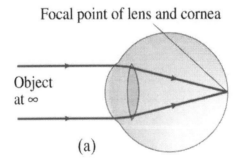

(a)

The near point is the closest distance at which the eye can focus clearly. The normal distance is about 25 cm. The far point is the farthest distance at which an object can be seen clearly. The normal distance is infinity. Nearsightedness occurs when a person's far point is too close.

Farsightedness occurs when an individual's near point is too far away.

Nearsightedness (*myopia*) can be corrected with a diverging lens. In diagram (a) below, an eye with myopia refracts light too much and causes the focal point to be located before the retina. Diagram (b) shows the correction lens for myopia. The lens refracts the light such that the light diverges before the cornea. Consequently, the higher refraction of the eye is compensated for and the focal point occurs at the retina, producing a clear image.

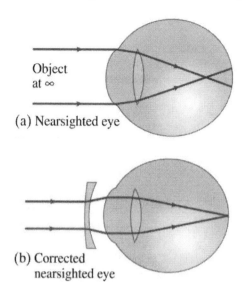

(a) Nearsighted eye

(b) Corrected
   nearsighted eye

Farsightedness (*hyperopia*) is corrected with a converging lens.

In diagram (c), hyperopia occurs when the eye refracts the incoming light too little, and the focal point occurs behind the retina. This can be corrected with a converging lens which brings the light rays to a more parallel orientation before entering the eye. The lower refractive index of the eye is accounted for, and the focal point occurs at the retina

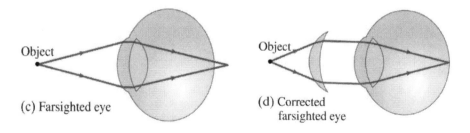

(c) Farsighted eye

(d) Corrected
   farsighted eye

Magnifying glass

A magnifying glass is a converging lens. It allows the user to focus on objects closer than the near point so that they create a larger image on the retina. The figure below demonstrates a magnifying glass in use.

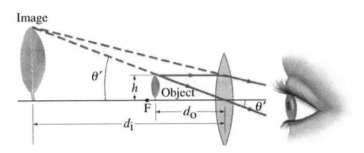

The power of a magnifying glass is described by its angular magnification:

$$M = \frac{\theta'}{\theta}$$

$$\theta \approx \frac{h}{f}$$

$$\theta' \approx \frac{25cm}{h}$$

If the eye is relaxed (N is the near point distance and f the focal length), magnification is given as:

$$M = \frac{\theta'}{\theta} = \frac{h/f}{h/N} = \frac{N}{f} = \frac{25cm}{f}$$

If the eye is focused at the near point, magnification is given as:

$$M = \frac{N}{f} + 1 = \frac{25cm}{f} + 1$$

Refracting telescope

A refracting telescope consists of two lenses at opposite ends of a long tube.

The objective lens is closest to the object, and the eyepiece is closest to the eye.

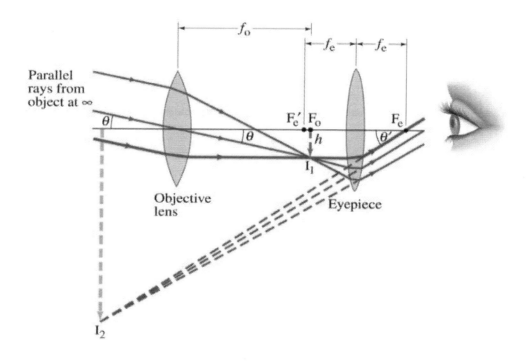

The magnification is given by:

$$M = \frac{\theta'}{\theta} = \frac{(h/f_e)}{(h/f_o)} = -\frac{f_o}{f_e}$$

Chapter Summary

Light, Refraction, and Reflection

- Light paths are rays.

- Visible spectrum of light ranges approximately from 400 nm to 750 nm.

- Two sources of light are coherent if they have the same frequency and maintain the same phase relationship.

- Index of refraction varies with wavelength, leading to dispersion.

- There are boundaries between different materials, as well as between regions of the same material that is under different conditions, such as temperature or pressure, which cause a change in the index of refraction.

- Index of refraction: $n = \dfrac{c}{v}$

- Law of refraction (Snell's Law): $n_1 \sin(\theta_1) = n_2 \sin(\theta_2)$

- Angle of reflection equals the angle of incidence.

- Total internal reflection occurs when the angle of incidence is greater than the critical angle:

$$\sin(\theta_C) = \frac{n_2}{n_1} \sin(90°) = \frac{n_2}{n_1}$$

Diffraction—Single-slit and Double-slit

- Wavelength of light in a medium with index of refraction n: $\lambda_n = \dfrac{\lambda}{n}$

- Wavelength can be measured precisely with a spectroscope.

- Young's double-slit experiment demonstrated interference:

    constructive interference occurs when: $d \sin(\theta) = m\lambda$, $m = 0, 1, 2, \ldots$

    and destructive interference when: $d \sin(\theta) = (m + \frac{1}{2})\lambda$, $m = 0, 1, 2, \ldots$

- Diffraction grating has many small slits or lines, and the same condition for constructive interference.

- Light bends around obstacles and openings in its path, producing diffraction patterns.

- Light passing through a narrow slit produces a bright central maximum of width:

$$\sin(\theta) = \frac{\lambda}{D}$$

- Interference can occur between reflections from the front and back surfaces of a thin film.

Polarization

- Light whose electric fields are all in the same plane is plane polarized.
- The intensity of plane polarized light is reduced after it passes through another polarizer:

$$I = I_o \cos^2(\theta)$$

o Light can also be polarized by reflection; it is completely polarized when the reflection angle is the polarization angle: $\tan(\theta_p) = n$

Mirrors

- Plane mirror: image is virtual, upright and the same size as the object.
- A real image means light passes through it.
  A virtual image means light does not pass through it.

- Spherical mirror can be concave or convex.

- Focal length of the mirror: $f = \frac{r}{2}$

- Mirror equation: $\frac{1}{d_o} + \frac{1}{d_i} = \frac{1}{f}$

- Magnification: $m = \frac{h_i}{h_o} = -\frac{d_i}{d_o}$

Lenses

- A converging lens focuses incoming parallel rays to a point.
  A diverging lens spreads incoming rays so that they appear to come from a point

- Power of a lens: $P = \dfrac{1}{f}$

- The thin lens equation is given by: $\dfrac{1}{f} - \dfrac{1}{d_i} = \dfrac{1}{d_o}$ or $\dfrac{1}{d_o} + \dfrac{1}{d_i} = \dfrac{1}{f}$

Lens Aberrations

- Spherical aberration occurs when rays far from axis do not go through the focal point.

- Chromatic aberration occurs when different wavelengths have different focal points.

Optical Devices

- Resolution of optical devices is limited by diffraction.
- Nearsighted vision is corrected by the diverging lens, farsighted by converging.

- Simple magnifier: object at focal point

$$M = \frac{\theta'}{\theta} = \frac{h/f}{h/N} = \frac{N}{f}$$

- Magnification:

$$M = \frac{\theta'}{\theta} = \frac{(h/f_e)}{(h/f_o)} = -\frac{f_o}{f_e}$$

Practice Questions

1. Which color of the visible spectrum has photons with the most energy?

    A. Violet   **B.** Green   **C.** Orange   **D.** Red   **E.** Yellow

2. An index of refraction of less than one for a medium implies that:

    A. the speed of light in the medium is less than the speed of light in a vacuum
    B. refraction is not possible
    C. the speed of light in the medium is the same as the speed of light in a vacuum
    D. the speed of light in the medium is greater than the speed of light in a vacuum
    E. reflection is not possible

3. The colors on an oil slick are caused by reflection and:

    A. refraction   **C.** diffraction
    B. polarization   **D.** interference   **E.** diffusion

4. Which of the following describes the best scenario if a person wants to start a fire using sunlight and a mirror?

    A. Use a concave mirror with the object to be ignited positioned at the center of **the** curvature of the mirror
    B. Use a concave mirror with the object to be ignited positioned halfway between the mirror and its center of curvature
    C. Use a plane mirror
    D. Use a convex mirror
    E. A fire cannot be started using a mirror since mirrors form only virtual images

5. A lens has a focal length of 2 m. What lens could you combine with it to get a combination with a focal length of 3 m?

    A. A lens of power 1/6 diopters   **C.** A lens of power –6 diopters
    B. A lens of power 6 diopters   **D.** A lens of power –1/6 diopters
                                      E. A lens of power 3 diopters

6. An incident ray traveling in the air makes an angle of 30° with the surface of a medium with an index $n = 1.73$. What is the angle that the refracted ray makes with the surface? (Use the index of refraction for air $n = 1$)

    A. 30°   **B.** $90 \sin^{-1}(0.5)$ **C.** 60°   **D.** $\sin^{-1}(0.5)$ **E.** 90°

7. A mirage is produced because:

    A. light travels faster through the air than through water

    B. images of water are reflected in the sky

    C. warm air has a higher index of refraction than cool air

    D. warm air has a lower index of refraction than cool air

    E. water from oceans and lakes is highly reflective

8. An object is viewed at various distances using a concave mirror with a focal length of 14 m. What happens when a candle is placed at the focus?

    A. Light rays end up parallel going to infinity

    B. Light rays meet at the focus

    C. An image is formed 7 m in front of the mirror

    D. An image is formed 7 m behind the mirror

    E. Light rays end up parallel going out 7 m on either side

9. A material which can rotate the direction of polarization of linearly polarized light is said to be:

    A. diffraction limited   **C.** circularly polarized

    B. dichroic   **D.** birefringent   **E.** optically active

10. When light enters a material of a higher index of refraction, its speed:

    A. increases   **C.** first increases then decrease

    B. stays the same   **D.** decreases

     E. first decreases then increase

11. What is the correct order of the electromagnetic spectrum from shortest to longest wavelength?

    A. Radio waves → X-rays → Ultraviolet radiation → Visible light → Infrared radiation → Microwaves → Gamma rays

    B. Gamma rays → X-rays → Visible light → Ultraviolet radiation → Infrared radiation → Microwaves → Radio waves

    C. Gamma rays → X-rays → Ultraviolet radiation → Visible light → Infrared radiation → Microwaves → Radio waves

    D. Visible light → Infrared radiation → Microwaves → Radio waves → Gamma rays → X-rays → Ultraviolet radiation

    E. Gamma rays → X-rays → Infrared radiation → Visible light → Ultraviolet radiation → Microwaves → Radio waves

12. The angle of incidence can vary between zero and:

A. 2π radians

B. π radians

C. $\pi/2$ radians

D. 1 radian

E. $3\pi/2$ radians

13. An amateur astronomer grinds a double-convex lens whose surfaces have radii of curvature of 40 cm and 60 cm. What is the focal length of this lens in air? (Use index of refraction for glass $n = 1.54$)

A. 44 cm

B. 88 cm

C. 132 cm

D. 22 cm

E. 1.32 cm

14. When light reflects from a stationary surface, there is a change in its:

I. frequency

II. speed

III. wavelength

A. I and II only

B. I and III only

C. III only

D. I, II and III

E. none of the above

15. If a distant galaxy is moving away from the Earth at 4,300 km/s, how do the detected frequency (f_{det}) and λ of the visible light detected on Earth compare to the f and λ of the light emitted by the galaxy?

A. The f_{det} is lower, and the λ is shifted towards the red end of the visible spectrum

B. The f_{det} is lower, and the λ is shifted towards the blue end of the visible spectrum

C. The f_{det} is the same, but the λ is shifted towards the red end of the visible spectrum

D. The f_{det} is the same, but the λ is shifted towards the blue end of the visible spectrum

E. The f_{det} and the λ are the same as the sources

Solutions

1. A is correct.

Violet light has the highest frequency of the visible light colors with a range of 668 to 789 THz. Because frequency is related to photon energy by:

$$E = hf$$

Violet light is also the most energetic of the visible light spectrum.

2. D is correct. The index of refraction for a given material is expressed as the speed of light in a vacuum divided by the speed of light in that material:

$$n = c / v$$

If the index of refraction is less than one, it implies that the speed of light in the material is greater than the speed of light in vacuum. However, this is never the case because the speed of light in a vacuum can never be exceeded.

3. D is correct. The colors observed on an oil slick pool are caused by reflection and thin film interference. This is the process by which the incoming light is reflected off the top and bottom layer of the oil slick and producing reflected waves in and out of phase. This phase change determines the interference (constructive or destructive) and colors form as a result.

4. B is correct. $f = \frac{1}{2}R$, where R is the radius of curvature

5. D is correct. The first lens has a power:

$$P_1 = 1 / f$$

$$P_1 = \frac{1}{2} D$$

For a combination of total power:

$$P_{tot} = 1 / f_{tot}$$

$$P_{tot} = 1/3 \ D$$

Thus,

$$P_2 = P_{tot} - P_1$$

$$P_2 = 1/3 \ D - 1/2 \ D$$

$$P_2 = -1/6 \ D$$

6. A is correct.

$$n_1 \sin \theta_1 = n_1 \sin \theta_2$$

$$(1) \sin (90° - 30°) = (1.73) \sin \theta_2$$

$$\sin (60°) = 1.73 \sin \theta_2$$

$$\sin \theta_2 = \sin (60°) / 1.73$$

$$\sin \theta_2 = 0.5$$

$$\theta_2 = \sin^{-1} (0.5)$$

$$\theta_2 = 30°$$

7. D is correct. A mirage is produced due to the higher index of refraction of cold air compared to warm air. As light from the sky goes through denser cold air and approaches the warm air (which is less dense and therefore has a lower refraction index) near the ground (generated by a hot surface of asphalt or sand), the light bends away from the warm air and the reflection of the sky can be observed on the ground.

8. A is correct.

Mirror equation:

$$1 / f = 1 / d_o + 1 / d_i$$

If the object is placed at the focus:

$$d_o = f$$

$$1 / f = 1 / f + 1 / d_i$$

$$1 / f - 1 / f = 1 / d_i$$

$$0 = 1 / d_i$$

Only if $d_i = \infty$ this is true.

This implies that no image is formed. Thus the light rays neither converge nor diverge and travel parallel to infinity.

9. E is correct. A material which can rotate the direction of polarization of linearly polarized light is said to be *optically active*.

10. D is correct.

When light enters a material of a higher index of refraction, its speed decreases.

11. C is correct. The correct order of the electromagnetic spectrum from shortest to longest wavelength is Gamma rays → X-rays → Ultraviolet radiation → Visible light → Infrared radiation → Microwaves → Radio waves

12. C is correct.

The angle of incidence ranges from 0° to 90°.

Convert degrees to radians:

$$0° = 0 \text{ radians}$$

$$(90° / 1)·(\pi / 180°) = \pi/2 \text{ radians}$$

---

13. A is correct.

Double convex lens:

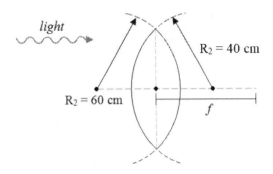

Lensmaker's formula:

$$1/f = (n-1) \cdot (1/R_1 - 1/R_2)$$

$$1/f = (1.54 - 1) \cdot (1/40 \text{ cm} - (1/-60 \text{ cm}))$$

$$1/f = -0.0225 \text{ cm}^{-1}$$

$$f = 44 \text{ cm}$$

If light passes through the center of the radii of curvature (as it does to R_2) before the curve itself in the lens then that R is negative by convention.

14. E is correct. Light does not experience a change in frequency, wavelength or speed when it reflects from a stationary surface.

15. A is correct.

The Doppler effect is qualitatively similar for both light and sound waves.

If the source and the observer move towards each other, the f_{det} is higher than the f_{source}.

If the source and the observer move away, the f_{det} is lower than the f_{source}.

Since the galaxy is moving away from the Earth, the f_{det} is lower.

The speed of light through space is constant ($c = \lambda f$).

A lower f_{det} means a longer λ_{det}, so the λ_{det} is longer than the λ_{source}.

The λ has been shifted towards the red end of the visible spectrum because red light is the visible light with the longest λ.

Chapter 10

Heat and Thermodynamics

- **The Basics of Thermal Physics**

- **Heat, Temperature and Thermal Energy**

- **Heat Capacity and Specific Heat**

- **Heat Transfer**

- **Thermodynamic Systems**

- **The Zeroth Law of Thermodynamics**

- **First Law of Thermodynamics: Conservation of Energy**

- **Second Law of Thermodynamics: Entropy**

- **The Third Law of Thermodynamics**

- **Enthalpy**

- **Gibbs Free Energy**

- **PV diagrams**

- **The Carnot Cycle**

- **The Kinetic Theory of Gases**

- **Coefficient of Linear Expansion**

- **Phase Diagram: Pressure and Temperature**

- **Latent Heat**

Notes

The Basics of Thermal Physics

Energy is defined as the ability to do work and can be classified as either kinetic or potential energy. Kinetic energy is the energy of an object in motion; for example, a rolling ball, moving the car and dropped coin all have kinetic energy. Potential energy is defined as the potential to do work. As discussed earlier, there are many forms of potential energy, including gravitational potential energy, spring potential energy, chemical potential energy, etc. For example, the hammer in the figure below initially has gravitational potential energy. When the hand holding the hammer relaxes, the hammer begins to move downward, converting its potential energy into kinetic energy.

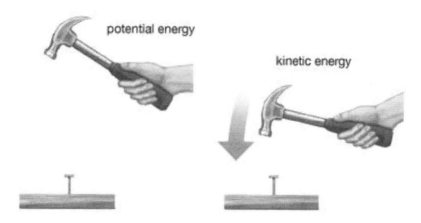

Thermal physics is the science of heat and the energy it retains. In all situations, the conservation of energy holds, meaning there is no loss of energy. However, in most real-life examples, non-conservative forces play a role and energy is not always converted into useful work. When these forces act on an object, the energy they use by acting over a distance cannot be regained—but that does not mean the energy disappears into thin air.

If a book is pushed along a table, a force of friction is exerted on the book.

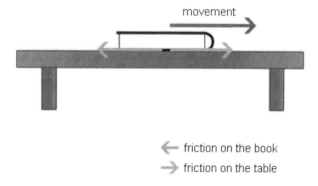

Depending on how much effort is put into pushing the book, it travels a certain distance, and then come to rest as it steadily decreases in velocity. The book comes to rest because there is a force of friction opposing its motion. As its velocity decreases, so do its kinetic energy ($\frac{1}{2}mv^2$). Conservation of energy must hold, so the loss in kinetic energy is energy being converted into heat.

However, neither the surface of the counter nor the bottom of the book feels tangibly warm, because more energy is needed to raise the temperature to where the difference can be felt. If the process is repeated back and forth over a period, the bottom of the book and the surface of the table begins to feel warm to the touch, because enough energy had been deposited to raise the temperature noticeably.

On a microscopic level, thermal energy is the energy related to the vibration of molecules and atoms. Every bit of matter is made of billions and trillions of small molecules, and even in solids these particles never stand perfectly still. The amount of movement an object has in its molecules relegates how much thermal energy the object holds.

The figure below displays a closed container of gas, in which the gas molecules are shown in random motion throughout the container.

The thermal energy of the gas is directly related to the *KE* of these molecules.

The more kinetic energy they have, the more thermal energy they have. With less kinetic energy, the gas has less thermal energy.

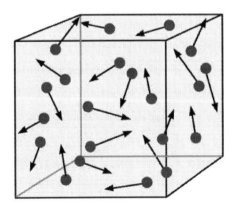

Heat, Temperature and Thermal Energy

Heat and temperature are often used interchangeably in everyday language. However, this usage is incorrect. *Heat* is a form of energy and exists independently from any medium.

Temperature is a measure of the kinetic energy in a specific medium and is thus dependent on the material itself. Temperature and heat are connected, but heat is the total energy due to molecular motion and temperature is the average measure of the energy stored within a certain substance. Some substances respond drastically to a change in thermal energy, and some have a subtler reaction. This all depends on the material and heat capacity, which is discussed later.

The measure of the quantity of thermal energy transmitted from one body to another is heat. An object does not "contain" heat, but it can have a certain amount of thermal energy. Heat can be measured in joules (J) but is also measured in calories (cal).

Conveniently, *calories* relate heat to change in temperature, which is often useful when solving problems in thermal physics. The definition of a calorie is the amount of heat needed to raise the temperature of one gram of water by one degree Celsius (g/°C).

$$1 \; cal = 1 \frac{g}{{}^\circ C} = 4.19 \; J$$

Food Calories are not the same as heat calories. Notice one is capitalized and, the other is not. This is similar to the relationship between kilograms and grams (1 Calorie = 1,000 calories). Another difference to note is that while Calories measure stored energy just as calories do, they also measure the energy stored in the chemical bonds of food that are broken down and stored when digested.

Regardless, Calories are still a measure of energy in a substance and can be converted to their equivalents of conventional energy.

For example, Calories contained in 5 lbs. of spaghetti have enough energy to brew a pot of coffee; calories in one piece of cheesecake can power a 60W incandescent light bulb for 1.5 hours; 217 Big Macs contain enough energy to drive a vehicle for 88 miles.

In the United States, the unit of temperature is the *Fahrenheit* (°F). However, the SI unit is the *Celsius* (°C). This is an easier system to remember, as water freezes at 0 °C and boils at 100 °C (instead of the 32 °F and 212 °F).

The conversion between the two scales of temperature is computed byg the relationship:

$$°F = \frac{9}{5}°C + 32$$

Another unit of temperature often used in scientific calculations is the *Kelvin*. This scale is often used when working with gases, as usually, very low temperatures are in question. Kelvin (K) is the measure of absolute temperature.

The coldest theoretical temperature any substance can have is *absolute zero*, and it is equal to 0 K. This is the same temperature as –273 °C!

The figure below shows three thermometers displaying equal temperatures in the three common units of temperature.

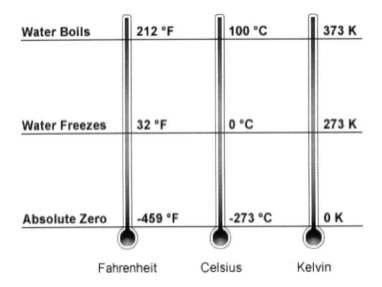

Temperature itself is the average amount of kinetic energy in the particles (molecules and atoms) that make up a material. At absolute zero, these particles will theoretically have no kinetic energy, and therefore no movement. Kelvin and Celsius use the same step in their degree measurements, which can make many calculations easier.

For example, a temperature difference is the same in Kelvin as it is in Celsius so when asked to calculate a temperature difference in either of these units you do not have to convert.

If required to convert from one to the other, the conversion can be performed by adding 273 to the Celsius temperature to get Kelvin:

$$K = {}^\circ C + 273$$

Another important note is that absolute zero can never be attained. Scientists have achieved temperatures very close to absolute zero but can never fully reach it.

For example, the lowest temperature ever recorded was in 2003, by a group of scientists from MIT. They successfully cooled sodium gas to a temperature of half-a-billionth of a degree above absolute zero, but not at absolute zero.

Heat Capacity and Specific Heat

The *heat capacity* of a substance is the ratio of the absorbed heat energy to the resulting temperature change. The SI unit for heat capacity is joule per Kelvin (J/K). When measuring the heat capacity of a substance, a variable must be held constant, since the heat capacity of a system depends on the temperature itself, the pressure and the volume of the system. To get a constant reading, gases and liquids are normally measured at constant volume and subjected to a certain pressure.

When pressure is held constant, the process to define a heat capacity is an *isobaric process*.

When the volume is held constant, it is an *isochoric process*. These are noted with either a c_p or a c_v, respectively.

A similar concept is *specific heat*. This is the measurement of heat needed to raise the temperature of a certain mass of a given substance (the heat capacity of a substance per unit of mass). Notice that the heat capacity and the specific heat of a substance are very similar. However, specific heat is the ratio of energy absorbed to the temperature rise per unit of mass of the substance, and heat capacity is the ratio of energy absorbed to the temperature rise.

The specific heat is a characteristic of the substance and thus does not change.

Below is a table of the specific heats of several common substances:

Specific heats of selected materials	
Material	**C(J/kg·K)**
Aluminum	879
Concrete	850
Diamond	509
Glass	840
Helium	5,193
Water	4,186

Substances such as metals (like copper) have a low specific heat because it does not take much energy to transfer the heat and excite the molecules, therefore raising the measurement of their average energy (raising their temperature). Materials that are difficult to heat, such as rubber, have a much higher specific heat because more energy is required to raise its temperature the same amount.

This is the reason for the *sea breeze effect*. The previous table shows that water has a much higher heat capacity than other common materials found on land. This means that it takes more energy to raise an ocean by 1 °C than it does to raise city sidewalks by the same amount.

Thus, during the day, land warms faster than water when subjected to the same amount of thermal energy from the sun. The hot land heats the air above it, causing it to rise and create a low-pressure system above it. The cooler water creates a high-pressure system, due to air cooling down and descending.

The difference in pressures creates a flow of air from the sea to the land during the day, which is a sea breeze. At night, the land cools faster than the water (due to its lower specific heat capacity), and the effect is reversed as air flows from land to sea.

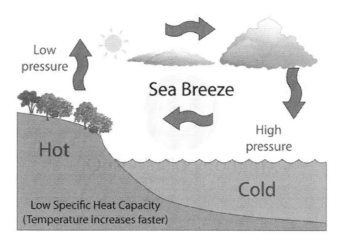

Using the specific heat of a substance (*c*), heat and temperature can be related in the equation:

$$Q = mc\Delta T$$

where Q is the heat transferred to the material (J), m is the mass of the object being heated (kg), and ΔT is the change in temperature (K).

For example, 3,200 J of heat is added to 1.0 kg of water (c = 4,190 J/kg·°C) at an initial temperature of 10 °C. By rearranging the equation for specific heat, the increase in temperature can be solved for.

$$\Delta T = \frac{Q}{mc}$$

$$\Delta T = \frac{3,200\ J}{1.0\ kg \cdot 4,190\ \frac{J}{kg} \cdot {}^{\circ}C}$$

$$\Delta T = 0.76\ {}^{\circ}C$$

Remember when solving for ΔT, that it stands for change in temperature. This value must be added to the initial temperature to find the final temperature or subtracted from the final to find the initial.

To fully analyze a reaction, it must be contained so that all of the products can be observed. A *calorimeter* is a special device that is considered ideally-insulated, such that any heat freed by the process taking place is transferred to either the other substances within the calorimeter or the calorimeter itself—but no heat is lost to the surroundings.

Since no thermal energy is lost, a scientist can measure the heat of a reaction by inserting a thermometer into a calorimeter and recording the temperature before and after the reaction takes place. A stirrer is used to ensure all contents of the calorimeter are well mixed and react uniformly. Below is an example of a calorimeter often used to demonstrate the concept:

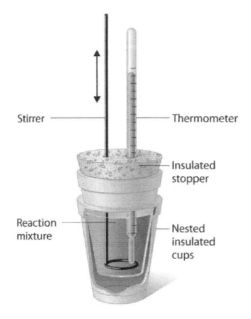

Heat Transfer

Heat can be transferred between two objects in three ways: conduction, convection or radiation.

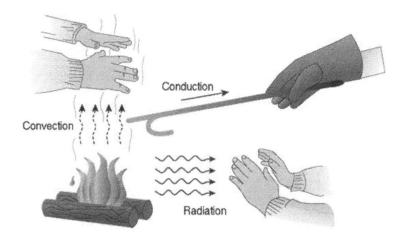

Conduction occurs when heat is transferred through direct contact. On a cold winter night, when a person wraps their hands around a cup of hot cocoa, their fingers warm up because they are in direct contact with the warm mug, which is in direct contact with the warm liquid. The same process is happening at a molecular level. The liquid in the mug contains heat energy, and molecules of the liquid are in constant motion. These molecules collide against the molecules in the mug, increasing their motion.

The action of the collisions gradually transfers some of the energy from the liquid molecules to the mug molecules. In the same way, the mug then transfers its heat to a persons' hands. They feel the transfer of energy as an increase in temperature; thus, their hands feel warm. The figure below gives a visual approximation of the process of conduction through a mug:

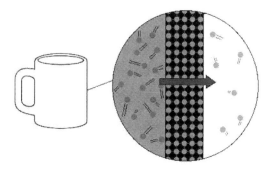

When heat is transferred by conduction, the rate of heat transfer (H) can be calculated. It is measured in joules per second, or watts (W).

This describes the amount of energy (heat) conducted during a set time interval:

$$H = \frac{kA\Delta T}{t}$$

where ΔT is the temperature difference across the object (K), A is the cross-sectional area (m^2), t is the thickness of the material (m), and k is the thermal conductivity of the material (J/s·m·k). This quantity is a characteristic of the material and is usually is given in the problem.

Below is a table of common values of thermal conductivities.

Thermal Conductivities of Selected Materials	
Material	**k (J/s·m·K)**
Aluminum	237
Concrete	1
Copper	386
Glass	0.9
Stainless Steel	16.5
Water	0.6

When calculating heat conduction through an object, it is important to note that the cross-sectional area refers to the area through which the heat is being conducted. In the case of the mug example, the heat is being conducted through its outer curved surface.

Therefore, the cross-sectional area is the circumference of the mug times its height. The thickness, in this case, is the thickness of the mug itself.

If the mug were set down on a table and the heat conduction to the table was to be calculated, then the cross-sectional area is the area of the bottom of the mug, rather the area of the sidewalls.

Convection is the process of transferring heat through the flow of energized molecules from one place to another. This is done through the movement of fluids. Remember that gas is also a fluid, as it can flow and change shape depending on its container.

For example, when a pot of water is placed on a stove, the water at the bottom starts to warm up first. As it warms, it rises and is replaced by cooler water. This circulation of water transfers the thermal energy from the bottom of the pot to the top and results in a closed pattern of fluid flow of *convection currents*.

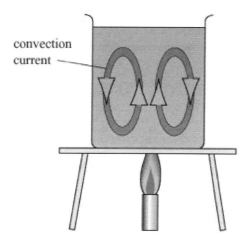

A convection oven works similarly, but with gas molecules instead of liquid molecules. Air is blown past a heating element to the oven chamber. When passing through the heating element, the air molecules are energized by the hot element. They are then circulated throughout the oven by the airflow provided by the fan until all of the molecules are energized to the same amount.

Although convection is similar to conduction, be sure to notice the difference. Conduction is the flow of heat between two materials in direct contact, while convection is the flow of energized molecules. When the energized molecules settle, they then deposit their energy through conduction.

Radiation is the transfer of energy through electromagnetic waves. Radiation is emitted from all objects or surfaces with heat energy. The more energy contained, the more radiation emitted. For example, a hot piece of metal radiates heat in the form of infrared electromagnetic waves. As the metal gets hotter, it also begins to radiate heat in the visual spectrum, thus making the metal appear "red hot."

Another well-known source of radiation is the Sun. It releases electromagnetic waves that travel through space, then through the atmosphere to heat Earth. Similarly, holding one's hands next to a fire heats them through radiation. Notice that radiation is the transfer of heat through electromagnetic waves, and therefore does not require a medium; thus, it can occur in a vacuum.

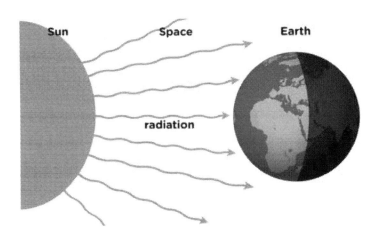

The power radiated by an object is related to its temperature and can be calculated by:

$$P = e\sigma A(T^4 - T_C^4)$$

where P is the power radiated (W), e is the emissivity of the radiator, σ is Stefan's constant equal to $5.67 \times 10^{-8}\ \dfrac{W}{m^2 K}$, A is the area of the radiating surface (m^2), T is the temperature of the radiator (K) and T_C is the temperature of the surroundings (K)

Thermodynamic Systems

A *thermodynamic system* is often used to describe thermodynamic processes and is a quantity of matter around which a boundary can be drawn. Thermodynamic systems can be isolated, closed or open. An isolated system has no transfer of heat, work or matter with its surroundings. A closed system may transfer heat and work to its surroundings but never matter. An open system can transfer all three to its surroundings.

State functions (i.e., state quantities), are a group of equations representative of the properties of a system, which depend only on the current state of the system, not on the way the current state was achieved. Thermodynamic state functions include enthalpy, entropy, and Gibbs free energy.

System	Exchanges with surrounding	Total amt. of Energy	Example	Illustration
Open	Energy & Matter	Does not remain constant	Solution kept in an open flask	
Closed	Only Energy	Does not remain constant	Solution kept in a sealed flask	
Isolated	Neither energy nor matter	Remains constant	Sealed flask kept in a thermos flask	

The Zeroth Law of Thermodynamics

The Zeroth Law is the logical predecessor of the First and Second Laws of Thermodynamics. The *Zeroth Law of Thermodynamics* states that if two systems are in thermal equilibrium with a third system, the two initial systems are in thermal equilibrium. This means that all three systems contain the same amount of heat energy (the same temperature) and do not exchange any heat. This is an observation and the fundamental idea behind thermodynamics.

The figure below demonstrates the Zeroth Law. If system A is in equilibrium with B, and system C is in equilibrium with B, then system A and C must be in equilibrium, and all three systems must be at the same temperature.

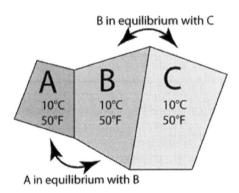

It is important to notice, however, that although no net transfer of heat occurs between systems in equilibrium, thermal energy is still technically transferring between the systems. This requires every unit of energy that is passed from any system to have the same value of energy passed back into the system.

This holds even if the two systems contain materials with different specific heats. This means that there must be a property that can be considered the same upon which heat transfer depends, and that property is temperature.

First Law of Thermodynamics: Conservation of Energy

Like matter, energy is always conserved. It can neither be created nor destroyed. The *First Law of Thermodynamics* relates closely to the *internal energy of a substance*. The internal energy refers to the microscopic energy of the disordered motion of particles. This energy cannot be seen and has no apparent effect on the motion of the object as a whole, but it does play a part in the thermodynamic properties of the substance. Internal energy is represented by the symbol (U).

For example, a glass of water does not look like it contains any kinetic or potential energy. However, on the atomic scale, its molecules are whizzing around any which way, moving at hundreds of meters per second. If the water is dumped out of the glass, its internal energy has no apparent effect on its motion.

Water

The First Law states that the internal energy of a system increases if heat is added to the system, or if work is done on the system. The difference between the amount of heat added to the system (Q) and the work done by the system (W) is equal to the total change in internal energy (ΔU):

$$\Delta U = \Delta Q - \Delta W$$

As with every energy, the unit of internal energy is the joule (J), although it is sometimes expressed using calories (cal).

By convention, work done by a system is negative, and work done on a system is positive. Occasionally, the above equation is written as $\Delta U = \Delta Q + \Delta W$, and ΔW is defined as the work done on the system.

Be sure to note which form is being used.

Using the quantities in this equation, it can be determined what a thermodynamic system is undergoing.

For example, in a chemical reaction, if ΔQ is some quantity less than zero, the reaction is losing heat. This reaction is exothermic and contains heat as a product.

If ΔQ is some quantity greater than zero, the reaction is absorbing heat from its surroundings. This is an endothermic reaction and contains heat as a reactant. The figure below depicts both types of reactions.

On the left, the reaction is *exothermic* because heat is produced and released to the surroundings from the system.

On the right, the reaction is *endothermic* because heat is absorbed from the surroundings.

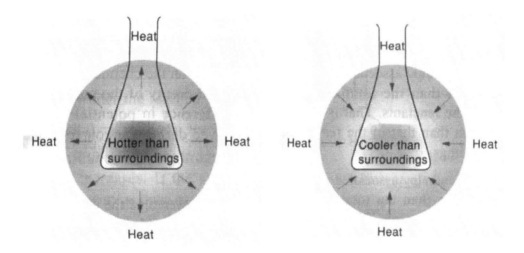

Second Law of Thermodynamics: Entropy

The *Second Law of Thermodynamics* states that in an isolated system (no transfer of heat, work, or matter), a process either increases in entropy or stays constant, but it never decreases. The only exception to this is an open system (heat, work, and matter can be transferred to surroundings), which can decrease in entropy only because it increases the entropy of its surroundings.

Regarding heat flow, the Second Law states that heat flows spontaneously from a hot object to a cold one, but it never spontaneously flows in the opposite direction.

For example, a bowl of ice cream never gets colder in a warm room; it gets warmer.

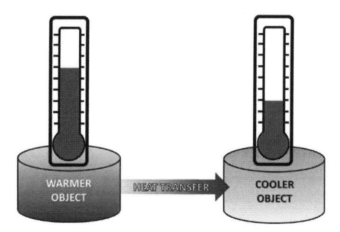

Entropy (S) is a measure of disorder within a system. In reality, it is more a measure of multiplicity and likelihood – how likely a system will resemble the same thing twice, or how likely a reaction is to happen.

The entropy of a natural system never decreases, as it is the natural tendency of all things to move towards maximum disorder – maximum entropy.

For example, a gas expands to fill a space, because there are then more ways it can arrange its given particles—more multiplicities.

Therefore, a solid has less entropy than a liquid, which has much less entropy than a gas.

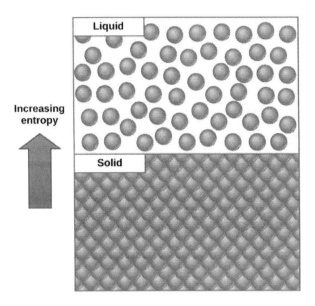

According to the Second Law of Thermodynamics, entropy is given by the equation (remember that entropy can stay constant or increase but never decrease):

$$\Delta S \geq \frac{Q}{T}$$

where ΔS is the change in entropy of a process or reaction (J/K), Q is the heat transferred (J), and T is the temperature (K).

Just because a system wants to increase in entropy does not mean that the system cannot become more orderly. It means that to do so; outside energy must be transferred into the system—it cannot do it on its own.

A *nonspontaneous process* requires energy or work to be added for it to occur.

A *spontaneous process* is the opposite and requires no energy input to occur.

For example, a valve connects a container with air and another container at a vacuum. When the valve is opened, the air flows from the container with air to the container at a vacuum. No work or energy is needed for this to happen.

The process is spontaneous; at the end of the reaction, the entropy has increased.

For the reverse to occur, energy must be added to the system to re-pressurize the original container with air.

Below is an example of a nonspontaneous reaction.

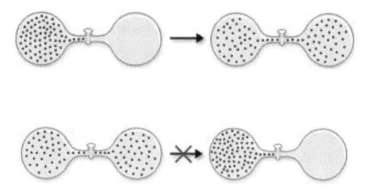

Another important idea to note is that the entropy of the universe always increases when a spontaneous process occurs.

This is expressed as:

$$\Delta S_{universe} > 0$$

The Third Law of Thermodynamics

The *Third Law of Thermodynamics* states that as the temperature of a system approaches absolute zero, the entropy approaches a constant value. Typically, this constant value is zero.

In this definition, the entropy of a system is related to the number of microstates possible. Microstates refer to all the atomic configurations possible. The equation represents this relationship:

$$S = k \cdot ln \ (\Omega)$$

where S is the entropy (J/K), k is Boltzmann's constant (1.381×10^{-23} J/K), and Ω is the number of microstates.

Only one microstate is possible at absolute zero, and so Ω equals 1:

$$S = k \cdot ln(1) = k \cdot 0 = 0$$

Therefore, the entropy of a system at absolute zero is zero. However, some systems have more than one minimum energy state. That is, as their temperature approaches absolute zero, the entropy levels off at a value other than zero.

It is impossible to cool any process to absolute zero in a finite number of steps. In the image on the left, $T = 0$ can be reached following an infinite number of steps (step lines between X_1 or X_2).

However, in the image on the right, $T = 0$ is reached by a finite number of steps, each getting closer and closer to zero, but never to zero.

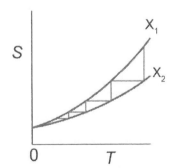 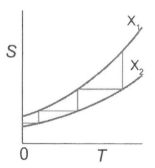

Enthalpy

The *enthalpy* (*H*) of a system is the amount of heat used at constant pressure in a system or reaction and is given in SI units of Joules. It describes the energy changes of the system, and can be written as:

$$\Delta U = \Delta H - P\Delta V$$

where ΔH is the change in enthalpy of a system (J), P is the pressure (Pa), and ΔV is the change in volume (m^3).

During an isobaric process (pressure is constant), such as in an open container, the change in enthalpy equals the amount of heat transferred during the process.

Most reactions do not give off a lot of gaseous products, and as a result, there is very little work associated with the reaction. This means that the change in energy of the system is equal to the change in enthalpy:

$$\Delta E \approx \Delta H$$

Since the enthalpy is equal to the transfer of thermal energy (heat), the reaction, the system displays can be determined. This only works at constant pressure. An exothermic reaction has a change in enthalpy less than zero. An endothermic reaction has a change in enthalpy greater than zero.

Since enthalpy is a state function, it represents a property of a system. It can be used to describe a reaction or an equation for a reaction.

Hess' Law states that the change of enthalpy in a reaction is equal to the sum of the products' enthalpy, minus the sum of the reactants' enthalpy:

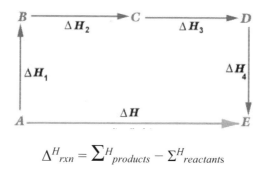

$$\Delta H_{rxn} = \sum H_{products} - \sum H_{reactants}$$

Gibbs Free Energy

J. Willard Gibbs was an American physicist who introduced the concept of free energy to thermodynamics. The equation for free energy is given by:

$$\Delta G = \Delta H - T\Delta S$$

where G is Gibbs free energy (J).

If at a given temperature and pressure, the change in G is negative, then the reaction is *spontaneous*.

If G is equal to zero, the reaction is at *equilibrium*.

If G is positive, the reaction is *nonspontaneous*.

Because Gibbs free energy depends on signs, its value can be calculated using estimates of values.

The table below gives a quick approximation for the value of the free energy, and whether the reaction is spontaneous or nonspontaneous.

ΔH	ΔS	Result
-	+	Spontaneous at all temperatures
+	+	Spontaneous at high temperatures
-	-	Spontaneous at low temperatures
+	-	Not spontaneous at any temperatures

PV Diagrams

A *PV diagram* shows the thermodynamic process by graphing pressure against volume. The work done by the system is equal to the area under the curve.

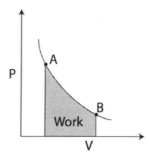

A process can be labeled with four titles: adiabatic, isothermal, isobaric and isochoric. An *isothermal reaction* keeps temperature constant ($\Delta T = 0$). This also means that the change in internal energy must stay the same, as an increase in thermal energy (heat) increases temperature ($\Delta U = 0$).

The PV diagram of an isothermal process is given below:

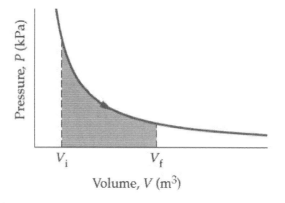

An *adiabatic process* is one in which there is no transfer of heat ($Q = 0$). This means that the change in energy is equal to the work. This process is often confused with the isothermal process because it is sometimes assumed that no transfer of heat means no change in temperature. However, this is not true—in isothermal instances, heat energy must be allowed into or out of the reaction to keep the temperature constant.

Unlike the isothermal reaction, an adiabatic process occurs quickly and has a PV graph much steeper than the isothermal process, but in the same shape. Adiabatic processes include a tire pump or a sharp expulsion of breath.

Adiabatic PV diagrams are often shown about isothermal lines called *isotherms*.

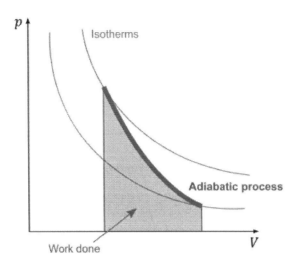

Isobaric reactions keep the pressure constant. When this occurs, the work is equal to the pressure times the change in volume ($W = P\Delta V$).

The graph of an isobaric reaction is a horizontal line. Some examples include a piston in an engine, or a flexible container open to Earth's atmosphere.

When pressure is constant, the PV graph of an isobaric process is a straight line.

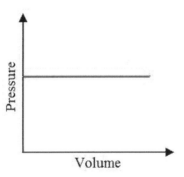

An *isochoric process* is also an isovolumetric process. This means the volume is kept constant. Since there is no movement, the work is zero, and all of the change in energy is due to the amount of heat added to the system ($W = 0$, $\Delta E = Q$).

Isochoric processes include those inside a closed and rigid container or a constant volume thermometer.

The graph of an isochoric reaction is a vertical line.

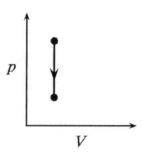

The processes, along with their relationships to the Ideal Gas Law, is below:

Process	Constant	PV Diagram	Ideal Gas Law	First Law of Thermodynamics
Isobaric	Pressure	Horizontal line	$V \alpha T$	$\Delta U = Q + W$
Isochoric	Volume	Vertical line	$P \alpha T$	$\Delta U = Q$
Isothermal	Temperature	Curved line	$PV \alpha T$	$\Delta U = 0$
Adiabatic	No heat exchanged	Curved line (jumps to different isotherm)	$PV = nRT$ (only "nR" are constant)	$\Delta U = W$

Types of Work Cycles

In cyclic reactions, the work done is the area enclosed in the graph.

These reactions are comprised of different processes, as shown below.

As seen in the diagram, work is done by the gas when the volume increases and the pressure decreases and is done on gas when volume decreases and the pressure increases.

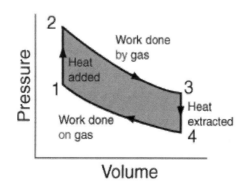

The Carnot Cycle

The *Kelvin-Planck statement* of the Second Law of Thermodynamics references heat engines. It states that it is impossible to extract an amount of heat from a "hot reservoir" (Q_2) and use all of it to do work. Some of this heat must be exhausted to a "cold reservoir" (Q_1).

A perfect heat engine uses all of the energy taken from the hot reservoir to do work. This is not possible because real heat engines lose some heat to the environment.

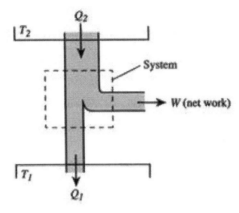

The *Carnot Cycle* represents the most efficient heat engine cycle. It is made of two isothermal processes and two adiabatic processes.

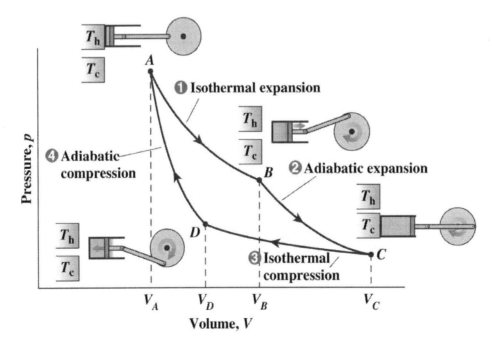

However, the Carnot cycle is an ideal situation and can never be perfectly replicated in real life.

To follow the Second Law, the *Carnot efficiency* sets a limiting value on the fraction of heat taken from the hot reservoir, which can be used for work:

$$n = \frac{T_H T_C}{T_H} \times 100\%$$

where n is the Carnot efficiency, T_H is the temperature of the hot reservoir (K), and T_C is the temperature of the cold reservoir (K).

To achieve this efficiency, the entire process must be reversible, and the change in entropy must be zero.

This is impossible, as no process of a real engine is reversible, and every process involves an increase in entropy because maximum entropy is the natural state of the universe.

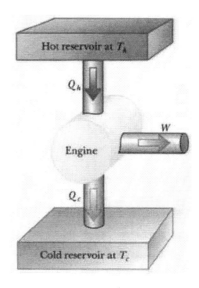

The Kinetic Theory of Gases

The Kinetic Theory of Gases relates the microscopic values of atomic kinetic energy to tangible quantities like temperature and pressure. There are four basic premises behind this theory:

1. Gases are made up of molecules. Molecules may be treated as perfect spheres of mass, and the space between each of these masses are many times greater than their diameters.

2. The motion of each molecule is random. There is no order or pattern to either their direction or magnitude of the velocity.

3. Molecules still follow Newton's Laws of Motion.

   Each molecule moves in a straight line with a constant velocity.

   If they collide, the molecules exert an equal but opposite force on one another.

4. The collisions of molecules are perfectly elastic—they lose no kinetic energy.

These rules display gases as ideal substances and only approximate their behavior. However, their description is remarkably accurate. Using these definitions, one can define and derive laws for a gas's behavior.

Ideal Gas Law

The *Ideal Gas Law* is used to explain the relationship between pressure (P), volume (V), and temperature (T). The gas law is expressed as:

$$PV = nRT$$

where n is the number of moles and R is the universal gas constant with a value of 8.314 J/mol·K.

One mole is equal to 6.023×10^{23} molecules. Technically, it is the number of hydrogen atoms in one gram of hydrogen. Because atoms are so small, it is much easier to count them in moles than it is to count them individually.

The Ideal Gas Law was found by examining the pressure exerted by a gas on a cylinder with a moving wall.

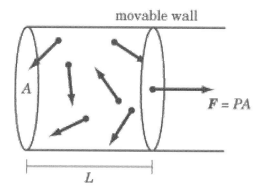

Since pressure is equal to $P = F/A$, the force that the gas exerts on the wall is equal to $F = PA$. If this force moves the wall back a length of L, then the volume of the cylinder increases by $\Delta V = LA$. By solving for A and plugging this back into the equation for force, the result is $F = P\Delta V L$. This is equal to $P\Delta V = FL$.

Previously, work been defined as force multiplied by a distance traveled. By pushing the wall a distance of L with a force of F, the gas has done work equal to FL. When gas does work, it symbolizes a change in energy. This means that if a change in PV is equal to a change in energy, then PV itself is the total energy of the gas. Regarding the ideal gas law, this also means that nRT is the expression for the total kinetic energy of the gas molecules as well.

The ideal gas law can also be related to the number of molecules (N) and the Boltzmann's constant (k) which has a value of 1.381×10^{-23} J/K:

$$PV = NkT$$

Other laws can be derived from the Ideal Gas Law, by holding a variable constant. The number of moles (n) and the gas constant (R) are already constant, so four more laws can be derived from the Ideal Gas Law: Boyle's Law, Charles' Law, Combined Gas Law, and the Closed Container Law.

Boyle's Law (isothermal process)

When using *Boyle's Law*, the temperature of a gas is held constant. It states that an increase in pressure causes a decrease in volume, or that a decrease in pressure causes an increase in volume. Boyle's Law is expressed as:

$$P_1V_1 = P_2V_2$$

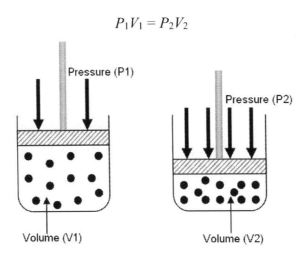

Charles' Law (isobaric process)

When gas is under constant pressure, its behavior can be approximated by *Charles' Law*. In this relationship, volume and temperature are directly proportional; when the temperature increases, the volume increases; when the temperature decreases, the volume decreases. Charles' Law is expressed as:

$$\frac{V_i}{T_f} = \frac{V_i}{T_f}$$

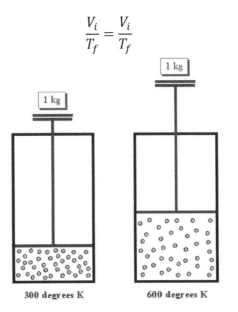

Closed Container Law (constant volume)

The *Closed Container Law* refers to situations in which the volume is constant. In such cases, pressure and temperature are directly proportional:

$$\frac{P_i}{T_i} = \frac{P_f}{T_f}$$

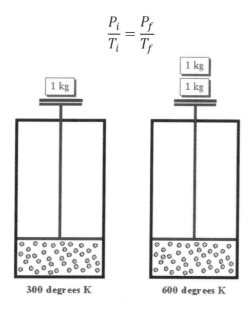

Combined Gas Law

The *Combined Gas Law* is a combination of Boyle's and Charles' Laws. It relates the pressure, volume, and temperature of a gas, and is expressed as:

$$\frac{P_i V_i}{T_i} = \frac{P_f V_f}{T_f}$$

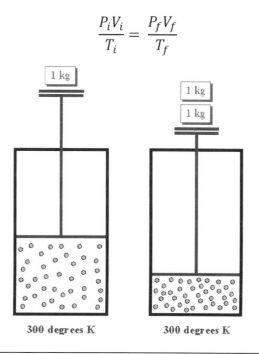

Coefficient of Linear Expansion

When a material changes temperature, it shrinks or expands, depending upon the temperature difference. As the temperature increases, the molecules within the material gain energy and vibrate at higher rates. This increases the distance between the molecules and causes the material to expand. If the material does not experience a phase change (liquid to gas), this expansion of material can be connected to the change in temperature.

The coefficient of expansion is a measurement of expansion or contraction per unit of length of a material that occurs when the temperature is increased or decreased by 1 °C. This is expansivity. The *coefficient of thermal expansion* (α) is given as:

$$\alpha_{linear} = \frac{\Delta l}{l_i \cdot \Delta T}$$

where α_{linear} is the coefficient of thermal expansion (K^{-1}), Δl is the change in length (m), l_i is the initial length (m), and ΔT is the change in temperature (K).

For example, in the figure below a bar of material is at an initial temperature, and has a length denoted as L.

If the bar is heated such that its temperature rises, it expands linearly by some length ΔL.

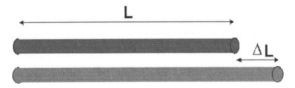

Objects can also undergo area expansion and volume expansion due to the same principles. The *coefficient of area expansion* is expressed as:

$$\alpha_{area} = \frac{\Delta A}{A_i \cdot \Delta T}$$

where α_{area} is the coefficient of thermal expansion (K^{-1}), ΔA is the change in area (m^2), A_i is the initial area (m^2) and ΔT is the change in temperature (K).

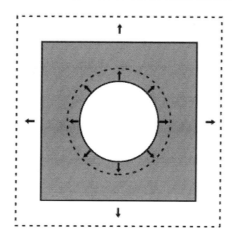

The *coefficient of volume expansion* is expressed as:

$$\alpha_{volume} = \frac{\Delta V}{V_i \cdot \Delta T}$$

where α_{volume} is the coefficient of thermal expansion (K^{-1}), ΔV is the change in volume (m^3), V_i is the initial volume (m^3), and ΔT is the change in temperature (K).

When designing products or structures that experience changes in temperature, thermal expansion is extremely important.

If the product design uses different materials with different thermal expansion coefficients, the design must also allow for a varying amount of component expansion and contraction.

If not, the components experience a great amount of stress when they attempt to expand and cannot. This makes the design and construction of bridges and aircraft extremely difficult.

Bridges in regions that get relatively cold have metallic joints where the bridge starts and ends.

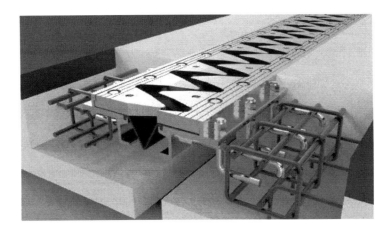

In the summer, these might be completely closed. However, in the winter, the thermal contraction of the bridge materials when subjected to cold air above and below cause the bridge to "shrink," and open a space up between these metal joints. This prevents the bridge from breaking because of material strain.

Phase Diagram: Pressure and Temperature

When an ice block is set out in the sun, it slowly absorbs the thermal energy through radiation and undergoes a series of phase changes. That is, it changes from a solid to a liquid, to a gas. Say the ice was in a freezer at a temperature of –20 °C.

Once it absorbs enough heat to melt (reaches 0 °C), its temperature remains constant until all of the molecules have reached a temperature of 0 °C.

Only when this occurs does the ice melt (point C). This is the horizontal plateaus in the graph below.

When the water changes to a gas (reaches 100 °C), it follows the same rule.

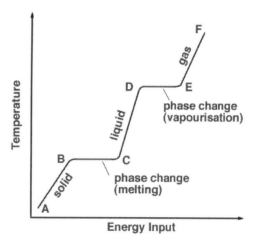

The *melting point* of a substance is the temperature at which it changes from a solid to a liquid, and it is the same temperature as the *freezing point*; the reverse reaction occurs at the same temperature. The *boiling point* (vaporization) of a substance is the temperature at which it changes phase from a liquid to a gas, and it is the same temperature as the *condensation point*.

Although the energy input (heat) increases with temperature, it never stays constant as the temperature does during a phase change.

As energy is constantly being added to the process, the substance uses the added heat to transition each molecule before increasing the temperature.

Technically, it converts the potential energy stored within each atom to kinetic energy before it changes phase.

A common way to display the phases of a substance is through a *phase diagram*. This is a graph plotted on a pressure vs. temperature plane. The plane is split into three disproportionate parts, which represent the phases of the substance.

Every point on the plane represents a possible combination of pressure and temperature for the system.

Below is a figure of a typical phase diagram:

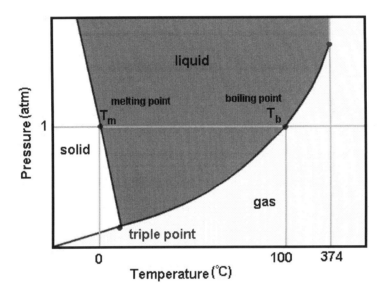

The melting point and boiling point of a substance are found by drawing a horizontal line at 1 atm of pressure, which is atmospheric pressure. Wherever the horizontal line intersects with a line on the phase diagram, the substance changes phases at that exact temperature.

The *triple point* is the point on the graph at which all three lines intersect and at which all three phases exist simultaneously.

The *critical point* on a phase diagram is the temperature, above which the substance is always a gas, regardless of pressure.

Latent Heat

The amount of heat required to perform a phase change is *latent heat*. The latent heat is known for most substances. In general, only computing the total heat is required for the reaction. The heat required to convert a substance from one phase to another is expressed as:

$$Q = m \cdot l$$

where *l* is the latent heat (J/kg), and *m* is the mass of the substance (kg).

If the particles get more excited (solid to liquid, liquid to gas) the change in entropy is always positive, because heat is being added to the system. For this process, the latent heat of fusion is used. The total heat required for this process is the heat of fusion.

If the particles get less excited (gas to liquid, liquid to solid) the change in entropy is always negative, because heat is being removed from the system.

A negative change in entropy results in a more ordered molecular structure of the substance. The total heat required for this process is the *heat of vaporization*.

Occasionally, a solid skips the liquid phase right to the gas phase; this phenomenon is *sublimation*. The heat required for sublimation is the sum of the heat of fusion and the heat of vaporization. The reverse reaction of sublimation is a *deposition*.

$$Q_{sub} = Q_{fus} + Q_{vap}$$

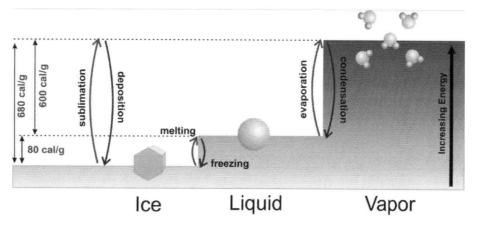

Latent heats are sometimes given in molar heat, or joules per mol (J/mol). Be sure to divide by the molecular weight of the substance if given a mass in grams. If any of these processes are reversed, the latent heat is given a negative sign.

For a process with multiple phase changes, the total heat of the reaction is the sum of the separate heats needed for each phase change and the addition of heat. For these types of problems, it is important to remember the First Law of Thermodynamics, which states that heat must be conserved (heat gained = heat loss), as well as the equation for heat ($Q = mc\Delta T$) where c is the specific heat capacity, and m is the mass. For example, to calculate the change in heat (change in entropy) when 2 kg of ice at 0 °C is warmed to 120 °C, a few equations must be set up, using a few known values.

- melting point = 0 °C

- boiling point = 100 °C

- latent heat of fusion = 3.33×10^5 J/kg

- latent heat of vaporization = 2.26×10^6 J/kg

- specific heat capacity = 4,186 J/kg °C

Heat required to phase change the ice into liquid water:

$$Q = m \, l_{fusion} = (2\text{kg}) \cdot (3.33 \times 10^5 \text{ J/kg}) = 6.66 \times 10^5 \text{ J}$$

Heat required to heat the water to its boiling point:

$$Q = mc\Delta T = (2 \text{ kg}) \cdot (4,186 \text{ J/kg °C}) \cdot (100 \text{ °C} - 0 \text{ °C}) = 837,200 \text{ J}$$

Heat required to phase change the liquid into gas:

$$Q = m \, l_{vap} = (2\text{kg}) \cdot (2.26 \times 10^6 \text{ J/kg}) = 4.52 \times 10^6 \text{ J}$$

Heat required to heat the water to 120 °C:

$$Q = mc\Delta T = (2 \text{ kg}) \cdot (4,186 \text{ J/kg °C}) \cdot (120 \text{ °C} - 100 \text{ °C}) = 167,440 \text{ J}$$

Therefore, the total heat required for the process to occur is the sum of the separate heats:

$$Q_{total} = Q_{fusion} + Q_{heat\_1} + Q_{vap} + Q_{heat\_2}$$

$$= 6.66 \times 10^5 + 837,200 + 4.52 \times 10^6 + 167,440 = 6,190,640 \text{ J}$$

Chapter Summary

Heat and Temperature

- Heat is the total energy due to molecular motion, and the temperature is the average measure of the energy stored within a certain substance.

- The calorie is the amount of heat needed to raise the temperature of one gram of water by one degree Celsius (g/°C).

- Kelvin (K) is the measure of absolute temperature. Absolute zero = 0 K.

- Kelvin and Celsius use the same step in their degree measurements.

- Specific heat is the ratio of energy absorbed to the temperature rise per unit of mass.

- The heat required to perform a phase change is latent heat (*l*):

$$Q = m \cdot l$$

- A calorimeter measures the heat of a reaction.

  - Temperature remains constant through a phase change.

- Phase diagram

  o Triple point: all three phases exist simultaneously.

  o Critical point: the substance is always a gas.

- Boltzmann's constant is 1.381×10^{-23} J/K: $PV = NkT$

- Coefficient of expansion: the expansion per unit of length of a material for an increase in temperature under constant pressure:

$$\alpha = \frac{\Delta l}{l_i \cdot \Delta T}$$

Heat Transfer

- Conduction - direct contact.

  The rate of heat transfer (*H*) by conduction: $H = \frac{kA\Delta T}{L}$

- Convection (energized particles from one place to another).

- Radiation (electromagnetic waves).

Laws of Thermodynamics

- Zeroth Law: two systems in thermal equilibrium with a third system are in thermal equilibrium.

- First Law: energy is always conserved: $\Delta U = Q - W$

  o Work done by a system ($-$)

  o Work done on a system ($+$)

  o $Q < 0$ exothermic

  o $Q > 0$ endothermic

- Second Law: entropy increases or stays constant, never decrease;

  o Entropy (*S*) is a measure of disorder within a system.

  o Natural tendency of all things to move towards maximum disorder: $\Delta S \geq \frac{Q}{T}$

  o $\Delta S_{universe} > 0$ spontaneous

  o $\Delta S_{universe} > 0$ at equilibrium

  o $\Delta S_{universe} > 0$ reverse process spontaneous

- Third Law: as the temperature of a system approaches absolute zero; the entropy approaches a constant value (typically zero).

$$S = k \cdot ln\ (\Omega)$$

where S is the entropy (J/K), k is Boltzmann's constant (1.381×10^{-23} J/K), and Ω is the number of microstates.

- The entropy of a system at absolute zero is zero. However, some systems have more than one minimum energy state.

Enthalpy

- Amount of heat used at constant pressure: $\Delta U = \Delta H - P\Delta V$

- $\Delta H < 0$ exothermic

- $\Delta H > 0$ endothermic

- Hess' Law: $\Delta H_{rxn} = \sum H_{products} - H_{reactants}$

Gibb's Free Energy

- $\Delta G = \Delta H - T\Delta S$

- G < 0 spontaneous

- G = 0 at equilibrium

- G > 0 nonspontaneous.

PV Diagram

- Work is the area under the curve.

- Isothermal - constant temperature: hyperbola

- Adiabatic - no transfer of heat: steeper hyperbola

- Isobaric - constant pressure: horizontal line

- Isochoric - constant volume: vertical line

The Carnot Cycle

- Most efficient heat engine cycle

- Two isothermal processes and two adiabatic processes

- Carnot Efficiency: $\frac{T_H T_C}{T_H} \times 100\%$

The Kinetic Theory of Gases

1. Gases are made up of molecules. Molecules may be treated as perfect spheres of mass, and the space between each of these masses are many times greater than their diameters.

2. The motion of each molecule is random. There is no order or pattern to either their direction or magnitude of the velocity.

3. Molecules follow Newton's Laws of Motion. Each molecule moves in a straight line with a constant velocity. If they collide, the molecules exert an equal but opposite force on one another.

4. The collisions of molecules are perfectly elastic—they lose no kinetic energy.

Coefficient of Linear Expansion

- *The coefficient of expansion* is a measurement of the expansion or contraction per unit of length of a material that occurs when the temperature is increased or decreased by $1°$ C. This term is expansivity.

$$\alpha_{linear} = \frac{\Delta l}{l_i \cdot \Delta T}$$

where α_{linear} is the coefficient of thermal expansion (K^{-1}), Δl is the change in length (m), l_i is the initial length (m), and ΔT is the change in temperature (K).

Phase diagram: Pressure and Temperature

- The *melting point* of a substance is the temperature at which it changes from a solid to a liquid, and it is the same temperature as the *freezing point*; the reverse reaction occurs at the same temperature.

  The *boiling point* (vaporization) of a substance is the temperature at which it changes phase from a liquid to a gas, and it is the same temperature as the *condensation point*.

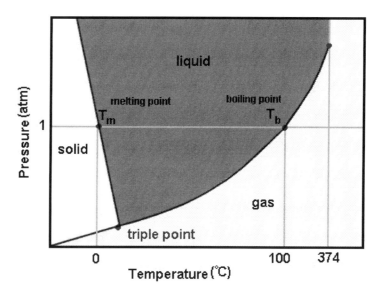

Latent Heat

- The amount of heat required to perform a phase change is *latent heat*. The latent heat is known for most substances.

  The heat required to convert a substance from one phase to another is expressed as:

$$Q = m \cdot l$$

  where *l* is the latent heat (J/kg), and *m* is the mass of the substance (kg).

Notes

Practice Questions

1. A mass of 0.2 kg ethanol, in the liquid state at its melting point of $-114.4\,°C$, is frozen at atmospheric pressure. What is the change in the entropy of the ethanol as it freezes? (Use the heat of fusion of ethanol $L_f = 1.04 \times 10^5$ J/kg)

    A. -360 J/K   **B.** 54 J/K   **C.** -131 J/K   **D.** -220 J/K   **E.** 285 J/K

2. Isobaric work is

    A. $Q - W$ **B.** $P\Delta V$ **C.** $P\Delta T$ **D.** $V\Delta P$ **E.** $Q + W$

3. An adiabatic process is performed on 9 moles of an ideal gas. The initial temperature is 315 K, and the initial volume is 0.70 m³. The final volume is 0.30 m³. What is the amount of heat absorbed by the gas? (Use the adiabatic constant for the gas = 1.44)

    A. -18 kJ   **B.** 32 kJ   **C.** 9 kJ   **D.** -32 kJ   **E.** 0 kJ

4. An 80 g aluminum calorimeter contains 360 g of water at an equilibrium temperature of 20 °C. A 180 g piece of metal, initially at 305 °C, is added to the calorimeter. The final temperature at equilibrium is 35 °C. Assume there is no external heat exchange. What is the specific heat capacity of the metal? (Use the specific heat capacity of aluminum = 910 J/kg·K and the specific heat of water $c = 4{,}190$ J/kg·K)

    A. 260 J/kg·K   **C.** 488 J/kg·K

    B. 324 J/kg·K   **D.** 410 J/kg·K   **E.** 535 J/kg·K

5. A chemist uses 120 g of water that is heated using 65 W of power with 100% efficiency. How much time is required to raise the temperature of the water from 20 °C to 50 °C? (Use specific heat of water $c = 4.186$ J/g·°C)

    A. 136 s   **B.** 182 s   **C.** 93 s   **D.** 232 s   **E.** 274 s

6. The Second Law of Thermodynamics leads to the following conclusion:

    A. the average temperature of the universe is increasing over time
    B. it is theoretically possible to convert heat into work with 100% efficiency
    C. disorder in the universe is increasing over time
    D. total energy of the universe remains constant
    E. entropy of the universe remains constant

7. The statement that 'heat energy cannot be completely transformed into work' is a statement of which thermodynamic law?

A. Third   **B.** Second   **C.** Zeroth   **D.** Fourth   **E.** First

8. What is the change in entropy when 20 g of water at 100 °C is turned into steam at 100 °C? (Use the latent heat of vaporization of water $L_v = 22.6 \times 10^5$ J/kg)

A. −346 J/K   **B.** 346 J/K   **C.** −80.8 J/K   **D.** 121 J/K   **E.** 0 J/K

9. A Carnot-efficiency engine is operated as a heat pump to heat a room in the winter. The heat pump delivers heat to the room at the rate of 32 kJ per second and maintains the room at a temperature of 293 K when the outside temperature is 237 K. The power requirement for the heat pump under these operating conditions is:

A. 6,100 W   **B.** 3,400 W   **C.** 7,300 W   **D.** 14,300 W   **E.** 11,450 W

10. Which of the following relationships is true for all types of Carnot heat engines?

I. $\eta = 1 - T_C / T_H$
II. $\eta = 1 - | Q_C / Q_H |$
III. $T_C / T_H = Q_C / Q_H$

A. I only   **B.** II only   **C.** III only   **D.** I, II and III   **E.** I and III only

11. What is the change of entropy associated with 8 kg of water freezing to ice at 0 °C? (Use the latent heat of fusion $L_f = 80$ kcal/kg)

A. 1.4 kcal/K   **C.** −2.3 kcal/K
B. 0 kcal/K   **D.** −1.4 kcal/K   **E.** 0.8 kcal/K

12. A Carnot-efficiency engine extracts 515 J of heat from a high-temperature reservoir during each cycle and ejects 340 J of heat to a low-temperature reservoir during the same cycle. What is the efficiency of the engine?

A. 67%   **B.** 21%   **C.** 53%   **D.** 17%   **E.** 34%

13. A glass beaker of unknown mass contains 65 ml of water. The system absorbs 1,800 cals of heat, and the temperature rises 20 °C. What is the mass of the beaker? (Use the specific heat of glass = 0.18 cal/g·°C and the specific heat of water $c = 1$ cal/g·°C)

A. 342 g   **B.** 139 g   **C.** 546 g   **D.** 268 g   **E.** 782 g

14. A 0.3 kg ice cube at 0 °C has sufficient heat added to result in total melting, and the resulting water is heated to 60 °C. How much total heat is added? (Use the latent heat of fusion for water L_f = 334 kJ/kg, the latent heat of vaporization for water L_v = 2,257 kJ/kg and the specific heat of water c = 4.186 kJ/kg·K)

    A. 73 kJ   **B.** 48 kJ   **C.** 176 kJ   **D.** 144 kJ   **E.** 136 kJ

15. The water flowing over a large dam drops a distance of 60 m. If all the gravitational potential energy is converted to thermal energy, by what temperature does the water rise? (Use acceleration due to gravity g = 10 m/s^2 and specific heat of water c = 4,186 J/kg·K)

    A. 0.34 °C   **B.** 0.44 °C   **C.** 0.09 °C   **D.** 0.14 °C   **E.** 0.58 °C

Solutions

1. C is correct.

Find the heat from phase change:

$$Q = mL_f$$

$$Q = (0.2 \text{ kg}) \cdot (1.04 \times 10^5 \text{ J/kg})$$

$$Q = 20{,}800 \text{ J}$$

Because the ethanol is freezing, Q should be negative due to heat being released.

$$Q = -20{,}800 \text{ J}$$

Find the change in entropy:

$$\Delta S = Q / T$$

$$\Delta S = -20{,}800 \text{ J} / (-114.4 \text{ °C} + 273 \text{ K})$$

$$\Delta S = -131 \text{ J} / \text{K}$$

2. B is correct.

$$W = P \Delta V$$

Isobaric means pressure is constant, and the volume is changing.

3. E is correct.

Adiabatic means that no heat enters or leaves the system.

$$Q = 0 \text{ kJ}$$

4. C is correct.

$$Q = mc\Delta T$$

Find the heat added to aluminum calorimeter:

$$Q_A = (0.08 \text{ kg}) \cdot (910 \text{ J/kg·K}) \cdot (35 \text{ °C} - 20 \text{ °C})$$

$$Q_A = 1{,}092 \text{ J}$$

Find the heat added to water:

$$Q_W = (0.36 \text{ kg}) \cdot (4{,}190 \text{ J/kg·K}) \cdot (35 \text{ °C} - 20 \text{ °C})$$

$$Q_W = 22{,}626 \text{ J}$$

Find total heat added to the system:

$$Q_{total} = Q_A + Q_W$$

$$Q_{total} = 1{,}092 \text{ J} + 22{,}626 \text{ J}$$

$$Q_{total} = 23{,}718 \text{ J}$$

Find specific heat of the metal:

$$Q = mc\Delta T$$

$$c = Q / m\Delta T$$

$$c = (23{,}718 \text{ J}) / [(0.18 \text{ kg}) \cdot (305 \text{ °C} - 35 \text{ °C})]$$

$$c = 488 \text{ J/kg} \cdot \text{K}$$

5. D is correct.

$$\text{Watt} = 1 \text{ J/s}$$

Thermal energy:

$$Q = \text{Power} \times \text{time}$$

$$Q = mc\Delta T$$

$$P \times t = mc\Delta T$$

$$t = (mc\Delta T) / P$$

$$t = [(120 \text{ g}) \cdot (4.186 \text{ J/g} \cdot \text{°C}) \cdot (50 \text{ °C} - 20 \text{ °C})] / (65 \text{ W})$$

$$t = 232 \text{ s}$$

6. C is correct.

The Second Law of Thermodynamics states that entropy is either constant or increasing over time. A constant entropy process is an idealized process and doesn't exist. Thus, entropy is always increasing over time.

7. B is correct.

The Second Law of Thermodynamics states that through thermodynamic processes, there is an increase in the sum of entropies of the system and thus no engine process is 100% efficient.

8. D is correct.

Find the heat from phase change:

$$Q = mL_f$$

$$Q = (0.02 \text{ kg}) \cdot (22.6 \times 10^5 \text{ J/kg})$$

$$Q = 45,200 \text{ J}$$

Because the water is vaporizing, Q should be positive due to heat being absorbed.

$$Q = 45,200 \text{ J}$$

Find the change in entropy:

$$\Delta S = Q / T$$

$$\Delta S = 45,200 \text{ J} / (100 \text{ °C} + 273 \text{ K})$$

$$\Delta S = 121 \text{ J} / \text{K}$$

A positive change in entropy indicates that the disorder of the isolated system has increased. When water evaporates into steam, the entropy is positive because the disorder of steam is higher than water.

9. A is correct.

Coefficient of performance assuming an ideal Carnot cycle:

$$C_p = Q_H / W$$

$$C_p = T_H / (T_H - T_C)$$

$$Q_H / W = T_H / (T_H - T_C)$$

$$W = Q_H \cdot (T_H - T_C) / T_H$$

$$W = (32 \times 10^3 \text{ J/s}) \cdot (293 \text{ K} - 237 \text{ K}) / (293 \text{ K})$$

$$W = 6,116 \text{ J/s} \approx 6,100 \text{ W}$$

10. D is correct.

Carnot efficiency engines can be written as:

$$\eta = 1 - T_C / T_H$$

$$\eta = 1 - | Q_C / Q_H |$$

Thus:

$$Q_C / Q_H = T_C / T_H$$

11. C is correct.

Find the heat from the phase change:

$Q = mL_f$

$Q = (8 \text{ kg}) \cdot (80 \text{ kcal/kg})$

$Q = 640 \text{ kcal/kg}$

Because the water is freezing, Q should be negative due to heat being released.

$Q = -640 \text{ kcal/kg}$

Find the change in entropy:

$\Delta S = Q / T$

$\Delta S = -640 \text{ kcal/kg} / (0 \text{ °C} + 273 \text{ K})$

$\Delta S = -2.3 \text{ kcal/K}$

A negative change in entropy indicates that the disorder of the isolated system has decreased. When water freezes the entropy is negative because water is more disordered than ice. Thus, the disorder has decreased, and entropy is negative.

12. E is correct.

$Q_H = 515 \text{ J}$

$Q_C = 340 \text{ J}$

Carnot cycle efficiency:

$\eta = (Q_H - Q_C) / Q_H$

$\eta = (515 \text{ J} - 340 \text{ J}) / (515 \text{ J})$

$\eta = 0.34 = 34\%$

13. B is correct.

$Q = (mc\Delta T)_{water} + (mc\Delta T)_{beaker}$

Change in temperature is the same for both:

$Q = \Delta T[(mc)_{water} + (mc)_{beaker}]$

$1{,}800 \text{ cal} = (20 \text{ °C}) \cdot [(65 \text{ g}) \cdot (1 \text{ cal/g·°C}) + (m_{beaker}) \cdot (0.18 \text{ cal/g·°C})]$

$90 \text{ cal/°C} = 65 \text{ cal/°C} + (m_{beaker}) \cdot (0.18 \text{ cal/g·°C})$

$25 \text{ cal/°C} / (0.18 \text{ cal/g·°C}) = (m_{beaker})$

$m_{beaker} = 139 \text{ g}$

14. C is correct.

Heat to melt the ice cube:

$$Q_1 = mL_f$$

Heat to raise the temperature:

$$Q_2 = mc\Delta T$$

Total heat:

$$Q_{total} = Q_1 + Q_2$$

$$Q_{total} = mL_f + mc\Delta T$$

$$Q_{total} = (0.3 \text{ kg}) \cdot (334 \text{ kJ/kg}) + (0.3 \text{ kg}) \cdot (4.186 \text{ kJ/kg} \cdot \text{K}) \cdot (60 \text{ °C} - 0 \text{ °C})$$

$$Q_{total} = (100.2 \text{ kJ}) + (1.257 \text{ kJ/K}) \cdot (60 \text{ K})$$

$$Q_{total} = 175.55 \text{ kJ} \approx 176 \text{ kJ}$$

15. D is correct.

$$PE = Q$$

$mgh = mc\Delta T$, cancel m from both sides of the expression

$$gh = c\Delta T$$

$$gh / c = \Delta T$$

$$\Delta T = [(10 \text{ m/s}^2) \cdot (60 \text{ m})] / 4{,}186 \text{ J/kg} \cdot \text{K}$$

$$\Delta T = 0.14 \text{ °C}$$

Please, leave your Customer Review on Amazon

Chapter 11

Atomic and Nuclear Structure

ATOMIC STRUCTURE AND SPECTRA

- **Emission Spectrum of Hydrogen: Bohr model**

- **Atomic Energy Levels**

ATOMIC NUCLEUS

- **Neutrons, Protons, Isotopes**

- **Atomic Number, Atomic Weight**

- **Nuclear Forces**

- **Radioactive Decay**

- **General Nature of Fission**

- **General Nature of Fusion**

- **Mass Deficit, Energy Liberated, Binding Energy**

- **Mass Spectrometer**

Notes

Atomic Structure and Spectra

The atomic structure was discovered by John Dalton in the early 1800s. Dalton reintroduced atomic theory to explain chemical reactions. His theory centered on the five main concepts:

1. All matter is made of indivisible particles of *atoms*.

2. An *element* is made up of identical atoms.

3. Different elements have atoms with different masses.

4. Chemical compounds are made of atoms in specific integer ratios.

5. Atoms are neither created nor destroyed in chemical reactions.

The *electron* was discovered by J. J. Thomson in the late 1800s. By performing cathode ray experiments (two of which are explained below), he discovered that the electron was negatively charged.

Thomson also measured the electron's charge-to-mass ratio and identified the electron as a fundamental particle.

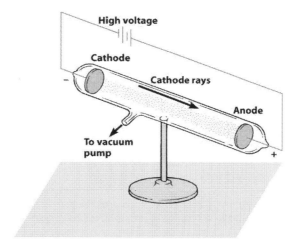

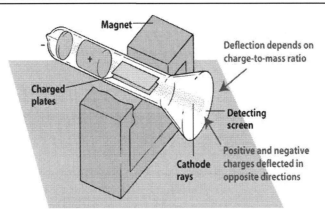

Around 1906, Robert Millikan was another scientist studying minuscule particles, specifically, charged oil droplets in an electric field. Millikan found that the charge on the oil droplets was a multiple of the electron charge. This finding, along with Thomson's results, was used to calculate the mass of the electron.

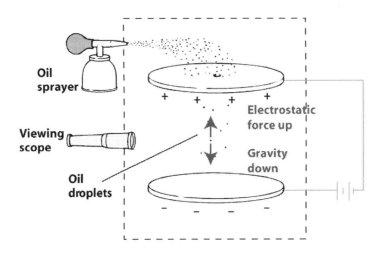

Thomson's result (charge-to-mass) was the quantity:

$$\frac{q}{m} = 1.7584 \times 10^{11} \frac{C}{kg}$$

Millikan's result (charge) was:

$$q = 1.60 \times 10^{-19} C$$

Combined, the mass of an electron is:

$$m = \frac{q}{1.7584 \times 10^{11}} = 9.11 \times 10^{-31} kg$$

Dalton claimed that atoms were indivisible, that there were no smaller quantities involved. However, Thomson's and Millikan's experiments, along with the discovery of the electron, proved that statement false.

The electron's mass is very small (no measurable volume), but there needs to be a nature of an atom's positive charge. Thomson came up with what is the "plum pudding" model. Thomson thought that electrons were embedded in a blob of positively charged matter like "raisins in plum pudding."

Ernest Rutherford, in 1907, conducted an experiment which scattered alpha particles by bouncing them off gold foil.

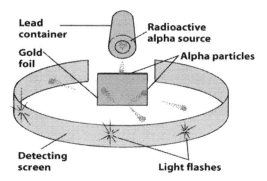

Most of the particles passed through without significant deflection, but a few scattered at large angles. Rutherford concluded that an atom's positive charge resides in a small nucleus that nonetheless contained most of the atom's mass (unlike the spread-out blob of matter containing electrons, as the plum pudding model suggested).

Later, he named these positive charges protons. James Chadwick, in 1932, added the existence of neutral neutrons in the nucleus to the previous atomic theories.

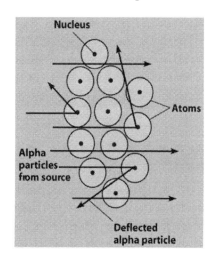

Emission Spectrum of Hydrogen; Bohr Model

The Bohr model is a depiction of the atom in which the electron orbits the nucleus in the same way that Earth orbits the Sun. Electrostatic attraction pulls the electron toward the nucleus. However, the electron orbits at high enough speeds to prevent it from crashing into the nucleus. The relationship of the electron orbit with respect to the nucleus leads to several important implications:

1. Electrons only exist in certain allowed orbits.

2. Within an orbit, the electron does not radiate.

3. Radiation is emitted or absorbed when changing orbits.

The first implication of the Bohr model is that electrons occupy different orbitals which determine their energy. These orbits are characterized by the orbital number n where n= 1 is equal to the ground state and represents the lowest energy level of the electron. The higher the orbital number of the electron, the higher energy it will have, as well as being further away from the nucleus.

The second implication is that the electron does not radiate while orbiting the nucleus. As mentioned in earlier chapters, accelerating electric charges emit energy in the form of electromagnetic radiation.

According to classical physics, the electron would, therefore, radiate away its energy (due to the energy radiated from centripetal acceleration) and crash into the nucleus. Bohr's model assumes that within the energy levels the electron does not radiate its energy and therefore stays in orbit.

The third implication of the Bohr model is that when changing energy levels, the electron must absorb or release some of its energy.

For example, for a ground state electron to achieve a higher orbital, it must absorb a photon (and thus absorb the photon's energy).

If the electron drops to a lower orbital, then the electron emits a photon equal to the energy difference between orbital levels.

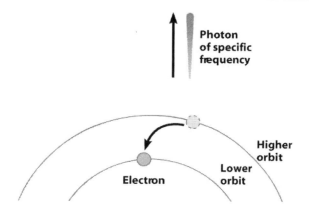

An important application of the Bohr model is in the identification of elements through their line spectrum. When a high potential difference energizes an element, the electrons are constantly being raised to higher energy levels and then dropping back to lower energies.

The photons released in the process contain specific energies which can be deduced by their frequency. These energies relate the energy differences in the different electron orbitals and allow quantization of the specific orbital energies.

For example, the figure below shows the line spectra of Hydrogen. The different series of light relates to the different orbital transitions of the Hydrogen's electrons.

Specifically, the Balmer series refers to the orbital transitions of electrons from any orbital back to $n = 2$.

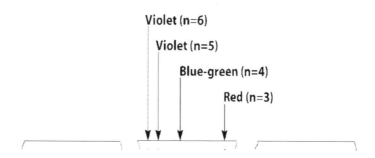

Atomic Energy Levels

The *quantum theory* of the atom declares there are a series of energy states that an electron can occupy. The lowest energy state is "ground state," and any higher states are "excited states." The energy of the photon emitted during a transition between energy levels equals the difference in state energies.

Below is an example of a hydrogen atom and its energy levels. The violet light represents the higher energy transitions (n = 5, 6 to n = 2) because violet has the highest energy of the visible spectrum.

Red light has lower energy than violet and is the result of a lower energy transition (n = 3 to n = 2).

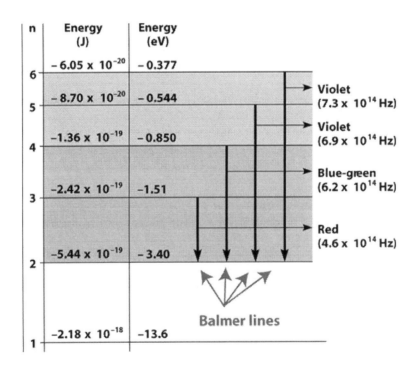

Bohr theory only holds for the line spectrum of H, because there are only two electrons. Once more electrons are added, the theory is not able to keep up with the complications of heavier atoms.

Further experiments have established wave-particle duality of light and matter. Young's two-slit experiment, discussed previously when introducing light wave theory, produced interference patterns for both photons and electrons.

Louis de Broglie, in 1923, suggested the existence of matter waves in regards to atomic theory. The wavelength is related to momentum, and the matter waves in atoms are standing waves. He came up with the formula for wavelength:

$$\lambda = \frac{h}{mv}$$

h = Planck's constant = 6.63×10^{-34} J·s

λ = Particle wavelength

m = mass

v = speed

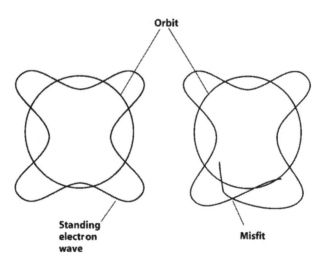

Wave mechanics was developed by Erwin Schrödinger. This method treats atoms as three-dimensional systems of waves and incorporates successful ideas of the Bohr model and much more.

Wave mechanics describes the hydrogen atom and many electron atoms, as well as forms the fundamental understanding of chemistry.

The quantum mechanics model is a visualization of wave functions and probability distributions.

Quantum numbers specify electronic quantum states, and electrons are delocalized.

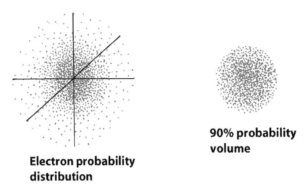

90% probability volume

Electron probability distribution

Quantum numbers are used to define and describe a certain electron in an atom.

The *principal quantum number*, given by the lowercase letter n, state the energy level (i.e., *shells*) in which the electron can most likely be found. It also represents an average distance from the nucleus.

The *angular momentum quantum number* is the second quantum number and is given by the lowercase letter l. It describes the spatial distribution of the particular orbits, which are labeled s, p, d, f, g, h, etc. These are *subshells*.

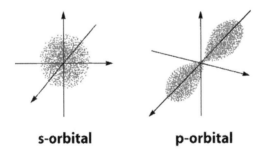

s-orbital   **p-orbital**

The *magnetic quantum number* is the third quantum number. It states the spatial orientation of the orbit within the energy (n) and the shape (l). The magnetic quantum number (m_l) divides the subshell even more into specific orbitals that hold the electron.

The number of orbitals is given by $2l + 1$. M_l has values of $-l$ to l, with increments of one including zero ($-l, .., 0, ..., +l$).

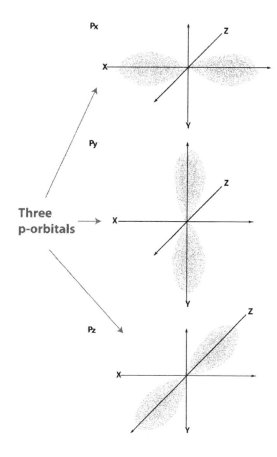

The *spin quantum number* is the fourth quantum number. It is either $+\frac{1}{2}$ or $-\frac{1}{2}$, and it stands for the electron spin orientation. There are only two values because an electron can only spin in one of two directions.

Because of this and *Pauli's exclusion principle*, which states that no two electrons in the same atom can have the same set of quantum numbers, each orbital can only contain two electrons, and they must have opposite spins.

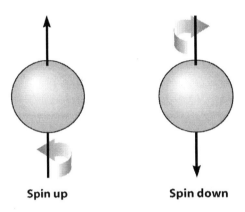

Spin up   **Spin down**

An *electron configuration* is an arrangement of electrons into atomic orbitals and specifies the atom's quantum state. The chemical properties of an atom are often determined by looking at the electronic structure.

When writing electron configurations, it is imperative to follow the Pauli exclusion principle: each electron has unique quantum numbers, a maximum of two electrons per orbital, one spins up, and one spins down.

Electrons fill available orbitals in order of increasing energy (n).

Each shell can only hold so many orbitals. Their capacities are as follows:

$s = 2$

$p = 6$

$d = 10$

$f = 14$

Each orbital can contain only two electrons. It is possible to fill only half an orbital, but it must be in the outer shell.

Example: strontium (38 electrons)

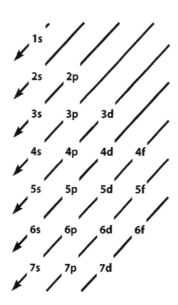

$$1s^2 2s^2 2p^6 3s^2 3p^6 4s^2 3d^{10} 4p^6 5s^2$$

The chemical properties of the elements can be understood by the periodic table. Most chemical reactions follow the rules aligned with their *valence electron configuration* — electrons in the outer orbits determine chemical properties. Elements always want to have full outer shells and will thus give their extra electrons away or take more from another element. Which of these occurs generally depends on how many valence electrons the element has.

In the periodic table, rows are *periods* and columns are *families* or *groups*. The families are:

Alkali metals (IA)

Alkaline earth (IIA)

Halogens (VIIA)

Noble gases (VIIIA)

A-group elements are the main group or the representative elements.

B-group elements are the transition elements or metals.

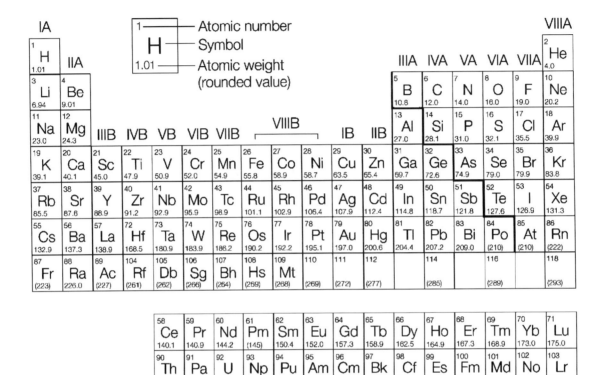

( ) represents an isotope

Noble gases (VIIIA) have completely-filled valence shells. This means they are inert or do not react easily with other elements.

Elements with 1 to 3 outer electrons will lose their valence electrons to become positive ions (such as metals).

Elements with 5 to 7 outer electrons tend to gain electrons and form negative ions (such as nonmetals).

Semiconductors are intermediate substances between metals and nonmetals.

Quantized energy levels for electrons

In 1900, Max Planck introduced *quantized energy*. In 1905, Einstein discovered that light was made up of quantized photons. He also found that higher frequency photons meant more energetic photons and derived the equation:

$$E = hf$$

h = Planck's constant = 6.63×10^{-34} J·s

E = Photon energy

f = Photon frequency

The distinct lines of the emission spectrum prove that electron energy is quantized into energy levels. If electron energy is not quantized, then a continuous spectrum would be observed.

The energy of a particular level is calculated using the quantum number, and given by the equation:

$$E_n = -\frac{13.6}{n^2} (eV)$$

The equation is negative, so all energies are negative. Negative energies mean that energy contributes to the "stability" of the system — the electron *binding energy*.

The more negative (lower) the energy, the more stable the orbit and the harder it is to knock out the electron.

The less negative (higher) the energy, the less stable the orbit and the easier it is to knock out the electron.

At the highest energy, 0 eV, there is no binding energy, so the electron dissociates.

For atoms other than hydrogen, the shape of the energy level curve stays the same. However, the numerator is a constant other than 13.6 eV.

The precise relationship for atoms other than hydrogen is:

$$E = -\frac{Z^2 R_E}{n^2}$$

where Z is the atomic number.

Higher Z values give more negative binding energy (more stable) because the more charge, the more electrostatic attraction.

Calculation of energy emitted or absorbed when an electron changes energy level

The wavelength of the emitted or absorbed radiation is governed by the *Rydberg formula*:

$$\frac{1}{\lambda} = R \left(\frac{1}{n_f^2} - \frac{1}{n_i^2} \right)$$

where λ is the wavelength, n_f is the final energy level, n_i is the initial energy level, and R is the Rydberg constant of $1.0973 \times 10^7 \, \text{m}^{-1}$.

The energy of the emitted or absorbed radiation is:

$$E = hf = hv = h\frac{c}{\lambda}$$

where E is energy, f and v both mean frequency and c is the speed of light.

Energy is emitted for transitions to lower energy levels ($n_f < n_i$) and absorbed for transitions to higher energy levels ($n_f > n_i$).

The photon energy can also be computed using the equation:

$$hf = E_H - E_L$$

Neutrons, Protons, Isotopes

The *nucleus* is made of protons and neutrons. *Protons* have a positive charge and a mass of:

$$m_p = 1.67262 \times 10^{-27} \text{ kg}$$

Neutrons are electrically neutral and slightly more massive than the proton:

$$m_n = 1.67493 \times 10^{-27} \text{ kg}$$

Neutrons and protons are collectively *nucleons* (as they reside in the nucleus). The different nuclei are *nuclides*. The number of protons defines an element and refers to the neutral atom (having no charge). If two atoms have the same number of protons, they are the same element.

An *isotope* is an atom that has the same atomic number as its counterpart on the periodic table, but which has a different number of neutrons. Isotopes often have similar chemical properties, but different stabilities. For instance, some isotopes decay and give off radiation particles, while others are stable and do not decay.

For many elements, several different isotopes exist in nature.

Natural abundance is the percentage of a particular element that consists of a particular isotope in nature.

$$
\begin{array}{llll}
{}^{14}_{7}N & \nearrow \ \textbf{99.63\%} & & \textbf{0.9963(14.00307 u)} \\
& \textbf{Natural abundances} & \textbf{Sum} & = \textbf{atomic weight} = \textbf{14.0067 u} \\
& \searrow & & \searrow \\
{}^{15}_{7}N & \textbf{0.37\%} & & \textbf{0.0037(15.00011 u)}
\end{array}
$$

Atomic Particles			
Name	Mass (amu)	Charge	Location
Proton	1	+1	In the nucleus
Neutron	1	0	In the nucleus
Electron	0	-1	Surrounding the nucleus

Atomic Number, Atomic Weight

The number of protons is what gives an element its *atomic number* (*Z*). So far, we have identified 113 elements. The number of nucleons is equal to the *atomic mass* number (*A*). This is found by adding the number of protons and neutrons. $N = A - Z$ give the neutron number. The *atomic weight* is the weighted average of *atomic mass* for all isotopes of a given atom and is used for an element. The atomic mass is used for an isotope.

A and *Z* are sufficient to specify a nuclide. Nuclides are symbolized as follows:

$$_{Z}^{A}X$$

X is the chemical symbol for the element; it contains the same information as *Z* but in a more recognizable form.

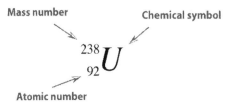

Because of wave-particle duality, the size of the nucleus is somewhat fuzzy. Measurements of high-energy electron scattering yield the radius to be:

$$r \approx (1.2 \times 10^{-15}\,m)(A^{\frac{1}{3}})$$

Masses of atoms are measured with reference to the carbon-12 atom, which is assigned a mass of exactly 12u. Where:

$$1\,u = 1.6605 \times 10^{-27}\,kg = 931.5\,MeV/c^2$$

From the table, the electron is considerably less massive than a nucleon.

Rest Masses in Kilograms, Unified Atomics Mass Units, and MeV/c^2			
	Mass		
Object	kg	amu	MeV/c^2
Electron	9.1094×10^{-31}	0.00054858	0.51100
Proton	1.67262×10^{-27}	1.007276	938.27
$_{1}^{1}H$ atom	1.67353×10^{-27}	1.007825	938.78
Neutron	1.67493×10^{-27}	1.008665	939.57

Nuclear Forces

There are two forces are at work in the nucleus: the strong nuclear force and the electromagnetic force.

The *strong nuclear force* binds the nucleons together and therefore contributes to the binding energy.

The *electromagnetic force* is due to electrostatic repulsion in the group of positively charged protons in the nucleus (like-charges repel).

The nucleus stays together because the strong nuclear force is much stronger than the electromagnetic repulsion. The strong force is short-ranged, less than 10^{-15} m.

The repulsion between proton particles that it overcomes is *proton-proton Coulomb repulsion*.

Proton-proton chain reaction

$$_1^1H + {}_1^1H \rightarrow {}_1^2H + {}_1^0e$$

$$_1^2H + {}_1^2H \rightarrow {}_2^3He + {}_0^1n$$

$$_2^3He + {}_2^3He \rightarrow {}_2^4He + 2{}_1^1H$$

Coulomb's Law relates the repulsion force on two charged particles depending on their charge and their distance from each other.

The force (F) is large when the distance (r) is small.

$$F_{Coulomb} = \frac{kq_1q_2}{r^2}$$

To compare how tightly bound different nuclei are, divide the binding energy by A to get the binding energy per nucleon.

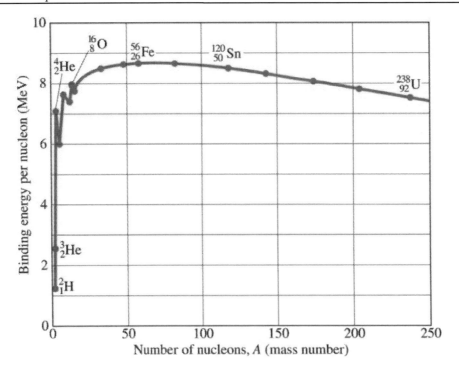

Chemical Reactions

To discuss chemical reaction, compounds and chemical change must be explained. The atom is the smallest elemental unit. A *molecule* is the smallest particle still retaining the characteristic chemical properties of a substance; they are combinations of atoms.

Some examples of molecules are oxygen and hydrogen gas which are diatomic molecules (made of two atoms), ozone which is a triatomic oxygen molecule (made of three atoms), and the noble gases such as helium and neon, which are monatomic molecules (made of one atom, as they do not bond).

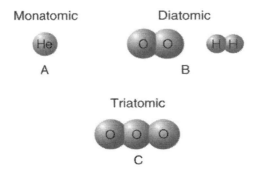

During chemical reactions, there is a formation and/or breaking of chemical bonds that form new molecules (*products*) from old ones (*reactants*).

Chemical energy is the internal bonding potential energy, and the chemical equation is a symbolic summary of the chemical reaction. A chemical reaction cannot be reversed.

For example, firewood burned to create carbon dioxide cannot be turned back into wood.

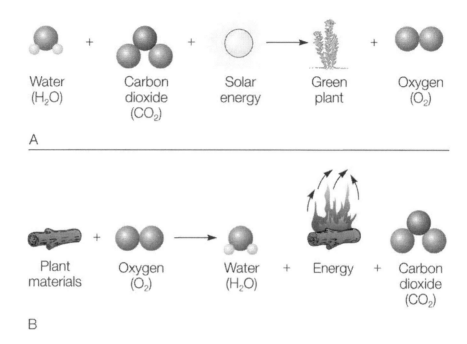

Valence electrons and ions are very important when it comes to chemical reactions. The outer electrons determine the chemical properties of an atom.

Dot notation shows how many electrons each element has in its outer shell.

From the periodic table, this is determined by moving from left to right, with each group receiving one more electron in its outer shell than the previous.

Notice in the diagram below that the transition metals are excluded.

Transition elements do not generally follow this rule.

The elements shown below are the main elements used when computing dot notation reactions.

H•									He:
Li•	Be•			B •	• C •	• N :	• O :	: F :	:Ne:
Na•	Mg•			Al •	• Si •	• P :	• S :	: Cl:	:Ar:
K•	Ca•			Ga•	•Ge•	•As:	•Se:	: Br:	: Kr:
Rb•	Sr•			In •	•Sn•	•Sb:	•Te:	: I :	:Xe:
Cs•	Ba•			Tl •	•Pb•	• Bi:	•Po:	: At:	:Rn:
Fr•	Ra•								

Atoms attempt to acquire a full outer shell of eight electrons. To do so, electrons can be gained, lost or shared in the process of reacting with another atom. When electrons are transferred, they must follow a few rules. The number of gained electrons must equal the number of lost electrons, and electrons are either lost or gained to form closed *octets*. This means a diatomic molecule will not be formed unless both octets are satisfied.

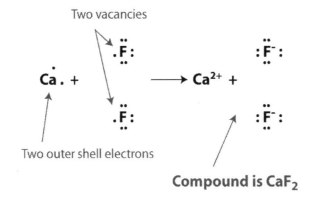

Compound is CaF$_2$

There are a few exceptions to this rule. Lithium and hydrogen are both most stable when they fill their first orbital, and therefore only have two electrons. Aluminum and boron both function very well with only six valence electrons. They still want all eight but will form stable compounds without them.

Some compounds have more than an octet—these are mostly in the halogen family. Another exception to the rule is noble gas compounds. For instance, xenon will react with six fluorine atoms to create xenon hexafluoride.

Depicted below is sodium (Na) reacting with another element and losing its one outer electron in the process. Sodium is now stable because it has eight electrons in its outer shell.

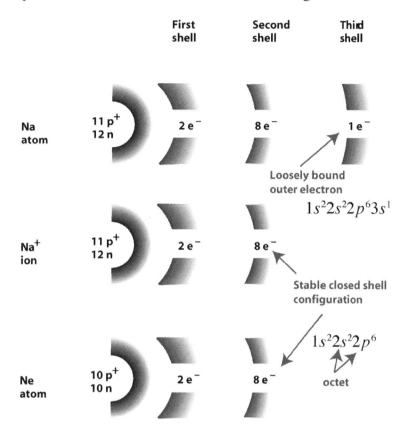

Chemical bonds are attractive forces that hold atoms together in compounds. They can be described regarding molecular (delocalized) or atomic (localized) orbitals. There are three types of chemical bonds: metallic, ionic and covalent.

Metallic bonds occur between metallic elements, and the outer electrons are allowed to move freely throughout the metal. It is almost as if all of the electrons are combined to form an "electron gas" that fills in the spaces within the rigid crystalline lattice of metal atoms. This allows the efficient conduction of heat and electricity.

When these types of bonds are formed, there is not just one molecule. Rather, these bonds will create an orderly geometric structure, as depicted below in the formation of sodium chloride, or NaCl.

Sodium loses an electron while chlorine gains one—both then have eight valence electrons.

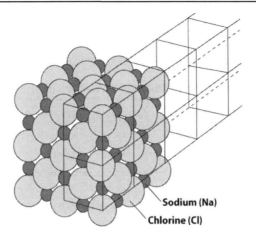

Sodium (Na)
Chlorine (Cl)

$$Na^{+1} + Cl^{-1} \rightarrow NaCl$$

A *covalent bond* is when electrons are shared between electrons, so both atoms achieve octets in their outside orbital. This overlap of shared electron clouds between nuclei yields net attraction.

Atoms within covalent compounds are electrically neutral, or nearly so.

Typically, this bonding occurs between nonmetallic elements.

A *covalent compound* is held together by covalent bonds which are represented by electron dot diagrams.

Bonding pairs are shared electrons, while lone (non-bonding) pairs are not shared.

The fluorine molecule: F_2

$$.\ddot{F}: + .\ddot{F}:$$

Lone (non-bonding) pairs

$$:\ddot{F}:\ddot{F}:$$

Bonding electron pair

Structures and compounds of nonmetallic elements combined with hydrogen:

Nonmetallic Elements	Element (E Represents Any Element of Family)	Compound
Family IVA: C, Si, Ge	·Ė·	H H:Ë:H H
Family VA: N, P, As, Sb	·Ë·	H:Ë:H H
Family VIA: O, S, Se, Te	·Ë·	H:Ë:H
Family VIIA: F, Cl, Br, I	·Ë:	H:Ë:

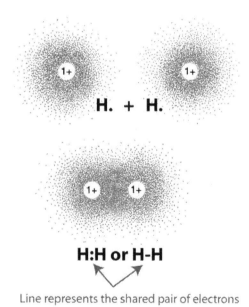

Line represents the shared pair of electrons

Some covalent bonds require the sharing of more than one electron pair. When this occurs, they are double or triple bonds. These bonds are symbolized by a single bar and represent two electrons.

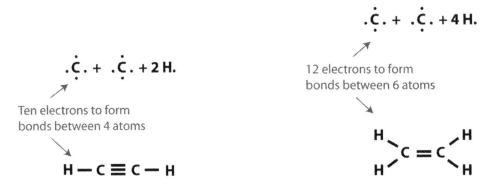

An *ionic bond* occurs when electrons are transferred between atoms.

The only force involved in ionic bonding is the electrostatic force—this is what binds the atoms together.

The reaction energy released during the reaction is equal to the heat of formation.

Each ionic reaction can be conceptually divided into half-reactions.

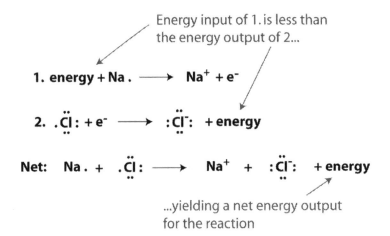

Ionic bonds characterize ionic compounds. They are commonly in the form of white, crystalline solids that are soluble in water.

Families IA and IIA lose electrons and form positive ions.

Families VIA and VIIA gain electrons to form negative ions.

Some ions are made up of more than one element and are *polyatomic ions*.

Common ions of some representative elements		
Element	**Symbol**	**Ion**
Lithium	Li	1+
Sodium	Na	1+
Potassium	K	1+
Magnesium	Mg	2+
Calcium	Ca	2+
Barium	Ba	2+
Aluminum	Al	3+
Oxygen	O	2–
Sulfur	S	2–
Hydrogen	H	1+ , 1–
Fluorine	F	1–
Chlorine	Cl	1–
Bromine	Br	1–
Iodine	I	1–

Common ions of some transition elements		
Single-Charge Ions		
Element	**Symbol**	**Charge**
Zinc	Zn	2+
Tungsten	W	6+
Silver	Ag	1+
Cadmium	Cd	2+
Variable-Charge Ions		
Chromium	Cr	2+ , 3+ , …
Manganese	Mn	2+ , 4+ , …
Iron	Fe	2+ , 3+
Cobalt	Co	2+ , 3+
Nickel	Ni	2+ , 3+
Copper	Cu	1+ , 2+
Tin	Sn	2+ , 4+
Gold	Au	1+ , 3+
Mercury	Hg	1+ , 2+
Lead	Pb	2+ , 4+

Some common polyatomic ions

Acetate $(C_2H_3O_2)^-$

Ammonium $(NH_4)^+$

Borate $(BO_3)^{3-}$

Carbonate $(CO_3)^{2-}$

Chlorate $(ClO_3)^-$

Chromate $(CrO_4)^{2-}$

Cyanide $(CN)^-$

Dichromate $(Cr_2O_7)^{2-}$

Hydrogen carbonate (or bicarbonate) $(HCO_3)^-$

Hydrogen sulfate (or bisulfate) $(HSO_4)^-$

Hydroxide $(OH)^-$

Hypochlorite $(ClO)^-$

Nitrate $(NO_3)^-$

Nitrite $(NO_2)^-$

Perchlorate $(ClO_4)^-$

Permanganate $(MnO_4)^-$

Phosphate $(PO_4)^{3-}$

Phosphite $(PO_3)^{3-}$

Sulfate $(SO_4)^{2-}$

Sulfite $(SO_3)^{2-}$

When writing a chemical formula for an ionic compound, list the elements in the compound and their proportions (subscripts). The proportions are decided by the amount of electron gain or loss. Always write the symbol for a positive ion first, followed by a negative ion symbol. Then, assign subscripts to assure the compound is electrically neutral.

For example, when magnesium and chloride react, the chemical formula for the compound is $MgCl_2$. This is because magnesium has two electrons to give away (Mg^{-2}), but chlorine only wants one to fill its orbital (Cl^{+1}). This means there must be two chlorines, and each will take one of magnesium's two extra electrons.

$$Ca \rightarrow Ca^{2+} \qquad Cl \rightarrow Cl^{-}$$

Forms +2 ion   Forms -1 ion

$$CaCl_2$$

+2+2(-1) = neutral compound

When compounds are formed, there is an unequal sharing of electrons. This is because of the difference in electronegativity in the elements involved in the reaction.

Electronegativity is the measure of an atom's ability to attract electrons.

The amount of difference reveals what bond is between the two atoms.

The meaning of absolute differences in electronegativity		
Absolute Difference	$\rightarrow$	**Type of Bond Expected**
1.7 or greater	means	ionic bond
between 0.5 and 1.7	means	polar covalent bond
0.5 or less	means	covalent bond

Below is a depiction of the electron cloud distribution for each different kind of bond.

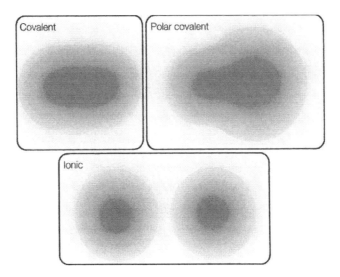

The electronegativity of each element can be found from the following table:

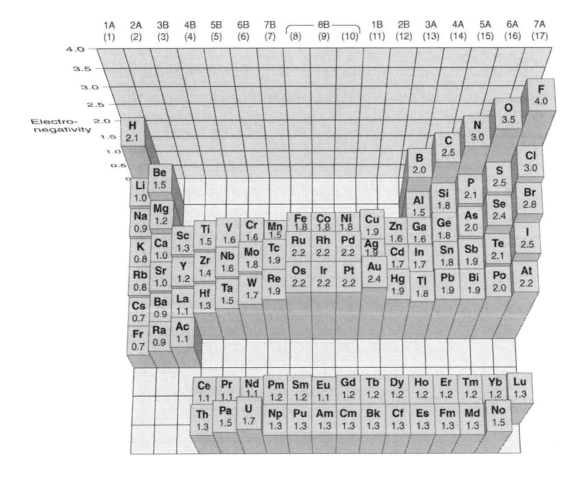

Naming Compounds

There are millions of different combinations of over 90 elements. Many of these have common names often related to historical usage (such as baking soda or washing soda). However, these common names are difficult to relate to the molecular composition.

The modern approach to naming compounds contains a systematic set of rules. These rules are different for ionic vs. covalent compounds, but there is one rule: the suffix "-ide" refers to a compound that contains only two different elements.

Ionic Compounds

1. Start with the name of the metal ion (the positive one) first, then add the nonmetal ion (the negative one).

2. Use a distinguisher for elements that have more than one common ion

   – Historical suffix usage

     • "-ic" for higher of two;

     • "-ous" for lower

   – Modern approach

     • English name of metal, followed by a Roman numeral indicating charge in parentheses

Modern names of some variable-charge ions	
Ion	**Name of Ion**
Fe^{2+}	Iron(II) ion
Fe^{3+}	Iron(III) ion
Cu^+	Copper(I) ion
Cu^{2+}	Copper(II) ion
Pb^{2+}	Lead(II) ion
Pb^{4+}	Lead(IV) ion
Sn^{2+}	Tin(II) ion
Sn^{4+}	Tin(IV) ion
Cr^{2+}	Chromium(II) ion
Cr^{3+}	Chromium(III) ion
Cr^{6+}	Chromium(VI) ion

Covalent compounds

    Covalent compounds are molecular or composed of two or more nonmetals.

    The same elements can combine to form some different compounds, depending on the concentration of each element involved.

    When naming covalent compounds, there are two rules to follow.

    Use the table below for the prefix and stem names:

1. The first element given in the formula is named first.

   - The subscript or concentration of the element is indicated by a Greek prefix

2. Only the stem name of the second element comes next.

   - a Greek prefix is used to indicate concentration

   - the suffix "-ide" is added to the end

Prefixes and element stem names			
Prefix	*Meaning*	*Element*	*Stem*
Mono-	1	Hydrogen	Hydr-
Di-	2	Carbon	Carb-
Tri-	3	Nitrogen	Nitr-
Tetra-	4	Oxygen	Ox-
Penta-	5	Fluorine	Fluor-
Hexa-	6	Phosphorus	Phosph-
Hepta-	7	Sulfur	Sulf-
Octa-	8	Chlorine	Chlor-
Nona-	9	Bromine	Brom-
Deca-	10	Iodine	Iod-

    Note: the a or o ending on the prefix if often dropped if the stem name begins with a vowel (e.g., "tetroxide," not "tetraoxide").

    Examples: carbon dioxide, carbon tetrachloride.

Radioactive Decay

Natural radioactivity is a spontaneous emission of particles or energy from an unstable nucleus. Towards the end of the 19th century, minerals were found that would darken a photographic plate even in the absence of light. This phenomenon is radioactivity.

When an atom is unstable, it will undergo *radioactive decay*. The maximum stability for a nucleon number is 2, 8, 20, 28, 50, 82 or 126. The higher the binding energy per nucleon, the more stable the nucleus. More massive nuclei require extra neutrons to overcome the Coulomb repulsion of the protons to be stable. There is a band of stability that depends on the ration of protons to neutrons that makes an atom stable. The Coulomb force is long-range; this is why extra neutrons are needed for stability in high-Z nuclei:

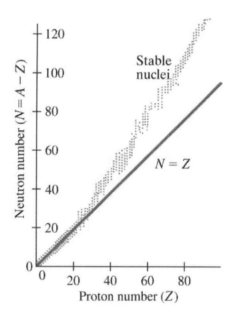

Pairs of protons and pairs of neutrons add stability to the atom.

Conversely, an odd number of both protons and neutrons makes a less stable atom.

For added stability, certain neutron-to-proton ratios are desired: 1:1 for isotopes with up to 20 protons and (1+1):1 for increasingly heavy isotopes.

Nuclei that are unstable decay; many such decays are governed by another force of the weak nuclear force. There are three types of decay: alpha, beta, and gamma decay.

All these forms of radiation are *ionizing radiation* because they ionize material that they go through.

Alpha emission is an expulsion of a helium nucleus. It is the least penetrating and can even be stopped by a piece of paper.

Beta emission is an expulsion of an electron. This is more penetrating than alpha decay and can be stopped by 1 cm of aluminum.

Gamma decay is an emission of a high energy photon (electromagnetic radiation). This is the most penetrating, and can only be stopped by a thick, dense shield (e.g., approximately 13.5 feet of water, 6.5 feet of concrete or about 1.3 feet of lead).

Radioactive Decay			
Unstable Condition	**Type of Decay**	**Emitted**	**Product Nucleus**
More than 83 protons	Alpha emission	${}^{4}_{2}\alpha$ (${}^{4}_{2}He$)	Lost 2 protons and 2 neutrons
Neutron-to-proton ratio too large	Beta emission	${}^{0}_{-1}\beta$ (${}^{0}_{-1}e$)	Gained 1 proton, no mass change
Excited Nucleus	Gamma emission	${}^{0}_{0}\gamma$	No change
Neutron-to-proton ratio too small	Other emission	${}^{0}_{1}e$	Lost 1 proton, no mass change

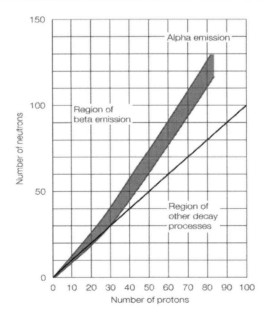

Alpha and beta rays are bent in opposite directions in a magnetic field, while gamma rays are not bent at all.

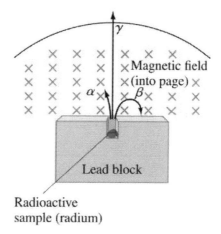

The *conservation of mass* dictates that the total atomic weight before the decay must equal the total atomic weight after. The *conservation of charge* dictates that the total atomic number before the decay must equal the total atomic number after.

A new conservation law that is evident by studying radioactive decay is that the total number of nucleons cannot change. Do not get thrown off by unfamiliar particles. If they have a weight and a charge, incorporate these numbers into calculations.

Test problems on identifying decay products are just math work.

The atomic number (*Z*; the bottom number) determines the element.

Alpha Decay

An example of alpha decay is radium-227 (^{227}Ra) decaying into radon-222 (^{222}Rn):

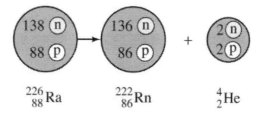

In general, alpha decay can be written:

$$^{A}_{Z}N \rightarrow\ ^{A-4}_{Z-2}N' +\ ^{4}_{2}He$$

Alpha decay occurs when the strong nuclear force cannot hold a large nucleus together. The mass of the parent nucleus is greater than the sum of the masses of the daughter nucleus and the alpha particle; this difference is the *disintegration energy*.

Alpha decay is much more likely than other forms of nuclear disintegration because the alpha particle itself is quite stable.

Some smoke detectors use alpha radiation—the presence of smoke is enough to absorb the alpha rays and keep them from striking the collector plate.

Beta Decay

Beta decay occurs when a nucleus emits an electron. An example is the decay of carbon-14 (^{14}C):

$$^{14}_{6}C \rightarrow {}^{14}_{7}N + e^- + neutrino$$

The nucleus still has 14 nucleons, but it has one more proton and one fewer neutron. This decay is an example of an interaction that proceeds via the weak nuclear force.

The electron in beta decay is not an orbital electron; it is created in the decay.

The fundamental process is a neutron decaying to a proton, electron, and neutrino:

$$n \rightarrow p + e^- + neutrino$$

The need for a particle such as a *neutrino* was discovered through analysis of energy and momentum conservation in beta decay—it could not be a two-particle decay. Neutrinos are notoriously difficult to detect. They interact only weakly, and direct evidence for their existence was not available for a long time.

The symbol for the neutrino is the Greek letter nu (v); using this, the beta decay of carbon-14 is written as (the bar over the neutrino means that it is an antineutrino):

$$^{14}_{6}C \rightarrow {}^{14}_{7}N + e^- + \overline{v}$$

Beta decay can also occur where the nucleus emits a positron rather than an electron:

$$^{19}_{10}Ne \rightarrow {}^{19}_{9}F + e^+ + \overline{v}$$

And a nucleus can capture one of its inner electrons:

$$_4^7Be + e^- \rightarrow {_3^7}Li + v$$

Gamma Decay

Gamma rays are very high-energy photons. They are emitted when a nucleus decays from an excited state to a lower state, just as electrons returning to a lower state emits photons.

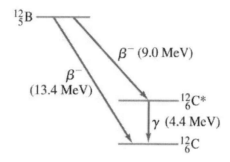

Half-life, stability, exponential decay, semi-log plots

An element's *half-life* is the amount of time required for ½ of a radioactive sample to decay.

For example, a 1 kg sample of an unstable isotope with a one-day half-life:

After 1 day - 500 g remain

After 2 days - 250 g remain

After 3 days - 125 g remain

Half-lives of some radioactive isotopes		
Isotope	**Half-Life**	**Mode of Decay**
$^{3}_{1}H$ (tritium)	12.26 years	Beta
$^{14}_{6}C$	5,730 years	Beta
$^{90}_{38}Sr$	28 years	Beta
$^{131}_{53}I$	8 days	Beta
$^{133}_{54}Xe$	5.27 days	Beta
$^{238}_{92}U$	4.51×10^{9} years	Alpha
$^{242}_{94}Pu$	3.79×10^{5} years	Alpha
$^{240}_{94}Pu$	6,760 years	Alpha
$^{239}_{94}Pu$	24,360 years	Alpha
$^{40}_{19}K$	1.3×10^{9} years	Alpha

Half-life graphs look like the following decreasing exponential:

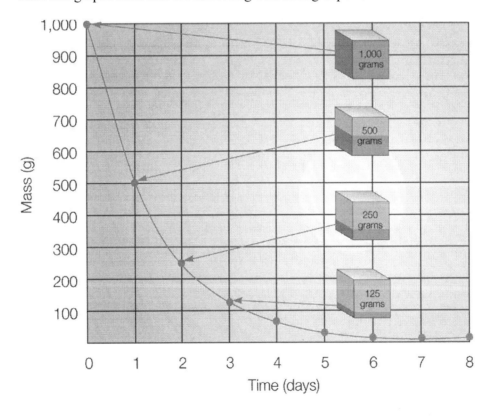

Nuclear decay is a random process; the decay of one nucleus is not influenced by the decay of any other.

Additionally, the decay rate is unaffected by temperature, pressure, volume or any other environmental factor.

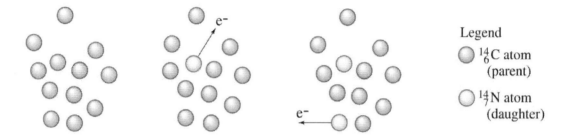

Legend

$^{14}_{6}C$ atom (parent)

$^{14}_{7}N$ atom (daughter)

Therefore, the number of decays in a short time interval is proportional to the number of nuclei present and to the time:

$$\Delta N = -\lambda N \Delta t$$

Here, λ is a constant characteristic of that particular nuclide, the decay constant.

This equation can be solved, using calculus, for N as a function of time:

$$N = N_0 e^{-\lambda t}$$

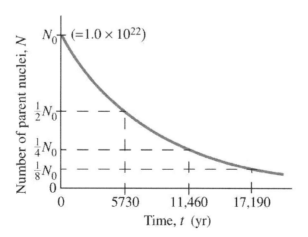

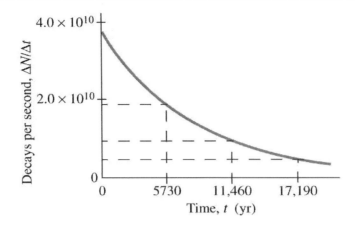

The half-life can be related to the decay constant:

$$T_{\frac{1}{2}} = \frac{\ln 2}{\lambda} = \frac{0.693}{\lambda}$$

It can also be written:

$$N_t = N_{t=0} \cdot \left(\frac{1}{2}\right)^{\#half-lives} = N_{t=0} \cdot \left(\frac{1}{2}\right)^{\frac{t}{half-life}}$$

where $N_{t=0}$ is the amount the original starting material, N_t is the amount of the original material that is still left, and t is time.

Although the above is the official half-life equation, some people prefer to multiply rather than to divide. Therefore, a more user-friendly equation is:

$$N_{t=0} = N_t \cdot 2^{\#half-lives} = N_t \cdot 2^{\frac{t}{half-life}}$$

For the test, semi-log plots convert exponential curves into straight lines.

- Something that curves up becomes a straight line with a positive slope.
- Something that curves down becomes a straight line with a negative slope.
- For exponential decay, a semi-log plot graphs the log of amount vs. time.
- For exponential decay, a semi-log plot is a straight line with a negative slope.
- The semi-log plot intercepts the x-axis where the original y-value is 1.

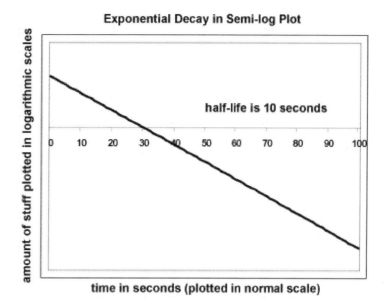

A decay series occurs when one radioactive isotope decays to another radioactive isotope, which decays to another and so on. This allows the creation of nuclei that otherwise would not exist in nature.

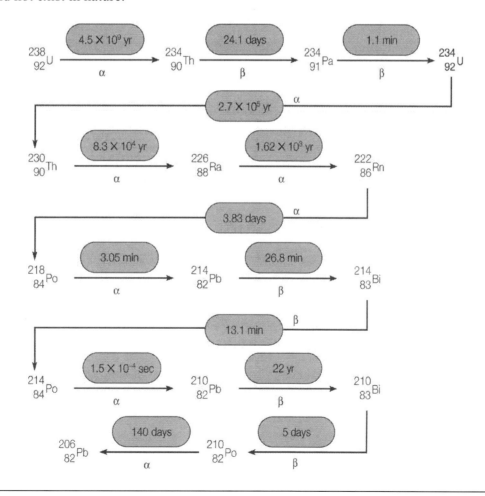

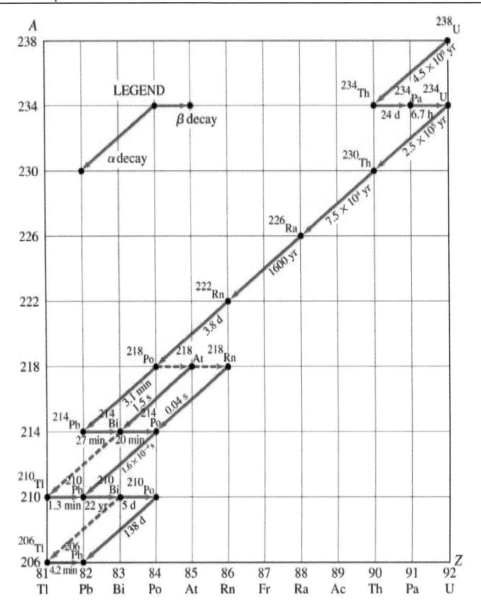

Radioactive dating can be done by analyzing the fraction of carbon in organic material that is carbon-14. The ratio of ^{14}C to ^{12}C in the atmosphere has been roughly constant over thousands of years.

A living plant or tree will constantly be exchanging carbon with the atmosphere and will have the same carbon ratio in its tissue. When the plant dies, this exchange stops.

^{14}C has a half-life of about 5,730 years; it gradually decays away and becomes a smaller and smaller fraction of the total carbon in the plant tissue. This fraction can be measured, and the age of the tissue deduced.

Objects older than about 60,000 years cannot be dated this way—there is too little ^{14}C remaining. Other isotopes are useful for geologic time scale dating, Uranium-238 has a half-life of 4.5×10^9 years and has been used to date the oldest rocks on Earth as about 4 billion years old.

When a nucleus decays through alpha emission, energy is released. Why is it that these nuclei do not decay immediately?

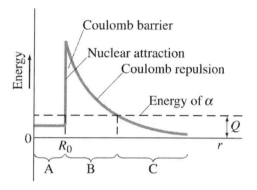

The answer is that although energy is released in the decay, there is still an energy barrier. The alpha particle can escape through a quantum mechanical phenomenon of tunneling. From the *Heisenberg uncertainty principle*, energy conservation can be violated, if the violation does not last long:

$$Q = M_p c^2 - (M_D + m_\alpha)c^2$$

The higher the energy barrier, the less time the alpha particle has to get through it, and the less likely that is to happen. This accounts for the extremely wide variation in half-lives for alpha decay.

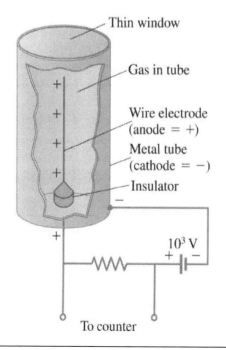

There are a few different methods to take measurements of decay. Ionization counters detect ions produced by radiation, such as a *Geiger counter*.

The Geiger counter is a gas-filled tube with a wire in the center. The wire is at high voltage; the case is grounded. When a charged particle passes through, it ionizes the gas. The ions cascade onto the wire, producing a pulse.

A *scintillation counter* uses a scintillator—a material that emits light when a charged particle goes through it. The scintillator is made light-tight, and the light flashes are viewed with a photomultiplier tube, which has a photocathode that emits an electron when struck by a photon, and then a series of amplifiers.

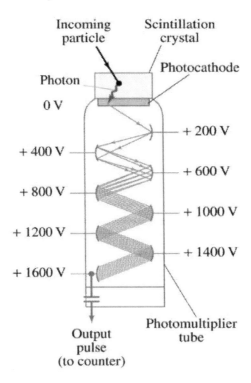

A *cloud chamber* contains a supercooled gas; when a charged particle goes through it, droplets form along its track.

Similarly, a *bubble chamber* contains a superheated liquid, which forms bubbles.

In either case, the tracks can be photographed and measured.

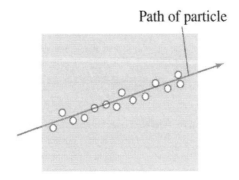

A *wire drift chamber* is similar to but vastly more sophisticated than, a Geiger counter. Many wires are present, some at high voltage and some grounded; in addition to the presence of a signal, the time it takes the pulse to arrive at the wire is measured, allowing a very precise measurement of position.

Radiation can be measured at the source. The activity is the number of disintegrations per unit time.

There are many different units of activity:

Names, symbols, and conversion factors for radioactivity			
Name	**Symbol**	**To Obtain**	**Multiply by**
Becquerel	Bq	Ci	2.7×10^{-11}
gray	Gy	rad	100
sievert	Sv	rem	100
curie	Ci	Bq	3.7×10^{10}
rem	rem	Sv	0.01
millirem	mrem	rem	0.001
rem	rem	millirem	1,000

Radiation is also measured where it is absorbed. Human exposure is measured in rem, but the SI unit is the millisievert. Another measurement is the absorbed dose—the effect the radiation has on the absorbing material. The rad, a unit of dosage, is the amount of radiation that deposits energy at a rate of 1.00×10^{-2} J/kg in any material. The SI unit for dose is the gray, Gy. The dosage is related to effects on organisms.

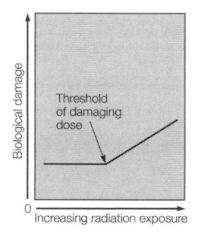
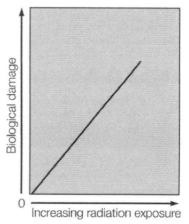

Approximate single dose, whole body effects of radiation exposure	
Level	**Comment**
0.130 rem	Average annual exposure to natural background radiation
0.500 rem	Upper limit of annual exposure to the general public
25.0 rem	Threshold for observable effects such as reduced blood cell count
100.0 rem	Fatigue and other symptoms of radiation sickness
200.0 rem	Definite radiation sickness, bone marrow damage, the possibility of developing leukemia
500.0 rem	The lethal dose for 50 percent of individuals
1,000.0 rem	Lethal dose for all individuals

Radiation damages biological tissue, but it can also be used to treat cancer and other diseases. It is important to be able to measure the amount, or dose, of radiation, received.

Relative Biological Effectiveness (RBE)	
Type	**RBE**
X- and γ rays	1
β (electrons)	1
Protons	2
Slow Neutrons	5
Fast Neutrons	≈ 10
α particles and heavy ions	≈ 20

The different effect types of radiation have on tissue varies. Gamma rays are often the most dangerous overall because they can penetrate the whole body; however, if ingested, alpha rays being the most damaging. To get the effective dose, the dose is multiplied by the relative biological effectiveness. If the dose is measured in rad, the effective dose is in rem; if the dose is grays, the effective dose is in Sieverts (Sv).

Cancer is sometimes treated with *radiation therapy* to destroy the cancerous cells. To minimize the damage to healthy tissue, the radiation source is often rotated, so it goes through different parts of the body on its way to the tumor.

Radioactive isotopes are widely used in medicine for diagnostic purposes. They can be used as non-invasive scans or tools to check for unusual concentrations that could signal a tumor or other problem. The radiation is detected with a gamma-ray detector.

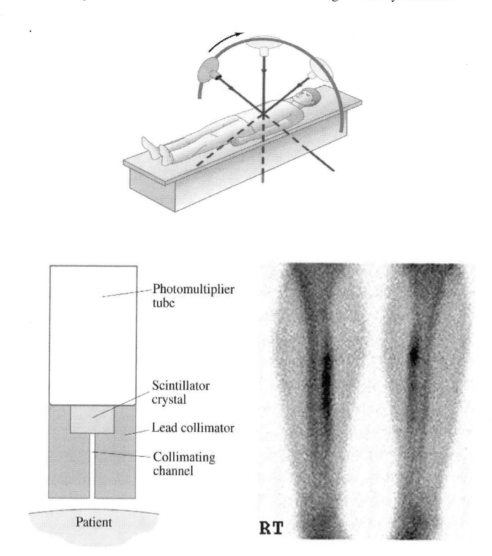

Radioactive tracers can also be detected using tomographic techniques, where a three-dimensional image is gradually built up through successive scans.

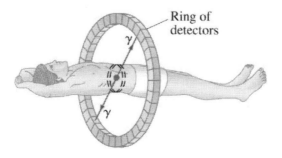

A proton in a magnetic field can have its spin either parallel or antiparallel to the field.

The field splits the energy levels slightly; the energy difference is proportional to the field magnitude.

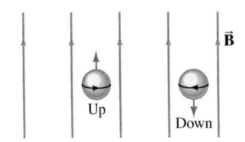

The object to be examined is placed in a static magnetic field, and radio frequency (RF) electromagnetic radiation is applied. When the radiation has the right energy to excite the spin-flip transition, many photons are absorbed. This is *nuclear magnetic resonance*.

The value of the field depends somewhat on the local molecular neighborhood; this allows information about the structure of the molecules to be determined.

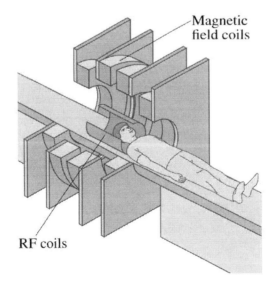

Magnetic resonance imaging works the same way; the transition is excited in hydrogen atoms, which are common in the human body.

Giving the field a gradient can contribute to image accuracy, as it allows determining the origin of a particular signal.

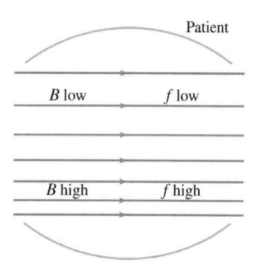

Technique	Optimal Resolution
Conventional X-ray	½ mm
CT scan, X-ray	½ mm
Nuclear medicine (tracers)	1 cm
SPECT (single photon emission)	1 cm
PET (positron emission)	2-5 mm
MRI (NMR)	½ - 1 mm
Ultrasound	0.3 – 2 mm

General Nature of Fission

There are two types of nuclear reactions: fission and fusion. Nuclear fission is the process whereby the nucleus of an atom is split into two smaller fragments. A nuclear reaction takes place when another nucleus or particle strike a nucleus.

For example, when the original nucleus is transformed into another, this is *transmutation*:

$$\ce{^4_2He} + \ce{^{14}_7N} \rightarrow \ce{^{17}_8O} + \ce{^1_1H}$$

Energy and momentum must be conserved in nuclear reactions.

$$a + X \rightarrow Y + b$$

The reaction energy, or Q-value, is the sum of the initial masses less the sum of the final masses, multiplied by c^2:

$$Q = (M_a + M_X - M_b - M_Y)c^2$$

If Q is positive, the reaction is exothermic and occurs regardless of how small the initial kinetic energy is.

If Q is negative, there is a minimum initial kinetic energy that must be available before the reaction can take place.

Neutrons are very effective in nuclear reactions, as they have no charge and therefore are not repelled by the nucleus.

Neutron captured by $^{238}_{92}U$.

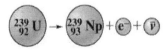

$^{239}_{92}U$ decays by β decay
to neptunium-239.

$^{239}_{93}Np$ itself decays by
β decay to produce
plutonium-239.

Nuclear fission occurs when one nucleus split apart. The energy released in a fission reaction is quite large. Also, since smaller nuclei are stable with fewer neutrons, several neutrons emerge from each fission as well. These neutrons can be used to induce fission in other nuclei, causing a chain reaction. This occurs when Uranium undergoes fission when struck by a free neutron.

The *critical mass* determines if the nuclei have sufficient mass and concentration to produce a chain reaction.

The *mass distribution of the fragments* shows that the first two pieces are large but usually unequal in size.

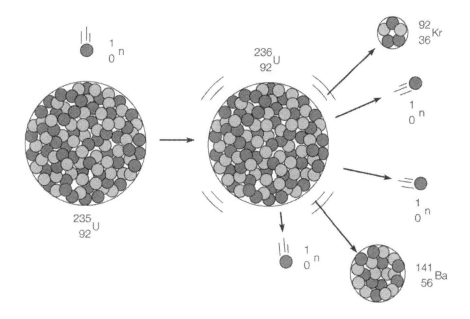

Nuclear energy is an interconversion of mass and energy. It is ultimately connected to the origins of the universe and the life cycles of the starts.

The *Big Bang theory* says that incredibly hot, dense, primordial plasma cooled, creating protons and neutrons. Continued cooling leads to hydrogen atoms which collapsed gravitationally into 1st generation stars.

The ultimate source of nuclear energy is a gravitational attraction. The mass deficit is the difference between the masses of reactants and products.

The binding energy is the energy required to break a nucleus into individual protons and neutrons. The ratio of binding energy to nucleon number tells you how stable a nucleus is. Iron-56 is the most stable nucleus:

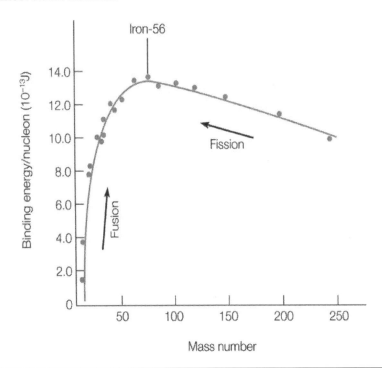

Isotope	Major Mode of Decay	Half-Life
Tritium	Beta	12.26 years
Carbon-14	Beta	5,930 years
Argon-41	Beta, gamma	1.83 hours
Iron-55	Electron capture	2.7 years
Colbalt-58	Beta, gamma	71 days
Colbalt-60	Beta, gamma	5.26 years
Nickel-63	Beta	92 years
Krypton-85	Beta, gamma	10.76 years
Strontium-89	Beta	5.4 days
Strontium-90	Beta	28 years
Yttrium-91	Beta	59 days
Isotope	**Major Mode of Decay**	**Half-Life**
Zirconium-93	Beta	9.5×10^5 years
Zirconium-95	Beta, gamma	65 days
Niobium-95	Beta, gamma	35 days
Technetium-99	Beta	2.1×10^5 years

Ruthenium-106	Beta	1 year
Iodine-129	Beta	1.6×10^7 years
Iodine-131	Beta, gamma	8 days
Xenon-133	Beta, gamma	5.27 days
Cesium-134	Beta, gamma	2.1 years
Cesium-135	Beta	2×10^6 years
Cesium-137	Beta	30 years
Cerium-141	Beta	32.5 days
Cerium-144	Beta, gamma	285 days
Promethium-147	Beta	2.6 years
Samarium-151	Beta	90 years
Europium-154	Beta, gamma	16 years
Lead-210	Beta	22 years
Radon-222	Alpha	3.8 days
Radium-226	Alpha, gamma	1,620 years
Thorium-229	Alpha	7,300 years
Thorium-230	Alpha	26,000 years
Uranium-234	Alpha	2.48×10^5 years
Uranium-235	Alpha, gamma	7.13×10^8 years
Uranium-238	Alpha	4.51×10^9 years
Neptunium-237	Alpha	2.14×10^6 years
Plutonium-238	Alpha	89 years
Plutonium-239	Alpha	24,360 years
Plutonium-240	Alpha	6,760 years
Plutonium-241	Beta	13 years
Plutonium-242	Alpha	3.79×10^5 years
Americium-241	Alpha	458 years
Americium-243	Alpha	7,650 years
Curium-242	Alpha	163 days
Curium-244	Alpha	18 years
Thorium-229	Alpha	7,300 years

To make a nuclear reactor, the chain reaction needs to be self-sustaining—it will continue indefinitely—but controlled. A *moderator* is needed to slow the neutrons; otherwise, their probability of interacting is too small. Common moderators are heavy water and graphite.

Unless the moderator is heavy water, the fraction of fissionable nuclei in natural uranium is too small to sustain a chain reaction, about 0.7%. It needs to be enriched to about 2–3%.

Neutrons that escape from the uranium do not contribute to fission. There is a critical mass below which a chain reaction will not occur because too many neutrons escape.

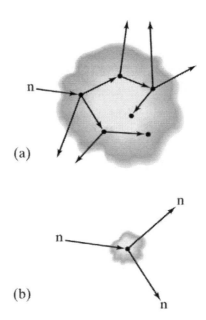

Finally, there are *control rods*, usually cadmium or boron, which absorb neutrons and can be used for fine control of the reaction, to keep it just barely critical.

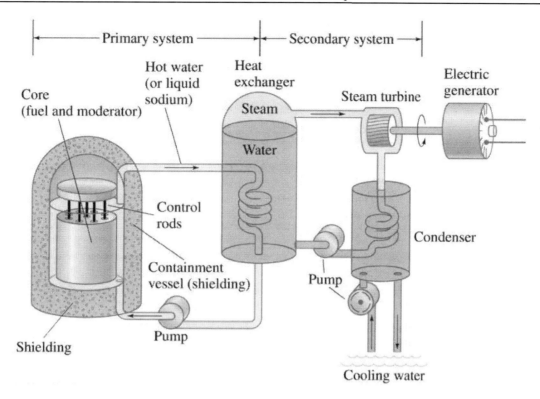

Some problems associated with nuclear reactors include the disposal of radioactive waste and the possibility of an accidental release of radiation.

An atomic bomb also uses fission, but the core is deliberately designed to undergo a massive uncontrolled chain reaction when the uranium is formed into a critical mass during the detonation process.

General Nature of Fusion

Nuclear fusion occurs when less massive nuclei form more massive nuclei. Nuclear fusion is the energy source for the Sun and other stars.

Fusion requires high temperature, high density, and sufficient confinement time.

Controlled fusion is usually studied with magnetic or inertial confinement.

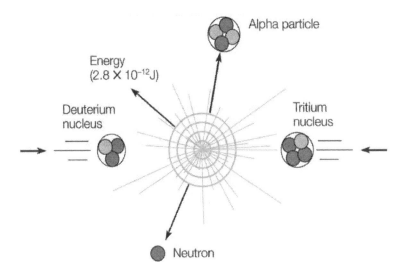

When light nuclei fuse to form heavier nuclei, they release energy in the process.

An example is the sequence of fusion processes that change hydrogen into helium in the Sun. They are listed here with the energy released in each:

$$^1_1H + ^1_1H \rightarrow ^2_1H + e^+ + v \qquad\qquad (0.42 \; \text{MeV})$$

$$^1_1H + ^2_1H \rightarrow ^3_2He + \gamma \qquad\qquad (5.49 \; \text{MeV})$$

$$^3_2He + ^3_2He \rightarrow ^4_2He + ^1_1H + ^1_1H \qquad (12.86 \text{ MeV})$$

The net effect is to transform four protons into a helium nucleus plus two positrons, two neutrinos, and two gamma rays.

$$4^1_1H \rightarrow ^4_2He + 2e^+ + 2v + 2\gamma$$

More massive stars can fuse heavier elements in their cores, all the way up to iron, the most stable nucleus.

Three fusion reactions are being considered for power reactors:

$$^2_1H + \ ^2_1H \rightarrow \ ^3_1H + \ ^1_1H \qquad \text{(4.03 MeV)}$$

$$^2_1H + \ ^2_1H \rightarrow \ ^3_2He + n \qquad \text{(3.27 MeV)}$$

$$^2_1H + \ ^3_1H \rightarrow \ ^4_2He + n \qquad \text{(17.59 MeV)}$$

These reactions use common fuels—deuterium or tritium—and release much more energy per nucleon than fission does.

A successful fusion reactor has not yet been achieved, but fusion (thermonuclear) bombs have been built. Several geometries for the containment of the incredibly hot plasma that must exist in a fusion reactor have been developed.

Mass Deficit, Energy Liberated, Binding Energy

Nuclear reactions are presented by balanced equations. The charge is always conserved, as is the mass number.

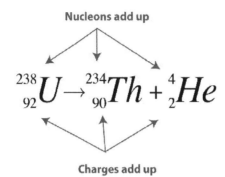

Names, symbols, and properties of particles in nuclear equations			
Name	Symbol	Mass Number	Charge
Proton	^1_1H (or ^1_1p)	1	1+
Electron	$^{\,\,0}_{-1}e$ (or $^{\,\,0}_{-1}\beta$)	0	1−
Neutron	^1_0n	1	0
Gamma Photon	$^0_0\gamma$	0	0

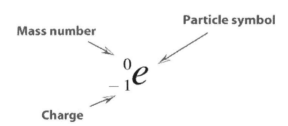

The difference in mass before and after a reaction is the mass deficit or mass defect. If the total mass before the reaction is different from the total mass after the reaction, then the difference in mass is made up for by energy.

Energy is liberated when mass is lost during a reaction because mass and energy are always conserved; the total mass and energy before a reaction is always the same as the total mass and energy after the reaction.

The energy that makes up for the mass deficit is calculated by:

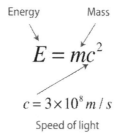

$$E = mc^2$$

Energy — Mass

$$c = 3 \times 10^8 \, m/s$$

Speed of light

The mass of the nucleons will always be greater than the mass of the atom. The mass has become energy, such as radiation or kinetic energy, released during the formation of the nucleus. This difference between the total mass of the constituents and the mass of the nucleus is the total binding energy of the nucleus.

The energy liberated is equal to the binding energy. The binding energy is used when converting ΔM into its equivalent in energy (ΔMc^2).

$$M_{nucleons} = M_{atom} + \text{binding energy}/c^2$$

Binding energy commonly refers to nuclear binding energy (the energy that binds the nucleons together). Binding energy per nucleon is strongest for Iron (Fe 56), and weakest for Deuterium (the 2-nucleon isotope of hydrogen).

Less commonly used is the electron binding energy. This is because electron binding energy is the ionization energy.

$$M_{nucleons} - M_{atom} = \text{mass deficit (also mass defect)} = \Delta M$$

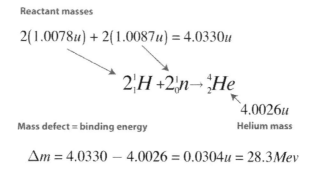

Reactant masses

$$2(1.0078u) + 2(1.0087u) = 4.0330u$$

$$2_1^1H + 2_0^1n \rightarrow {}_2^4He$$

4.0026u

Mass defect = binding energy   Helium mass

$$\Delta m = 4.0330 - 4.0026 = 0.0304u = 28.3 Mev$$

Mass Spectrometer

Mass spectrometry is a chemistry technique used to identify the chemicals in a substance. A mass spectrometer is a device that measures the mass-to-charge ration of a sample, as well as the number of ions in gas-phase. This produces a mass spectrum.

A magnetic field can deflect charged particles. A mass spectrometer works by turning atoms into ions, increasing their acceleration, so they all have the same kinetic energy, and deflecting them with a magnetic field. It creates ions by removing electrons from the atom—even if an atom normally forms a negative ion, a mass spectrometer usually works with positive ions.

Once their paths are deflected, their mass can be calculated because the force of deflection is known, and the curve of their deflection path is used to separate the atoms. The lighter the ion, the more it is deflected.

The greater the positive charge on the ion, the more the magnetic field deflects it.

A mass spectrum is then produced, which is a bar graph.

The graph gives the concentration of the atom, organized by their mass-to-charge ratio:

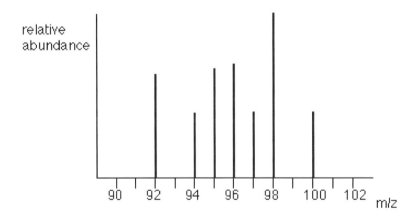

Chapter Summary

Atoms

- Nuclei contain protons and neutrons—nucleons.

- Total number of nucleons, A, is atomic mass number.

- Number of protons, Z, is atomic number.

- Isotope notation: $^{A}_{Z}X$

- Nuclear masses are measured in u; ^{12}C is defined with a mass of 12 amu.

- $1\ amu = 1.6605 \times 10^{-27}\ kg = 931.5\ MeV/c^2$

- Difference between the mass of the nucleus and mass of its constituents is binding energy.

Decay

- Unstable nuclei decay through alpha, beta or gamma emission.

- An alpha particle is a helium nucleus; a beta particle is an electron or positron; a gamma ray is a highly energetic photon.

- Nuclei are held together by the strong nuclear force; the weak nuclear force is responsible for beta decay.

- Electric charge, linear and angular momentum, mass-energy and nucleon number are all conserved.

- Radioactive decay is a statistical process.

- The number of decays per unit time is proportional to the number of nuclei present: $N = N_0 e^{-\lambda t}$

- The half-life is the time it takes for half the nuclei to decay.

Nuclear Reactions

- Nuclear reaction occurs when nuclei collide, and different nuclei are produced.

- Reaction energy or Q-value:

$$Q = M_p c^2 - (M_D + m_a)c^2$$

- Fission is when the heavy nucleus splits into two intermediate-sized nuclei.

  o Chain reactions occurred when neutrons emitted in a fission trigger more reactions.

  o Critical mass is the minimum mass needed to sustain a chain reaction.

  o A moderator is used to slow the neutrons, so collisions are more likely.

- Fusion is when small nuclei combine to form larger ones.

  o Sun's energy comes from fusion reactions.

  o Useful fusion reactor has not yet been built.

  o Radiation damage is measured using dosimetry.

  o Effect of absorbed dose depends on the radiation.

Practice Questions

1. In a nuclear reaction, the mass of the products is less than the mass of the reactants. Why is this not observed in a chemical reaction?

A. In chemical reactions, the mass is held constant by the nucleus
B. In chemical reactions, the mass deficit is balanced by a mass surplus
C. The mass deficit in chemical reactions is too small to be observed
D. The mass does not convert to energy in chemical reactions
E. None of the above are true

2. The isotope $^{13}_{7}N$ decays by positron emission to what isotope?

A. $^{14}_{6}C$ **B.** $^{11}_{7}N$ **C.** $^{13}_{6}C$ **D.** $^{12}_{6}C$ **E.** $^{12}_{7}N$

3. The radioactive gas radon is:

    I. more hazardous to smokers than nonsmokers
    II. the single greatest source of human radiation exposure
    III. a product of the radioactive decay series of uranium

A. I only   **B.** II only   **C.** III only   **D.** I and III only   **E.** I, II and III

4. Which of the following statements best describes the strong nuclear force?

A. The strength of the force increases with distance
B. The force is very strong and is effective over a large range of distances
C. The electrical force is stronger than the nuclear force
D. The force is very strong but is effective only within a short range of distances
E. None of the above are true statements

5. Natural line broadening can be understood in terms of the:

A. Schrodinger wave equation   **C.** de Broglie wavelength
B. Pauli exclusion principle   **D.** uncertainty principle   **E.** quantum numbers

6. A blue photon has a:

A. longer wavelength than a red photon and travels with a greater speed
B. longer wavelength than a red photon and travels with the same speed
C. shorter wavelength than a red photon and travels with a greater speed
D. longer wavelength than a red photon and travels with a lower speed
E. shorter wavelength than a red photon and travels with the same speed

7. Which type of nuclear radiation is powerful light energy that is *not* deflected as it passes between electrically-charged plates?

 A. Gamma **B.** Beta **C.** Alpha **D.** Nuclide **E.** None of the above

8. The main reason that there is a limit to the size of a stable nucleus is the:

 A. weakness of the electrostatic force
 B. weakness of the gravitational force
 C. short-range effect of the strong nuclear force
 D. limited range of the gravitational force
 E. long-distance effect of the strong nuclear force

9. Elements combine in fixed mass ratios to form compounds. This requires that elements:

 A. have unambiguous atomic numbers
 B. are always chemically active
 C. are composed of continuous matter without subunits
 D. are composed of discrete subunits called atoms
 E. none of the above are required

10. What is a rem?

 A. A unit for measuring rapid electron motion
 B. The number of radiation particles absorbed per second
 C. The number of radiation particles emitted per second
 D. The maximum exposure limit for occupational safety
 E. A unit for measuring radiation exposure

11. The intensity of X-rays, gamma rays, or any other radiation is:

 A. inversely proportional to the square of the distance from the source
 B. inversely proportional to the distance from the source
 C. directly proportional to the square of the distance from the source
 D. directly proportional to the distance from the source
 E. inversely proportional to the cube of the distance from the source

12. Ionizing radiation is:

 A. a neutron that has acquired a charge, resulting in the formation of an ion
 B. high-energy radiation that removes electrons from atoms or molecules
 C. radiation that only interacts with ions
 D. equivalent to a proton
 E. released by ions and reacts with nuclei

13. What nucleus results when ^{55}Ni decays by positron emission?

    A. ^{55}Ca   **B.** ^{55}Ni   **C.** ^{55}Co   **D.** ^{55}Fe   **E.** None of the above

14. Which of the following types of radiation has the highest energy?

    A. γ rays   **C.** α particles

    B. Visible light rays   **D.** β particles   **E.** All have the same energy

15. If a star has a peak intensity at 580 nm, what is its temperature? (Use Wien's displacement constant $b = 2.9 \times 10^{-3}$ K·m)

    A. 5,000 °C   **B.** 2,000 °C   **C.** 5,000 °F   **D.** 2,000 K   **E.** 5,000 K

Solutions

1. D is correct.

Mass is conserved in a chemical reaction; no particles are created or destroyed. The atoms are rearranged to form products from reactants.

In nuclear reactions, the mass difference is due to mass converting into energy.

2. C is correct.

Positron emission occurs during β^+.

The decay equation:

$$^{13}_{7}\text{N} \rightarrow {}^{13}_{6}\text{C} + e^+ + v_e$$

A proton converts into a neutron and a positron is ejected with an electron neutrino. The daughter nuclide is ^{13}C.

3. E is correct.

Radon gas is a natural decay product of uranium that accounts for the greatest source of yearly radiation exposure in humans. Radon is more hazardous to smokers due to the combined carcinogenic effects of smoking and radiation exposure.

4. D is correct. The strong nuclear force is the strongest of the four fundamental forces. However, it only acts within a small range of distance (about the diameter of the nucleus).

5. D is correct.

Natural line broadening is the extension of a spectral line over a range of frequencies. This occurs due in part to the uncertainty principle, which relates the time in which an atom is in an excited state to the energy of its emitted photon.

$\Delta E \Delta t > \hbar / 2$

where $\hbar$ is reduced Planck's constant

Because energy is related to frequency by:

$E = hf$

where h is Planck's constant

The range of frequencies observed (broadening) is due to the uncertainty in energy outlined by the uncertainty principle.

6. E is correct.

Speed is constant for all electromagnetic waves and only changes due to the transmission medium, not the frequency or wavelength of the wave.

Blue photons have higher energy and thus higher frequencies than red light due to:

$$E = hf$$

However, the frequency is inversely proportional to wavelength:

$$\lambda = c / f$$

Thus, blue photons have shorter wavelengths than red photons due to their higher frequencies.

7. A is correct.

Gamma radiation is a high energy electromagnetic wave, and as such it has no charge and will not deflect within an electric field.

8. C is correct.

Nuclei with atomic numbers over 83 are inherently unstable and thus radioactive. This limit in size is because the strong nuclear force has a very short range and as the nucleus gets larger, the strong nuclear force cannot overcome the Coulomb repulsion from the protons within the nucleus.

9. D is correct.

A mass of an element or compound can be measured by its molar mass. The molar mass relates the mass of the element or compound to a discrete number of subunits (atoms for elements, molecules for compounds).

10. E is correct.

The rem is short for the Roentgen equivalent in man and is designed to measure the biological damage of ionizing radiation. It does not measure the number of particles absorbed or emitted, nor is it the maximum occupational safety exposure limit for radiation.

11. A is correct.

The intensity of electromagnetic radiation concerning distance from the point source:

$$I = S / 4\pi r^2$$

where I = intensity, S = point source strength, and r = radial distance from the point source

The intensity of the radiation from the point source is inversely proportional to the square of the distance away from the point source.

12. B is correct.

Ionizing radiation can be high energy charged particles (alpha, beta) or high energy electromagnetic waves (X-rays, gamma rays).

All are termed ionizing because they possess enough energy to remove electrons from atoms or molecules and ionize them.

13. C is correct.

Nuclear reaction:

$$^{55}_{28}\text{Ni} \rightarrow {}^{55}_{27}\text{Co} + e^+ + v_e$$

where Co = product, e^+ = positron and v_e = electron neutrino

In positron emission (β^+ decay), a proton in the nucleus converts to a neutron while releasing a positron and an electron neutrino.

The atomic number decreases by one, but the mass number stays constant.

14. A is correct.

Gamma rays are high energy electromagnetic waves. They have the highest energy of all radiation (e.g., alpha, beta, and electromagnetic spectrum).

15. E is correct.

Use Wien's Displacement Law:

$$\lambda_{max} = b / T$$

$$T = (2.9 \times 10^{-3}\,\text{K·m}) / (580 \times 10^{-9}\,\text{m})$$

$$T = 5,000$$

Notes

Notes

Appendix

Common Physics Formulas & Conversions

Constants and Conversion Factors

1 unified atomic mass unit	1 u (or Dalton) = 1.66×10^{-27} kg
	1 u = 931 MeV/c^2
Proton mass	$m_p = 1.67 \times 10^{-27}$ kg
Neutron mass	$m_n = 1.67 \times 10^{-27}$ kg
Electron mass	$m_e = 9.11 \times 10^{-31}$ kg
Electron charge magnitude	$e = 1.60 \times 10^{-19}$ C
Avogadro's number	$N_0 = 6.02 \times 10^{23}$ mol^{-1}
Universal gas constant	R = 8.31 J/(mol·K)
Boltzmann's constant	$k_B = 1.38 \times 10^{-23}$ J/K
Speed of light	$c = 3.00 \times 10^8$ m/s
Planck's constant	$h = 6.63 \times 10^{-34}$ J·s
	$h = 4.14 \times 10^{-15}$ eV·s
	$hc = 1.99 \times 10^{-25}$ J·m
	$hc = 1.24 \times 10^3$ eV·nm
Vacuum permittivity	$\varepsilon_0 = 8.85 \times 10^{-12}$ C^2/N·m^2
Coulomb's law constant	$k = 1/4\pi\varepsilon_0 = 9.0 \times 10^9$ N·m^2/C^2
Vacuum permeability	$\mu_0 = 4\pi \times 10^{-7}$ (T·m)/A
Magnetic constant	$k' = \mu_0/4\pi = 10^{-7}$ (T·m)/A
Universal gravitational constant	$G = 6.67 \times 10^{-11}$ m^3/kg·s^2
Acceleration due to gravity at Earth's surface	g = 9.8 m/s^2
1 atmosphere pressure	1 atm = 1.0×10^5 N/m^2
	1 atm = 1.0×10^5 Pa
1 electron volt	1 eV = 1.60×10^{-19} J
Balmer constant	B = 3.645×10^{-7} m
Rydberg constant	R = 1.097×10^7 m^{-1}
Stefan constant	$\sigma = 5.67 \times 10^{-8}$ W/m^{2}K^4

Units			Prefixes	
Name	**Symbol**	**Factor**	**Prefix**	**Symbol**
meter	m	10^{12}	tera	T
kilogram	kg	10^{9}	giga	G
second	s	10^{6}	mega	M
ampere	A	10^{3}	kilo	k
kelvin	K	10^{-2}	centi	c
mole	mol	10^{-3}	milli	m
hertz	Hz	10^{-6}	micro	μ
newton	N	10^{-9}	nano	n
pascal	Pa	10^{-12}	pico	p
joule	J			
watt	W			
coulomb	C			
volt	V			
ohm	Ω			
henry	H			
farad	F			
tesla	T			
degree Celsius	°C			
electronvolt	eV			

Values of Trigonometric Functions for Common Angles

θ	$\sin \theta$	$\cos \theta$	$\tan \theta$
0°	0	1	0
30°	1/2	$\sqrt{3}/2$	$\sqrt{3}/3$
37°	3/5	4/5	3/4
45°	$\sqrt{2}/2$	$\sqrt{2}/2$	1
53°	4/5	3/5	4/3
60°	$\sqrt{3}/2$	1/2	$\sqrt{3}$
90°	1	0	∞

Newtonian Mechanics

		a = acceleration
	$v = v_0 + a\Delta t$	A = amplitude
Translational Motion	$x = x_0 + v_0\Delta t + \dfrac{1}{2}a\Delta t^2$	E = energy
	$v^2 = v_0^2 + 2a\Delta x$	F = force
	$\vec{a} = \dfrac{\sum \vec{F}}{m} = \dfrac{\vec{F}_{net}}{m}$	f = frequency
		h = height
	$\omega = \omega_0 + \alpha t$	I = rotational inertia
	$\theta = \theta_0 + \omega_0 t + \dfrac{1}{2}\alpha t^2$	J = impulse
Rotational Motion	$\omega^2 = \omega_0^2 + 2\alpha\Delta\theta$	K = kinetic energy
	$\vec{\alpha} = \dfrac{\sum \vec{\tau}}{I} = \dfrac{\vec{\tau}_{net}}{I}$	k = spring constant
		ℓ = length
		m = mass
Force of Friction	$\left|\vec{F}_f\right| \leq \mu\left|\vec{F}_n\right|$	N = normal force
Centripetal Acceleration	$a_c = \dfrac{v^2}{r}$	P = power
		p = momentum
Torque	$\tau = r_\perp F = rF \sin\theta$	L= angular momentum
		r = radius of distance
Momentum	$\Delta\vec{p} = m\vec{v}$	T = period
Impulse	$\vec{J} = \Delta\vec{p} = \vec{F}\Delta t$	t = time
		U = potential energy
Kinetic Energy	$K = \dfrac{1}{2}mv^2$	v = velocity or speed
		W = work done on a
Potential Energy	$\Delta U_g = mg\Delta y$	system
Work	$\Delta E = W = F_\parallel d = Fd\cos\theta$	x = position
		y = height
Power	$P = \dfrac{\Delta E}{\Delta t} = \dfrac{\Delta W}{\Delta t}$	

$\alpha = angular$

Simple Harmonic Motion	$x = A\cos(\omega t) = A\cos(2\pi f t)$	*acceleration*
Center of Mass	$x_{cm} = \dfrac{\sum m_i x_i}{\sum m_i}$	$\mu = coefficient\ of$
Function of Time Function of Time Angular Momentum	$L = I\omega$	*friction* $\theta = angle$
Angular Impulse	$\Delta L = \tau\Delta t$	$\tau = torque$ $\omega = angular\ speed$
Angular Kinetic Energy	$K = \dfrac{1}{2}I\omega^2$	
Work	$W = F\Delta r\ \cos\theta$	
Power	$P = Fv\ \cos\theta$	
Spring Force	$\left|\vec{F}_s\right| = k\left|\vec{x}\right|$	
Spring Potential Energy	$U_s = \dfrac{1}{2}kx^2$	
Period of Spring Oscillator	$T_s = 2\pi\sqrt{m/k}$	
Period of Simple Pendulum	$T_p = 2\pi\sqrt{\ell/g}$	
Period	$T = \dfrac{2\pi}{\omega} = \dfrac{1}{f}$	
Gravitational Body Force	$\left|\vec{F}_g\right| = G\dfrac{m_1 m_2}{r^2}$	
Gravitational Potential Energy of Two Masses	$U_G = -\dfrac{Gm_1 m_2}{r}$	

Electricity and Magnetism

Electric Field	$\vec{E} = \dfrac{\vec{F}_E}{q}$	$A = area$
		$B = magnetic\ field$
		$C = capacitance$
Electric Field Strength	$\left|\vec{E}\right| = \dfrac{1}{4\pi\varepsilon_0}\dfrac{|q|}{r^2}$	$d = distance$
		$E = electric\ field$
Electric Field Strength	$\left|\vec{E}\right| = \dfrac{|\Delta V|}{|\Delta r|}$	$\epsilon = emf$
		$F = force$
Electrostatic Force Between Charged Particles	$\left|\vec{F}_E\right| = \dfrac{1}{4\pi\varepsilon_0}\dfrac{|q_1 q_2|}{r^2}$	$I = current$
		$l = length$
Electric Potential Energy	$\Delta U_E = q\Delta V$	$P = power$
		$Q = charge$
Electrostatic Potential due to a Charge	$V = \dfrac{1}{4\pi\varepsilon_0}\dfrac{q}{r}$	$q = point\ charge$
		$R = resistance$
Capacitor Voltage	$V = \dfrac{Q}{C}$	$r = separation$
		$t = time$
Capacitance of a Parallel Plate Capacitor	$C = \kappa\varepsilon_0\dfrac{A}{d}$	$U = potential\ energy$
		$V = electric\ potential$
Electric Field Inside a Parallel Plate Capacitor	$E = \dfrac{Q}{\varepsilon_0 A}$	$v = speed$
		$\kappa = dielectric\ constant$
Capacitor Potential Energy	$U_C = \tfrac{1}{2}Q\Delta V = \tfrac{1}{2}C(\Delta V)^2$	$\rho = resistivity$
		$\theta = angle$
Current	$I = \dfrac{\Delta Q}{\Delta t}$	$\Phi = flux$
Resistance	$R = \dfrac{\rho l}{A}$	
Power	$P = I\Delta V$	

Current	$I = \dfrac{\Delta V}{R}$
Resistors in Series	$R_s = \displaystyle\sum_i R_i$
Resistors in Parallel	$\dfrac{1}{R_p} = \displaystyle\sum_i \dfrac{1}{R_i}$
Capacitors in Parallel	$C_p = \displaystyle\sum_i C_i$
Capacitors in Series	$\dfrac{1}{C_s} = \displaystyle\sum_i \dfrac{1}{C_i}$
Magnetic Field Strength	$B = \dfrac{\mu_0 I}{2\pi r}$
Magnetic Force	$\vec{F}_M = q\vec{v} \times \vec{B}$ $\vec{F}_M = \lvert q\vec{v} \rvert \lvert \sin\theta \rvert \lvert \vec{B} \rvert$ $\vec{F}_M = I\vec{l} \times \vec{B}$ $\vec{F}_M = \lvert I\vec{l} \rvert \lvert \sin\theta \rvert \lvert \vec{B} \rvert$
Magnetic Flux	$\Phi_B = \vec{B} \cdot \vec{A}$ $\Phi_B = \lvert \vec{B} \rvert \cos\theta \lvert \vec{A} \rvert$
Electromagnetic Induction	$\epsilon = \dfrac{-\Delta \Phi_B}{\Delta t}$ $\epsilon = Blv$

Fluid Mechanics and Thermal Physics

Density	$\rho = \dfrac{m}{V}$	$A = area$
Pressure	$P = \dfrac{F}{A}$	$c = specific\ heat$
		$d = thickness$
		$e = emissivity$
Absolute Pressure	$P = P_0 + \rho g h$	$F = force$
Buoyant Force	$F_b = \rho V g$	$h = depth$
Fluid Continuity Equation	$A_1 v_1 = A_2 v_2$	$k = thermal\ conductivity$
		$K = kinetic\ energy$
Bernoulli's Equation	$P_1 + \rho g y_1 + \dfrac{1}{2}\rho v_1^2 = P_2 + \rho g y_2 + \dfrac{1}{2}\rho v_2^2$	$l = length$
		$L = latent\ heat$
Heat Conduction	$\dfrac{Q}{\Delta t} = \dfrac{kA\Delta T}{d}$	$m = mass$
		$n = number\ of\ moles$
		$n_c = efficiency$
Thermal Radiation	$P = e\sigma A(T^4 - T_C^4)$	$N = number\ of\ molecules$
Ideal Gas Law	$PV = nRT = Nk_B T$	$P = pressure\ or\ power$
		$Q = energy\ transferred\ to$
Average Energy	$K = \dfrac{3}{2}k_B T$	$a\ system\ by\ heating$
		$T = temperature$
Work	$W = -P\Delta V$	$t = time$
Conservation of Energy	$\Delta E = Q + W$	$E = internal\ energy$
Linear Expansion	$\Delta l = al_o \Delta T$	$V = volume$
Heat Engine Efficiency	$n_c = |W/Q_H|$	$v = speed$
		$W = work\ done\ on\ a$
		$system$
Carnot Heat Engine Efficiency	$n_c = \dfrac{T_H - T_C}{T_H}$	$y = height$
		$\sigma = Stefan\ constant$
Energy of Temperature Change	$Q = mc\Delta T$	$\alpha = coefficient\ of\ linear$
		$expansion$
Energy of Phase Change	$Q = mL$	$\rho = density$

Optics

Wavelength to Frequency	$\lambda = \dfrac{v}{f}$	d = separation
		f = frequency or focal length
Index of Refraction	$n = \dfrac{c}{v}$	h = height
		L = distance
Snell's Law	$n_1 \sin \theta_1 = n_2 \sin \theta_2$	M = magnification
		m = an integer
Thin Lens Equation	$\dfrac{1}{s_i} + \dfrac{1}{s_0} = \dfrac{1}{f}$	n = index of refraction
		R = radius of curvature
Magnification Equation	$|M| = \left|\dfrac{h_i}{h_o}\right| = \left|\dfrac{s_i}{s_o}\right|$	s = distance
		v = speed
Double Slit Diffraction	$d \sin \theta = m\lambda$	x = position
	$\Delta L = m\lambda$	λ = wavelength
		θ = angle
Critical Angle	$\sin \theta_c = \dfrac{n_2}{n_1}$	
Focal Length of Spherical Mirror	$f = \dfrac{R}{2}$	

Acoustics

Standing Wave/ Open Pipe Harmonics	$\lambda = \dfrac{2L}{n}$	f = frequency L = length
Closed Pipe Harmonics	$\lambda = \dfrac{4L}{n}$	m = mass M = molecular mass
Harmonic Frequencies	$f_n = n f_1$	n = harmonic number
Speed of Sound in Ideal Gas	$v_{sound} = \sqrt{\dfrac{yRT}{M}}$	R = gas constant T = tension
Speed of Wave Through Wire	$v = \sqrt{\dfrac{T}{m/L}}$	v = velocity y = adiabatic constant
Doppler Effect (Approaching Stationary Observer)	$f_{observed} = \left(\dfrac{v}{v - v_{source}}\right)f_{source}$	λ = wavelength
Doppler Effect (Receding Stationary Observer)	$f_{observed} = \left(\dfrac{v}{v + v_{source}}\right)f_{source}$	
Doppler Effect (Observer Moving towards Source)	$f_{observed} = \left(1 + \dfrac{v_{observer}}{v}\right)f_{source}$	
Doppler Effect (Observer Moving away from Source)	$f_{observed} = \left(1 - \dfrac{v_{observer}}{v}\right)f_{source}$	

Modern Physics

		B = Balmer constant
Photon Energy	$E = hf$	
		c = speed of light
Photoelectric Electron Energy	$K_{max} = hf - \phi$	E = energy
		f = frequency
Electron Wavelength	$\lambda = \dfrac{h}{p}$	
		K = kinetic energy
		m = mass
Energy Mass Relationship	$E = mc^2$	
		p = momentum
Rydberg Formula	$\dfrac{1}{\lambda} = R\left(\dfrac{1}{n_f^2} - \dfrac{1}{n_i^2}\right)$	R = Rydberg constant
		v = velocity
Balmer Formula	$\lambda = B\left(\dfrac{n^2}{n^2 - 2^2}\right)$	λ = wavelength
		$\emptyset$ = work function
Lorentz Factor	$\gamma = \dfrac{1}{\sqrt{1 - \dfrac{v^2}{c^2}}}$	γ = Lorentz factor

Geometry and Trigonometry

Rectangle	$A = bh$	$A = area$
		$C = circumference$
Triangle	$A = \dfrac{1}{2}bh$	$V = volume$
		$S = surface\ area$
Circle	$A = \pi r^2$	$b = base$
	$C = 2\pi r$	$h = height$
Rectangular Solid	$V = lwh$	$l = length$
		$w = width$
Cylinder	$V = \pi r^2 l$	$r = radius$
	$S = 2\pi rl + 2\pi r^2$	$\theta = angle$
Sphere	$V = \dfrac{4}{3}\pi r^3$	
	$S = 4\pi r^2$	
Right Triangle	$a^2 + b^2 = c^2$	
	$\sin\theta = \dfrac{a}{c}$	
	$\cos\theta = \dfrac{b}{c}$	
	$\tan\theta = \dfrac{a}{b}$	

Notes

Physics Glossary

A

Absolute humidity (or saturation value) − the maximum amount of water vapor that could be present in 1 m³ of the air at any given temperature.

Absolute magnitude − a classification scheme which compensates for the differences in the distance to stars; calculates the brightness that stars would appear to have if they were all at a defined, standard distance of 10 parsecs.

Absolute scale − temperature scale set so that zero is the theoretical lowest temperature possible (this would occur when all random motion of molecules has ceased).

Absolute zero − the theoretical lowest temperature possible, at which molecular motion vanishes; −273.16 °C or 0 K.

Absorptance − the ratio of the total absorbed radiation to the total incident radiation.

Acceleration − the rate of change of velocity of a moving object concerning time; the SI units are m/s²; by definition, this change in velocity can result from a change in speed, a change in direction or a combination of changes in both speed and direction.

Acceleration due to gravity − the acceleration produced in a body due to the Earth's attraction; denoted by the letter g (SI unit − m/s²); on the surface of the Earth, its average value is 9.8 m/s²; increases when going towards the poles from the equator; decreases with altitude and with depth inside the Earth; the value of g at the center of the Earth is zero.

Achromatic − capable of transmitting light without decomposing it into its constituent colors.

Acoustics − the science of the production, transmission, and effects of sound.

Acoustic shielding − a sound barrier that prevents the transmission of acoustic energy.

Adiabatic − any change in which there is no gain or loss of heat.

Adiabatic cooling − the decrease in temperature of an expanding gas that involves no additional heat flowing out of the gas; the cooling from the energy lost by expansion.

Adiabatic heating − the increase in temperature of the compressed gas that involves no additional heat flowing into the gas; the heating from the energy gained by compression.

Afocal lens − a lens of zero convergent power whose focal points are infinitely distant.

Air mass – a large, more or less uniform body of air with nearly the same temperature and moisture conditions throughout.

Albedo – the fraction of the total light incident on a reflecting surface, especially a celestial body, which is reflected in all directions.

Allotropic forms – elements that can have several different structures with different physical properties (e.g., graphite and diamond).

Alpha (α) particle – the nucleus of a helium atom (two protons and two neutrons) emitted as radiation from a decaying heavy nucleus (α-decay).

Alternating current – an electric current that first moves in one direction, then in the opposite direction with a regular frequency.

Amorphous – term that describes solids that have neither definite form nor structure.

Amp – unit of electric current; equivalent to coulomb/second.

Ampere – the full name of the unit amp; the SI unit of electric current; one ampere is the flow of one coulomb of charge per second.

Amplitude – the maximum absolute value attained by the disturbance of a wave or by any quantity that varies periodically.

Amplitude (of an oscillation) – the maximum displacement of a body from its mean position during an oscillatory motion.

Amplitude (of waves) – the maximum displacement of particles of the medium from their mean positions during the propagation of a wave.

Angle of contact – the angle between tangents to the liquid surface and the solid surface inside the liquid; both the tangents are drawn at the point of contact.

Angle of incidence – the angle of an incident (arriving) ray or particle to a surface; measured from a line perpendicular to the surface (the normal).

Angle of reflection – the angle of a reflected ray or particle from a surface; measured from a line perpendicular to the surface (the normal).

Angle of refraction – the angle between the refracted ray and the normal.

Angle of repose – the angle of inclination of a plane with the horizontal such that a body placed on the plane is on the verge of sliding but does not.

Angstrom – a unit of length; $1 = 10^{-10}$ m.

Angular acceleration − the rate of change of angular velocity of a body moving along a circular path; denoted by a.

Angular displacement − the angle described at the center of the circle by a moving body along a circular path. It is measured in radians.

Angular momentum − also a moment of momentum; the cross-product of position vector and momentum.

Angular momentum quantum number − from quantum mechanics model of the atom, one of four descriptions of the energy state of an electron wave; describes the energy sublevels of electrons within the main energy levels of an atom.

Angular velocity − the rate of change of angular displacement per unit of time.

Annihilation − a process in which a particle and an antiparticle combine and release their rest energies in other particles.

Antineutrino − the antiparticle of neutrino; has zero mass and spin ½.

Archimedes principle − a body immersed in a fluid experiences an apparent loss of weight which is equal to the weight of the fluid displaced by the body.

Astronomical unit − the radius of the Earth's orbit is defined as one astronomical unit (A.U.).

Atom − the smallest unit of an element that can exist alone or in combination with other elements.

Atomic mass unit − relative mass unit (amu) of an isotope based on the standard of the ^{12}C isotope; one atomic mass unit (1 amu) = 1/12 the mass of a ^{12}C atom = 1.66×10^{-27} Kg.

Atomic number − the number of protons in the nucleus of an atom.

Atomic weight − weighted average of the masses of stable isotopes of an element as they occur in nature; based on the abundance of each isotope of the element and the atomic mass of the isotope compared to carbon-12.

Avogadro's number − the number of carbon-12 atoms in exactly 12.00 g of C that is 6.02×10^{23} atoms or other chemical units; the number of chemical units in one mole of a substance.

Avogadro's Law − under the same conditions of temperature and pressure, equal volumes of all gases contain an equal number of molecules.

Axis − the imaginary line about which a planet or other object rotates.

B

Background radiation – ionizing radiation (e.g., alpha, beta, gamma rays) from natural sources.

Balanced forces – when some forces act on a body and the resultant force is zero; see *Resultant forces*.

Balmer lines – lines in the spectrum of the hydrogen atom in the visible range; produced by the transition between n 2 and n = 2, with n being the principal quantum number.

Balmer series – a set of four line spectra; narrow lines of color emitted by hydrogen atom electrons as they drop from excited states to the ground state.

Bar – a unit of pressure; equal to 10^5 Pascals.

Barometer – an instrument that measures atmospheric pressure; used in weather forecasting and determining elevation above sea level.

Baryon – subatomic particle composed of three quarks.

Beat – a phenomenon of the periodic variation in the intensity of sound due to the superposition of waves differing slightly in frequency; rhythmic increases and decreases of volume from constructive and destructive interference between two sound waves of slightly different frequencies.

Bernoulli's theorem – states that the total energy per unit volume of a non-viscous, incompressible fluid in a streamline flow will remain constant.

Beta (β) particle – high-energy electron emitted as ionizing radiation from a decaying nucleus (β-decay); also a beta ray.

Big bang theory – current model of galactic evolution in which the universe is assumed to have been created by an intense and brilliant explosion from a primeval fireball.

Binding energy – the net energy required to break a nucleus into its constituent protons and neutrons; also the energy equivalent released when a nucleus is formed.

Black body – an ideal body which would absorb all incident radiation and reflect none.

Black body radiation – electromagnetic radiation emitted by an ideal material (the black body) that perfectly absorbs and perfectly emits radiation.

Black hole – the remaining theoretical core of a supernova that is so dense that even light cannot escape.

Bohr model – model of the structure of the atom that attempted to correct the deficiencies of the solar system model and account for the Balmer series.

Boiling point – the temperature at which a phase change of liquid to gas takes place through boiling; the same temperature as the condensation point.

Boundary – the division between two regions of differing physical properties.

Boyle's Law – for a given mass of a gas at constant temperature, the volume of the gas is inversely proportional to the pressure.

Brewster's Law – states that the refractive index of a material is equal to the tangent of the polarizing angle for the material.

British thermal unit (Btu) – the amount of energy or heat needed to increase the temperature of one pound of water one degree Fahrenheit.

Brownian motion – the continuous random motion of solid microscopic particles when suspended in a fluid medium due to their ongoing bombardment by atoms and molecules.

Bulk's modulus of elasticity – the ratio of normal stress to the volumetric strain produced in a body.

Buoyant force – the upward force on an object immersed in a fluid.

C

Calorie – a unit of heat; 1 Calorie = 4.186 joule.

Candela – the SI unit of luminous intensity defined as the luminous intensity in a given direction of a source that emits monochromatic photons of frequency 540×10^{12} Hz and has a radiant intensity in that direction of 1/683 W/sr.

Capacitance – the ratio of charge stored per increase in potential difference.

Capacitor – electrical device used to store charge and energy in the electrical field.

Capillarity – the rise or fall of a liquid in a tube of very fine bore.

Carnot's theorem – no engine operating between two temperatures can be more efficient than a reversible engine working between the same two temperatures.

Cathode rays – negatively charged particles (electrons) that are emitted from a negative terminal in an evacuated glass tube.

Celsius scale of temperature – the ice-point is taken as the lower fixed point (0 °C), and the steam-point is taken as the upper fixed point (100 °C); the interval between the ice-point and the steam-point is divided into 100 equal divisions; the unit division on this scale is 1 °C; previously called the centigrade scale; the relationship relates the temperatures on the Celsius scale and the Fahrenheit scale, C/100 = (F – 32) / 180; the temperature of a healthy person is 37 °C or 98.6 °F.

Centrifugal force – an apparent outward force on an object in circular motion; a consequence of the third law of motion.

Centripetal force – the radial force required to keep an object moving in a circular path.

Chain reaction – a self-sustaining reaction where some of the products can produce more reactions of the same kind (e.g., in a nuclear chain reaction, neutrons are the products that produce more nuclear reactions in a self-sustaining series).

Charles' Law – for a given mass of a gas at constant pressure, the volume is directly proportional to the temperature.

Chromatic aberration – an optical lens defect causing color fringes due to the lens bringing different colors of light to focus at different points.

Circular motion – the motion of a body along a circular path.

Closed system – the system which cannot exchange heat or matter with the surroundings.

Coefficient of areal expansion – the fractional change in surface area per degree of temperature change; see *Coefficient of thermal expansion.*

Coefficient of linear expansion – the fractional change in length per degree of temperature change; see *Coefficient of thermal expansion.*

Coefficient of thermal expansion – the fractional change in the size of an object per degree of change in temperature at a constant pressure; the SI unit is K^{-1}.

Coefficient of volumetric expansion – the fractional change in volume per degree of temperature change; see *Coefficient of thermal expansion.*

Coherent source – a source in which there is a constant phase difference between waves emitted from different parts of the source.

Compression – a part of a longitudinal wave in which the density of the particles of the medium is higher than the normal density.

Compressive stress – a force that tends to compress the surface as the Earth's plates move into each other.

Condensation (sound) – a compression of gas molecules; a pulse of increased density and pressure that moves through the air at the speed of sound.

Condensation (water vapor) − where more vapor or gas molecules are returning to the liquid state than are evaporating.

Condensation nuclei − tiny particles such as tiny dust, smoke, soot or salt crystals suspended in the air on which water condenses.

Condensation point − the temperature at which a gas or vapor changes back to liquid; see *Boiling point*.

Conduction − the transfer of heat from a region of higher temperature to a region of lower temperature by increased kinetic energy moving from molecule to molecule.

Constructive interference − the condition in which two waves arriving at the same place at the same time and in phase add amplitudes to create a new wave.

Control rods − rods inserted between fuel rods in a nuclear reactor to absorb neutrons and control the rate of the nuclear chain reaction.

Convection − transfer of heat from a region of higher temperature to a region of lower temperature by the displacement of high-energy molecules (e.g., the displacement of warmer, less dense air (higher kinetic energy) by cooler, denser air (lower kinetic energy)).

Conventional current − the opposite of electron current; considers an electric current to consist of a drift of positive charges that flow from the positive terminal to the negative terminal of a battery.

Coulomb − unit used to measure the quantity of electric charge; equivalent to the charge resulting from the transfer of 6.24 billion particles such as the electron.

Coulomb's Law − relationship between charge, distance, and magnitude of the electrical force between two bodies; the force between any two charges is directly proportional to the product of charges and inversely proportional to the square of the distance between the charges.

Covalent bond − a chemical bond formed by the sharing of a pair of electrons.

Covalent compound − chemical compound held together by a covalent bond or bonds.

Crest − the point of maximum positive displacement on a transverse wave.

Critical angle − the limit to the angle of incidence when all light rays are reflected internally.

Critical mass − the mass of fissionable material needed to sustain a chain reaction.

Curvilinear motion − the motion of a body along a curved path.

Cycle − a complete vibration.

Cyclotron − a device used to accelerate the charged particles.

D

De-acceleration − negative acceleration when the velocity of a body decreases with time.

Decibel − unit of the sound level; if P1 & P2 are two amounts of power, the first is said to be n decibels greater, where n = 10 log10 (P1/P2).

Decibel scale − a nonlinear scale of loudness based on the ratio of the intensity level of a sound to the intensity at the threshold of hearing.

Density − the mass of a substance per unit volume.

Destructive interference − the condition in which two waves arriving at the same point at the same time out of phase add amplitudes that cancel to create zero total disturbance; see *Constructive interference*.

Dewpoint temperature − the temperature at which condensation begins.

Dew − condensation of water vapor into droplets of liquid on surfaces.

Diffraction − the bending of light around the edge of an opaque object.

Diffuse reflection − light rays reflected in many random directions, as opposed to the parallel rays reflected from a perfectly smooth surface such as a mirror.

Diopter − unit of measure of the refractive power of a lens.

Direct current − an electrical current which always flows in one direction.

Direct proportion − when two variables increase or decrease together in the same ratio (at the same rate).

Dispersion − the splitting of white light into its component colors of the spectrum.

Displacement − a vector quantity for the change in the position of an object as it moves in a particular direction; also the shortest distance between the initial position and the final position of a moving body.

Distance − a scalar quantity for the length of the path traveled by a body irrespective of the direction it goes in.

Doppler effect − an apparent change in the frequency of sound or light due to the relative motion between the source of the sound or light and the observer.

E

Echo − a reflected sound that can be distinguished from the original sound, usually arriving 0.1 s or more after the original sound.

Einstein mass-energy relation − $E = mc^2$; E is the energy released, m is the mass defect and c is the speed of light.

Elastic potential energy − the potential energy of a body by its configuration (i.e., shape).

Elastic strain − an adjustment to stress in which materials recover their original shape after stress is released.

Electric circuit − consists of a voltage source that maintains an electrical potential, a continuous conducting path for a current to follow and a device where the electrical potential does work; a switch in the circuit is used to complete or interrupt the conducting path.

Electric current − the flow of electric charge; the electric force field produced by an electrical charge.

Electric field line − an imaginary curve tangent to which at any given point gives the direction of the electric field at that point.

Electric field lines − a map of an electric field representing the direction of the force that a test charge would experience; the direction of an electric field shown by lines of force.

Electric generator − a mechanical device that uses wire loops rotating in a magnetic field to produce electromagnetic induction to generate electricity.

Electric potential energy − potential energy due to the position of a charge near other charges.

Electrical conductors − materials that have electrons that are free to move throughout the material (e.g., metals); allows electric current to flow through the material.

Electrical energy − a form of energy from electromagnetic interactions.

Electric force − a fundamental force that results from the interaction of electrical charges; it is the most powerful force in the universe.

Electrical insulators − electrical nonconductors, or materials that obstruct the flow of electric current.

Electrical nonconductors − materials that have electrons that do not move easily within the material (e.g., rubber); also electrical insulators.

Electrical resistance − the property of opposing or reducing electric current.

Electrolyte – water solution of ionic substances that will conduct an electric current.

Electromagnet – a magnet formed by a solenoid that can be turned on and off by turning the current on and off.

Electromagnetic force – one of four fundamental forces; the force of attraction or repulsion between two charged particles.

Electromagnetic induction – the process in which current is induced in a coil whenever there is a change in the magnetic flux linked with the coil.

Electromagnetic waves – the waves which are due to oscillating electrical and magnetic fields and do not need any material medium for their propagation; can travel through a material medium (e.g., light waves and radio waves); travel in a vacuum with a speed of 3×10^8 m/s.

Electron – subatomic particle that has the smallest negative charge possible; usually found in an orbital of an atom but is gained or lost when atoms become ions.

Electron configuration – the arrangement of electrons in orbits and sub-orbits about the nucleus of an atom.

Electron current – the opposite of conventional current; considers electric current to consist of a drift of negative charges that flows from the negative terminal to the positive terminal of a battery.

Electron pair – a pair of electrons with different spin quantum numbers that may occupy an orbital.

Electron volt – the energy gained by an electron moving across a potential difference of one volt; equal to 1.60×10^{-19} Joules.

Electronegativity – the comparative ability of atoms of an element to attract bonding electrons.

Electrostatic charge – an accumulated electric charge on an object from a surplus of electrons or a deficiency of electrons.

Element – a pure chemical substance that cannot be broken down into anything simpler by chemical or physical means; there are over 100 known elements, the fundamental materials of which all matter is made.

Endothermic process – the process in which heat is absorbed.

Energy – the capacity of a body to do work; a scalar quantity; the SI unit is the Joule; there are five forms: mechanical, chemical, radiant, electrical and nuclear.

Escape velocity − the minimum velocity with which an object must be thrown upward to overcome the gravitational pull and escape into space; the escape velocity depends on the mass and radius of the planet/star, but not on the mass of the body being thrown upward.

Evaporation − process of more molecules leaving a liquid for the gaseous state than returning from the gas to the liquid; can occur at any given temperature from the surface of a liquid; takes place only from the surface of the liquid; causes cooling; faster if the surface of the liquid is large, the temperature is higher, and the surrounding atmosphere does not contain a large amount of vapor of the liquid.

Exothermic process − the process in which heat is evolved.

F

Fahrenheit scale of temperature − the ice-point (lower fixed point) is taken as 32 °F, and the steam-point (upper fixed point) is taken as 212 °F; the interval between these two points is divided into 180 equal divisions; the unit division on the Fahrenheit scale is 1 °F; the relationship relates the temperatures on the Celsius scale and the Fahrenheit scale, $C/100 = (F − 32)/180$; the temperature of a healthy person is 37 °C or 98.6 °F.

Farad − the SI unit of capacitance; the capacitance of a capacitor that, if charged to 1 C, has a potential difference of 1 V.

Faraday − the electric charge required to liberate a gram equivalent of a substance; 1 Faraday = 96,485 coulomb/mole.

Fermat's principle − an electromagnetic wave takes a path that involves the least time when propagating between two points.

First Law of Motion − every object remains at rest or in a state of uniform straight-line motion unless acted on by an unbalanced force.

Fluid − matter that can flow or be poured; the individual molecules of a fluid can move, rolling over or by one another.

Focus − the point to which rays that are initially parallel to the axis of a lens or mirror converge or from which they appear to diverge.

Force − a push or pull which tends to change the state of rest or of uniform motion, the direction of motion or the shape and size of a body; a vector quantity; the SI unit is a Newton, denoted by N; one N is the force which when acting on a body of mass 1 kg produces an acceleration of 1 m/s².

Force of gravitation − the force with which two objects attract each other by their masses; acts even if the two objects are not connected; an action-at-a-distance force.

Fracture strain − an adjustment to stress in which materials crack or break as a result of the stress.

Fraunhofer lines − the dark lines in the spectrum of the sun or a star.

Freefall − the motion of a body falling to Earth with no other force except the force of gravity acting on it; all free-falling bodies are weightless.

Freezing point − the temperature at which a phase change of liquid to solid takes place; the same temperature as the melting point for a given substance.

Frequency − the number of oscillations completed in 1 second by an oscillating body.

Frequency (of oscillations) − the number of oscillations made by an oscillating body per second.

Frequency (of waves) − the number of waves produced per second.

Friction − the force that resists the motion of one surface relative to another with which it is in contact; caused by the humps and crests of surfaces, even those on a microscopic scale; the area of contact is very small, and the consequent very high pressure leads to local pressure welding of the surface; in motion the welds are broken and remade continually.

Fuel rod − long zirconium alloy tubes containing fissionable material for use in a nuclear reactor.

Fundamental charge − the smallest common charge known; the magnitude of the charge of an electron and a proton, which is 1.60×10^{-19} coulombs.

Fundamental frequency − the lowest frequency (longest wavelength) at which a system vibrates freely and can set up standing waves in an air column or on a string.

Fundamental properties − a property that cannot be defined in simpler terms other than to describe how it is measured; the fundamental properties are length, mass, time and charge.

G

g – symbol representing the acceleration of an object in free fall due to the force of gravity; its magnitude is 9.80 m/s^2.

Gamma (γ) ray – a high energy photon of very short wavelength electromagnetic radiation emitted by decaying nuclei (γ-decay).

Gases – a phase of matter composed of molecules that are relatively far apart moving freely in constant, random motion and have weak cohesive forces acting between them, resulting in the characteristic indefinite shape and indefinite volume of a gas.

Graham's Law of Diffusion – the rate of diffusion of a gas is inversely proportional to the square root of its density.

Gram-atomic weight – the mass in grams of one mole of an element that is numerically equal to its atomic weight.

Gram-formula weight – the mass in grams of one mole of a compound that is numerically equal to its formula weight.

Gram-molecular weight – the gram-formula weight of a molecular compound.

Gravitational constant G – appears in the equation for Newton's Law of Gravitation; numerically, it is equal to the force of gravitation, which acts between two bodies with a mass of 1 kg each separated by a distance of 1 m; the value of G is 6.67×10^{-11} Nm^2/kg^2.

Gravitational potential at a point – the amount of work done against the gravitational forces to move a particle of unit mass from infinity to that point.

Gravitational potential energy – the potential energy possessed by a body by its height from the ground; equals *mgh*.

Gravity – the gravitational attraction at the surface of a planet or other celestial body.

Greenhouse effect – the process of increasing the temperature of the lower parts of the atmosphere through redirecting energy back toward the surface; the absorption and re-emission of infrared radiation by carbon dioxide, water vapor, and a few other gases in the atmosphere.

Ground state – the energy state of an atom with its electrons at the lowest energy state possible for that atom.

H

Half-life − the time required for one-half of the unstable nuclei in a radioactive substance to decay into a new element.

Heat − a form of energy that makes a body hot or cold; measured by the temperature-effect, it produces in any material body; the SI unit is the Joule (J).

Heisenberg uncertainty principle − states that there is a fundamental limit to the precision with which certain pairs of physical properties of a particle (i.e., complementary variables) can be known simultaneously (e.g., one cannot measure both the exact momentum and the exact position of a subatomic particle at the same time – the more one is certain of one, the less certain one can be of the other).

Hertz − unit of frequency (Hz); equivalent to one cycle per second.

Hooke's Law − within the elastic limit, stress is directly proportional to strain.

Horsepower − unit of power; 1 hp = 746 Watts.

Humidity − the ratio of water vapor in a sample of air to the volume of the sample.

Huygens' principle − each point on a light wavefront can be regarded as a source of secondary waves, the envelope of these secondary waves determining the position of the wavefront at a later time.

Hypothesis − a tentative explanation of a phenomenon that is compatible with the data and provides a framework for understanding and describing that phenomenon.

I

Ice-point − the melting point of ice under 1 atm pressure; equal to 0 °C or 32 °F.

Ideal gas equation − $PV = nRT$.

Impulse − equal to the product of the force acting on a body and the time for which it acts; if the force is variable, the impulse is the integral of Fd_t from t_0 to t_1; the impulse of a force acting for a given time interval is equal to change in momentum produced over that interval; $J = m(v - u)$, assuming that the mass m remains constant while the velocity changes from v to u; the SI units are kg m/s.

Impulsive force − the force which acts on a body for a very short time but produces a large change in the momentum of the body.

Incandescent − matter emitting visible light as a result of high temperature (e.g., a light bulb, a flame from any burning source, the Sun).

Incident ray − line representing the direction of motion of incoming light approaching a boundary.

Index of refraction − the ratio of the speed of light in a vacuum to the speed of light in a material.

Inertia − the property of matter that causes it to resist any change in its state of rest or of uniform motion; there are three kinds of inertia: the inertia of rest, the inertia of motion and the inertia of direction; the mass of a body is a measure of its inertia.

Infrasonic − sound waves at a frequency below the range of human hearing (less than 20 Hz).

Insulators − materials that are poor conductors of heat or electricity (e.g., wood or glass); materials with air pockets slow down the movement of heat because the air molecules are far apart.

Intensity − a measure of the energy carried by a wave.

Interference − the redistribution of energy due to the superposition of waves with a phase difference from coherent sources, resulting in alternate light and dark bands.

Intermolecular forces − forces of interaction between molecules.

Internal energy – the sum of the kinetic energy and potential energy of all molecules of an object.

Inverse proportion − the relationship in which the value of one variable increases while the value of a second variable decreases at the same rate (in the same ratio).

Ionization − process of forming ions from molecules.

Ionized − an atom or a particle that has a net charge because it has gained or lost electrons.

Isobaric process − in which pressure remains constant.

Isochoric process − in which volume remains constant.

Isostasy − a balance or equilibrium between adjacent blocks of Earth's crust.

Isothermal process − in which temperature remains constant.

Isotope − atoms of the same element with the same atomic number (i.e., number of protons) but with a different mass number (i.e., number of neutrons).

J

Joule − the unit used to measure work and energy; can also be used to measure heat; 1 J = 1N·m.

Joule's Law of Heating – states that the heat produced when a current (I) flows through a resistor (R) for a given time (t) is given by $Q = I^2Rt$.

K

Kelvin scale of temperature − the ice-point (the lower fixed point) is taken as 273.15 K, and the steam-point (the upper fixed point) is taken as 373.15 K; the interval between these two points is divided into 100 equal parts; each division is equal to 1K.

Kelvin's statement of Second Law of Thermodynamics − it is impossible that, at the end of a cycle of changes, heat has been extracted from a reservoir and an equal amount of work has been produced without producing some other effect.

Kepler's laws of planetary motion − the three laws describing the motion of the planets.

Kepler's First Law – in planetary motion, each planet moves in an elliptical orbit, with the Sun located at one focus.

Kepler's Second Law – a radius vector between the Sun and a planet moves over equal areas of the ellipse during equal time intervals.

Kepler's Third Law – the square of the period of an orbit is directly proportional to the cube of the radius of the major axis of the orbit.

Kilocalorie − the amount of energy required to raise the temperature of 1 kg of water by 1 °C; 1 Kcal = 1,000 calorie.

Kilogram − the fundamental unit of mass in the metric system of measurement.

Kinetic energy − energy possessed by a body due to its motion; KE = $\frac{1}{2}mv^2$, where m is mass and v is velocity.

L

Laser – a device that produces a coherent stream of light through stimulated emission of radiation.

Latent heat – energy released or absorbed by a body during a constant-temperature phase change.

Latent heat of vaporization – the heat absorbed when one gram of a substance changes from the liquid phase to the gaseous phase; also, the heat released when one gram of gas changes from the gaseous phase to the liquid phase.

Latent heat of fusion – the quantity of heat required to convert one unit mass of a substance from a solid state to a liquid state at its melting point without any change in its temperature; the SI unit is $J\ kg^{-1}$.

Latent heat of sublimation – the quantity of heat required to convert one unit of mass of a substance from a solid state to a gaseous state without any change in its temperature.

Law of Conservation of Energy – states that energy can neither be created nor destroyed, but can be transformed from one form to another.

Law of Conservation of Mass – states that mass (including single atoms) can neither be created nor destroyed in a chemical reaction.

Law of Conservation of Matter – states that matter can neither be created nor destroyed in a chemical reaction.

Law of Conservation of Momentum – states that the total momentum of a group of interacting objects remains constant in the absence of external forces.

Lenz's Law – states that the induced current always flows in such a direction that it opposes the cause producing it.

Light-year – the distance that light travels in a vacuum in one year (365.25 days); approximately 9.46×10^{15} m.

Line spectrum – an emission (of light, sound or other radiation) spectrum consisting of separate isolated lines (discrete frequencies or energies); can be used to identify the elements in a matter of unknown composition.

Lines of force – lines drawn to make an electric field strength map, with each line originating on a positive charge and ending on a negative charge; each line represents a path on which a charge would experience a constant force; having the lines closer together indicates a stronger electric field.

Liquids − a phase of matter composed of molecules that have interactions stronger than those found in gas but not strong enough to keep the molecules near the equilibrium positions of a solid, resulting in the characteristic definite volume but the indefinite shape of a liquid.

Liter − a metric system unit of volume; usually used for liquids.

Longitudinal strain − the ratio of change in the length of a body to its initial length.

Longitudinal waves − the wave in which the particles of the medium oscillate along the direction of propagation of a wave (e.g., sound waves).

Loudness − a subjective interpretation of a sound that is related to the energy of the vibrating source, related to the condition of the transmitting medium and the distance involved.

Luminosity − the total amount of energy radiated into space each second from the surface of a star.

Luminous − an object or objects that produce visible light (e.g., the Sun, stars, light bulbs, burning materials).

Lyman series − a group of lines in the ultraviolet region in the spectrum of hydrogen.

M

Magnetic domain − tiny physical regions in permanent magnets, approximately 0.01 to 1 mm, that have magnetically aligned atoms, giving the domain an overall polarity.

Magnetic field − the region around a magnet where other magnetic objects experience its magnetic force; a model used to describe how magnetic forces on moving charges act at a distance.

Magnetic poles − the ends, or sides, of a magnet about which the force of magnetic attraction seems to be concentrated.

Magnetic quantum number − from quantum mechanics model of the atom, one of four descriptions of the energy state of an electron wave; describes the energy of an electron orbital as the orbital is oriented in space by an external magnetic field, a kind of energy sub-sublevel.

Magnetic reversal − the changing of polarity of the Earth's magnetic field as the north magnetic pole and the south magnetic pole exchange positions.

Magnetic wave − the spread of magnetization from a small portion of a substance where an abrupt change in the magnetic field has taken place.

Magnification − the ratio of the size of the image to the size of the object.

Magnitude − the size of a measurement of a vector; scalar quantities that consist of a number and unit only.

Malus Law – states that the intensity of the light transmitted from the analyzer varies directly as the square of the cosine of the angle between the plane of transmission of the analyzer and the polarizer.

Maser − microwave amplification by stimulated emission of radiation.

Mass − the quantity of matter contained in a body; the SI unit is the kg; remains the same everywhere; a measure of inertia, which means resistance to a change of motion.

Mass defect − the difference between the sum of the masses of the individual nucleons forming a nucleus and the mass of that nucleus.

Mass number − the sum of the number of protons and neutrons in a nucleus; used to identify isotopes (e.g., Uranium-238).

Matter − anything that occupies space and has mass.

Mean life − the average time during which a system, such as an atom or a nucleus, exists in a specified form.

Mechanical energy − the sum of the potential energy and the kinetic energy of a body; energy associated with the position of a body.

Mechanical wave − those waves that need a material medium for their propagation (e.g., sound waves and water waves); also elastic waves.

Megahertz − unit of frequency; equal to 106 Hertz.

Melting point − the temperature at which a phase change of solid to liquid takes place.

Metal − matter having the physical properties of conductivity, malleability, ductility, and luster.

Meter − the fundamental metric unit of length.

MeV − unit of energy; equal to 1.6×10^{-13} joules.

Millibar − a measure of atmospheric pressure equivalent to 1,000 dynes per cm^2.

Miscible fluids − fluids that can mix in any proportion.

Mixture − matter made of unlike parts that have a variable composition and can be separated into their component parts by physical means.

Model − a mental or physical representation of something that cannot be observed directly; usually used as an aid to understanding.

Modulus of elasticity − the ratio of stress to the strain produced in a body.

Modulus of rigidity − the ratio of tangential stress to the shear strain produced in a body.

Mole − the amount of a substance that contains Avogadro's number of atoms, ions, molecules or any other chemical unit; 6.02×10^{23} atoms, ions or other chemical units.

Momentum − a measure of the quantity of motion in a body; the product of the mass and the velocity of a body; SI units are kg·m /s.

Monochromatic light − consisting of a single wavelength.

N

Natural frequency − the frequency of oscillation of an elastic object in the absence of external forces; depends on the size, composition, and shape of the object.

Negative electric charge − one of the two types of electric charge; repels other negative charges and attracts positive charges.

Negative ion − atom or particle that has a surplus or imbalance of electrons and a negative charge.

Net force − the resulting force after all vector forces have been added; if a net force is zero, all the vector forces have canceled, and there is not an unbalanced force.

Newton (N) − a unit of force defined as kg·m/s^2; 1 Newton is needed to accelerate a 1 kg mass by 1 m/s^2.

Newton's First Law of Motion − a body continues in a state of rest or of uniform motion in a straight line unless it is acted upon by an external (unbalanced) force.

Newton's Law of Gravitation − the gravitational force of attraction acting between any two particles is directly proportional to the product of their masses and inversely proportional to the square of the distance between them; the force of attraction acts along the line joining the two particles; real bodies having spherical symmetry act as point masses with their mass assumed to be concentrated at their center of mass.

Newton's Second Law of Motion − the rate of change of momentum is equal to the force applied; the force acting on a body is directly proportional to the product of its mass and acceleration produced by force in the body.

Newton's Third Law of Motion − states that to every action there is an equal and opposite reaction; the action and the reaction act on two different bodies simultaneously.

Noise − sounds made up of groups of waves of random frequency and intensity.

Non-uniform acceleration − when the velocity of a body increases by unequal amounts in equal intervals of time.

Non-uniform speed − when a body travels unequal distances in equal intervals of time.

Non-uniform velocity − when a body covers unequal distances in equal intervals of time in a particular direction, or when it covers equal distances in equal intervals but changes its direction.

Normal − a line perpendicular to the surface of a boundary.

Nuclear energy − the form of energy from reactions involving the nucleus.

Nuclear fission − the splitting of a heavy nucleus into more stable, lighter nuclei with an accompanying release of energy.

Nuclear force − one of four fundamental forces; a strong force of attraction that operates over very short distances between subatomic particles; overcomes the electric repulsion of protons in a nucleus and binds the nucleus together.

Nuclear fusion − nuclear reaction of low mass nuclei fusing to form a more stable and more massive nucleus with an accompanying release of energy.

Nuclear reactor − a steel vessel in which a controlled chain reaction of fissionable materials releases energy.

Nucleons − a collective name for protons and neutrons in the nucleus of an atom.

Nucleus − the central, positively charged, dense portion of an atom; contains protons and neutrons.

O

Ohm − unit of resistance; 1 ohm = 1volt/ampere.

Ohm's Law – states that the current flowing through a conductor is directly proportional to the potential difference across the ends of the conductor.

Open system − a system across whose boundaries both matter and energy can pass.

Optical fiber − a long, thin thread of fused silica; used to transmit light; based on total internal reflection.

Orbital − the region of space around the nucleus of an atom where an electron is likely to be found.

Origin − the only point on a graph where the x and the y variables both have a value of zero at the same time.

Oscillatory motion – the to and fro motion (periodic in nature) of a body about its mean position; also vibratory motion.

P

Pascal − a unit of pressure, equal to the pressure resulting from a force of 1 Newton acting uniformly over an area of 1 m^2.

Pascal's Law – states that the pressure exerted on a liquid is transmitted equally in all directions.

Paschen series − a group of lines in the infrared region in the spectrum of hydrogen.

Pauli exclusion principle − no two electrons in an atom can have the same four quantum numbers; a maximum of two electrons can occupy a given orbital.

Peltier effect − the evolution or absorption of heat at the junction of two dissimilar metals carrying current.

Period (of a wave) − the time taken by a wave to travel through a distance equal to its wavelength; denoted by T; period of a wave = 1/frequency of the wave.

Period (of an oscillation) − the time taken to complete one oscillation; does not depend upon the mass of the bob and amplitude of oscillation; directly proportional to the square root of the length and inversely proportional to the square root of the acceleration due to gravity.

Periodic wave − a wave in which the particles of the medium oscillate continuously about their mean positions regularly at fixed intervals of time.

Periodic motion − a motion which repeats itself at regular intervals of time.

Permeability − the ability to transmit fluids through openings, small passageways or gaps.

Phase – when the particles in a wave are in the same state of vibration (i.e., in the same position and the same direction of motion).

Phase change − the action of a substance changing from one state of matter to another; always absorbs or releases internal potential energy that is not associated with a temperature change.

Photons − quanta of energy in the light wave; the particle associated with light.

Photoelectric effect − the emission of electrons in some materials when the light of a suitable frequency falls on them.

Physical change − a change of the state of a substance but not in the identity of the substance.

Planck's constant − proportionality constant in the ratio of the energy of vibrating molecules to their frequency of vibration; a value of 6.63×10^{-34} J·s.

Plasma − a phase of matter; a very hot highly ionized gas consisting of electrons and atoms that have been stripped of their electrons because of high kinetic energies.

Plasticity − the property of a solid whereby it undergoes a permanent change in shape or size when subjected to a stress.

Plastic strain − an adjustment to stress in which materials become molded or bent out of shape under stress and do not return to their original shape after the stress is released.

Polarized Light − light whose constituent transverse waves are all vibrating in the same plane.

Polaroid − a film that transmits only polarized light.

Polaroid or polarizer − a device that produces polarized light.

Positive electric charge − one of the two types of electric charge; repels other positive charges and attracts negative charges.

Positive ion − atom or particle that has a net positive charge due to an electron or electrons being torn away.

Positron – an elementary particle having the same mass as that of an electron but equal and positive charge.

Potential Energy – energy possessed by a body by its position or configuration; see *Gravitational potential energy* and *Elastic potential energy*.

Power – scalar quantity for the rate of doing work; the SI unit is Watt; 1 W = 1 J/s.

Pressure – a measure of force per unit area (e.g., kilograms per square meter (kg/m^2).

Primary coil – part of a transformer; a coil of wire connected to a source of alternating current.

Primary colors – three colors (red, yellow and blue) which can be combined in various proportions to produce any other color.

Principal quantum number – from quantum mechanics model of the atom, one of four descriptions of the energy state of an electron wave; describes the main energy level of an electron regarding its most probable distance from the nucleus.

Principle of calorimetry – states that if two bodies of different temperature are in thermal contact, and no heat is allowed to go out or enter into the system, then heat lost by the body with higher temperature is equal to the heat gained by the body of lower temperature (i.e., heat lost = heat gained).

Progressive wave – a wave which transfers energy from one part of a medium to another.

Projectile – an object is thrown into space either horizontally or at an acute angle and under the action of gravity; the path followed by a projectile is its trajectory; the horizontal distance traveled by a projectile is its range; the time is taken from the moment it is thrown until the moment it hits the ground is its time of flight.

Proof – a measure of ethanol concentration of an alcoholic beverage; double the concentration by volume (e.g., 50% by volume is 100 proof).

Properties – qualities or attributes that, taken together, are usually unique to an object (e.g., color, texture, and size).

Proportionality constant – a constant applied to a proportionality statement that transforms the statement into an equation.

Pulse – a wave of short duration confined to a small portion of the medium at any given time; also a wave pulse.

Q

Quanta − fixed amounts; usually referring to fixed amounts of energy absorbed or emitted by matter.

Quantum limit − the shortest wavelength; present in a continuous x-ray spectrum.

Quantum mechanics − model of the atom based on the wave nature of subatomic particles and the mechanics of electron waves; also wave mechanics.

Quantum numbers − numbers that describe the energy states of an electron; in the Bohr model of the atom, the orbit quantum numbers could be any whole number (e.g., 1, 2, 3, etc.); in the quantum mechanics model of the atom, four quantum numbers are used to describe the energy state of an electron wave (*n*, *m*, *l,* and *s*).

Quark − one of the hypothetical basic particles; has a charge with magnitudes of one-third or two-thirds of the charge on an electron.

R

Rad − a measure of radiation received by a material (radiation-absorbed dose).

Radiant energy − the form of energy that can travel through space (e.g., visible light and other parts of the electromagnetic spectrum).

Radiation − the emission and propagation of waves transmitting energy through space or some medium.

Radioactive decay − the natural, spontaneous disintegration or decomposition of a nucleus.

Radioactive decay constant − a specific constant for a particular isotope that is the ratio of the rate of nuclear disintegration per unit of time to the total number of radioactive nuclei.

Radioactive decay series − series of decay reactions that begins with one radioactive nucleus that decays to a second nucleus that decays to a third nucleus and so on, until a stable nucleus is reached.

Radioactive decay law − the rate of disintegration of a radioactive substance is directly proportional to the number of undecayed nuclei.

Radioactivity − spontaneous emission of particles or energy from an atomic nucleus as it disintegrates.

Rarefaction − a part of a longitudinal wave in which the density of the particles of the medium is less than the normal density.

Real image − an image generated by a lens or mirror that can be projected onto a screen.

Rectilinear motion − the motion of a body in a straight line.

Reflected ray − a line representing the direction of motion of light reflected from a boundary.

Refraction − the bending of a light wave, a sound wave or another wave from its straight-line path as it travels from one medium to another.

Refractive index − the ratio of the speed of light in a vacuum to that in the medium.

Relative density – (i.e., *specific gravity*) is the ratio of the density (mass of a unit volume) of a substance to the density of given reference material. *Specific gravity* usually means relative density with respect to water. The term *relative density* is more common in modern scientific usage.

Relative humidity − the percentage of the amount of water vapor present in a certain volume of the air to the amount of water vapor needed to saturate it.

Resolving power − a quantitative measure of the ability of an optical instrument to produce separable images of different points of an object.

Resonance − when the frequency of an external force matches the natural frequency of the body.

Restoring force − the force which tends to bring an oscillating body to its mean position whenever it is displaced from the mean position.

Resultant force − a single force, which acts on a body to produce the same effect on it as done by all other forces collectively; see *Balanced forces*.

Reverberation − apparent increase in the volume of sound caused by reflections from the boundary surfaces, usually arriving within 0.1 seconds after the original sound.

Rigid body − an idealized extended body whose size and shape is fixed and remains unaltered when forces are applied.

S

Saturated air − air in which an equilibrium exists between evaporation and condensation; the relative humidity will be 100 percent.

Saturated solution − the apparent limit to dissolving a given solid in a specified amount of water at a given temperature; a state of equilibrium that exists between dissolving solute and solute coming out of solution.

Scalar quantity − a physical quantity described completely by its magnitude.

Scientific law − a relationship between quantities; usually described by an equation in the physical sciences; describes a wider range of phenomena and is more important than a scientific principle.

Scientific principle − a relationship between quantities concerned with a specific or narrow range of observations and behavior.

Second − the standard unit of time in both the metric and English systems of measurement.

Second law of motion − the acceleration of an object is directly proportional to the net force acting on that object and inversely proportional to the mass of the object.

Secondary coil − part of a transformer; a coil of wire in which the voltage of the original alternating current in the primary coil can be stepped up or down by way of electromagnetic induction.

Second's pendulum − a simple pendulum whose period on the surface of the Earth is 2 seconds.

Semiconductors − elements whose electrical conductivity is intermediate between that of a conductor and an insulator.

Shear strain − the ratio of the relative displacements of one plane to its distance from the fixed plane.

Shear stress − the restoring force developed per unit area when deforming force acts tangentially to the surface of a body, producing a change in the shape of the body without any change in volume.

Siemens − the derived SI unit of electrical conductance; equal to the conductance of an element that has a resistance of 1 ohm; also written as ohm^{-1}.

Simple harmonic motion − the vibratory motion that occurs when the restoring force is proportional to the displacement from the mean position and is directed opposite to the displacement.

Simple pendulum – a heavy point mass (actually a small metallic ball), suspended by a light inextensible string from the frictionless rigid support; a simple machine based on the effect of gravity.

Snell's Law – states that the ratio of sin i to sin r is a constant and is equal to the refractive index of the second medium concerning the first.

Solenoid – a cylindrical coil of wire that becomes electromagnetic when a current is run through it.

Solids – a phase of matter with molecules that remain close to fixed equilibrium positions due to strong interactions between the molecules, resulting in the characteristic definite shape and definite volume of a solid.

Sonic boom – sound waves that pile up into a shock wave when a source is traveling at or faster than the speed of sound.

Specific gravity – see *Relative density*.

Specific heat – the amount of heat energy required to increase the temperature of 1 g of a substance by 1 °C; each substance has its specific heat value.

Speed – a scalar quantity for the distance traveled by a body per unit of time; if a body covers the distance in time, then its speed is given by distance/time; SI units are m/s.

Spin quantum number – from quantum mechanics model of the atom, one of four descriptions of the energy state of an electron wave; describes the spin orientation of an electron relative to an external magnetic field.

Standing waves – the condition where two waves of equal frequency traveling in opposite directions meet and form stationary regions of maximum displacement due to constructive interference and stationary regions of zero displacement due to destructive interference.

State of motion – when a body changes its position concerning a fixed point in its surroundings; the states of rest and motion are relative to the frame of reference.

State of rest – when a body does not change its position with respect to a fixed point in its surrounding; the states of rest and motion are relative to the frame of reference.

Steam-point – the temperature of steam over pure boiling water under 1 atm pressure; taken as the upper fixed point (100 °C or 212 °F) for temperature scales.

Stefan-Boltzmann Law – the amount of energy radiated per second per unit area of a perfectly black body, is directly proportional to the fourth power of the absolute temperature of the surface of the body.

Superconductors – some materials in which, under certain conditions, the electrical resistance approaches zero.

Super-cooled – water in the liquid phase when the temperature is below the freezing point.

Supersaturated – containing more than the normal saturation amount of a solute at a given temperature.

Surface tension – the property of a liquid due to which its surface behaves like a stretched membrane.

T

Temperature – a numerical measure of the hotness or coldness of a body; according to the molecular model, it is a measure of the average kinetic energy of the molecules of the body; heat flows from a body at higher temperature to a body at a lower temperature.

Tensional stress – the opposite of compressional stress; occurs when one part of a plate moves away from another part that does not move.

Tesla – the SI unit of magnetic flux density; the magnetic flux density of a magnetic flux of 1 Wb through an area of 1 m^2.

Thermal Capacity – the quantity of heat required to raise the temperature of the whole body by one degree (1 K or 1 °C).

Thermal equilibrium – when two bodies in contact are at the same temperature, and there is no flow of heat between them; also, the common temperature of the bodies in thermal equilibrium.

Thermal expansion – the increase in the size of an object when heated.

Thermometer – a device used for the numerical measurement of temperature; the mercury thermometer is commonly used.

Third Law of Motion – whenever two objects interact, the force exerted on one object is equal in size and opposite in direction to the force exerted on the other object; forces always occur in matched pairs that are equal and opposite.

Total internal reflection – condition where all light is reflected from a boundary between materials; occurs when light travels from a denser to a rarer medium, and the angle of incidence is greater than the critical angle.

Transformation of energy – the conversion of one form of energy into another (e.g., when a body falls, its potential energy is converted to kinetic energy).

Transverse wave – wave in which the particles of the medium oscillate in a direction perpendicular to the direction of propagation of the wave (e.g., water waves, light waves, radio waves).

Trough – the point of maximum negative displacement on a transverse wave.

U

Ultrasonic – sound waves too high in frequency (above 20,000 Hz) to be heard by the human ear.

Unbalanced forces – when some forces act on a body and the resultant force is not zero.

Uniform acceleration – when the velocity of a body increases by equal amounts in equal intervals of time.

Uniform circular motion – the motion of an object in a circular path with uniform speed; accelerated motion.

Uniform speed – when a body travels equal distances in equal intervals of time.

Uniform velocity – when a body travels along a straight line in a particular direction and covers equal distances in equal intervals of time.

Universal law of gravitation – every object in the universe is attracted to every other object with force directly proportional to the product of their masses and inversely proportional to the square of the distance between the centers of the two masses.

Unpolarized light – light consisting of transverse waves vibrating in all possible random directions.

V

Van der Waals force − general term for weak attractive intermolecular forces.

Vapor − the gaseous state of a substance that is normally in a liquid state.

Vector quantity − a quantity which needs both magnitude and direction to describe it.

Velocity − distance traveled by a body in a particular direction per unit time; the displacement of the body per unit time; a vector quantity; the SI units are m/s.

Vibration − a back and forth motion that repeats itself.

Virtual image − an image formed when the reflected or refracted light rays appear to meet; this image cannot be projected on a screen.

Volt − unit of potential difference equivalent to joules/coulomb.

Voltage drop – the difference in electric potential across a resistor or other part of a circuit that consumes power.

W

Watt − SI unit for power; equivalent to joule/s.

Wave − a disturbance or oscillation that moves through a medium.

Wavelength − the distance between the two nearest points on a wave which are in the same phase; the distance between two adjacent crests or two adjacent troughs.

Wave (mechanical) – a periodic disturbance produced in a material medium due to the vibratory motion of the particles of the medium.

Wave mechanics − alternate name for quantum mechanics derived from the wavelike properties of subatomic particles.

Wave motion − the movement of a disturbance from one part of a medium to another involving the transfer of energy but not the transfer of matter.

Wave period − the time required for two successive crests or other successive parts of the wave to pass a given point.

Wave velocity − the distance traveled by a wave in one second; it depends on the nature of the medium through which it passes.

Weight − the force with which a body is attracted towards the center of the Earth; the SI unit is N; the gravitational units are kg·wt and g·wt; the weight of a body is given by *mg*.

Weightlessness − the state when the apparent weight of a body becomes zero; all objects while falling freely under the action of gravity are seemingly weightless.

Wien's Displacement Law – states that for a black body, the product of the wavelength corresponding to its maximum radiance and its absolute temperature is constant.

Work − work is done when a force acting on a body displaces it; Work = Force × Displacement in the direction of the force; work is a scalar quantity; the SI unit is Joule.

Y

Young's modulus of elasticity − the ratio of normal stress to the longitudinal strain produced in a body.

Z

Zeeman effect − the splitting of the spectral lines in a spectrum when the source is exposed to a magnetic field.

Zeroth Law of Thermodynamics – states that if body A is in thermal equilibrium with body B, and B is also in thermal equilibrium with C, then A is necessarily in thermal equilibrium with C.

Please, leave your Customer Review on Amazon

Notes

Notes

33873079R00314

Made in the USA
Middletown, DE
19 January 2019